State of
the Environment
1982

The Conservation Foundation is a nonprofit research and communications organization dedicated to encouraging human conduct to sustain and enrich life on earth. Since its founding in 1948, it has attempted to provide intellectual leadership in the cause of wise management of the earth's resources.

State of the Environment 1982

A Report from
The Conservation Foundation

Washington, D.C.

State of the Environment 1982

Copyright © 1982 by The Conservation Foundation

International Standard Book Number: 0-89164-070-3

All rights reserved. No part of this book may be reproduced in any form without the permission of The Conservation Foundation.

Cover design by Sally A. Janin

Graphics by Forte, Inc., Alexandria, Virginia

Typeset by VIP Systems, Alexandria, Virginia

Printed by Todd/Allan Printing Company, Washington, D.C.

The Conservation Foundation
1717 Massachusetts Avenue, N.W.
Washington, D.C. 20036

Library of Congress Cataloging in Publication Data
Main entry under title:

State of the environment 1982.

   Includes bibliographies.
1. Environmental policy—United States.
2. Environmental protection—United States.
I. Conservation Foundation.
HC110.E5S69   1982   363.7'00973   82-8257
ISBN 0-89164-070-3 (pbk.)

Contents

Figures

Agriculture and Forestry

Land

The Urban Environment

The Reagan Administration and Institutional Change

The data used in preparing the figures published in this report are available from The Conservation Foundation.

Foreword

The Conservation Foundation has consistently striven for careful, objective analysis of resource and environmental problems and policies. This report, with its examination of environmental conditions and trends, its attention to the status of natural resources, and its concern with scientific, legal, and other issues, is typical of much of the Foundation's work.

In one sense, however, this report is unlike anything we have ever done. Neither we nor any other institution outside of government has previously attempted such an ambitious, comprehensive assessment of the nation's environment. Our decision to do so now represents a major undertaking for the Foundation, a commitment to try to assure the continued availability to the public of data vitally necessary to the formulation of environmental policies. We hope thereby to help make possible an informed debate in a period of intense polarization.

One of the most worrisome new directions of federal policy is a significant reduction in environmental research and a discontinuance of many public information services. Both collection and dissemination of environmental data have been downgraded. No private effort can fully replace government as a source of comprehensive data about the environment, and one must hope that federal policymakers will come eventually to appreciate the need for expanded data collection, both to inform decisions and to assure a more substantive public debate. For the present, there remains a serious vacuum which this report is intended to help fill.

We began work on this report in the late fall of 1981. The report is almost entirely the product of the Foundation's own interdisciplinary staff of economists, scientists, lawyers, political scientists, writers, and federal program specialists. The project director was Edwin H. Clark, II, an economist and senior associate, who collaborated closely with Terry Davies, Foundation executive vice president. Contributors to the report were: Virginia Coull, Janet M. Fesler, Meredith Golden, Jennifer A. Haverkamp, Frances H. Irwin, Richard A. Liroff, Michael Mantell, Robert J. McCoy, Phyllis Myers, John H. Noble, Clem L. Rastatter, Michael Rawson, Barbara K. Rodes, William E. Shands, Grant P. Thompson, and Daniel B. Tunstall. Assistance was also provided by two outside consultants, Perry Hagenstein and Roger McManus, and by several interns, including Karen Stray-Gunderson, Philip Schiliro, John Foggle, and Tom Gherlein.

Each chapter was reviewed by at least three outside experts, many of whom provided valuable comments and suggestions. For review and comment, we are grateful to: James Banks, Sandra S. Batie, John Clark, Timothy Conlon, Jack Cremeans, David Doniger, Don Dworsky, Loran Frazer, Campbell Gibson, Roy Mack Gray, Dwight Hair, Curtis Haymore, Robert G. Healy, Larry Hill, T. Destry Jarvis, William Lienesch, Alec McBride, Robert C. Mitchell, Sharon Newsome, Robert Parke, Clay Peters, George Peterson, Paul R. Portney, Veronica Pye, Robert A.F. Reisner, Leslie Rice, Neil R. Sampson, John Scheibel, Stanley Senner, Donald W. Smith, James N. Smith, Richard Smith, Rochelle Stanfield, Howard Sumka, Ron Tipton, James Tripp, Jacqueline M. Warren, and Gregory Whetstone.

The manuscript was typed on extremely tight schedules by Jenny Billet, Tony Brown, Lynnette Clemens, Marie DiCocco, Gwen Harley, Debbie Johnson, and Andee Shetzich.

* * *

Contributors of unrestricted gifts to the Foundation provided the major portion of financial support for this project. Additional supporters included the George Gund Foundation; the Rockefeller Brothers Fund, which contributed toward the research for the chapter on water; and the Guenther Fund, which provided partial support for research on the chapter dealing with the urban environment. We are deeply grateful for this support. Responsibility for the contents of the report is exclusively that of The Conservation Foundation.

William K. Reilly
President
The Conservation Foundation
June 1982

Overview

At a time when a new generation of environmental problems demands attention, the search for solutions has been lost in a storm of attacks and counterattacks. The bipartisan consensus that supported federal protection of the environment for more than a decade has been broken by an Administration that has given priority to deregulation, defederalization, and defunding domestic programs.

Reagan Administration initiatives have polarized relations between the executive branch and conservationists in Congress and throughout the country. The polarization has disrupted the communication necessary to formulate and carry out environmental programs. It has distracted attention from environmental assessment and from problems that vitally affect human health and the quality of life.

Without question, the Reagan Administration has introduced a fundamental discontinuity into national resource and environmental policy. It has pursued its domestic goals with such single-mindedness, so aggressively, as to allow conservationists no alternative but to protest. After firing virtually the entire staff of the Council on Environmental Quality (CEQ), the Administration reduced CEQ's personnel and funding levels by more than 50 percent. At the Environmental Protection Agency, the 1983 budget calls for a 40 percent reduction from the 1981 level for research and development; cuts already made have done away with the noise control program, sharply reduced efforts to deal with toxic substances, and cast doubt on the agency's ability to fulfill its mandates under the Clean Air and Clean Water Acts. At the Department of Energy, programs in energy conservation and renewable energy sources have given way to increased spending for nuclear reactor research. At the Department of the Interior, the emphasis has been on selling off federal land, encouraging accelerated mineral exploration and extraction, and making the national parks more comfortable for tourists; the tendency has been either to neglect or to exploit natural resources.

The Administration's sweeping changes in environmental policies and priorities make the careful documentation of environmental conditions and trends even more necessary now than in the past. In the midst of highly charged arguments about new directions, a source of reliable, credible, objective data is crucial. With this report, The Conservation Foundation hopes to provide such a source for 1982.

Our report describes major resource and environmental problems facing the United States, presents data to show whether the problems are getting better or worse, and discusses institutional changes and options that affect environmental and resource policy. Its intent is to provide an objective description of the state of the U.S. environment. We have not emphasized the global environment, but hope to do so in the future.

The initiatives of the Reagan Administration, important as they are, are difficult to assess in an objective report on the state of the environment. It is inherently more difficult to report on the implications of policy changes than on the effects of changes in air quality or agricultural production. Eventually, changes in environmental policy will result in changes in the physical environment, but it takes time for this to happen, and even more time for these changes to be detected, analyzed, and reported. The physical changes described in this report, for example, reflect policies adopted three or five or ten years ago. The effects of some policy decisions, such as reduced research on toxic substances, may never be detected, even though such decisions may have serious consequences.

Although the current state of the environment defies simple characterization, three principal conclusions can be drawn:

- The nation has made impressive progress in its attack on some conventional environmental problems. Even where pollution levels have remained the same, progress is still worthy of note in the face of a 40 percent real increase in Gross National Product (GNP) since 1970.
- At the same time, many new and serious problems have been identified.
- The information base on which sound environmental policy depends, always inadequate, is deteriorating.

Progress on Conventional Problems

Emissions of most major air pollutants have continued to decline, at least as estimated by EPA. Data from 23 metropolitan areas show that particulate emissions dropped 56 percent between 1970 and 1980, partly because of a decrease in the burning of coal and solid waste. With a 24-percent decline in ambient sulfur dioxide levels from 1974 to 1980, most urban areas have now reached EPA's primary, health-based standards.

Available data show no similarly significant progress toward water quality goals. Still, even to hold the *status quo* is an achievement in the face of significant economic and population growth since 1970. Moreover, there is episodic evidence across the country that some of the worst pollution problems may be easing. Salmon have reappeared in New England rivers. Eutrophication of Lakes Ontario and Erie has slowed. And the ecological productivity of some estuaries—for example, near Pensacola, Florida—is returning.

The 1979-80 jump in energy prices had the predictable effect of encouraging conservation. The fuel economy of new automobiles has continued to improve, and industrial fuel use has shown markedly greater efficiency. Crude oil imports were 16 percent less in 1981 than in 1980. Energy consumption per dollar of GNP (adjusted for inflation) was down 4 percent.

More land, both public and private, has become available for outdoor recreation. In December 1980, 104 million acres of federally owned lands in Alaska were added to the nation's park, forest, wilderness, and wildlife systems. Meanwhile, state and local governments, often with federal support, have moved to protect sensitive lands; by 1979, 31 coastal states and territories had adopted statutes for the protection of wetlands.

After falling in 1980, agricultural productivity, as measured by yield per acre, increased in 1981, pushing total agricultural production to a nearly record high. In contrast, largely because of fewer housing starts, timber harvest declined in 1980, and probably in 1981 as well.

Continuing Problems

Available data continue to show losses in jobs, population, and capital investment in many of the nation's central cities. Fiscal problems are chronic. The viability of many state and municipal governments has been further jeopardized by cutbacks in federal assistance, tax losses (not only from the lack of economic growth but from changes in the federal tax structure), and citizen opposition to tax increases. Nevertheless, even some of the most troubled central cities are experiencing significant revitalization in areas that a decade ago appeared hopelessly overwhelmed by poverty.

A very old problem, soil erosion, has grown more acute, even as agricultural production reaches record high levels. Most of the erosion comes from our most productive farmland; half of it from the Corn Belt and Northern Plains, though areas from Maine to Washington are also experiencing serious problems. Particularly disturbing is the fact that the use of soil conservation measures such as contour plowing and windbreaks is declining, largely because of the poor economic condition of farmers and because these techniques are incompatible with modern agricultural equipment. An exception is the adoption of "conservation tillage" techniques on an increasing number of farms.

Energy efficiency in the United States has generally improved, but federal research on both energy conservation and renewable energy resources has been all but eliminated. Except for the addition of 159 million barrels to the Strategic Petroleum Reserve, there has been little evidence of government planning to deal with another sudden cutoff of Middle Eastern oil. Federal programs to help the poor meet their energy bills have suffered the same fate as most other social welfare programs, thus increasing the likelihood that efforts to rationalize energy pricing will be achieved at the expense of those least able to pay.

Nearly 35 million people live in areas that will be unable to meet the air quality standards for protection of human health from ozone by 1987, even if existing automobile emission standards are met. The Reagan Administration has advocated a relaxation of emission standards for gasoline and diesel automobiles and trucks, which would delay attainment of the ambient standards in major metropolitan areas. Meanwhile, a number of major stationary sources of air pollution continue to violate prevailing emission standards. Business investment in pollution control, as measured by percentage of GNP, declined in 1980 and probably declined still further in 1981.

In the past five years, two major laws have been passed to deal with hazardous waste disposal. Implementation of both has been slow. Meanwhile, old hazardous waste sites continue to threaten many communities, and much of the waste now being generated is disposed of under environmentally unsafe conditions.

Pollution has also adversely affected the National Park System. Land development outside park boundaries, as well as overuse of sensitive areas within parks, is degrading natural and historic resources. Beaches are littered and springs polluted at Rio Grande

Wild and Scenic River. Tons of fossil material are taken each year from the Petrified Forest. The clarity of water at Crater Lake has declined measurably in recent years.

Many other sensitive land areas are feeling the pressures of development. Along the Atlantic and Gulf coasts, the nearly 300 barrier islands that serve as the nation's first defense against ocean storms are being urbanized at a pace far greater than mainland areas. Since 1950, barrier island development has proceeded at an estimated rate of 6,000 acres annually, much of it aided by federal funds.

The New Agenda

Our perception of environmental problems changes constantly. Shifts in economic and demographic conditions, new scientific and technological discoveries, the introduction of new commercial products, local crises that suddenly illuminate national concerns—all inevitably expose new problems even as they force us to redefine old ones.

The unprecedented population increase in nonmetropolitan areas has brought to national attention the limitations of small local governments. Nonmetropolitan growth has also made an issue of the availability of prime farmland.

The redefinition of environmental problems is most obvious in air and water pollution control. Until the past five or six years, air pollution concerns were concentrated on five pollutants emitted in large volumes. Water pollution control efforts were similarly limited to a small number of traditional water problems such as oxygen depletion, sediment, and coliform bacteria. The gradual discovery that a variety of metals and organic chemicals are polluting both air and water, and that these substances pose potentially severe human health threats, has markedly changed the perception of what needs to be done to deal with air and water pollution. As this report indicates, control efforts have not yet adjusted to this changed perception.

The still-unfolding discovery of the nature and dimensions of the toxics problem has focused attention on aspects of the environment previously neglected. Most people spend most of their lives indoors, but air pollution control efforts under the Clean Air Act have been devoted exclusively to the quality of outdoor air. Occupational health programs have dealt with air quality in factories for some time, but evidence is now accumulating that residences and offices may also be places where people are exposed to significant amounts of toxic pollutants. Similarly, until recently, groundwater, the source of drinking water for half the nation's population, has been presumed safe. Toxic contamination of groundwater is now recognized as a problem in many locations, forcing the abandonment of hundreds of drinking wells supplying millions of people. Groundwater supplies in some places—in many parts of the Southwest and Great Plains, for example—also are being threatened by depletion.

Government environmental programs are compartmentalized, usually into air, water, land disposal, and so forth. One characteristic of toxic substances, however, is that they tend to be present in more than one part of the environment, so, for example, efforts to control toxic water pollutants may result in increased toxic air pollution. What's more, air pollutants may be a significant source of water pollution, as in the case of acid rain. Data on PCBs in the Great Lakes Basin suggest that 60 to 90 percent of the total PCB input to Lakes Superior and Michigan may come from the atmosphere. To date, problems like these, affecting more than one part of the environment, have been attacked by neither the federal nor state governments.

The highest priority on the new agenda is the development of more efficient programs that will address environmental problems more comprehensively. We need to examine increased use of market mechanisms, greater integration of both statutory authorities and organizational arrangements, and a wide range of incentives to improve the way our environmental and resource laws are implemented.

Information for Environmental Policy

Scientific ignorance or uncertainty characterizes most environmental problems. We do not know much about how to predict the transport of pollutants in air or water, we do not have good ways of measuring or predicting the amount of soil erosion from a field, we do not know the habitat requirements of many endangered species, we have only rudimentary knowledge of how heat circulates inside buildings. The gaps in scientific knowledge are most severe with respect to toxic substances. Many potentially toxic chemicals have not been tested at all, many more have not been tested adequately, and, even for those that have been subjected to the most extensive tests, we are often unsure what the tests mean for human health.

Our monitoring of environmental problems is even more deficient than our scientific knowledge. We have no monitoring data sufficient to describe accurately the extent or developing seriousness of any environmental problem. The single national water quality monitoring network often fails to provide useful information on several of the major traditional water pollutants, because the monitors generally are some distance removed from where the pollutants are discharged. EPA's estimates of air pollution emissions are simply rough approximations. They have been drastically revised, for all years back to 1970, three times in the past two years. Each change showed more improvement in air pollution control than the previous set of figures, but the reasons for the changes have not been documented. Except for a few pesticides, there is no reliable national monitoring of toxic chemicals.

Government planning efforts are a third source of information for environmental policy. Planning both uses and produces information. In the past few years, planning programs under the Resources Conservation Act (for farmland), the Resources Planning Act (for forests and rangelands), and the Federal Land Policy and Management Act (for federal lands managed by the Bureau of Land Management) have not only tried to introduce a greater degree of rationality and predictability to government programs but also have triggered the collection of a great deal of new and relevant information. These programs supplemented other planning efforts such as the A-95 review of federal projects by state and regional agencies, multi-agency river basin planning, and water pollution control planning under Section 208 of the Clean Water Act. Many of these planning efforts have failed to bring about the coordination and policy cohesion that their supporters had anticipated, but the need persists for resource planning guided by accurate information.

All these types of information—scientific, monitoring, and planning—either have been or are likely to be severely set back by budget cuts. Scientific research on environmental problems has been among the hardest hit of the generally hard-hit environmental programs. Some monitoring programs, such as the national water quality monitoring network (NASQAN), have already been curtailed, and many more are threatened. The 208 planning program (aimed at controlling nonpoint water pollution or runoff) is ending; the A-95 program (under which all relevant government bodies in an area were routinely consulted about federal plans, to ensure coordination and avoid duplication) is about to be eliminated; and the future of some of the more recently established programs is in doubt.

Because of the budget cuts, the information base for environmental policy, always weak, is likely to be even weaker in the future. We will be less able to sort out important problems from unimportant ones, less able to tell which environmental programs are working effectively and which are not. Perhaps most important, the perennial dilemma of whether available information is sufficient to justify action will become more pervasive and difficult.

Not to take action is itself a decision. To decide to wait for more information is, in fact, a decision not to take action. But the less adequate the available information, the more the decision to take or not take action will be based, even more than in the past, on ideology or the instincts or self-interest of decision makers.

The Urgency of Action

Environmental programs are not an expendable indulgence of an affluent society. The basic purpose of environmental programs is to protect us from ourselves by assuring that our activities do not destroy the natural functions on which we depend.

Resource policies are inseparable from environmental policies. One function of environmental policies is to assure the availability of such vital resources as clean water and an adequate supply of food and timber. Conversely, wasteful and inefficient resource use is a major contributor to environmental problems. The wise use of the earth's resources is a key element in a wise environmental policy.

Delays in pursuing environmental programs may have serious consequences. At stake are human health, the condition of our farms and forests and rivers, and irreplaceable natural areas and animal species. Not only are the stakes high; many decisions are irreversible. A wetland filled, a historic building razed, a species that becomes extinct, are forever gone. Wilderness once developed takes generations to revert back to wilderness. Once contaminated, groundwater may be unusable for centuries. Changes in global climate produced by human activities may be irreversible.

Policy Changes

President Reagan's determined campaign to diminish federal involvement and reduce domestic expenditures has brought deep cutbacks in environmental programs. It is the Administration's view that environmental protection measures have imposed unacceptable burdens on the economy, particularly on industry. It seeks, therefore, both to ease regulatory requirements affecting industry and to assign priority to mineral exploration and extraction in the management of federal lands.

Consistent with this view, the Administration looks to the private market and to state and local governments to assume some of the eliminated federal functions. For many environmental programs, however, it was the failure of the private market that led to government action in the first place, and failures or inaction of state and local governments that led to federal intervention. Although federal efforts have themselves often merited criticism, there is need to determine, in each case, whether the private sector or states or localities will, in fact, act more effectively.

First, the private sector. There are, indeed, things that the market can do well. Energy pricing can and probably should be left to market forces, although it is not clear that the Administration will take measures (such as natural gas deregulation) that will lead to a free energy market. Also, it is not clear that the market will work effectively for such important energy users as rental housing and commercial office space, where those who make the decisions about design, insulation, and heating and cooling systems are not the ones who pay the fuel bills. There is, however, no market for clean air or water or for wilderness, and no market is likely to develop. Nor is research—on energy, for example—likely to be supported adequately by corporations, because no single company can capture the full benefits of research that does not result in a specific product or process change. The market has failed to provide many other societal needs, such as decent housing for a large number of Americans.

As for state and local governments, most are fiscally strapped, and the reduction of federal assistance will reduce state and local budgets and staffs at the same time that demands on them are increased. Few of these governments are in a position to replace federal expenditures for environmental and resource protection or to establish regulatory standards that may be perceived as driving prospective economic development to other jurisdictions.

The connection between federal programs to protect the environment and the physical quality of the environment has been amply documented. For example, although air quality improvements have not come cheaply, the air today is far cleaner than it would have been if the Clean Air Act had not been implemented. Environmental programs are sometimes cumbersome, legalistic, or bureaucratic. But overall data indicate they have been working. Critics within and outside the Reagan Administration argue that the cost of environmental programs has been excessive. But with the critics now responsible for executing environmental policies, one awaits a clear, well thought-out philosophy of environmental protection. A year and a half into the Administration's term, no hierarchy of environmental priorities or concept of a positive federal role in maintaining and enhancing the nation's environment is yet discernible.

Chapter 1

Underlying Trends

Population and economic trends are two of the fundamental determinants of both resource consumption and environmental degradation. The number of people in the United States, their ages, where they live, and how much money they have to spend substantially influence how we use our land, the characteristics of our urban areas, the amount of energy and other natural resources we consume, and the amount of air, water, and other pollution we produce. Our economic situation affects the ability of industries to invest in pollution abatement facilities, of government to provide a wide range of environmental amenities, and the willingness of voters to support programs that attempt to limit environmental degradation. The quality of the environment and the efficiency with which we use natural resources are, in turn, important factors in determining our economic viability and overall quality of life.

POPULATION

In April 1980, the U.S. Census Bureau conducted the 20th Census of the U.S. population. The counts are now in, and they document some major changes taking place in the growth, location, and age of the U.S. population.

Three major shifts are confirmed by the data. We are still a growing country, but at some of the lowest rates in history. While the bulk of the population lives in metropolitan areas, our non-metropolitan areas are now growing faster. And, not surprisingly, we are an aging society.

Population Growth

The population of the United States on April 1, 1980, was estimated at 226,504,825, an 11.4 percent increase over the 1970 count. This rate of increase was the second lowest ever recorded for the United States since counting began in 1790. (See figure 1.1) The only lower increase, 7.2 percent, was registered during the Depression years of the 1930s. Yet even the small rate of increase between 1970 and 1980 added more than 23 million people to the population—the third largest numerical increase in our history.*

The United States population has increased by approximately 50 percent since 1950. We remain the fourth most populated country

Figure 1.1
U.S. Population Growth, 1790-1980

Million people

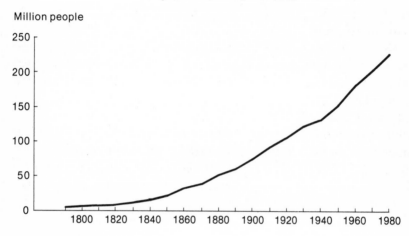

Average annual rate of growth
in percent

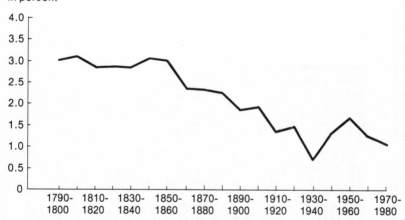

Source: U.S. Department of Commerce, Bureau of the Census

---

* The two larger numerical increases were during the 1950s, with 27.8 million people added, and during the 1960s, with 23.9 million added.

in the world, behind China, India, and the Soviet Union.[1] If things seem more crowded than they used to, it is because they are. We averaged 42.6 people per square mile in 1950; now there are 64.

The most important reason for the declining rate of population growth has been the decline in the natural rate of growth (figure 1.2), resulting from fewer children being born per family. In 1980, the total fertility rate was 1.8, meaning that, on the average, American women would have 1.8 live births during their lifetime. This rate is far lower than the rate of 2.5 in 1970, 3.4 in 1960, and 3.3 in 1950, and below the rate (2.1) that would eventually result in zero population growth if there were no net immigration.

The decline in the rate of natural growth is making immigration a more important component in the rate of population growth. Legal immigration accounted for nearly one-fourth of the total increase in population over the past five years. Although the immigration laws set a quota of 270,000 net immigrants per year, the actual amount of immigration has been much higher due to families of American citizens entering outside the quota, and to the increasing numbers of refugees. The United States has made special exceptions

Figure 1.2
Components of Population Change, 1955-1981

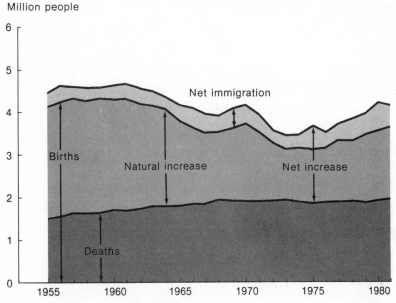

Source: U.S. Department of Commerce, Bureau of the Census

to the quota for large numbers of Vietnamese and Cubans. There is also a significant amount of illegal entry into the country, perhaps as large as the number of legal entrants, and, although many of these illegal aliens choose to stay, they may not be fully counted in the Census.[2]

Population Distribution

Changes in population tend to follow cycles, not straight lines. The rapid rate of population growth during the late 1950s and early 1960s was followed by a period of declining growth rates in the late 1960s and 1970s. Regional and local concentrations of population, too, have changed. The apparently unending growth in urbanization and the movement of jobs and people from the South to the North and West have stopped, and in the case of regional shifts the trend is now in the other direction.

Regional Shifts

Where people live has changed significantly during the past 10 to 15 years. The West and the South are now the fastest-growing regions of the country (figure 1.3). Their combined population, for the first time, is greater than the combined population of the Northeast and North Central regions. In fact, during the late 1970s, the Northeast experienced a net loss in population.

The fastest-growing states are Wyoming, Arizona, Nevada, and Florida. New York, the District of Columbia, and Rhode Island lost population, and Pennsylvania, Ohio, and Massachusetts had virtually the same number of people in 1980 as they did in 1970.*[3] As a result, the center of the population moved west and south— from southern Illinois across the Mississippi River into Jefferson County, Missouri.[4]

These population shifts have been influenced by many factors. The West and the South generally have better climates, a lower cost of living, and more new jobs. Federal government purchases of goods and services, military spending, and growth in transfer payments have influenced this migration. Many of the rapidly growing areas are also less afflicted by the congestion, crime, and pollution of the older industrial settlements. In public opinion polls taken

---

*In an apparent deviation from this general trend, population grew during the 1970s in the northern New England states—Vermont, New Hampshire, and Maine—by 17 percent.

Figure 1.3
Population Growth by Region, 1950-1980

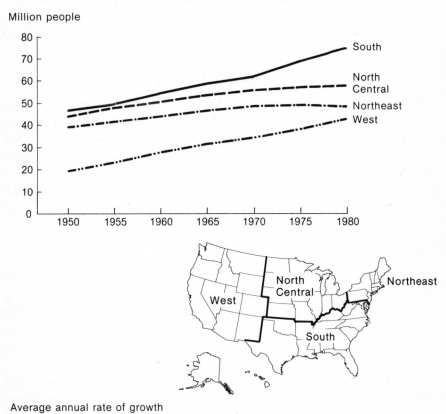

Million people

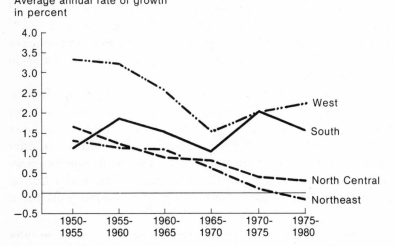

Average annual rate of growth
in percent

Source: U.S. Department of Commerce, Bureau of the Census

during the late 1950s and the 1960s, Americans said they wanted to live in smaller places, with higher quality environmental amenities (less noise, air pollution, smog, congestion, and water pollution).[5] These factors favored growth in the South and West. They also favored growth in smaller cities. The result has been an explosion of new and fast-growing metropolitan areas.

Metropolitan Areas

Three-quarters of the population (or 169,430,000 people) live in metropolitan areas. The character of these areas is changing. Standard Metropolitan Statistical Areas (or SMSAs) almost always include a city or urbanized area of 50,000 persons or more, the county containing the urban center, and neighboring counties closely associated with the central area by daily commuting ties. There are now 318 SMSAs, at least one in every state of the country. In 1950, there were 169; in 1970, 243. Two-thirds of the most recently designated SMSAs are located in the South and West.[6]

The 25 SMSAs that grew fastest during the 1970s are also in the South and West, with 10 in Florida and 5 in Texas (figure 1.4). Three of the fastest-growing metropolitan areas registered increases of more than 350,000: Houston, Phoenix, and Ft. Lauderdale. In almost every case the SMSAs with declining populations are located in the North and North Central regions of the country.[7] These SMSAs include New York, Philadelphia, Detroit, Cleveland, Boston, St. Louis, Pittsburgh, Newark, Milwaukee, and Buffalo.

Within metropolitan areas, suburban areas are growing faster than central cities. They now account for 44.7 percent of the population, up from 37.2 percent in 1970 and 30.6 percent in 1960.[8] Suburban areas have become the primary growth centers of our society: in population, commerce, industry, and services.

Even in the Northeast, where population is declining, suburban areas in general grew. In the North Central region, the suburbs of Chicago, Detroit, St. Louis, Minneapolis-St.Paul, and Cleveland gained population, while their central cities lost at rates ranging from 11 percent to 28 percent.[9]

In the rapidly growing SMSAs of the West and South, it was principally the suburban areas that did the growing. The suburbs of Denver grew by 60 percent, while the central city lost 2.8 percent of its population. Dallas suburbs grew by 47.4 percent, while the central city grew a modest 3.7 percent. Only where cities such as Houston aggressively annexed nearby territory did the central cities

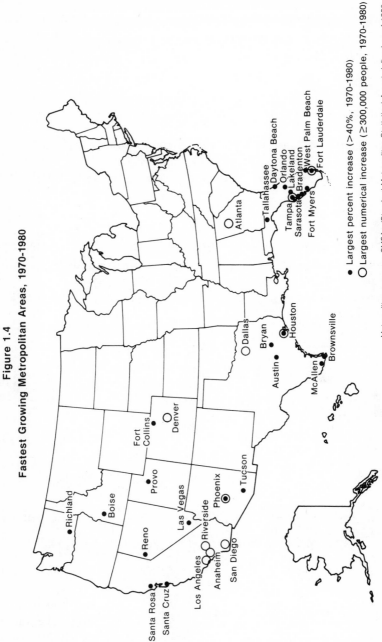

Figure 1.4
Fastest Growing Metropolitan Areas, 1970-1980

● Largest percent increase (>40%, 1970-1980)
○ Largest numerical increase (≥300,000 people, 1970-1980)

Metropolitan areas are SMSAs (Standard Metropolitan Statistical Areas) defined as of 1980.
Source: U.S. Department of Commerce, Bureau of the Census

grow substantially.[10]

As a result, the density of central cities across the country is declining. Since 1950, density in the central cities has dropped almost half, from 7,517 to 4,167 people per square mile in 1978. At the same time, density in the suburbs increased from 175 to 223 people per square mile.[11]

Nonmetropolitan Areas

For the first time in history, nonmetropolitan areas of the country are growing faster than metropolitan areas (figure 1.5). While the United States as a whole grew by 11.4 percent (1.08 percent a year) during the 1970s, nonmetropolitan areas grew by 15.1 percent (1.46 percent a year). This is a remarkable shift from a nonmetropolitan growth rate of 0.30 percent per year in the 1950s and 0.43 percent per year in the 1960s. Much of this nonmetropolitan growth occurred in counties adjacent to SMSAs and is thought to be an extension of the drawing power of the SMSA for jobs and services. But a large portion of the increase occurred in the least populated counties of the country.[12]

Figure 1.5

Population Growth in Metropolitan and Nonmetropolitan Areas, 1950-1980

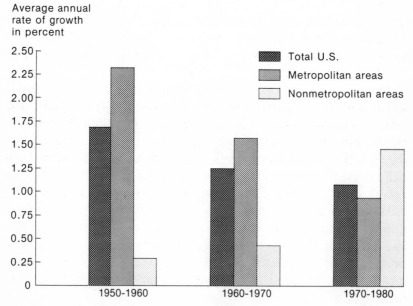

Source: U.S. Department of Agriculture, Economic Research Service

The growth of nonmetropolitan areas has been widespread. Forty-six states registered higher rates of growth in nonmetropolitan counties in the 1970s than in the 1960s. The exceptions were Rhode Island, Connecticut, New Jersey and Indiana. Places like the Ozarks, the Texas hill country, Northern Michigan, the Tennessee Valley, and the intermountain regions of the West are examples of high growth areas.[13]

This rural growth does not signal a back-to-farming movement. The number of people employed in farming has continued to decline at the same time that rural growth has been occurring.[14] People are moving to nonmetropolitan areas to participate in a variety of economic activities and have in the process created more complex and perhaps more stable economies than those based primarily on agriculture. In fact, those nonmetropolitan counties dependent primarily on agriculture are continuing to lose population. People are finding jobs in construction (recreation, resort, retirement, second home); light industry; state universities; new energy and mineral developments; and social services and businesses to support the growing rural population. Many of the new rural settlers are retired persons living on pensions or social security. And, of course, many rural residents commute to jobs in metropolitan areas.

As a result of these population shifts, many sparsely settled areas of the country are now undergoing intensive development. Populations along the Gulf and Pacific coasts are increasing rapidly.[15] Population growth in Alaska, on barrier islands along the Atlantic and Gulf Coasts, on the steep slopes of the Rocky Mountains, and in other areas is stimulating substantial development.

Many of these shifts are creating significant impacts on the environment. They are resulting in the development of new lands that were previously inhospitable: lands that were too hot (Florida and the Southwest); without water (the arid and semiarid Southwest); inaccessible (barrier islands); too cold (Alaska); or subject to high risk of natural disasters (floodplains and hurricane and earthquake zones). The inhospitality of these lands was a form of protection from human development. With the aid of advanced technology, humans have overcome natural forces and have changed the quality and extent of these fragile lands, altered their natural biota, and brought pollution to areas that were relatively untouched. In many places, new development is substantially affecting traditional patterns of life.

Age of the Population

The U.S. population as a whole is getting older (figure 1.6). The median age of the population in 1980 was 30.0 years; in 1970, it was 28.0; and in 1960, 29.5.

The change is only partially a result of people living longer (life expectancy increased from 70.9 years in 1970 to 73.6 years in 1980). Another important factor is that the declining birth rate decreased the proportion of young people.

Since 1970, there has been a continual decrease in the total number of people under the age of 15. This decrease results both from the decrease in birth rates and from the fact that the people born during the "baby boom" of the 1950s are past 15. People between 25 and 34 years old now form the second largest 10-year age group in our society. By 1990, this group will be 35 to 44, thus further increasing the median age.

This is the age group that caused crowded primary and secondary schools in the 1950s and 1960s, crowded colleges in the late 1960s and early 1970s, and expanded the supply of new job applicants throughout the 1970s. They then created a demand for apartments

Figure 1.6
Population by Age and Sex, 1960 and 1980

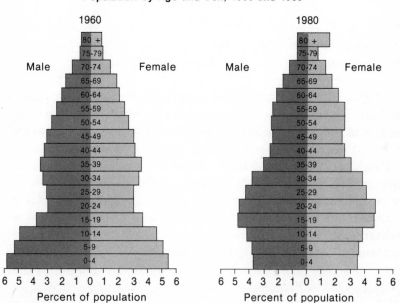

Source: U.S. Department of Commerce, Bureau of the Census

and multifamily dwellings. Now this group is ready to buy homes. Their choices in housing location (center city, suburb, nonmetropolitan area) and type of housing (single family, multifamily, mobile home) will be the most important factor in determining the shape of human settlements for decades to come.

Household Formation

An important development greatly influencing the growth and location of housing, particularly in central cities, is the rapid growth in the number of households.* Although the growth in total population has slowed, the rate of household formation has increased rapidly. Both young and old have been moving out of larger family households to set up private housekeeping. This change has been rapid. In the 1960s, when population grew at a rate of 1.3 percent per year, the number of households grew at a rate of 1.9 percent per year. In the 1970s, with population growing at a rate of 0.8 percent per year, the number of households grew at a rate of 2.3 percent.[16]

As the number of households has increased and the number of children per family has declined, household size has also declined. In 1960, the average household had 3.29 persons; in 1980 it had 2.75 persons, a decline of 16 percent.[17]

ECONOMICS

At the beginning of 1982, the United States was experiencing the second recession in as many years—a new record—and there were more people unemployed than at any time since the Depression of the 1930s.[18] During the past two years, the rate of economic growth has been down; interest rates have been at record high levels; and the rate of inflation has been higher than at any time since the end of World War II.[19]

The Reagan Administration has adopted a series of economic policies that involve a combination of large tax cuts (particularly for businesses and higher income taxpayers), substantial reductions in all of the federal budget except for defense, a significant increase in defense expenditures, and a freeing of businesses from government regulations. At the same time, to dampen inflation, the Federal

---

* A household is defined as one or more persons living together in a single housing unit. Therefore, the number of households is equal to the number of occupied housing units.

Reserve Bank has been maintaining very tight control on the money supply.

The goal of the Administration's program is to stimulate more business investment, which will result, it is argued, in higher levels of output and a resurgence in the rate of economic growth. Current economic trends and the Administration's policies have important implications for efforts to preserve and improve our natural and human environment.

Gross National Product (GNP)

The U.S. economy has almost reached a $3 trillion Gross National Product (having passed $1 trillion in 1971), although much of the apparent increase since 1970 has resulted from inflation rather than real growth (figure 1.7).* Real economic growth rates over the past decade have varied considerably. The rate of real growth has been negative in 4 years during this period, compared to 1 year out of the previous 15. The average growth rate was somewhat lower than the longer-term trend, 3.0 percent per year (from 1971 to 1981) compared to an average of 3.4 percent over the preceeding 20 years. Since 1973, the average growth rate has been even lower—2.3 percent per year.

A high level of GNP indicates that we are producing lots of goods and services, thus consuming large amounts of natural resources, and, probably, producing large amounts of pollution. When looking at the environmental trends reported in the rest of this book, it is important to remember that the real level of GNP has grown by about 40 percent since 1970.[20] Given such an increase, pollution levels also might be expected to increase substantially in the absence of environmental controls, and even relatively unimpressive improvements in environmental quality may represent a significant accomplishment. In some cases, however, apparent environmental improvements—cleaner air, for example—may result from a reduction in the amount of activity creating pollution rather than from real improvements in pollution control.

A strong economy, represented by a growing GNP, creates a number of opportunities for environmental improvement. Economic growth brings about the construction of new production facilities, which often tend to be cleaner than older ones. And rapidly growing

*GNP is a measure of the value of all the goods and services produced by the economy that enter the marketplace.

Figure 1.7
Gross National Product, 1955-1981

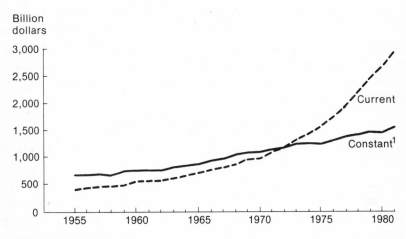

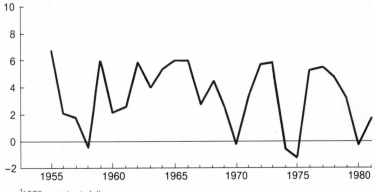

[1] 1972 constant dollars
1981 preliminary

Source: Executive Office of the President, Council of Economic Advisors

economies are usually better able to divert resources to programs such as environmental improvement. In a stagnant economy, these resources have to be drawn from some competing use, often against substantial resistance.

Industrial Production and Productivity

The nation's economic growth is not shared equally by all economic sectors (Figure 1.8). The communication sector has grown at almost three times the rate of all industry; other service-type sectors are

Figure 1.8

Growth in Industrial Output by Industry, 1968-1978

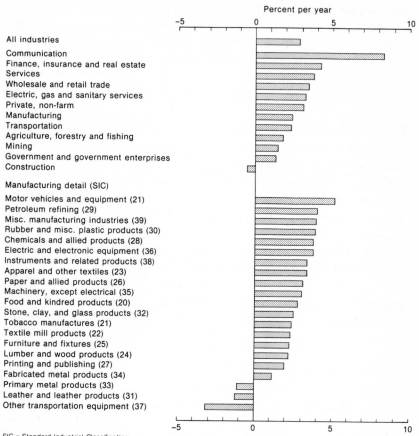

SIC = Standard Industrial Classification

Source: U.S. Department of Commerce, Bureau of Industrial Economics

also growing rapidly. Agriculture, government, and mining have grown most slowly, and construction has actually declined. The four fastest-growing sectors (communication, finance, services, and trade) increased their proportion of total industrial output from 42.84 percent in 1958 to 48.42 percent in 1978. The four slowest-growing sectors (agriculture, mining, government, and construction) decreased their proportion from 28.18 percent to 20.70 percent over the same period.

These statistics support the common observation that the U.S. economy is becoming increasingly service oriented. From an environmental perspective, this trend has positive implications. The most rapidly growing sectors are, in general, less environmentally destructive than the slowest-growing sectors.

The shift to service industries is not taking place at the expense of the manufacturing sector. In fact, manufacturing has grown faster than the average of all industries, increasing its proportion of total industrial output from 22.81 percent to 24.62 percent from 1958 to 1978 (this proportion fell slightly between 1968 and 1978).

Within the manufacturing sector, the fastest-growing subsector from 1968 to 1978 was motor vehicles and equipment, although this performance has not continued over the past three years. Chemicals, petroleum refining, plastics, electrical equipment, and miscellaneous manufacturing also grew faster than the average, with rates between 3.75 and 4.00 percent per year. Some of these faster growing industries—for instance, chemicals and petroleum refining—have caused serious pollution problems. But so have such slow-growing industries as primary metals (which includes both iron and steel production and nonferrous metals).

One of the major factors underlying our overall economic problems has been the reduced rate of productivity growth in the economy. Productivity—as measured by real output per hour worked—grew at a relatively consistent rate of around 3.13 percent from 1948 to 1968. Since 1968, the average rate has been only 1.3 percent, less than half the previous level.[21] This lower rate places a severe constraint on overall economic growth, on the ability of people to increase their real incomes, and on our willingness (and ability) to free resources to deal with environmental problems and other social issues.

The reasons for the reduced rate of productivity growth are not clear. Some of the most commonly mentioned factors are insufficient investment; lower expenditures for research and development; the entry of large numbers of younger, less experienced workers into the labor force; the economic shock caused by higher energy prices; and health and environmental regulation.*

Reduced productivity and higher inflation rates are the two chief economic factors used in arguments opposing environmental pro-

---

*There may be additional reasons in specific industries. For instance, the reduced productivity in mining (which includes oil extraction) is probably at least partially caused by the fact that an increased proportion of these minerals are taken from lower grade deposits as better deposits are exhausted.

grams. To at least some extent, the productivity argument has some legitimacy—although not necessarily as it is usually used. During the 1970s, we placed much more emphasis than we had in the past on producing cleaner air, water, and other environmental amenities as well as more goods and services. The standard productivity measure, however, ignores the benefits of a cleaner environment. If there were some way of including these benefits, the apparent drop in productivity would not be as great.*

Investment

Business investment in equipment and buildings has recently been a higher percentage of the nation's GNP than it was in the early 1960s, although current rates are still considered inadequate to support a vigorously growing economy.** The proportion of this investment devoted to pollution abatement equipment has declined from a high of over 4.4 percent in 1975 to an average of 3.1 percent in the past three years.[22]

The rate of investment has several implications for environmental programs. Some of these are favorable; some unfavorable. New plants are often more efficient in their use of energy, water, and other scarce natural resources than are older plants. And, because they usually have to satisfy stringent environmental standards, new plants typically emit fewer pollutants. The location of new plants is also important. They are predominantly being located outside of central cities and away from the older industrial areas of the Northeast and Midwest.[23] These shifts are seriously affecting the economic viability of some older areas (see chapter 8). The shifts also mean that, while new plants may not be contributing to air and water pollution in the more polluted areas of the country, they are emitting these pollutants in areas that previously were often relatively pollution free.

Housing is another form of investment that can have important

---

*On the other hand, it is also true that further environmental improvements are becoming more expensive, which implies that the productivity of resources devoted to these outputs will be declining as well.

**An increasing proportion of this investment has gone for equipment rather than structures. Since equipment has a shorter economic life, the growth in usable capital stock has not kept pace with the growth in investment. The increased emphasis on equipment may also indicate that more of the investment is being devoted to fixing up old plants rather than building new ones. In many cases, the older facilities remain less productive than new ones, even after these investments are made.

environmental implications. Many new housing units are built far from central cities. This results in increased sprawl and attendant land-use conflicts, loss of economic activity for the central urban areas, and increased automobile travel.[24] After reaching a historic peak of 2.4 million units in 1972, the number of housing starts has fallen off substantially (figure 1.9). However, the number of single-family units—those that consume the most land—has fallen less rapidly.

One major reason for the slump in housing starts is, of course, high interest rates. High rates discourage all types of investment, but they have a particularly severe effect on the housing and automobile sectors. During periods of high interest rates, businesses tend to keep older (and often dirtier) plants in operation longer, rather than investing in new facilities; homeowners tend to rehabilitate existing structures rather than building new ones; and government finds it more difficult to make investments in a wide range of environmental facilities such as wastewater treatment plants and parks.

Figure 1.9
New Housing Starts, 1955-1980

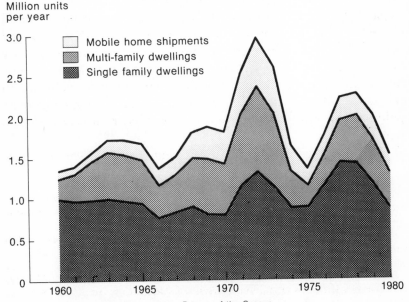

Source: U.S. Department of Commerce, Bureau of the Census

Employment and Unemployment

While our labor force continues to grow (at a rate of about 2 million persons per year), an increasing number of workers have been unable to find jobs. In the last half of the 1970s, the unemployment rate averaged 6.7 percent, compared to 4.8 percent for the 1960s—a difference of approximately 3 million workers. The 1981-1982 recession has created the largest number of unemployed since the Depression.[25]

There have also been some significant changes in the location of new jobs and the types of activities in which people are being employed. New jobs are shifting away from the Northeast and North Central states and to the South and Southwest (figure 1.10). Employment in traditionally more polluting industries is following the same general trend, again indicating that major pollution sources are shifting into less polluted areas.*

Inflation

In the last half of the 1970s, the consumer price index was increasing, on an average, nearly seven times faster than it did during the first half of the 1960s. By 1980, it was increasing at a rate that the United States had not experienced in 35 years. The 1981-1982 recession brought the rate of inflation down, but this may be only a temporary phenomenon. The most important single component in the inflation of the 1970s was the rapid increase in the cost of energy, the composite price of which increased 158 percent, compared to 82 percent for all other consumer prices.[26]

Inflation has a generally negative impact on environmental programs. People tend to be more concerned about maintaining their own real standard of living, and therefore resist attempts to divert personal or public funds to environmental programs, particularly when the costs of these programs are rapidly increasing. Environmental programs have also been blamed for contributing to inflation, creating additional pressure to relax them.

Personal Income and Expenditures

For the second time in the last two decades, in 1980 the average

---

*The high growth rates in mining in the South Central region most likely reflect the fact that the statistics on mining employment include petroleum exploration, which has increased significantly in the traditional oil-producing states since 1973.

per capita real disposable income was lower than the year before (the first time this occurred during the period was in 1974).*

Since 1960, the proportion of income spent on such necessities as food and clothing has decreased (from 33 percent to 27 percent), while the proportion spent on housing, transportation, and medical expenses has increased (from 29 to 36 percent).[27] The increased expenditures for housing reflect a combination of factors: the desire for more space, generally higher housing prices, and higher interest rates on mortgages. The higher proportion of income spent on "housing operation" over the same period reflects, in large part, higher expenditures for energy—resulting both from increased energy consumption and higher energy prices. These expenditures (including fuel oil, coal, electricity, and gas) have grown from a total of $12.1 billion (or 3.7 percent of personal consumption expenditures) in 1960 to $63.3 billion (or over 4.1 percent) in 1979.

The increased expenditures on transportation include both higher expenditures on motor vehicles and parts (from 6 percent of total expenditures in 1960 to 7.0 percent in 1978) and on gasoline and oil (from 3.7 percent in 1960 to 4.5 percent in 1979).[28] However, expenditures on automobiles have fluctuated widely during recent years, and the higher expenditures on gasoline and oil have resulted more from increased prices than from increased consumption. The average number of passenger miles driven per vehicle has leveled off, and gasoline consumption per mile driven for private automobiles has fallen (because of more efficient automobiles) since 1973 (figure 1.11)**.

Another trend, paralleling the population and employment shifts discussed earlier, has been an evening-out of income levels among regions of the country. Per capita incomes have tended, on the average, to grow more rapidly in the South and West, thus reducing U.S. regional income disparaties.

Government Expenditures

Federal, state, and local governments have taken an increasingly

---

* Real disposable income is the amount of real income people have available for purchasing goods or services (or for savings) after taking account of inflation and payments to and from government (for example, income taxes and social security and welfare payments).

**See chapter 5 for futher information about energy consumption.

Figure 1.10
Employment Changes by Region and by Selected Industries, 1972-1980

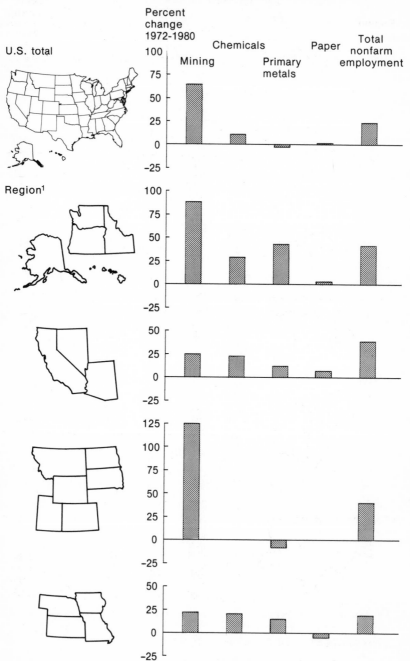

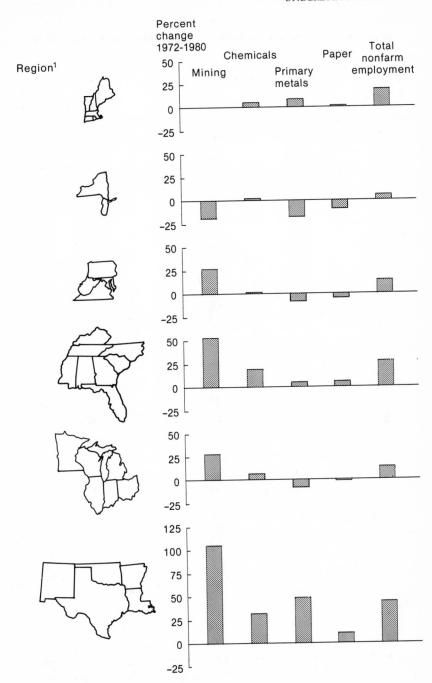

[1] U.S. Environmental Protection Agency regions.

Source: U.S. Department of Labor, Bureau of Labor Statistics

Figure 1.11

Miles Traveled and Gasoline Consumed per Passenger Car, 1967-1980

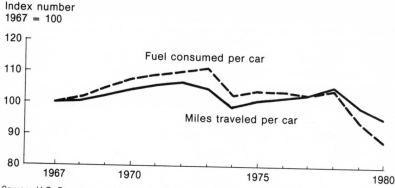

Source: U.S. Department of Transportation, Federal Highway Administration

larger proportion of our GNP over the past 25 years. From the late 1950s to the late 1970s, the ratio of total government receipts to GNP increased from .26 to .32. Most of the increase has gone to payments for income maintenance programs, such as social security, and interest on the national debt.[29]

Government purchase of goods and services has only increased from 19.7 percent of GNP in the late 1950s to 20.3 percent in the late 1970s, when it began falling again.[30] Some of the increase went for environmental programs: between 1960 and 1979, the proportion of government expenditures for recreation increased from 0.66 percent to 0.94 percent, and for sewage treatment from 0.67 percent to 1.05 percent.[31] On the other hand, the proportion of expenditures allocated to natural resources and to sanitation decreased.

Economic Impacts of Pollution Control Programs

Environmental programs in general, and pollution control programs in particular, are frequently accused of being responsible for many of our recent economic problems. The Bureau of Economic Analysis estimates that the nation spent $55.7 billion (or about 2 percent of GNP) for pollution control in 1980—equivalent to $26.5 billion in 1972 dollars (figure 1.12). There has been substantial debate on the economic impact of these expenditures. Some argue that the funds are diverted from alternative uses such as investments in new plants and equipment and, therefore, lower the rate of economic growth and increase the rate of inflation.

The most recent analysis of these impacts, like most of those

Figure 1.12

**Pollution Abatement and Control Expenditures, 1972-1979
(in 1972 constant dollars)**

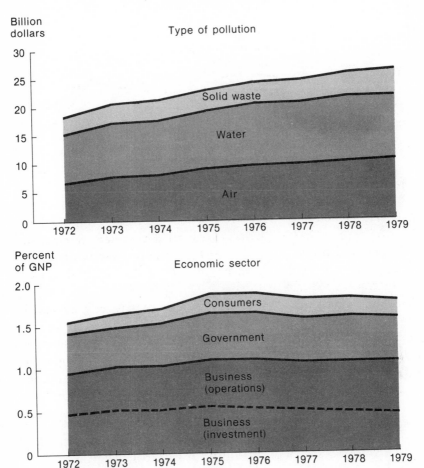

Source: U.S. Department of Commerce, Bureau of Economic Analysis

undertaken earlier, indicates that they are not significant. The programs have some economic impact, but it is much smaller and less serious than is often claimed (figure 1.13). The analysis is based on a comparison between projected economic performance without pollution control programs and the actual and projected performance with the programs in effect.*

---

*This analysis was conducted using a large-scale computer model of the United States economy by Data Resources, Inc., an independent consulting firm that does substantial amounts of work for both private industry and government.

Figure 1.13

**Estimated Impact of Pollution Control Programs on the
Economy, 1970-1987**

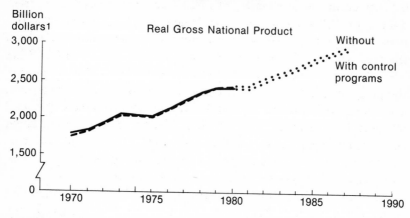

Billion
dollars1   Real Gross National Product

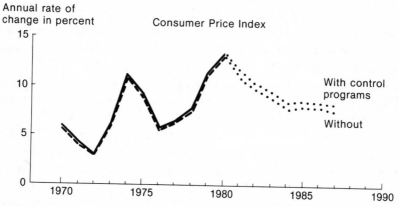

Annual rate of
change in percent   Consumer Price Index

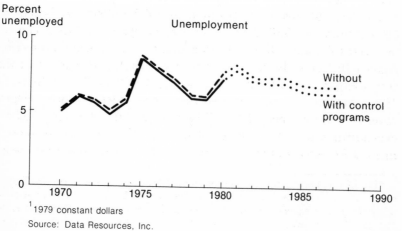

Percent
unemployed   Unemployment

1 1979 constant dollars

Source: Data Resources, Inc.

The study concluded that in 1981 the real Gross National Product was 0.2 percent lower, the Consumer Price Index was increasing 0.5 percentage points faster, business fixed investment in constant dollars was 0.8 percent higher, and the unemployment rate was 0.3 percentage points lower with the programs than would have been the case without them. Over the past 10 years, the real GNP has been slightly higher than it otherwise would have been because of the programs, but since 1976 it has been growing at a slower rate, and from 1981 onward will probably fall slightly below the level it would have attained without the programs. Business investment and various measures of inflation are higher because of pollution control programs throughout the entire period of analysis. Unemployment is lower by an average of 0.2 percentage points.

Although such analyses represent the best that can be done with currently available information and analytical tools, they do not take into account some potentially important considerations. For instance, they do not take account of any of the benefits provided by environmental programs. Although it is not possible to measure actual benefits, the Council on Environmental Quality (CEQ) estimated that the benefits of air quality improvement were $21.4 billion a year by 1978, and those from water quality improvement would be $12.3 billion a year (in 1978 dollars) by 1985.[32]

The macroeconomic analyses also do not completely reflect the impact of pollution control programs on industries that may be particularly affected by these programs. But here, too, evidence indicates that the impacts are less serious than originally feared. For instance, in 1978 CEQ reported that the iron and steel industry would have to invest $6.8 billion in 1975 dollars, equivalent to $9.9 billion in 1980 dollars, for air and water pollution control between 1975 and 1983.[33] A more recent Environmental Protection Agency (EPA) study, based on a survey of firms, estimated that the actual expenditures from 1974 and 1983 will be $8.5 billion (in 1980 dollars), 14 percent less than the earlier estimate, which covered a shorter period.*[34] CEQ reported that pollution control expenditures would consume 20 percent of total industry investment; EPA estimates that this proportion will be about 10 percent.

---

*The EPA estimates of pollution control expenditures in past years are significantly higher than those reported in surveys undertaken by the Bureau of Economic Analysis (BEA). If the EPA historical estimates are replaced by the results of the BEA surveys, the total for 1975-83 investments becomes $5.58 billion in 1980 dollars, 44 percent less than the 1978 CEQ-reported estimate.[35]

Similarly, in 1978 CEQ reported that between 1975 and 1983 the pulp and paper industry would have to invest the equivalent of $9.4 billion (in 1980 dollars) for air and water pollution control.[36] The most recent EPA analysis indicates that from 1970 through 1983 these expenditures will amount to only $6.2 billion, a 34 percent decrease from the earlier estimate.*[38]

Such direct comparisons are not available for other industries, but there is substantial evidence that the same conclusions apply—namely, that the costs and impacts of pollution control regulation are often less than earlier estimates indicated. For instance, metal finishing was thought to be one of the most severely affected industrial categories, requiring investment of $460 million (1977 dollars) for water pollution control, with annual compliance costs of $129 million, and forced closure of as many as 20 percent of the firms.[39] EPA now expects most firms to be able to adopt lower-cost control technologies, which in many cases provide the added benefit of allowing valuable metals to be captured and recycled.[40]

There is an increasing number of examples of individual plants in many different industries adopting innovative technologies that are much lower in cost than standard approaches and that frequently reclaim valuable materials and energy that were formerly wasted.[41] Some of these pollution control efforts even generate profits for the firms installing them.

LOOKING TO THE FUTURE

Population and economic projections are always problematic. Few people anticipated the reduced birth rates of the 1970s. Economic projections have been notoriously inaccurate, even for as little as a year into the future.

Nevertheless, all signs indicate that we can essentially expect our recent population and economic trends to continue, at least during the next decade or two. The population growth rate will probably keep falling—approaching zero by 2020, if net immigration is ignored. And the economy, though it should improve, will most likely not repeat the robust performance of the mid-1960s.

The U.S. population will likely be between 251 million and 288 million by the year 2000.[42] If current rates of natural increase and

---

*Again, the EPA estimates for investments made from 1970 through 1980 are much higher than those reported by the Bureau of Economic Analysis. If the BEA figures for 1975 through 1978 are combined with EPA's estimates for 1979-83, the total becomes $3.7 billion in 1980 dollars, 61 percent less than the 1978 CEQ-reported estimates.[37]

net immigration continue, the number would be about 265 million, and the median age of the population will have increased from 30.0 to 35.5 years.* During the next 5 to 10 years, we should see an echo of the 1950s "baby boom," as many women born during that earlier boom, having postponed their families, decide to have children before leaving the child-bearing ages. But this echo will be muted: there is no reason to expect a return to the large families of the 1950s and 1960s.

The South and the West should continue to experience the most rapid growth rates (figure 1.14). During the 1980s, the South should gain 13.2 million people (17.5 percent), the West 8.8 million (or 20.4 percent), while the North Central region should increase by only 1.6 million (2.8 percent) and the Northeast continue to decline (by 1.8 million, or 3.8 percent). The most important factor in these projections is net immigration among the different regions, which is influenced in large part by the formation of new jobs.

We can be less confident about our economic future. The official government forecasts are rosy—showing us pulling out of the current recesssion in 1982 and then beginning a period of rapid economic growth with low unemployment and inflation. Private forecasters are less optimistic. If we can avoid disruptions like the energy crunch

Figure 1.14
Population Growth and Projections by Region, 1950-1990

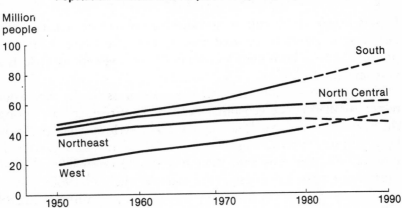

Source: U.S. Bureau of the Census and the Joint Center for Urban Studies of MIT and Harvard University

---

*These projections assume a slight increase in average life expectancy, no change in net immigration, and a fertility rate at replacement levels of 2.1.

of the early 1970s, conditions will probably improve over the next couple of years. The recent changes in federal tax policy should stimulate increased investment, and labor productivity should improve. But we will probably continue to experience lower overall growth rates and higher inflation, unemployment, and interest rates than we did during the 1960s.

This conclusion suggests that environmental programs will continue to face strong opposition. Costly regulations will be strongly opposed; government budgets will remain very tight; high interest rates will make pollution control investments particularly expensive; and slow rates of economic growth will force these programs into harder competition for the resources they need. Overall, our environmental policies will have to be very sensitive to this situation and to the need for balancing environmental improvements against their economic costs.

The need to balance, however, does not imply that we should disregard environmental concerns, as some opponents would seem to suggest. In the long run, a healthy environment is necessary for a healthy economy. We cannot maintain a growing population at a higher standard of living without adequate natural resources—adequate in both quantity and quality. And, as chapter 9 indicates, people in the United States still strongly support environmental programs. As we begin to work ourselves out of the current economic difficulties, we can only expect this support to increase.

The prospects for the United States, all in all, look tight, but relatively favorable. Some recent analyses of global prospects are much less encouraging. Worldwide, we are experiencing rapid population growth, natural resource consumption, and environmental destruction. Unless significantly slowed or reversed, these trends point toward very serious problems in the future. Less-developed countries are industrializing rapidly and experiencing the same types of pollution problems the United States has been attempting to deal with. These global problems can, in turn, have very important implications for our country. As chapter 6 indicates, some parts of our economy are becoming more dependent on global economic conditions. And, as chapter 2 points out, we are becoming more aware of global environmental problems, where pollutants emitted anywhere on earth can have an impact on the United States. Thus, we can ill afford to shrug off analyses of global problems. If their projections prove to be accurate, our situation will be much less attractive than we otherwise might expect.

FURTHER READING

The U.S. Census Bureau is the source of most basic reports on population growth and distribution, although many other organizations and scholars analyze how and why the trends are changing. A good starting point for current data is the *Statistical Abstract of the United States*, published annually by the Census Bureau and available through the U.S. Government Printing Office. The first chapter is on population (growth, distribution, and mobility), the second chapter deals with vital statistics (births, deaths, marriages, divorces) and the third with immigration—the three basic components of population change. The *Statistical Abstract* also contains a guide to sources of data and an appendix on statistical methodology and reliability. The monthly journal *American Demographics* is a good source for keeping up to date with current research on population trends. Another useful reference for both United States and international trends is *The Bulletin*, prepared by the Population Reference Bureau, Washington, D.C.

The Census Bureau conducts a complete count of the United States population through the decennial census as required in Article I of the Constitution. The national summary decennial population figures from the "1980 Census of Population and Housing" will be released late in 1982 as Chapters A, B, C, and D in the *U.S. Census of Population, 1980*, available from the U.S. Government Printing Office. Some of the national figures and those for a number of large SMSAs were released in a preliminary report, *Provisional Estimates of Social, Economic, and Housing Characteristics, Supplementary Report from the 1980 Census of Population and Housing*, PHC 80-51-1 (Washington, D.C.: U.S. Department of Commerce, Bureau of the Census, April 1982).

Most population trends, however, are based on data collected by the Census Bureau in a monthly sample survey of 85,000 households, called the "Current Population Survey" (CPS). From these data the Census Bureau prepares a series of reports, the "Current Population Reports" (CPR); the P-20, P-23, and P-25 series include reports on population growth, distribution, projections, and social characteristics.

Studies from the Center for Demographic Studies (CDS), a research and analysis staff within the Census Bureau, provide more detailed reviews of selected demographic issues. See, for example, "Population Deconcentration" (CDS-81-5), by John F. Long (Washington, D.C.: U.S. Department of Commerce, Bureau of the Census, 1981).

Another useful source of population data is the Population Studies group of the U.S. Department of Agriculture's Economic Research Service. See, for example, testimony by Calvin Beale prepared for the U.S., Congress, House, Committee on Public Works and Transportation, Subcommittee on Economic Development, *Projected Changes in the Economy, Population, Labor Market, and Work Force and Their Implications for Economic Development Policy*, Hearings, 97th Cong., 1st sess., November 1981, pp. 169-207.

The most important and comprehensive review of population distribution issues is found in *Population, Distribution and Policy*, Volume 5 in a series of eight research papers prepared by the Commission on Population Growth and the American Future (Washington, D.C.: U.S. Government Printing Office, 1972). Other readings in this field include David L. Brown and John M. Wardwell, eds., *New Directions in Urban-Rural Migration: The Population Turnaround in Rural America* (New York, N.Y.: Academic Press, 1980) and Andrew J. Sofranko and James D. Williams, eds., *Rebirth of Rural America: Rural Migration in the Midwest* (Ames, Iowa: Iowa State University, North Central Regional Center for Rural Development, 1980).

Relating changes in population to changes in environmental stress and environmental quality is a very difficult task. The most recent comprehensive review in this field is a study by the National Academy of Sciences, Assembly of Behavioral and Social Science, *Population Redistribution and Public Policy* (Washington, D.C.: National Academy Press, 1980).

The most useful government sources of macroeconomic data are the annual Council of Economic Advisors *Economic Report of the President*, issued each year in January (Washington, D.C.: U.S. Government Printing Office) and the monthly *Survey of Current Business* (Washington, D.C.: U.S. Government Printing Office), published by the Department of Commerce, Bureau of Economic Analysis.

The main government analyses of economic data and conditions are found in the annual *Economic Report of the President* and in various committee prints published by the Joint Economic Committee. The federal budget and general economic conditions are also extensively reviewed outside government. Perhaps the most thorough analyses are those provided by the Brookings Institution in its annual report,

Setting National Priorities (Washington, D.C.: Brookings Institution) and the American Enterprise Institute, *Annual Contemporary Economic Problems*, edited by William Fellner (Washington, D.C.: American Enterprise Insitute).

Most of the books published on environmental economics focus on such microeconomic issues as the costs and benefits of individual programs and analyses of alternative regulatory approaches like effluent charges and property rights. However, the Council on Environmental Quality has traditionally had a chapter analyzing macroeconomic concerns in its annual report, *Environmental Quality* (Washington, D.C.: U.S. Government Printing Office), and Resources for the Future has published several macroeconomic perspectives, the most recent being Henry M. Peskin, Paul R. Portney, Allen V. Kneese, eds., *Environmental Regulation and the U.S. Economy* (Baltimore, Md.: published for Resources for the Future by the Johns Hopkins University Press, 1981), a collection of articles by individual economists, presenting their perspectives on some of the major economic issues affecting environmental programs. Data collected on actual environmental expenditures are published in the monthly *Survey of Current Business*. The February issue usually contains an article estimating total expenditures, with a two-year lag (that is, the article published in 1982 reports 1980 expenditures), and the May issue reports on actual business investment for pollution control the previous year and on expected investments during the current year. The Bureau of Census, Industry Division, publishes the results of its annual survey of business expenditures in *Costs and Expenditures for Pollution Abatement* (MA-200 Series) and Environmental Quality Control. The latest industry survey is for FY 1980. Additional surveys will no longer be undertaken because of budget cuts.

Major recent long-term projections of population, natural resources, and environmental conditions are found in *Global 2000* (Washington, D.C.: U.S. Government Printing Office, 1980), a report prepared by the Council on Environmental Quality and the Department of State, and in various publications in the Worldwatch Institute Paper series, particularly Lester R. Brown and Pamela Shaw, *Six Steps to a Sustainable Society*, Worldwatch Paper 48 (Washington, D.C.: Worldwatch Institute, March 1982).

TEXT REFERENCES

1. U.S. Department of Commerce, Bureau of the Census, *Demographic Estimates for Countries with a Population of 10 Million or More: 1981* (Washington, D.C.: U.S. Government Printing Offices, 1981), p. 12.

2. Leon F. Bouvier, "The Impact of Immigration on U.S. Population Size," in *Population Trends and Public Policy* (Washington, D.C.: Population Reference Bureau, 1981).

3. Philip M. Hauser, "The Census of 1980," *Scientific American* 245(5):56 (1980).

4. U.S. Department of Commerce, Bureau of the Census, *Statistical Abstract of the United States: 1981*, 102d ed. (Washington, D.C.: U.S. Government Printing Offices, 1981), p.7

5. Council on Environmental Quality, *Environmental Trends* (Washington, D.C.: U.S. Government Printing Offices, 1981), p. 45.

6. U.S. Department of Commerce, Bureau of the Census, *1980 Census of Population*, Supplementary Report PC80-S1-5 (Washington, D.C.: U.S. Government Printing Offices, 1981), pp. 1-46.

7. U.S. Department of Commerce, Bureau of the Census, *U.S. Department of Commerce News*, CB 81-52 (Washington, D.C.: Bureau of the Census, 1981), pp. 1-7.

8. U.S. Department of Commerce, Bureau of the Census, *1980 Census of Population*, Supplementary Report PC80-S1-5, p. 1.

9. Philip M. Hauser, "The Census of 1980," p. 57.

10. *Ibid.*, p. 57, and U.S. Department of Commerce, Bureau of the Census, *Population Profile of the United States: 1980* (Washington, D.C.: U.S. Government Printing Offices, 1980), p. 9.

11. Council on Environmental Quality, *Environmental Trends*, p. 48.

12. Testimony of Calvin L. Beale, U.S. Department of Agriculture before the U.S., Congress, House Committee on Public Works and Transportation, Subcommittee on Economic Development, "Population Change in Rural America and Implications for Economic Development," November 1981, p. 4.

13. Council on Environmental Quality, *Environmental Trends*, p. 11.

14. James D. Schaub, *The Nonmetro Labor Force in the Seventies*, Rural Development Research, Report No. 33 (Washington, D.C.: U.S. Department of Agriculture, Economic Research Service, Economic Development Division, 1981), pp. 2-4.

15. U.S. Department of Commerce, Bureau of the Census, *Statistical Abstract of the United States: 1980*, p. 8.

16. Council on Environmental Quality, *Environmental Trends*, p. 51.

17. U.S. Department of Commerce, Bureau of the Census, *1980 Census of Population*, Supplementary Report PC80-S1-5, p. 3.

18. Council of Economic Advisors, *Economic Report of the President: 1982* (Washington, D.C.: U.S. Government Printing Office, 1982), p. 266.

19. *Ibid.*, pp. 295, 310.

20. *Ibid.*, p. 234.

21. *Ibid.*, p. 278.

22. Gary L. Rutledge and Betsy D. O'Connor, "Plant and Equipment Expenditures by Business for Pollution Abatement, 1973-1980, and Planned 1981," *Survey of Current Business* 61(6):20-21 (1981).

23. Extrapolations from regional employment data in M.F. Petrulis, *Regional Manufacturing Employment Growth Patterns*, Rural Development Research Report No. 13 (Washington, D.C.: U.S. Department of Agriculture, Economics, Statistics, and Cooperatives, Service, 1979), pp. 1-14.

24. Council on Environmental Quality, *Environmental Trends*, p. 45.

25. Council of Economic Advisors, *Economic Report of the President: 1982*, pp. 266, 269.

26. *Ibid.*, 294.

27. *Ibid.*, pp. 248-249.

28. U.S. Department of Commerce, Bureau of Economic Analysis, *The National Income and Product Accounts of the United States, 1929-1976 Statistical Tables* (Washington, D.C.: U.S. Government Printing Offices, 1981), p. 91, and U.S. Department of Commerce, Bureau of Economic Analysis, *The National Income and Production, 1976-79*, Special Supplement to the *Survey of Current Business* (Washington, D.C.: U.S. Government Printing Offices, 1980), pp.16-17.

29. Council of Economic Advisors, *Economic Report of the President: 1982*, pp. 233, 320.

30. *Ibid.*, p. 233.

31. U.S. Department of Commerce, Bureau of Economic Analysis, *The National Income and Product Accounts, 1929-1976 Statistical Tables*, pp. 153-165, and U.S. Department of Commerce, Bureau of Economic Analysis, *The National Income and Product Accounts 1976-79*, pp., 32-33.

32. Council on Environmental Quality, *Environmental Quality—1979* (Washington, D.C.: U.S. Government Printing Office, 1979), p. 655.

33. *Ibid.*, p.437. The 1978 estimates were adjusted to 1980 dollars using the implicit price deflators for pollution control investment developed by the Department of Commerce, Bureau of Economic Analysis, *Survey of Current Business* 61(6):23 (1981).

34. Temple, Barker, and Sloan, Inc., "An Economic Analysis of Proposed Effluent Limitations Guidelines, New Source Performance Standards, and Pretreatment Standards for the Iron and Steel Point Source Category," prepared for the U.S. Environmental Protection Agency, Office of Planning and Evaluation, December 1980, pp. III-5, IV-2. (Washington, D.C.: U.S. Environmental Protection Agency, 1980).

35. *Survey of Current Business* 61(6):19-30 (1981).

36. Council on Environmental Quality, *Environmental Quality—1978*, p. 437.

37. *Survey of Current Business* 61(6):19-30 (1981).

38. U.S. Environmental Protection Agency, Office of Policy Analysis, *Cost of Clean Air and Water Report*, Draft (Washington, D.C.: U.S. Environmental Protection Agency, 1982), p. 813.

39. Council on Environmental Quality, *Environmental Quality—1978*, p. 438.

40. Information provided by U.S. Environmental Protection Agency, Office of Planning and Evaluation, May 13, 1982.

41. For example, see the annual awards presented by the Environmental Industry Council, 1825 15th Street, N.W., Suite 210, Washington, D.C., 20006.

42. Information provided by U.S. Department of Commerce, Bureau of the Census, April 1982. May 26, 1982

FIGURE REFERENCES

Figure 1.1

U.S. Department of Commerce, Bureau of the Census, *Statistical Abstract of the United States: 1981*, 102d ed. (Washington, D.C.: U.S. Government Printing Office, 1982), Table I, p. 5.

Figure 1.2

U.S. Department of Commerce, Bureau of the Census, *Statistical Abstract of the United States: 1981*, 102d ed. (Washington, D.C.: U.S. Government Printing Office, 1982), Table 3, p. 6.

Figure 1.3

U.S. Department of Commerce, Bureau of the Census, *Statistical Abstract of the United States: 1981*, 102d ed. (Washington, D.C.: U.S. Government Printing Office, 1982), Table 8, p. 9.

Figure 1.4

U.S. Department of Commerce, Bureau of the Census, *Commerce News*, CB81-52 (Washington, D.C.: U.S. Department of Commerce, March 19, 1981), p. 3.

Figure 1.5

(1950-1970)—Calvin L. Beale and Glenn V. Fuguitt, "The New Pattern of Nonmetropolitan Population Change" (Madison, Wis.: University of Wisconsin, Center for Demography and Ecology, 1975). (1970-1980)—U.S. Department of Agriculture, Economic Research Service, Population Studies Group, unpublished data.

Figure 1.6

(1960)—U.S. Department of Commerce, Bureau of the Census, *1960 Census of Population* (Washington, D.C.: Bureau of the Census), Vol. II, Part 1. (1980)—U.S. Department of Commerce, Bureau of the Census, *Population Profile of the United States: 1980*, Series P-20, No. 363 (Washington, D.C.: U.S. Government Printing Office, June, 1981).

Figure 1.7

Executive Office of the President, Council of Economic Advisors, *Economic Report of the President, February, 1982* (Washington, D.C.: U.S. Government Printing Office, February, 1982), Table B-2, p. 235.

Figure 1.8

U.S. Department of Commerce, Bureau of Industrial Economics, *1981 U.S. Industrial Outlook for 200 Industries with Projections for 1985* (Washington, D.C.: U.S. Government Printing Office, January, 1981), Chart 1, p. xxii. Industrial "output" measures constant dollar gross product originating in the industry.

Figure 1.9

Data Resources, Inc., *U.S. Long Term Reviews, Spring 1981* (Lexington, Mass.: Data Resources, Inc., 1981), Table 6, pp. 111.12-111.13.

Figure 1.10

U.S. Department of Labor, Statistics Office of Employment and Trends, information provided by BLS 790 computer program.

Figure 1.11

U.S. Department of Transportation, Federal Highway Administration, Federal Highway Statistics Division, "Highway Statistics" (Washington, D.C.: U.S. Government Printing Office, 1980), Table VM-1.

Figure 1.12

Gary L. Rutledge and Susan L. Trevathan, "Pollution Abatement and Control Expenditures, 1972-79," *Survey of Current Business*, 61(3):19-27 (1981).

Figure 1.13

Data Resources, Inc., *The Macroeconomic Impact of Federal Pollution Control Programs: 1981 Assessment* (prepared for the U.S. Environmental Protection Agency, Washington, D.C.: U.S. Environmental Protection Agency, 1981), pp. 18, 20.

Figure 1.14

U.S. Department of Commerce, Bureau of the Census, *Statistical Abstract: 1980*, 101st ed. (Washington, D.C.: U.S. Government Printing Office, 1980), p. 10 and Gregory Jackson, et al., MIT-Harvard Joint Center for Urban Studies, *Regional Diversity: Growth in the United States, 1960-1990* (Boston, Mass.: Auburn House, 1981), pp. 26, 28.

Chapter 2

Air Quality

Over the past two decades, the number of motor vehicles in the United States has increased; the national economy has expanded; and we have made considerable progress in improving our air quality—at least with respect to the most common pollutants. These observations should not lull us into complacency. Many areas still experience pollution levels above the standards established to protect human health. Achieving further improvements, and in many cases merely maintaining the improvements already achieved, will be more difficult. And we have only begun to recognize how serious some unaddressed problems may be. As more is learned about these problems, our air quality programs may need significant adjustment, modifications, and, in some cases, expansion.

This is a particularly critical time for air quality programs. They are being strongly attacked as a source of serious economic problems. The federal Clean Air Act is due for revision. The Reagan Administration, along with congressional opponents of the program, is proposing a number of changes that would restrict the federal government's involvement in cleaning up the air, reduce the stringency of some of the requirements currently in the statute, and make little or no effort to deal with newer problems.

TRENDS IN AIR QUALITY

The one available national index on air quality indicates that progress in controlling air pollution has been significant, at least on the basis of the number of days in which pollution levels are very high in a number of our major metropolitan areas. The value of this index, called the Pollution Standards Index (PSI), is determined by the particular pollutant (of five "criteria pollutants") having the highest concentration relative to its primary air quality standard.[1]* If the

---

*The "primary" standard for ambient air quality is set at a level to protect human health from adverse effects of a pollutant. The pollutants included in the index are total suspended particulates, sulfur dioxide, ozone, carbon monoxide, and nitrogen dioxide.

air quality equals the primary standard for that pollutant, the index has a value of 100; it if is twice the standard, the index has a value of 200; and so forth. The index scale is divided into five ranges varying from "good" (0 to 49) to "hazardous" (300 +). Data from 23 metropolitan areas that have monitored air quality for seven or more years show considerable reductions in pollution levels, as measured by the average number of days in which index readings for the combined 23 cities were in the unhealthful, very unhealthful, and hazardous ranges (figure 2.1). From 1974 through 1980, the average number of days of elevated risk declined by 39 percent, from 97 to 59, in the 23 cities.[2]*

Some cities have demonstrated remarkable progress. For example, the number of days in the three highest risk categories in New York City was 270 in 1975 and 131 in 1980 (a drop of 51 percent); in Portland, Oregon, the number of days in these categories was 131 in 1974 and 55 in 1980 (a drop of 58 percent); in Chicago, 240 days in 1974 and 48 in 1980 (a drop of 80 percent). Although Los Angeles' air quality improved, that city still had 221 days in the three highest categories in 1980 (compared to nearly 300 in 1974). Houston's air, in contrast to that of most cities, became more unhealthy, with the number of days in the three highest categories increasing from 35 to 101 between 1974 and 1980.

Some of these results could reflect changes in weather conditions, though the trends do seem to be positive overall. Also, it is not known how many people in these cities are actually exposed to the measured levels of pollution.[3] We monitor places, not people; the number of places is limited; often, their locations do not reflect actual human exposure. There are few measures of indoor exposure, and data from monitors are not weighted to take population concentrations into account. Thus, we really have only a limited idea of how many people are exposed to what levels of pollution.

Trends for Individual Pollutants

The amount of progress that has been achieved varies from one type of pollutant to another. Individual pollutants can be measured in light of both measured ambient air concentration and the estimated amounts of the pollutant being emitted. The former is a more direct

---

*The cities in this composite index were selected on the basis of the availability of monitoring data, not on the basis of their population, location, or air quality characteristics. The overall trend might or might not be the same if data were included from a different group or a larger number of cities.

Figure 2.1

**Air Quality in 23 Metropolitan Areas, 1974-1980, as Measured by the
Pollutant Standards Index (PSI)**

Average number of days per
year in PSI categories

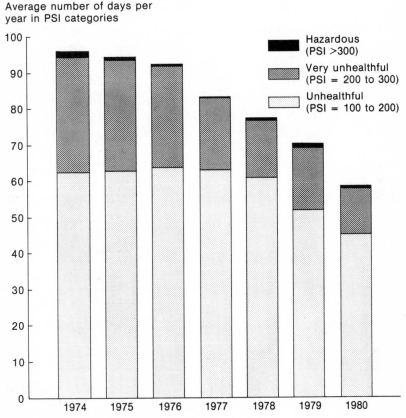

Source: Council on Environmental Quality

measure of how close we are getting to having clean air. The latter
reflects what our regulatory programs have accomplished in limiting
emissions from specific sources.

Emission and concentration trends do not always coincide. The
differences result, in part, from meteorological factors (such as changes
in temperature, wind patterns, and precipitation) and from changes
in the relative location of pollution sources and ambient monitors.
The ambient concentrations also reflect the contribution of sources,
such as dust from fields, that are not regulated and are not usually
included in emission estimates.

There are a number of problems with the data on emissions and
ambient concentrations. For instance, there is little information

about actual emissions, and the emission estimates are precisely that—estimates. As such, they are only as accurate as the assumptions underlying them. These assumptions evidently are changed periodically, because the estimates of the Environmental Protection Agency (EPA) keep changing, sometimes dramatically. For example, figure 2.2 displays two recent EPA estimates of carbon monoxide emissions. The 1980 estimate shows only a slight decline in emissions between 1970 and 1978; the 1982 estimate shows a substantial decline in this period.* In the following pages, the discussion of emission trends for individual pollutants relies on 1982 EPA estimates, but the apparent volatility of these estimates should be borne in mind.

The quality and comparability of data on ambient air quality depend on, among other factors, the proper siting of monitors, the reliability and uniformity of equipment, and the techniques used to identify both deficiencies in equipment and human errors. A 1979 study reported that 72 percent of 243 monitors inspected were sited incorrectly; 58 percent of the equipment in use was not certified by EPA; 81 percent of the sites examined had one or more problems that could adversely affect data reliability.[5] The number and location of ambient measurements may change substantially over time. Any interpretation of data on ambient air quality, therefore, must recognize these problems.**

Particulates (TSPs)

Perhaps the most dramatic reduction in air pollution has been achieved for "particulates." Particulates are solid particles or liquid droplets small enough to remain suspended in air. They can be emitted directly or formed from such gaseous precursors as sulfur dioxide. They can irritate the human respiratory system and contribute to acute respiratory illness. Prolonged inhalation of some types of airborne particulates may increase both the incidence and severity of chronic respiratory diseases. About two-thirds of the

---

*Unfortunately, EPA does not publicly document how its emission estimates are made, what changes are made in preparing the estimates from year to year, or how the changes in methods influence the emission levels.

It appears as if the estimate changes shown in figure 2.2 resulted from the agency's adopting a new model for estimating vehicle emissions which incorporates revised vehicle emission rates per mile for all model years up to 1979 and provides for a different allocation of vehicle miles traveled between light and heavy-duty vehicles.[4]

**EPA and the states have sought to improve monitoring systems, and in May 1979 EPA issued a regulation requiring establishment of standardized monitoring programs.[6]

Figure 2.2
EPA Estimates of Carbon Monoxide Emissions

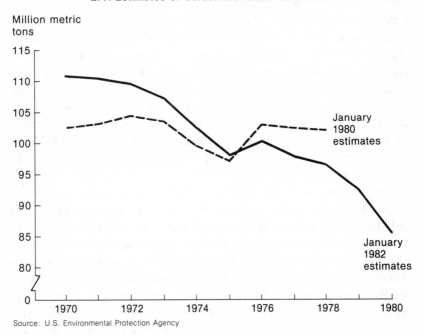

Million metric tons

January 1980 estimates

January 1982 estimates

1970   1972   1974   1976   1978   1980

Source: U.S. Environmental Protection Agency

nation's man-made particulate emissions are from stationary industrial sources; about 18 percent, from vehicles; about 5 percent,
from solid waste disposal.[7]

Ambient levels of particulates were 31 percent lower in 1980
than they were in 1960 (figure 2.3).* Three-fourths of this change
occurred between 1960 and 1971, as a result of conversions from
coal to cleaner fuels and of state and local governments' requiring
emission reductions.[8]

Estimated particulate emissions decreased by 56 percent between
1970 and 1980 (figure 2.4), a decline attributable to pollution
controls placed on coal-burning facilities and industrial processes
and to decreases in the burning of coal and solid waste.[9] General
economic conditions and changing fuel prices may also have had an
impact. The failure of ambient levels to drop by an equivalent
proportion most likely results from the contribution of fugitive
(nonstack) industrial emissions and of windblown dust. The amount
of progress varies substantially from region to region: the Northeast,

---

*The data for 1960-71 are from 95 monitors in urban areas; for 1972-76, from over 3,000
sites; for 1977-80, from 1,925 sites.

Figure 2.3

National Ambient Concentrations of Total Suspended Particulates, Nitrogen Dioxide, and Sulfur Dioxide, 1960-1980

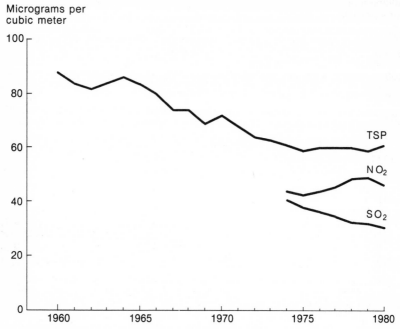

Data may not be strictly comparable. TSP (total suspended particulates) data for 1960-1971 are based on 95 sites. Data for 1972-1976 are based on more than 3,000 sites. For 1977-1980, there were 1,925 sites. The annual standard for TSP is 75 micrograms per cubic meter.

SO_2 (sulfur dioxide) data are based on 84 sites, all in urban areas. The annual standard for SO_2 is 80 micrograms per cubic meter.

NO_2 (nitrogen dioxide) data are based on 338 sites. The annual standard for NO_2 is 100 micrograms per cubic meter.

Source: U.S. Environmental Protection Agency

Great Lakes, and South have shown substantial improvements, while the West, where agricultural and natural sources contribute wind-blown particulates, has shown little progress.

In 1980, 211 counties or portions of counties (out of the more than 3,000 counties in the United States) failed to attain the primary air quality standard for particulates.[10] The National Commission on Air Quality (NCAQ)* projected that approximately 27 major metropolitan and 40 less-populated areas are certain to miss the 1982 deadline for attainment. Another 25 areas could also miss it. The primary reasons for not meeting the deadline are apparently

---

*The commission was established by Congress in 1977 to evaluate implementation of the Clean Air Act. It published its final report in March 1981.

Figure 2.4
National Air Pollutant Emissions, 1970-1980

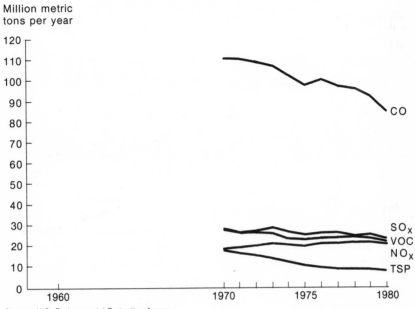

Source: U.S. Environmental Protection Agency

the failure of some industrial sources (primarily steel and utilities) to control fugitive emissions from industrial processes and the problem of controlling dust from such sources as unpaved roads, stockpiles, and fields.

Sulfur Dioxide (SO₂)

High concentrations of sulfur dioxide (SO_2), when found with high concentrations of particulates, are thought to cause increased death rates, particularly among people with heart and lung disease. Even at lower concentrations, sulfur dioxide is associated with noticeable increases in acute and chronic respiratory diseases.[11] It reacts in the atmosphere to form sulfates (and related compounds) that may create serious health risks. Sulfates also contribute to visibility problems and to acid rain. Eighty percent of SO_2 emissions result from combustion of fossil fuels, principally by electric utilities.[12]

The United States has made considerable progress in the last 15 years in reducing sulfur dioxide pollution. Ambient levels decreased 58 percent between 1966 and 1971.[13] The rapid improvement during this period apparently resulted primarily from the use of cleaner fuels in most urban areas, as local and state regulations prompted switches from coal and high-sulfur oil to natural gas and low-sulfur oil. Moreover, major new sources of SO_2 pollution, such as power plants that burn fossil fuels, tended to locate outside the more heavily polluted urban areas. The construction of tall smokestacks to disperse emissions over a wider area also helped to reduce recorded levels of SO_2 pollution. However, these smokestacks may be contributing to acid rain problems (see below).[14]

From 1974 to 1980, EPA found that ambient SO_2 levels decreased 24 percent (figure 2.3).*[15] As a result, most urban areas have attained the primary SO_2 standards and are now trying to maintain these levels. EPA estimates that sulfur oxide emissions were approximately 15 percent lower in 1980 than they had been in 1970 (figure 2.4).[16]**

NCAQ projects that 4 major urban areas (Pittsburgh, Indianapolis, Gary, and Chicago), and areas near nonferrous smelters in 5 western states, will definitely exceed (with another 24 areas possibly exceeding) the primary air quality standards for sulfur dioxide in 1982.[17] The main reasons for these continued problems include delays in developing state implementation plans, disputes over control requirements, and polluters' failures to comply with the control requirements of existing state plans.

Nitrogen Dioxide (NO$_2$)

In striking contrast to particulates and SO_2, nitrogen dioxide levels nationwide appear to have risen in recent years.† Nitrogen dioxide can irritate the lungs, contribute to respiratory difficulty, and lower resistance to respiratory infections. It also contributes to the oxidants in smog. About half of the nation's nitrogen oxide (NO_2)‡ emissions are from vehicles; the rest are primarily from power plants.[18] EPA reports that ambient NO_2 levels increased by a total of 5.7 percent between 1974 and 1980 (figure 2.3).[19] EPA does not have nation-

---

*The 1966-71 data are based on monitors in 32 urban locations; the 1974-80 data, on 84 monitors.
**Air quality standards have been established for sulfur dioxide, but EPA sometimes refers to emissions of sulfur oxides; sulfur dioxide is the preponderant component of these emissions.
†The nitrogen dioxide measurements from 1974 to 1980 are based on 338 monitors.
‡Air quality standards have been established for nitrogen dioxide, but EPA sometimes refers to emissions of nitrogen oxides; nitrogen dioxide is the preponderant component of these emissions.

wide ambient data prior to 1974 but nevertheless estimates (on the basis of its emission estimates) that ambient levels of NO_2 increased a total of 20 percent between 1970 and 1980.[20] The emission estimates show an increase of 9.7 percent between 1975 and 1979, 16.2 percent between 1970 and 1979, and a slight decline between 1979 and 1980 (figure 2.4).[21]

The increased emissions came primarily from motor vehicles and electric power stations.[22] Although the emission rates for both automobiles (per mile traveled) and utilities (per amount of energy consumed) declined during this period, these declines were more than offset by the increased number of miles traveled and amount of electricity generated.

In 1980, seven counties exceeded the primary ambient standard for nitrogen dioxide.[23] NCAQ projects that most of these counties will meet the standard by 1990 if EPA establishes stricter nitrogen oxide emission standards for light and heavy trucks beginning with 1986 models. States are depending on federal motor vehicle emission standards to help them attain the ambient standard for nitrogen dioxide, since emissions of this pollutant from stationary sources probably will increase. The federal standards for motor vehicles, and other components of the Clean Air Act's emission control program for vehicles, are targets of the Reagan Administration's "regulatory relief" program and proposed Clean Air Act amendments.

Ozone

A principal component of smog, ozone is one of the most pervasive pollutants. It is not emitted directly but is the product of photochemical reactions between nitrogen oxides and volatile organic compounds (VOCs).[24] Industrial processes emit nearly half of the man-made VOCs; vehicles emit just over one-third; the rest come from other sources.[25] Ozone impairs breathing and severely irritates mucous membranes of the nose and throat.

Ambient levels of ozone were 9.9 percent lower in 1979 than they had been in 1974; they rose slightly in 1980 (figure 2.5).[26]* At the same time, the emissions of volatile organic compounds that react with nitrogen dioxide to form ozone were 8.4 percent lower in 1980 than they had been in 1974 (figure 2.4).[27] The increased number of miles driven during this period would have caused a substantial increase in total emissions if federally required pollution

---

*Based on measurements at 122 sites nationwide.

Figure 2.5

National Ambient Concentrations of Carbon Monoxide and Ozone, 1970-1980

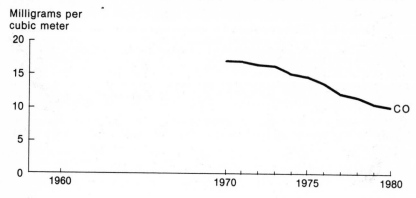

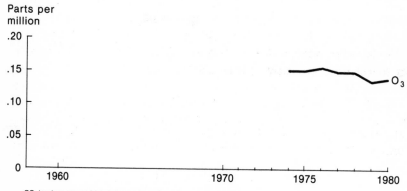

CO (carbon monoxide) data are based on the second highest 8-hour average level at 91 sites. The 8-hour standard for CO is 10 milligrams per cubic meter.

O_3 (ozone) data are based on the second highest daily maximum 1-hour concentration at 122 sites. The 1-hour standard is 0.12 parts per million.

Source: U.S. Environmental Protection Agency

control devices had not forced a significant reduction in the emission rate per mile driven.

In 1977, over 140 million people lived in areas exceeding the primary air quality standard for ozone. NCAQ projects that 31 metropolitan areas are certain to exceed the standard in 1982; another 17 will probably exceed it (figure 2.6).[28] Of these areas, 7 (the major northeastern metropolitan areas between Philadelphia and southwest Connecticut, sections of southern California, and Houston), containing nearly 35 million people, are expected to exceed the primary air quality standard in 1987. An additional 7 metropolitan areas may also be in that situation.

The major hopes for lowering ozone levels are new controls on

Figure 2.6
Areas Not Meeting Ozone Standards, Projections for 1982 and 1987

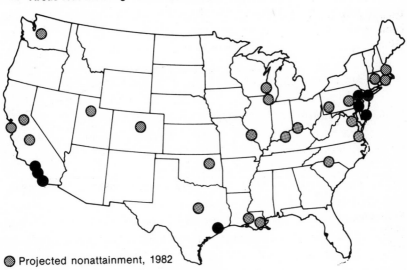

⬤ Projected nonattainment, 1982
● Projected nonattainment, 1982 and 1987

Source: U.S. National Commission on Air Quality

stationary sources of volatile organic compounds, controls on auto emissions, and motor vehicle inspection and maintenance programs.

Carbon Monoxide (CO)

Measured concentrations of the third automobile-related pollutant, carbon monoxide (CO), have decreased significantly since 1970. Motor vehicles are the major source of carbon monoxide, which interferes with the absorption of oxygen by red blood cells, thereby slowing reflexes, weakening judgment, and causing drowsiness. High levels of inhalation can cause death.

Ambient levels of carbon monoxide* decreased 40.6 percent between 1970 and 1980, although EPA estimates that national emissions declined only 23 percent during this period.[29] (Compare figures 2.4 and 2.5.) The apparent inconsistency between these trends results from the fact that the total emissions are the product of a rapidly decreasing trend, the average rate of emission per mile driven, and a less rapidly increasing trend, the total number of miles driven; whereas the location of the ambient monitors in traffic-

---

*Measured at 91 urban sites.

saturated downtown areas results in their reflecting only the lower emission rates, because the number of miles driven in these areas has generally not increased. The impact of the statutorily mandated pollution control standards is demonstrated in figure 2.7, which shows EPA estimates of highway vehicle emissions with and without the standards.

Measurements of ambient levels of carbon monoxide can vary considerably within a region, depending on traffic patterns and the location of monitors. In 1980, CO levels in 145 counties or parts of counties exceeded the health-based ambient standard, 39 of these by more than 100 percent.[30]

NCAQ estimates that 28 metropolitan areas will not meet the ambient standards by 1982. NCAQ has also noted that at least 22 areas have recorded carbon monoxide readings more than 150 percent higher than the standard.[31] Major metropolitan areas have recorded the highest levels, but smaller, rapidly growing areas have also recorded high levels. Assuming that the motor vehicle emission standard for carbon monoxide does not change and that motor vehicle

Figure 2.7
Carbon Monoxide Emissions from Highway Vehicles, 1970-1979

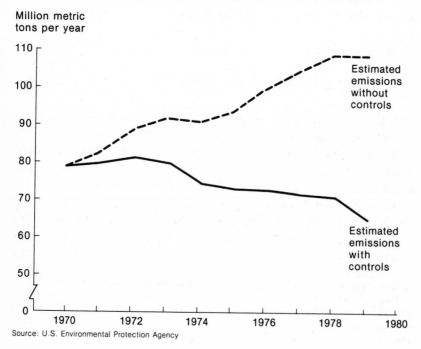

Million metric
tons per year

Estimated emissions without controls

Estimated emissions with controls

Source: U.S. Environmental Protection Agency

inspection and maintenance programs are implemented, only Los Angeles and part of Denver would still exceed the standard by 1987.

PROSPECTS AND ISSUES

Although we can justifiably take pride in many of our accomplishments in cleaning up the air, we are unlikely in many densely populated places to attain health-based standards for some of the five criteria pollutants and still have major problems that have not been addressed. Moreover, our accomplishments will not endure if controls are loosened. For pollutants related to motor vehicles, for instance, the projections presented above assume that strict auto emission standards will be retained, that vehicles will comply with these standards, and that state and local inspection and maintenance programs will be implemented to ensure compliance.* If any of these assumptions proves false (for instance, as a result of eased statutory requirements), the number of areas exceeding the standards could increase significantly.

The National Commission on Air Quality examined the impact of relaxing the nitrogen oxide auto emission standard for gasoline engines to 2.0 grams per mile (1980 standard) from the 1.0 level for 1981 required by statute, in combination with not establishing stricter emission standards for light and heavy trucks after 1986.[36] In these circumstances, two representative cities, Phoenix and Philadelphia, projected to attain the ambient standard under the existing requirement (by the early 1990s) would exceed it by 34 percent and 22 percent, respectively. St. Louis, also examined by NCAQ, would still meet the standard, but its ambient level of NO_2 would increase 13 percent. The NCAQ analyses indicate that a large number of other cities also would not meet the standard.

A four-year relaxation of the current emission standard for carbon monoxide, from 3.4 to 7 grams per mile, would cause similar attainment problems, according to a survey of 32 state and local agencies by the National Governors' Association, the State and Territorial Air Pollution Program Administrators, and the Association of Local Air Pollution Control Officials.[37] Of 21 respondents performing detailed analyses, 8 concluded that relaxing this stan-

---

*Actual emissions from automobiles usually exceed applicable emission standards.[32] Nevertheless, substantial abatement of automotive emissions has occurred.[33] Inspection and maintenance programs have been quite controversial,[34] but studies in Portland (Oregon) and California indicate that these programs make a substantial contribution to reduced levels of automotive emissions.[35]

dard, which is already met by most 1981 cars, would cause substantial attainment delays. Four others predicted shorter delays (six months or less) and 9 projected no delays. Of those not performing detailed analyses, 6 predicted no problems from the relaxation, and 5 offered no predictions.

There is also great uncertainty about the extent to which stationary sources actually comply with their emission limits. Most attainment projections assume full compliance, but noncompliance is common, apparently much more so than EPA recognizes. In 1979, EPA reported that 92 percent of major sources of air pollution were in compliance; an investigation by the U.S. General Accounting Office (GAO) concluded that the national compliance rate was considerably less.[38] In two regions, for example, half of the sources EPA reported as complying with their abatement schedules were, according to GAO, violating those schedules. GAO noted that EPA's own compliance monitoring program showed that 22 percent of sources classified by states as "in compliance" were not. Noncomplying sources, as compared to sources in compliance, produced disproportionately large amounts of emissions.[39] Improper operation and maintenance of equipment at sources that have installed controls is also a major source of excess emissions.[40]

In the past, EPA has focused its efforts on the larger (or "major") sources of air pollution. Beginning in 1977, the agency targeted major noncomplying sources for judicial or administrative enforcement action as part of its "Major Source Enforcement Effort."[41] Lawsuits against major polluters, particularly large steel companies, led to negotiated settlements, committing companies to install pollution control equipment.

There are a number of indications, however, that EPA is reducing these efforts. Although federal, state, and local governments share responsibility for enforcement, the agency is currently emphasizing the state role, and has asked the U.S. Justice Department to drop nearly 50 pending cases.[42] Simultaneously, EPA is reducing both its own enforcement budget and the amount of funds being made available to state authorities (see chapter 9).

State and local agencies often rely on EPA enforcement activities to support their programs. Because of the substantial time and resources needed to pursue judicial remedies, for example, they rely heavily on administrative solutions.[43] In many cases, it is the threat of possible federal action that encourages a polluter to cooperate. If negotiations fail, EPA often provides technical and legal assistance for any ensuing enforcement actions. The availability of this support apparently is being reduced.

Continuation of current auto emission standards, retention of inspection and maintenance programs for automobiles, tough deadlines for compliance by existing stationary sources, and many more issues have been discussed by Congress as part of a thorough legislative review of the Clean Air Act. Other key issues include the following:

- procedures for setting ambient air quality standards;
- procedures for controlling hazardous emissions;
- deadlines for attaining air quality standards;
- sanctions EPA can impose on states for failure to develop adequate attainment plans;
- procedural requirements for EPA approval of state plans and for state or EPA approval of permits for new air pollution sources;
- preventing significant deterioration of air quality in areas where the air is cleaner than national air quality standards;
- protecting visibility;
- acid rain.

Environmentalists, industry, and state and local officials have moved into the legislative fray with their own conclusions and recommendations.[44] The Reagan Administration did not develop a comprehensive legislative proposal of its own, but supported legislation proposed in the House of Representatives that would significantly weaken the act. Senator Robert T. Stafford (R.-Vermont), chairman of the Senate Environment and Public Works Committee, on the other hand, has repeatedly expressed his desire to "fine tune" and not weaken the act.

The conclusions of the Clean Air Act debate may well be the most important factor influencing what the quality of our air will be in the future. In the 1970s, the federal government adopted a precautionary approach to air quality problems, often taking a strong stand to protect human health on the basis of uncertain evidence. The legislation also emphasized tight deadlines and tough standards, which frequently seemed to give little weight to concerns about high costs, lack of technical solutions, and other arguments.

We have already seen some changes in this approach, as more weight is given to economic considerations and deadlines are postponed. How far should these changes go? There will always be uncertainty. How should we make decisions in the face of this uncertainty—in a way that emphasizes the protection of health and the environment, or in a way that emphasizes avoiding unnecessary costs? Economic considerations always have been and always will be a relevant factor. But how much weight should they have in pollution control decisions? It will be difficult for regulatory agencies to meet deadlines with sensitive and well-supported proposals when budgets are tightened. How much discretion should be given to the agencies under such conditions?

The way in which Congress answers these questions, and the extent to which it establishes mechanisms for dealing with emerging problems, will determine whether the 1980s will see continued progress in improving our air, or whether we will be hard pressed just to maintain what we have already achieved.

Since the passage of amendments to the Clean Air Act in 1970, some air quality problems have remained substantially unaddressed, and scientists have identified additional ones that merit government attention. For example, fears have been expressed about the proliferation of unregulated toxic air pollutants. When researchers began linking declining fish populations to lake acidification in New York's Adirondack Mountains, concern intensified about "acid rain." Scientists have also warned about the possible warming of the earth's atmosphere caused by emissions of carbon dioxide when fossil fuels are burned. In 1974, researchers first published the hypothesis that chlorofluorocarbons might destroy the earth's stratospheric ozone layer. Finally, when insulation of homes and offices increased, in response to rising energy prices, attention began to focus on human exposure to high levels of indoor pollutants.

The Clean Air Act scarcely addresses these issues. Some of them may simply require traditional regulatory responses at a time when the federal government is reluctant to issue new regulations. Others transcend state and national boundaries, require concerted global cooperation, or otherwise call for new kinds of responses. Designing appropriate policies will be a major challenge of the 1980s.

Unregulated Pollutants

Little has been done to control air pollutants that may be less common than the criteria pollutants but that may be more toxic. Two problems of particular concern are fine particles and hazardous pollutants.

Scientists have recognized in recent years that smaller particulates are a potentially greater threat to human health and welfare than are larger particulates. The existing air quality standard for particulates, however, does not distinguish particles of different sizes. "Fine" particles, those having diameters of less than 2.5 microns, are especially troublesome. These particles, produced by burning fossil fuels, may contain such toxic substances as lead, vanadium, manganese, and polycyclic organic compounds that can cause cancer, birth defects, and other chronic health problems.[45] Fine particles are more likely than large particles to reach deeply into the lungs and cause respiratory difficulties. Sulfur dioxide and nitrogen dioxide emissions from power plants and other sources can be converted in the atmosphere into fine sulfate and nitrate particles; these, in turn, may not only affect health, but form acid rain.

Fine particles can also markedly reduce visibility. For example, the addition of only 2 micrograms per cubic meter of sulfate particulates can reduce long-range visibility by as much as 45 percent— from 200 miles to 110 miles.[46] Impacts are less severe over shorter distances; yet even at 50 miles, 2 micrograms per cubic meter of sulfates added to the air reduce visibility by 18 percent. Total particulate levels have decreased nationwide. There is evidence, however, indicating that levels of small particulates have increased in some areas, such as the Southwest and nonurban areas of the East, and visibility has been deteriorating.[47]

Fine particles are of special concern because of the projected increase of diesel engines on the nation's roads. Diesels emit from 30 to 100 times more particulates, by mass, than catalyst-equipped gasoline engines, and many of the particles are quite small.[48] EPA has issued a standard for 1985 autos and light-duty trucks which, if implemented, would reduce emissions 80 percent from uncontrolled levels. But there is considerable controversy over the availability of technology to meet this standard.[49]

EPA staff, reviewing the existing air quality standard for particulates, have suggested development of a new standard that recognizes the greater risk from smaller particulates—specifically, those smaller than 10 microns in diameter. The suggested standard, although focusing on smaller particulates, would, in some cases, allow total particulate levels to be higher than under the existing standard.[50] Environmentalists have been particularly concerned that EPA may drop the existing standard before the new one is in place, creating a regulatory gap. The gap would occur because of the time that the states would need to establish monitoring networks, designate nonattainment areas, and revise state implementation plans.[51]

EPA has authority under the Clean Air Act to set emission standards for hazardous pollutants, even in the absence of ambient air quality standards. But the agency has rarely exercised this power. Since 1970, EPA has listed only 7 pollutants as hazardous, and has issued emission standards for only 4—asbestos, beryllium, mercury, and vinyl chloride. There are many more candidates.[52] In 1979, based on a survey of the synthetic organic compounds emitted by chemical manufacturing plants and its own review of other possibly hazardous pollutants, EPA identified 43 chemicals for priority consideration.[53] The agency has begun to assess the risks from several of these substances, but has yet to take regulatory action.

In fact, EPA generally has acted on hazardous pollutants only when prodded by Congress and by petitions and lawsuits filed by environmental groups.[54] Some of the factors slowing EPA's efforts to control hazardous substances apparently stem from disagreements about how much weight should be given to economic considerations, the higher priority assigned by the agency to setting emission standards for new sources of pollution, the tradition within the agency of establishing controls on an industry-by-industry rather than a substance-by-substance basis, and disagreement over how the agency should strike a balance between controlling high risks to a small number of people against lower risks to a larger population.[55]

Regardless of the status of EPA's regulatory program, we continue to learn more about hazardous air pollutants. There is some evidence that these pollutants can have serious impacts on our aquatic environments. The release of mercury through the burning of coal and crude oil, and through smelting, cement manufacture, and incineration of solid waste, may already have sufficiently elevated mercury concentrations to make fish from many areas unfit for human consumption.[56] Scientific models suggest that levels of cadmium and zinc in Lake Michigan will reach concentrations toxic to zooplankton within 30 to 80 years, depending on the rate of increase at which these metals are emitted into the air.[57] Some research indicates that 60 to 90 percent of the highly toxic polychlorinated biphenyls (PCBs) in Lakes Michigan and Superior are deposited from the atmosphere.[58] Thus, not only do hazardous pollutants create potentially serious health risks while in the air, they may also eventually concentrate in some other part of the environment and cause additional problems.

The possible development of the synthetic fuels industry means that we are likely to see more new sources emitting hazardous pollutants. For example, oil shale plants are expected to emit radionucleides, polycyclic organic matter, trace metals (arsenic, cadmium, mercury, beryllium, selenium, and so on), and other such substances. Coal liquefaction plants emit polycyclic aromatic hydrocarbons, carbonyl sulfide, hydrogen sulfide, and phenols.[59] It is unclear how rapidly synfuel plants will be put into operation; it is even less clear that sufficient attention is being given to setting the standards necessary to ensure that their operation will be safe.

Should standards for unregulated pollutants be set at the national level? The health risks are often quite localized, being limited—at least in terms of the direct effect—to the immediate vicinity of the particular plant emitting pollutants. One approach, therefore, would be to delegate regulatory responsibility to the state or local air pollution control agency. This option has the apparent advantage of allowing controls to be tailored to specific situations. However, it has the disadvantages of not dealing adequately with those problems that are not localized (fine particles, for instance, may travel hundreds of miles) and of possibly imposing demands for scientific and engineering expertise on local agencies that are not well equipped to handle them. Where similar problems are repeated at many different sites, there might be inefficient duplication of efforts.

No matter what level of government deals with setting standards, some of the problems that have stymied EPA will not go away, particularly the question of how much effort should be made to reduce risks to small groups of people, and the amount of attention that should be given to economic considerations.

"Acid Rain"

"Acid rain" is a controversial issue for a number of reasons. We know that it exists and can cause serious environmental problems, but we are uncertain about its sources. The acidic particles may be carried long distances, so the areas suffering damage may be far removed (often in another state or country) from the area causing the problem. And it will be very expensive to deal with acid rain. Decisions whether to require suspect sources to reduce their emissions must be made in the face of much uncertainty.[60] Those urging reductions fear that inaction will result in the destruction of fish populations in thousands of lakes, and hint that destruction of fish, like the death of a canary in a coal mine, is an indicator of worse consequences to follow.

Rain and snow are naturally slightly acidic, measuring between

5.6 and 5.7 on the pH scale.* Acid rain and snow contain elevated concentrations of sulfuric and nitric acid, with pH readings below 5.6. The most serious problems in the United States occur in New York's Adirondack Mountains and much of the rest of the Northeast (affecting southeastern Canada as well), where sulfuric acid is the principal component of acid rain (see figure 2.8), and in the West, where nitric acid is the principal component.

Much of the acid begins as sulfur oxides and nitrogen oxides. These are converted in the atmosphere into sulfates and nitrates, which interact with moisture to form sulfuric and nitric acid. Or sulfur and nitrogen compounds in gaseous or particulate form can be deposited or absorbed directly onto terrestrial surfaces and subsequently come into contact with moisture, forming acid.

Electric utilities account for over 65 percent of the sulfur dioxide and 31 percent of nitrogen oxide emissions in the United States created by human activity.[61] Motor vehicles contribute 40 percent of the man-made nitrogen oxides. Coal burning is the source of 90 percent of the utilities' sulfur dioxide emissions, and 71 percent of their nitrogen oxide emissions. Many of these utility emissions occur in the Ohio River Valley (figure 2.8). Although sulfur and nitrogen compounds are produced naturally, it is generally agreed that the acid rain in the northeastern United States and southeastern Canada comes primarily from man-made sources. The relative importance of such sources for western acid rain is less clear.

The acid deposition problem is thought largely to be a long-distance one. The power plants of the Ohio River Valley, for example, are blamed for effects in the Adirondacks and eastern Canada. But the transformation of acid rain's precursors and their transport in the atmosphere are not well understood by scientists, and there is some disagreement over the relative contributions of distant and local sources to the acid rain problems of the Northeast.[62]

The best-documented impacts of acid rain are on aquatic systems. The adversity of the impacts depends, in part, on a system's buffering capacity. If the soil in a watershed contains limestone or other alkaline substances that neutralize acidity, the system's lakes will acidify less rapidly than lakes in less buffered watersheds. The seriousness of the problem in the Adirondacks and many other areas is related to poor buffering capacity.

---

* The pH scale is logarithmic, that is, a change from 6.0 to 5.0 represents a 10-fold increase in acidity. (Neutral solutions have a pH of 7.0, and vinegar has a pH between 2.4 and 3.4.)

Many Adirondack lakes have become quite acidic. Their fish populations have declined and in some cases disappeared entirely. Acids interfere with the reproductive cycles of fish; high concentrations of acids released during spring thaws can be fatal to populations already under stress.[63] Acids also release metals from soils, sometimes in levels toxic to fish, and harm amphibians, aquatic plants, and microorganisms.[64]

Less understood and documented are the impacts of acid rain on forests, crops, and soils. Laboratory studies have demonstrated both beneficial and adverse effects on vegetation and soils; few field studies exist.[65]

Acid precipitation might have indirect effects on human health, resulting from the contamination of fish and water supplies by leached toxic metals such as lead and mercury. But there has been no clear evidence of such effects where contamination has been found.[66]

There are several policy options for addressing acid deposition problems. Further research could be required before reductions are sought in emissions from sources suspected of contributing to acid rain problems. Provisions of the Clean Air Act arguably could be used to promote reductions in emissions from suspect sources, but it may be necessary to amend the act to obtain adequate abatement of emissions from those sources.

The Acid Precipitation Act of 1980[67] established an Interagency Task Force on Acid Precipitation, one purpose of which is to develop a 10-year research plan. A draft plan was issued in January 1981.[68] Beyond this, there has been little further action because EPA and others argue that the scientific uncertainty and likely high abatement costs make it unreasonable to adopt regulations to reduce emissions from suspected contributors. EPA says it is considering accelerating its research efforts, but critics claim that the plan is so vague that, even when completed, it will contribute little to our understanding of what, if any, abatement strategy we should follow.[69]

The National Academy of Sciences has advocated a more aggressive approach. In a report released in September 1981, its Committee on the Atmosphere and the Biosphere concluded that there is "overwhelming" circumstantial evidence supporting claims that power plant emissions help form acid rain, and that the "picture is disturbing enough to merit prompt tightening of restrictions on atmospheric emissions from fossil fuels and other large sources such as metal smelters and cement manufacture."[70] The committee ob-

Figure 2.8
Acid Precipitation in North America

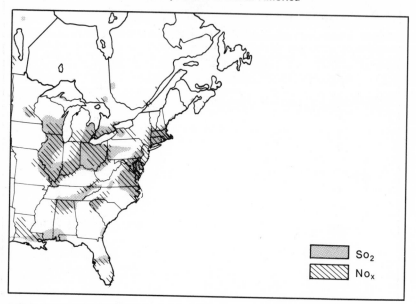

Location of emissions of sulfur dioxide (SO$_2$) and nitrous oxides (NO$_x$)

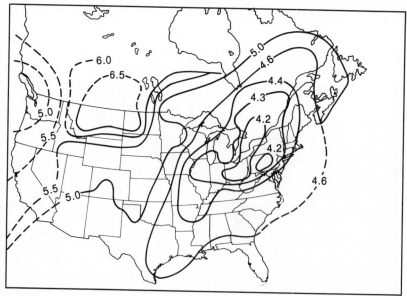

Acidity of North American precipitation (pH)

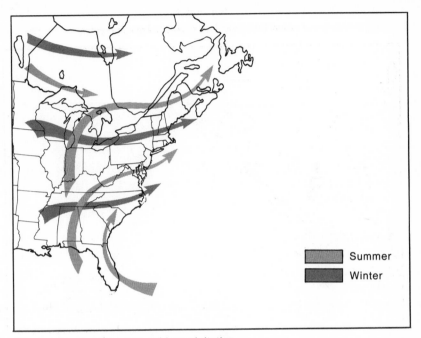

Wind patterns relevant to acid precipitation

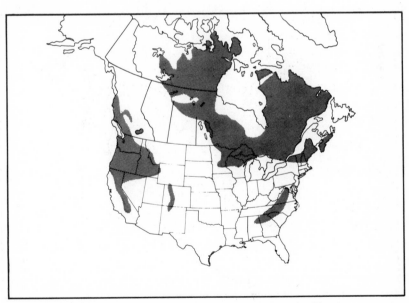

Approximate areas in North America containing lakes sensitive to acid precipitation

Source: Environment Canada and the Canada/United States Co-ordinating Committee on Transboundary Air Pollution, Impact Assessment Work Group

served: "Emissions of sulfur and nitrogen oxides at current or accelerated rates, in the face of clear evidence of serious hazard to human health and to the biosphere, will be extremely risky from a long-term economic standpoint as well as from the standpoint of biosphere protection."[71]

The Canadian government believes that the United States should act quickly to reduce emissions from midwestern pollution sources. One hundred forty acidified lakes in Canada have lost fish populations; nine Nova Scotia rivers with pH levels below 4.7 are barren; thousands of lakes are threatened and could become devoid of fish by the end of the decade.[72] Emissions from some Canadian facilities, particularly large smelters, contribute to acid precipitation in the United States. But the Canadians claim that the United States exports far greater amounts of acid rain to Canada, and that Canada has already ordered emission reductions for the worst of its polluters. In August 1980, the United States and Canada signed a memorandum indicating both governments' intention to negotiate a cooperative agreement on air pollution that crosses their borders. Several work groups were established to identify possible measures for inclusion in the agreement. The Canadians are concerned that the activity of the work groups and the overall negotiation process have slowed substantially since January 1981.[73]

The Clean Air Act does not deal adequately with problems like the long-range transport of acid rain and its precursors. The act focuses mainly on ground level air quality near emission sources. Indeed, as noted earlier, sometimes tall stacks have been constructed to satisfy local abatement requirements, and these stacks have vented pollutants high into the atmosphere where they are more readily transported long distances. Although several sections of the Clean Air Act do address interstate and international pollution impacts, EPA has made little use of these provisions, and only then in response to one state's complaining about emissions from its neighbors.* Acid rain also is not the type of problem apparently anticipated by the statute. The statute's applicable provisions tend to focus on violations of air quality standards in one state caused by specific

---

*For example, New York and Pennsylvania have filed petitions complaining about emissions from utilities and industrial facilities in Ohio, Indiana, Michigan, Tennessee, and West Virginia;[74] Connecticut and New Jersey have protested a New York utility's proposals to burn higher sulfur fuel oil;[75] New York, Pennsylvania, Massachusetts, and the Province of Ontario have challenged emission limit relaxations for two power plants in Cleveland, Ohio.[76]

sources in another, and the existing air quality standards do not address acid rain directly. Any proposals to deal with acid rain are also hindered by the fact that it is difficult to identify the specific sources responsible for distant adverse impacts, and there is no agreement on how much pollution abatement would be required in order to avoid the problem.

Two general approaches have been suggested for dealing with the problem of acid rain.[77] The first uses a technology standard; the second, an emission standard.

Under the first approach, the specific sources thought to be major contributors to the acid rain problem would be required to adopt some specific control technology such as a scrubber (to remove sulfur oxides from flue gas) or some means of "washing" coal (which would remove part of the sulfur before the coal is burned). The scrubber method would be much more expensive than washing. These particular technologies would only be appropriate in the eastern part of the United States, where sulfur appears to be the primary problem.* Even within this area, it would be difficult to identify the specific sources that should adopt the required technology. The advantage of applying technology standards is that the controls could be implemented relatively quickly.

The second approach does not specify the technology to be used, but provides an emission limit that designated sources must achieve, however they think best. Both these approaches have two major problems: the need to determine what sources will be covered by the standard and the question of how stringent the standards should be.

One way to designate the sources to be covered is to use a particular category of sources—for instance, large power plants. Senator Daniel P. Moynihan (D.-New York) has introduced a bill that would require the largest of these plants in about 16 eastern states to reduce their emissions by 85 percent.[79] This could produce moderate to large emission reductions relatively quickly. It would probably be less expensive than the technology standard approach. Its expense could be reduced even further if sources could agree among themselves that those facing particularly high abatement costs could continue to exceed the standard, if others, having lower abatement costs,

---

*Some scientists contend that even a significant reduction of sulfur-oxide emissions may not reduce acid rain, because only a fraction of the NO_x and SO_2 are converted to strong acids. The fraction converted appears to depend on the concentration of strong oxidants, and their concentration is dependent on the availability of NO_x.[78]

achieved compensating reductions below the standard.*

Another way to designate sources is to apply the emission limitation to an entire geographical area and allow state or local authorities to determine which particular emissions should be reduced to meet this standard. This approach is taken in several recent proposals for reducing acid rain in the Northeast. For instance, Senator George J. Mitchell (D.-Maine) has introduced a bill prohibiting increased nitrogen oxide emissions and requiring reduced sulfur dioxide emissions in 31 states east of the Mississippi River and in the District of Columbia.[81] The National Governors' Association is preparing a similar, though less stringent, proposal focusing on 23 states.[82]

Geographical designation does not eliminate the problem of identifying the specific sources that must reduce emissions, but assigns this responsibility to state or regional authorities instead of the federal government.** These authorities may or may not be in a better position to bear the responsibility. The geographical approach can also run into difficulties if the emission rates, from which the reductions are to be calculated, are not well defined. Finally, there is the problem of determining how large a reduction is necessary.

The Office of Technology Assessment (OTA) has estimated that the Mitchell bill would cost $3.3 to $4.1 billion per year and the Moynihan bill $2.2 to $2.6 billion per year, depending on the approaches the states take to achieving the targeted emission reductions. OTA's analysis assumes no interstate trading. If interstate trading were to occur, costs could be reduced to $3.1 billion annually under the Mitchell bill and $1.7 billion annually under the Moynihan bill. The Mitchell bill would require sulfur dioxide emissions to be reduced 10 million tons below 1980 levels and the Moynihan bill an estimated 8.2 million tons.[83]

Global Atmospheric Problems

Some of the air pollution problems that we are facing extend over even broader areas than acid rain. They are truly global problems,

---

*This could be done under EPA's "controlled trading" policy, which permits polluters to develop cooperatively more cost-effective abatement strategies than otherwise would be available.[80]

**The state or regional authority can, in turn, employ an emission standard or technology standard approach in dealing with individual sources. As applied to utilities, for instance, the latter might involve directing them to give priority to cleaner plants over dirtier plants in meeting electrical demands, providing incentives to retire older, heavier-pol-

caused by pollutants emitted anywhere in the world. The impacts, as well, are distributed worldwide.

The Greenhouse Effect

One global problem is the buildup of carbon dioxide (CO_2) in our atmosphere. Scientists fear that this buildup will trap some of the earth's heat, warm the earth's surface, and might, ultimately, cause melting of the polar ice caps, flooding of coastal areas, and the creation of deserts in many inland areas. This process is called "the greenhouse effect."

Carbon dioxide is not normally considered a pollutant. It is the primary product of most combustion—of fossil fuels, for example—and is created by many natural biological activities. We have, in fact, been so little concerned about carbon dioxide in the past that the preferred method of controlling carbon monoxide emissions from automobiles is to convert them to carbon dioxide.

Natural biological activities such as the respiration of mammals and the decay of vegetation account for over 95 percent of the carbon dioxide released to the atmosphere.[84] Why, then, is there so much concern about the 3 to 3.5 percent of emissions resulting from the burning of fossil fuels? The reason is that the natural biological activities eliminate as much carbon dioxide as they release, as plants use the carbon for their growth, releasing free oxygen. Fossil fuel combustion provides no such offsets. Although the biosphere probably absorbs about half of these emissions, the rest remain in the atmosphere. And, except for absorption by natural biological processes, there is no known feasible method of removing carbon dioxide from source emissions once it has been formed.

Recent scientific studies attempting to link increased CO_2 concentrations, rising temperatures, and other important natural phenomena indicate that the carbon dioxide buildup may become a very serious problem. The models used in these studies are limited, but most atmospheric scientists agree on rough estimates of the temperature changes expected from increased CO_2 concentrations.[85]* One study predicted that a 2.5 percent annual increase in fossil fuel consumption (comparable to recent trends) would create CO_2 concentrations by the middle of the next century twice as high as those

luting, coal-fired power plants, and limiting emission increases resulting from plants switching to coal.

*NASA scientists have found that temperature increases in the last 20 years are consistent with those calculated on their atmospheric model of the greenhouse effect.[86]

of the preindustrial level.* This doubling could increase average annual global surface temperature by 4° Fahrenheit or more,[88] making the temperature higher than it has been for over 100,000 years.[89] Because there is little historical experience to draw on, scientists find it difficult to predict all of the consequences of such a temperature change. But the West Antarctic ice sheet would probably melt, causing a rise in sea levels, and significant coastal flooding. Shifts in weather patterns could substantially affect the production capacity of existing agricultural regions. All of this, in turn, would have substantial socioeconomic impacts.[90]

At present, the only feasible way of limiting carbon dioxide concentrations is to reduce the amount of carbon dioxide we produce, particularly to get energy from fossil fuels. For this reason, President Carter's Council on Environmental Quality recommended in January 1981 that the United States incorporate concern about CO_2 levels into its energy policy planning; strive to keep its energy options open; not become committed to an extended period of unrestricted fossil fuel use; and vigorously pursue energy conservation and renewable energy technologies.[91] But the Department of Energy's 1981 national energy plan merely states there is considerable controversy over the significance of projected growth in CO_2 emissions and that long-term research on the effects of this buildup is being conducted "to develop an early understanding of potentially adverse impacts and quantitative relationships."[92]

Depletion of Stratospheric Ozone by Chlorofluorocarbons

The large-scale release of chlorofluorocarbons (CFCs) into the atmosphere also may be causing a global problem. In 1974, two scientists hypothesized that CFCs migrate slowly into the stratosphere where—through multiple, complex chemical reactions—they react with and thereby destroy ozone.[93] Although ozone, the major component of smog, is undesirable near the earth's surface, its presence in the stratosphere serves to reduce the amount of ultraviolet radiation reaching the earth's surface and thereby protects us from skin cancer and other harmful effects, such as reduced agricultural and marine productivity.

---

*Since the beginning of the industrial revolution about 180 years ago, the concentration of carbon dioxide in the atmosphere is estimated to have increased 15 to 25 percent. The concentration is known to have increased 7.0 percent between 1958 and 1979. The principal cause of these changes is believed to be the burning of fossil fuels.[87]

Chlorofluorocarbons are man-made chemicals. They served as the propellant in most aerosol products until this use was banned by the U.S. Environmental Protection Agency and the U.S. Food and Drug Administration; they are still used in aerosols in many other countries. Many countries continue to make extensive, and increasing, use of CFCs as industrial solvents, in producing rigid and flexible synthetic foams, as the cooling fluid in many refrigerators and air conditioners, for some types of insulation, and for numerous other purposes. Although the total amount of CFCs used in the United States fell after the ban on aerosol uses (the United States accounts for about one-third of the world's aerosol use), the amount consumed in nonaerosol uses continues to advance rapidly.[94] Worldwide use is estimated to be growing at 5 to 11 percent a year, although this growth rate has fallen during the recent recessions.[95]

The National Academy of Sciences (NAS) has studied the problem of CFCs for several years.[96] Its 1979 report concluded that continuing CFC emissions at 1977 rates would eventually result in ozone depletion of about 16.5 percent (with a 95 percent probability that the level would fall within a range of 5 to 28 percent depletion). One-fourth of this depletion would occur within 15 years; one-half, within 35 years. If emissions increased at a rate of 7 percent annually to the year 2000, there would be a 75 percent probability that ozone depletion would eventually exceed 30 percent.[97]* In its 1979 report, the academy further predicted that a 16 percent ozone depletion would result in several hundred thousand additional cases of nonmelanoma skin cancer annually and in possibly several thousand additional cases of melanoma skin cancer in the United States alone. More recent analyses indicate that the amount of ozone depletion would be less than this estimate, but still project about a 5 to 10 percent loss even with no growth in emissions over the 1977 level.[98]

CFCs may also contribute to the "greenhouse effect." Trace gases, including CFCs, are thought to trap heat from the earth's surface. Some analyses have indicated that the effect of trace gases may be nearly as great as that from combustion of fossil fuels in warming the global atmosphere.[99]

Because 98 percent of CFC emissions occur when CFCs are used, rather than when they are manufactured, the only feasible way of

---

*U.S. production of CFCs was expected to grow at a 7 percent annual rate in the absence of regulatory controls, and total world emissions in the absence of controls are expected to grow 9 percent annually during the next decade.

reducing release is usually to substitute other materials.[100] This may be relatively easy in some cases, but not in others. Some cooling equipment, such as that used for home and supermarket air conditioning, already uses a coolant that is not considered a threat to the ozone layer. Recycling and substitution are also possible for industrial solvents. Insulating materials that do not use CFCs are readily available, although they are less efficient.

The 1977 amendments to the Clean Air Act specifically authorize EPA regulation if CFCs can be reasonably anticipated to affect the stratosphere, and if this effect may endanger public health or welfare. The agency, however, has yet to respond with any specific proposal, in part because of the scientific uncertainty that remains, in part because of the large economic costs that might result from further regulation, in part because of substantial political pressure opposing any action, and in part because the United States acting alone will accomplish little if other nations do not follow suit. The last factor now carries less weight because, as noted below, other countries have begun to cut back on production and use of CFCs. Scientific uncertainty remains, because all depletion projections are based solely on mathematical models.[101]

In October 1980, EPA did issue an "advance notice of proposed rulemaking," which identified and solicited comments on the several different approaches the agency could take in dealing with CFCs.[102] One approach was to "wait and see," taking no action until there is better evidence that the ozone depletion theory is valid.[103] Although imposing few economic costs, this approach, if other countries followed suit, would permit unrestrained growth in CFC emissions. But some maintain it could take 10 years or more to accumulate the necessary evidence. Since CFCs take many years to migrate to the stratosphere, by the time the agency received the information it needed enough CFCs would already have been released to make the problem significantly more severe than if production were limited.

EPA presented two alternative policy options: to limit production to, or reduce it from, current levels. EPA has not followed up on its notice, and Congress is considering amendments to the Clean Air Act that would require EPA to consider additional scientific findings before it takes regulatory action.[104]

Although EPA is procrastinating, other countries are beginning to act. The European Economic Community (EEC), which was responsible for 30 percent of world production and 39 percent of world CFC use in 1977, has begun to eliminate the use of CFCs in aerosols.[105] (For example, West Germany reported reductions of 40 percent by 1980, Denmark 48 percent by 1979, and the Netherlands a projected 50 percent by 1981, compared to 1976 levels.)[106] The EEC countries and Japan have agreed not to increase CFC production capacity,[107] and the Commission of the European Communities reportedly is developing draft directives for limiting use of CFCs in foam plastics, refrigeration, and solvents.[108] The United Nations Environment Programme has begun work on a worldwide convention for the protection of the ozone layer. The convention is expected to result in agreements to participate in a range of research and information exchange activities, with more specific and controversial topics addressed in subsequent protocols. The first meeting of the technical and legal working group is being held in 1982.[109]

Indoor Air Pollution

Although most people spend much more of their lives indoors than outdoors, there has, until recently, been little interest in the problem of indoor air pollution. Yet indoor air is contaminated with a number of potentially hazardous pollutants, often at much higher concentrations than can be found in outdoor air. These potential pollutants include such substances as radon (from soil, water, and building materials), respirable particulates (from tobacco smoke and combustion), carbon monoxide and nitrogen dioxide (from gas stoves), formaldehyde (from insulation, plywood, particle board, and home furnishings), airborne microorganisms, and allergens.[110] Indoor concentrations of radon, the decay products of which can be inhaled in fine particles and may cause lung damage, are often 10 times greater than outdoor concentrations. Indoor levels of nitrogen dioxide from gas stoves have been measured at levels exceeding the outdoor air quality standards.

Growing emphasis on energy conservation in homes and offices may well be making the problems worse. Increasing the amount of insulation in buildings, and reducing their air leakage, tends to raise pollution levels by reducing the amount of cleaner air coming in from outside. Moreover, some of the materials used for insulation are themselves sources of pollutants.

There is some evidence that human exposure to indoor contaminants may significantly affect health and sometimes cause premature death, although the magnitude of these effects cannot yet be quantitatively estimated. Because of the absence of research on exposure,

it is difficult to establish defensible standards for indoor pollutants.*
It would also be very difficult to enforce such standards if they could
be established.

A National Academy of Sciences panel concluded that such exposure ought to be reduced, and that individuals, manufacturers,
building designers and contractors, and government should all take
responsibility for doing so. Depending on the particular pollutant
and its source, we can often reduce exposure by using different
materials or by increasing the amount of ventilation and air cleaning.
Ambient air contributes to indoor air pollution, and indoor and
outdoor pollutants may interact physiologically and chemically. For
these reasons, the NAS panel observed that the existence of substantial indoor exposure is not a reason to relax national outdoor
ambient air quality standards.

The extent to which government should attempt to take action
on this issue is unclear. In many cases, individuals are unable to
detect the pollutant, may not be aware of the problems it causes
even if they can, and in any case may be unable to take any action
to correct the problem. In other cases—tobacco smoke, for example—individuals may have full information and be able to do something about it. The appropriate amount of government involvement,
if any, might well differ for such different types of situations.

Different levels of government have advantages in dealing with
different types of indoor air pollution problems. Some local governments have begun to deal with specific problems—tobacco smoke,
for example—in public buildings. Massachusetts has prohibited the
use of an insulation material that may cause cancer. The Consumer
Product Safety Commission subsequently took nationwide action.
Nonetheless, government will undoubtedly move very slowly and
carefully in this area. To do otherwise would be considered by most
people to be an unwarranted invasion of privacy, and could create
personnel and financial demands beyond any currently feasible levels.

FURTHER READING

The most comprehensive review of progress and problems in implementing the Clean Air Act is the report of the National Com-

---

*It is unclear how much research EPA will conduct on indoor air pollution. EPA allegedly
barred one of its principal proponents of additional research from attending an international
conference on indoor pollution, and contemplates spending no money on research in this
area in fiscal year 1983.[111]

mission on Air Quality, *To Breathe Clean Air* (Washington, D.C.: U.S. Government Printing Office, March 1981). Detailed reports on particular topics, prepared under contract to the commission, are listed in the back of the volume and are available from the Department of Commerce's National Technical Information Service. The National Academy of Sciences was asked by Congress to conduct a study parallel to the research of the commission, on prevention of significant deterioration. The results are published in *On Prevention of Significant Deterioration of Air Quality* (Washington, D.C.: National Academy Press, 1981). An overview of many legal and institutional air quality issues, incorporating regulations, court decisions, and other basic documents, is Phillip D. Reed and Gregory Wetstone, eds., *Air and Water Pollution Control Law: 1982*, published by the Environmental Law Institute (Suite 600, 1346 Connecticut Avenue, N.W., Washington, D.C. 20036).

Environmental, business, and state and local government groups have developed their own conclusions and recommendations concerning the Clean Air Act. Capsule summaries of environmentalist and business views are found in the congressional briefing books of the National Clean Air Coalition (530 7th Street, S.E., Washington, D.C. 20003) and the National Environmental Development Association Clean Air Act Project (3 National Press Building, Washington, D.C. 20045). These and other groups' positions are elaborated in hearings conducted by the U.S. Congress, Senate Committee on Environment and Public Works, *Clean Air Act Oversight*, 97th Cong. 1st Sess., April-July 1981, Serial No. 97-H12.

Three recent Conservation Foundation publications addressing Clean Air Act issues include: Richard A. Liroff, *Air Pollution Offsets: Trading, Selling and Banking* (1980); Robert D. Friedman, *Sensitive Populations and Environmental Standards* (1981); and Daniel Swartzman, Richard A. Liroff, and Kevin G. Croke, eds., *Cost-Benefit Analysis and Environmental Regulations: Politics, Ethics, and Methods* (1982).

Many books and reports discuss risks from unregulated air pollutants. The National Academy of Sciences report *Diesel Cars: Benefits, Risks, and Public Policy* (Washington, D.C.: National Academy Press, 1982) discusses particulate emissions from diesel engines. This study may be out of date with respect to its conclusions about the availability of technology to reduce emissions of particulates. Fine particulates and other pollutants from stationary sources are examined in Richard Wilson, et al., *Health Effects of Fossil Fuel*

Burning: Assessment and Mitigation (Cambridge, Mass.: Ballinger Publishing Company, 1980). Another report on fossil fuel combustion, which details information on the impact of air pollution on aquatic ecosystems, is the National Academy of Sciences, *Atmosphere-Biosphere Interactions: Toward a Better Understanding of the Ecological Consequences of Fossil Fuel Combustion* (Washington, D.C. National Academy Press, 1981).

Conflicting points of view on the sources and impacts of acid deposition, and on appropriate policies for reducing and mitigating adverse impacts, are summarized in U.S. Comptroller General of the United States, *The Debate Over Acid Precipitation: Opposing Views, Status of Research* (Washington, D.C.: U.S. General Accounting Office, September 11, 1981). The National Academy of Sciences report on atmosphere-biosphere interactions, mentioned above, also reviews much information on acid deposition. Policy options for responding to acid deposition are outlined in Gregory Wetstone and Phillip D. Reed, *Institutional Aspects of Transported Pollutants: An Examination of Transport Reduction Strategies* (Washington, D.C.: Environmental Law Institute, 1981).

The Council on Environmental Quality's *Global Energy Futures and the Carbon Dioxide Problem* (Washington, D.C.: U.S. Government Printing Office, 1981) provides a brief introduction to and contains a useful bibliography on the "greenhouse effect." More recent scientific findings on the greenhouse effect have been reported in *Science* magazine.

The best sources of information on depletion of stratospheric ozone by chlorofluorocarbons are several reports by the National Academy of Sciences. See, for example, *Protection Against Depletion of Stratospheric Ozone by Chlorofluorocarbons* (Washington, D.C.: National Academy of Sciences, 1979). New scientific developments on ozone depletion are often reported in *Science* magazine. Economic and regulatory aspects of chlorofluorocarbon control were reviewed for EPA by the Rand Corporation in *Economic Implications of Regulating Chlorofluorocarbon Emissions from Nonpropellant Applications* (Santa Monica, Calif.: Rand Corporation, 1980).

The National Academy of Sciences has produced the most comprehensive review of indoor air quality issues: *Indoor Pollutants* (Washington, D.C.: National Academy Press, 1981).

TEXT REFERENCES

1. For a description of the index and its limitations, see Council on Environmental Quality, *Environmental Quality—1980* (Washington, D.C.: U.S. Government Printing Office, 1980), pp. 155-158.

2. These data, and the others reported in the text, are based on the Council on Environmental Quality's as yet unpublished UPGRADE analysis of the U.S. Environmental Protection Agency's air quality data bank, SAROAD (Storage n Retrieval of Aerometric Data); Council on Environmental Quality, *Environmental Quality—1980*, pp. 147-152; and previous CEQ annual reports.

3. The PSI index uses the highest reading from the many monitors in a region, and this reading may not be representative of regional air quality.

4. Information provided by the U.S. Environmental Protection Agency, Office of Air, Noise, and Radiation, the National Air Data Branch, and the Emission Control Technology Division.

5. U.S. Comptroller General, *Air Quality: Do We Really Know What It Is?* (Washington, D.C.: General Accounting Office, 1979), pp. ii-iii.

6. 44 Fed. Reg. 27558-27569 (1979).

7. These emission estimates for 1980 are from the U.S. Environmental Protection Agency, *National Air Pollutant Emission Estimates, 1940-1980* (Research Triangle Park, N.C.: U.S. Environmental Protection Agency, Office of Air Quality Planning and Standards, 1982), Tables 2-6. (Hereafter cited as *Emission Estimates*, 1940-1980.)

8. U.S. Environmental Protection Agency, Office of Air, Noise, and Radiation, unpublished analysis.

9. See U.S. Environmental Protection Agency, *Trends in the Quality of the Nation's Air—A Report to the People* (Washington, D.C.: U.S. Government Printing Office, 1980), p. 5. (Hereafter cited as *Report to the People*.) Unless otherwise indicated, this publication is the basis for the discussion of particulates in this paragraph of the text. For the data, see *Emission Estimates, 1940-1980*, Table 1.

10. A table of the attainment status of areas for all the criteria pollutants, based on EPA data, is found in the final report of the National Commission on Air Quality, *To Breathe Clean Air* (Washington, D.C.: U.S. Government Printing Office, 1981), p. 114. (Hereafter referred to as *NCAQ Report*.) A primary standard has been established for a 24-hour period and on an annual basis, but the NCAQ report does not indicate which of these standards has not been attained.

11. *Report to the People*, p. 6.

12. *Emission Estimates, 1940-1980*, Table 3.

13. U.S. Environmental Protection Agency, Office of Air, Noise, and Radiation, unpublished data.

14. For a summary of the 429 tall stacks, by height and industry, see Council on Environmental Quality, *Environmental Quality—1980*, p. 175. EPA has taken a long time to publish regulations implementing the Clean Air Act's provisions regarding tall stacks. Proposed rules were published in January 1979, but final rules were not published until February 1982. See 47 Fed. Reg. 5864-5869 (1982).

15. U.S. Environmental Protection Agency, Office of Air, Noise, and Radiation, unpublished data.

16. *Emission Estimates, 1940-1980*, Table 1.

17. *NCAQ Report*, p. 129.

18. *Emission Estimates, 1940-1980*, Table 4.

19. U.S. Environmental Protection Agency, Office of Air, Noise, and Radiation, unpublished data.

20. *Ibid.*

21. *Emission Estimates, 1940-1980*, Table 1.

22. These explanations of the emission trends are from *Report to the People*, p. 13.

23. *NCAQ Report*, pp. 129-130.

24. In 1979, EPA revised the previous air quality standard for photochemical oxidents, converting it to a standard for ozone. See 44 Fed. Reg. 8210-8221 (1979).

25. *Emission Estimates, 1940-1980*, Table 5. For discussion of the role of natural sources as smog precursors, see Basil Dimitriades, "The Role of Natural Organics in Photochemical Air Pollution," *Journal of the Air Pollution Control Association* 31(3):229-235 (1981).

26. U.S. Environmental Protection Agency, Office of Air, Noise, and Radiation, unpublished analysis. Based on the composite average of the second highest daily maximum hour ozone values.

27. *Emission Estimates, 1940-1980*, Table 1.

28. *NCAQ Report*, pp. 121, 127.

29. *Emission Estimates, 1940-1980*, Table 1, and Environmental Protection Agency, Office of Air, Noise, and Radiation, unpublished data.

30. *NCAQ Report*, pp. 128-129.

31. *Ibid.*, p. 114.

32. *NCAQ Report*, pp. 199-200.

33. *Ibid.*, p. 28.

34. Maintenance programs in the May 1981, 31(5) and September 1981, 31(9) issues of the *Journal of the Air Pollution Control Association*.

35. *NCAQ Report*, p. 209.

36. *Ibid.*, p. 129.

37. "States' Survey Indicates Problems in Some Areas if Emission Limit Eased," *Environment Reporter—Current Developments*, December 25, 1981, p. 1030. For additional statistics from the survey see "States Say 5252 Would Sharply Increase CO, NO^x, Prolong Nonattainment," *Inside E.P.A. Weekly Report*, February 26, 1982, pp. 14-15.

38. See U.S. Comptroller General, *Improvements Needed in Controlling Major Air Pollution Sources* (Washington, D.C.: General Accounting Office, 1979), pp. ii, 5-6. For results of a later EPA study showing substantial noncompliance at sources where pollution control equipment had been installed, see *NCAQ Report*, p. 230; and Renelle Rae, "Enforcement," in Phillip D. Reed and Gregory Wetstone, eds., *Air and Water Pollution Control Law: 1981* (Washington, D.C.: Environmental Law Institute, 1981), p. 715.

39. U.S. Comptroller General, *Ibid.*, pp. 6, 10.

40. "EPA Finds Most Sources Exceed Air Limits, Maps Plans to Combat Excesses," *Inside E.P.A. Weekly Report*, March 28, 1980, p. 1.

41. For summary statistics describing the results of EPA's actions, see Rae, "Enforcement."

42. *Environment Reporter—Current Developments*, Nov. 27, 1981, p. 937.

43. *NCAQ Report*, p. 233.

44. For an overview of the diverse views, see U.S., Congress, Senate, Committee on Environment and Public Works, *Clean Air Act Oversight*, Hearings, 97th Cong., 1st sess., 1981.

45. *NCAQ Report*, p. 74.

46. National Research Council, Commission on Natural Resources, Environmental Studies Board, Committee on Prevention of Significant Deterioration of Air Quality, *On Prevention of Significant Deterioration of Air Quality* (Washington, D.C.: National Academy Press, 1981), p. 28. This committee has recommended development of a PSD increment for fine particulates. See p. xix of its report.

47. *Report to the People*, p. 4.

48. *NCAQ Report*, pp. 216-217.

49. *Ibid.*, p. 30; see also *NRDC v. Costle*, 11 ELR 20361 (D.C. Cir., 1981); National Research Council, Health Effects Panel of the Diesel Impacts Study Committee, *Health Effects of Exposure to Diesel Exhaust* (Washington, D.C.: National Academy Press, 1981);

and Eliot Marshall, "Safe to Delay 1985 Diesel Rule, Study Says," *Science* 215(4531):268-69 (1982).

50. "EPA Staff Would Relax Particulate Standards in Shift to Fine-Particle Measure," *Inside E.P.A. Weekly Report*, June 26, 1981, p. 1. The new standard would be for "total thoracic deposited particles," those going beyond the mouth and nasal cavities into the lungs. EPA staff have characterized the new standard as a relaxation.

51. *Environment Reporter—Current Developments*, November 27, 1981, pp. 934-35; and "Staff Supports TSP Enforcement Until New Particulate Standard in Place," *Inside E.P.A. Weekly Report*, February 26, 1982, pp. 3-4.

52. *NCAQ Report*, pp. 76-78.

53. The list is reproduced in *NCAQ Report*, p. 78, and is supplemented by the four substances named in Section 122 of the Clean Air Act. A summary of estimated emissions of these substances is reproduced in the "Toxic Substances" section of the National Clean Air Coalition congressional briefing book on the Clean Air Act. (See FURTHER READINGS section of this chapter.) The emission estimates in the briefing book are taken from two compilations of reports for EPA by SRI International, Inc. and SAI, Inc., both titled "Human Exposures to Atmospheric Concentrations of Selected Chemicals."

54. *NCAQ Report*, p. 76.

55. These factors are cited in Gregory Wetstone, "National Emission Standards for Hazardous Air Pollutants," in Phillip D. Reed and Gregory Wetstone, *Air and Water Pollution Control Law: 1981*. For further discussion of the role of economic considerations, see this source, and the *NCAQ Report*, pp. 76-78.

56. National Research Council, Commission on Natural Resources, Board on Agriculture and Renewable Resources, Committee on the Atmosphere and the Biosphere, *Atmosphere-Biosphere Interactions: Toward a Better Understanding of the Ecological Consequences of Fossil Fuel Combustion* (Washington, D.C.: National Academy Press, 1981), p. 3. (Hereafter cited as *NAS Fossil Fuel Combustion Report.*)

57. *Ibid.*, p. 4.

58. See Steven J. Eisenreich, et al., "Airborne Organic Contaminants in the Great Lakes Ecosystem," *Environmental Science and Technology* 15(1):30-38 (1981).

59. Federal Interagency Committee on Health and Environmental Effects of Energy Technologies, cited in SRI International, "Health-Effects Research and Standard Setting at EPA" (Report to the National Commission on Air Quality, December 1980), pp. III-43-44. More detailed information on synthetic fuels is found in David Masselli and Norman L. Dean, Jr., *The Impacts of Synthetic Fuels Development* (Washington, D.C.: National Wildlife Federation, 1981).

60. A comprehensive summary of many of the arguments over acid rain, and the evidence supporting them, is found in a report by the U.S. Comptroller General, *The Debate Over Acid Precipitation: Opposing Views, Status of Research* (Washington, D.C.: General Accounting Office, September 11, 1981). (Hereafter cited as *GAO Acid Rain Report.*) See also, Bette Hileman, "Acid Precipitation," *Environmental Science and Technology* 15(10):1119-24 (1981); Lois R. Ember, "Acid Pollutants: Hitchhikers Ride the Wind," *Chemical and Engineering News* 59(37):20-31 (1981); Environmental Protection Agency, *Acid Rain* (Washington, D.C.: U.S. Government Printing Office, 1980) (hereafter cited as "EPA Acid Rain Brochure"); Gregory Wetstone, "Air Pollution Control Laws in North America and The Problem of Acid Rain and Snow," 10 ELR 5001 (1980); and Ellis B. Cowling, "Acid Precipitation in Historical Perspective," *Environmental Science and Technology* 16(2):110A-123A (1982).

61. The information in this paragraph and the next in the text is drawn from the *GAO Acid Rain Report*, p. 27.

62. *Ibid.*, pp. 29-31. See also, Richard A. Kerr, "Tracing Sources of Acid Rain Causes Big Stir," *Science* 215(4534):881 (1982).

63. "EPA Acid Rain Brochure," p. 16.

64. *GAO Acid Rain Report*, p. 7.

65. *Ibid.*, pp. 9-10; "EPA Acid Rain Brochure," pp. 20-22.

66. *GAO Acid Rain Report*, p. 12.

67. Title VII of the Energy Security Act of 1980, 42 U.S.C., sec. 8701 (1981).

68. "National Acid Precipitation Assessment Plan" (Washington, D.C.: Interagency Task Force on Acid Precipitation, 1981), available from the Council on Environmental Quality.

69. This criticism has been made by the JASON group, a prestigious committee of physicists reporting to the federal government. See J. Chamberlain, et al., "The Physics and Chemistry of Acid Precipitation" (Washington, D.C.: Draft Technical Report for the Department of Energy, September 1981), p. 6. The report is noted in "Edwards Asks ERAB to Examine Acid Rain, New High Level Study Revealed," *Inside Energy Weekly Report*, November 13, 1981, pp. 7-8.

70. *NAS Fossil Fuel Combustion Report*, pp. 3, 7.

71. *Ibid.*, p. 3.

72. See Ember, "Acid Pollutants: Hitchhikers Ride the Wind," p. 22.

73. *GAO Acid Rain Report*, p. 43. For more details on 1981 bilateral developments, see Gregory Wetstone, "Interstate and International Air Pollution," in Phillip D. Reed and Gregory Wetstone, *Air and Water Pollution Control Law: 1981*.

74. 46 Fed. Reg. 24602-24604 (1981).

75. 45 Fed. Reg. 53138-53145 (1980).

76. 46 Fed. Reg. 37642-37651 (1981).

77. For discussion of additional regulatory alternatives, see Gregory Wetstone and Phillip D. Reed, "Institutional Aspects of Transported Pollutants: An Examination of Transport Reduction Strategies, Prepared for the National Commission on Air Quality" (Washington, D.C.: Environmental Law Institute, 1981). See also, Gregory Wetstone, "Legislative Options for Controlling Long Range Air Pollution Problems," prepared for "The Challenge of Atmospheric Deposition" Conference, May 20, 1981, Chicago, Illinois.

78. *JASON Report*, pp. 3-4.

79. The paragraphs in the text describing the Mitchell bill (S. 1706) and the Moynihan bill (S. 1709) are based on prepared testimony of Robert M. Friedman, director of the Office of Technology Assessment's study of long-range transport before the U.S., Senate, Committee on Environment and Public Works, 97th Cong., 1st sess., October 29, 1981.

80. See Richard A. Liroff, *Air Pollution Offsets: Trading, Selling and Banking* (Washington, D.C.: The Conservation Foundation, 1980) and Richard A. Liroff, "The Bubble Concept for Air Pollution Control: A Political and Administrative Perspective," prepared for Annual Meeting of the Air Pollution Control Association, Philadelphia, Pennsylvania, 1981.

81. *Ibid.*

82. "State Group Informally Backs NGA Acid Rain Plan, Joint Meeting to be Held," *Inside E.P.A. Weekly Report*, December 25, 1981, p. 9, and "NGA Scraps 5-million Ton Reduction Target in Revised Acid Rain Plan," *Inside E.P.A. Weekly Report*, February 26, 1982, p. 1.

83. Testimony of OTA project director, Robert M. Friedman.

84. Council on Environmental Quality, *Global Energy Futures and the Carbon Dioxide Problem* (Washington, D.C.: U.S. Government Printing Office, January 1981), p. 4. (Hereafter referred to as *CEQ CO^2 Report*.)

85. *Ibid.*, p. 9. See also Stephen Budiansky, "Climate Modeling," *Environmental Science & Technology* 14(5):501-7 (1980).

86. Their results are reported in J. Hansen, et al., "Climate Impact of Increasing Atmospheric Carbon Dioxide," *Science* 213(4511):957-66 (1981). These findings are also discussed in "Evidence is Found of Warming Trend," *New York Times*, October 19, 1981.

87. *CEQ CO^2 Report*, pp. 1, 6, and sources cited therein.

88. *Ibid.*, p. 10.

89. *Ibid.*

90. *CEQ CO²* Report, pp. 21-22. See also "Is Antarctica Shrinking?" *Newsweek*, October 5, 1981, pp. 72-74, and G. Kukla and J. Gavin, "Summer Ice and Carbon Dioxide," *Science* 214(4520):497-503 (1981).

91. *CEQ CO² Report*, pp. 66-67. CEQ also urged greater global cooperation on the CO² question.

92. U.S. Department of Energy, *Environmental Trends to the Year 2000: A Supplement to the National Energy Policy Plan* (Washington, D.C.: U.S. Government Printing Office, 1981), p. 9. For further discussion of policy options for CO_2 control, see the three articles on the greenhouse effect in *Technology Review* 84(2) (1981).

93. Alan S. Miller, Natural Resources Defense Council, testimony before the U.S., Congress, Senate Committee on Environment and Public Works, Subcommittee on Toxic Substances and Environmental Oversight, *Hearing on the Impact of Chlorofluorocarbon Emissions on the Stratosphere*, 97th Cong., 1st sess., July 23, 1981, p. 2.

94. Much of the summary that follows is taken from EPA's Advanced Notice of Proposed Rulemaking regarding possible production restrictions on ozone-depleting chlorofluorocarbons, 45 Fed. Reg. 66725-66734 (1980). (Hereafter referred to as "EPA Chlorofluorocarbons Notice.")

95. "CFC Regulation Not Expected, Further Regulation Needed," *Air/Water Pollution Report*, March 8, 1982, p. 94.

96. See *Stratospheric Ozone Depletion by Halocarbons: Chemistry and Transport*, and *Protection Against Depletion of Stratospheric Ozone by Chlorofluorocarbons* (Washington, D.C.: National Academy of Sciences, 1979).

97. Data from the NAS study are cited in "EPA Chlorofluorocarbons Notice."

98. This estimate is found in "World Meterological Organization Third Statement on Modification of the Ozone Layer Due to Human Activities and Some Geophysical Consequences," *International Environment Reporter*, February 10, 1982, pp. 91-94. See also, "Science Panel Concludes Fluorocarbons Won't Deplete Ozone as Fast as Expected," *Wall Street Journal*, April 1, 1982.

99. See "Earth's Atmosphere May be Heating Faster Than Thought, Scientists Say," *Washington Post*, November 28, 1981.

100. "EPA Chlorofluorocarbons Notice."

101. For discussion of some of the difficulties in modeling the impact of chlorofluorocarbons on stratospheric ozone, see Stephen Budiansky, "Ozone Modeling," *Environmental Science and Technology* 14(6)645-7 (1981). For discussion of ozone trends between 1970 and 1979, see "New Satellite May Finally Determine Whether Man is Damaging Ozone Layer," *New York Times*, October 20, 1981, and *International Environment Reporter*, February 10, 1982, pp. 91-94. See also, J. W. Waters, et al., "Chlorine Monoxide Radical, Ozone, and Hydrogen Peroxide: Stratospheric Measurements by Microwave Limb Sounding," *Science* 214(4516): 61-4 (1981).

102. "EPA Chlorofluorocarbons Notice."

103. *Ibid.*

104. "New Clean Air Bill Includes Language Restricting Further Non-Aerosol Rules." See *Environment Reporter—Current Developments*, January 15, 1982, p. 1154.

105. "EPA Chlorofluorocarbons Notice."

106. Commission on the European Communities, "Communication to the Council on Chlorofluorocarbons in the Environment," *International Environment Reporter*, June 10, 1981, pp. 909-13.

107. Alan S. Miller, Natural Resources Defense Council, supplemental comments before the U.S., Congress, Senate Committee on Environment and Public Works, Subcommittee on Toxic Substances and Environmental Oversight, *Hearings on the Impact of Chlorofluorocarbon Emissions on the Stratosphere*, 97th Cong., 1st sess., July 23, 1981, p. 7.

108. "New Limits on CFC's," *International Environment Reporter*, July 8, 1981, p. 920.

109. *Ibid.*, and letter from Alan S. Miller, Natural Resources Defense Council, to Richard A. Liroff, December 31, 1981.

110. The information on indoor air pollutants in the first five paragraphs of text is based on National Research Council, Assembly of Life Sciences, Board on Toxicology and Environmental Health Hazards, Committee on Indoor Pollutants, *Indoor Pollutants* (Washington, D.C.: National Academy Press, 1981). See also Stephen Budiansky, "Indoor Air Pollution," *Environmental Science and Technology* 14(9):1023-27 (1980).

111. See "EPA Said to Bar Official from Meeting," *Science* 214(4521):639 (1981), and "Gorsuch Reportedly Zeros Out Indoor Air R&D for FY83, Despite NAS Report," *Inside E.P.A. Weekly Report*, September 4, 1981, p. 5.

FIGURE REFERENCES

Figure 2.1

Council on Environmental Quality, UPGRADE analysis of the U.S. Environmental Protection Agency's air quality data bank, *SAROAD* (Storage and Retrievel of Aerometric Data), Council on Environmental Quality, *Environmental Quality—1980* (Washington, D.C.: U.S. Government Printing Office, 1981), pp. 148-152 and previous CEQ annual reports.

PSI is a highly summarized health-related index based on direct measurements of five criteria pollutants: carbon monoxide, sulfur dioxide, total suspended particulates, photochemical oxidants or ozone, and nitrogen dioxide. The PSI for one day will rise above 100 when any one of the five criteria pollutants (at any one station in an SMSA) reaches a level judged to have adverse short-term effects on human health.

An index of 0-99 signifies good or moderate air quality.

An index of 100-199 signifies unhealthful air quality.

An index of 200-299 signifies very unhealthful air quality.

An index equal to or more than 300 signifies hazardous air quality.

PSI is designed for the daily reporting of air quality to advise the public of potentially acute, but not chronic, health effects. PSI is not used to rank air pollution in various cities. To properly rank the air pollution problems in different cities, one should rely not just on air quality data but should also include all data on population characteristics, daily population mobility, transportation patterns, industrial composition, emission inventories, meteorological factors, and the spatial representativeness of air monitoring sites.

The PSI analysis for 1974-1980 is based on standards applicable during 1980, not on standards applicable at the time of monitoring. The primary standard for ozone was relaxed in 1979 from 160 to 240 micrograms per cubic meter per hour.

The SMSAs shown here were chosen according to availability of trend data. For some of these SMSAs data are imputed for years when carbon monoxide or ozone were monitored for less than 300 days. Other major SMSAs not shown here may have many days of unhealthful air, but comparable data for 1974-1980 are not available in SAROAD.

Note that the average PSI values do not represent an average SMSA, but an average of 23 SMSAs.

Figure 2.2

U.S. Environmental Protection Agency, *National Air Pollutant Emission Estimates, 1940-1980* (Research Triangle Park, N.C.: U.S. Environmental Protection Agency, Office of Air Quality Planning and Standards, January 1982), Table 1, p. 21. U.S. Environmental Protection Agency, *National Air Pollutant Emission Estimates, 1970-1978* (Research Triangle Park, N.C.: U.S. Environmental Protection Agency, Office of Air Quality Planning and Standards, 1980), p. 2.

EPA does not publish complete documentation on how emission estimates are made for the major air pollutants. They also do not publicly document changes made in preparing the estimates from year to year and how the changes in methods influence the emission levels. So we do not know exactly why the emission estimates shown in figure 2.2 vary so dramatically.

Emissions of carbon monoxide (CO) and volatile organic compounds (VOC) come primarily from motor vehicles. The mathematical model used to estimate motor vehicle emissions (Mobile 1) has been replaced with a new model (Mobile 2). Mobile 2 incorporates newer test data from 1975, 1976, 1977, 1978, and 1979 vehicles; it provides for a different allocation of vehicles miles travelled between light and heavy duty vehicles; and it disaggregates the early years (pre 1968-74) into three internally comparable categories based on emission standards for those years: pre-1968 and 1969; 1970 and 1971; and 1972 to 1974.

This increased last characteristic is probably the critical assumption that increased the CO estimates for the first half of the 1970s by 10 to 12 percent. Mobile 1 assumed that light-duty, gasoline-powered vehicles manufactured before 1968 generated CO at a rate of 84 grams/mile, and that 1968-1974 vehicles generated CO at a rate of 62 grams/mile. The newer model, Mobile 2, assumes pre-1968 vehicles generated CO at 90 grams/mile; 1970-1971 vehicles at 58 grams/mile; and 1972-1974 vehicles at 53 grams/mile. This disaggregation appears to increase estimates for the earlier years. The two models (Mobile 1 & 2) give about the same estimates for 1975. Mobile 2 gives 1980-1981 vehicles (20 grams/mile) because of more recent test data. The two models, not surprisingly, get close together around 1985 when an increasing number and percentage of vehicles are expected to emit CO at about 20 grams per mile.

Figure 2.3

U.S. Environmental Protection Agency, *1980 Ambient Assessment-Air Portion* (Research Triangle Park, N.C.: U.S. Environmental Protection Agency, Office of Air Quality Planning and Standards, February, 1981).

Figure 2.4

U.S. Environmental Protection Agency, *National Air Pollutant Emission Estimates, 1940-1980* (Research Triangle Park, N.C.: U.S. Environmental Protection Agency, Office of Air Quality Planning and Standards, January 1982), Table 1, p. 2.

Figure 2.5

U.S. Environmental Protection Agency, *1980 Ambient Assessment-Air Portion* (Research Triangle Park, N.C.: U.S. Environmental Protection Agency, Office of Air Quality Planning and Standards, February 1981) and unpublished data from Office of Air Quality Planning and Standards.

Figure 2.6

U.S. National Commission on Air Quality, *To Breathe Clean Air* (Washington, D.C.: U.S. Government Printing Office, March 1981), p. 122.

Figure 2.7

U.S. Environmental Protection Agency, Office of Air Quality Planning and Standards, *National Air Pollutant Emission Estimates, 1970-1979* (Research Triangle Park, N.C.: U.S. Environmental Protection Agency, Office of Air Quality Planning and Standards, March 1981), p. 34.

Figure 2.8

Environment Canada, *Downwind, The Acid Rain Story* (Ottawa, Ontario: Canadian Minister of Supply and Services, 1981), and unpublished, updated data. Canada/United States Coordinating Committee on Transboundary Air Pollution, Impact Assessment Work Group I, *Memorandum of Intent on Transboundary Air Pollution, Phase II Interim Working Paper* (Washington, D.C.: Canadian Embassy, Environmental Counsel, October 1981), pp. 2-2, 2-4, 2-11.

Chapter 3

Water Resources

How do we ensure the adequacy of our water resources—their quantity and quality? An adequate supply of water is fundamental to the way we live, our food supply, the viability of many businesses, and the way in which we spend our leisure time. And such factors as the continued growth and regional shifts in our population and economy (see chapter 1), and changes taking place in energy and agricultural activities (see chapters 5 and 6), are placing increased demands on both the quality and quantity of our freshwater supplies.

During the past decade, there were serious droughts in many parts of the United States—so serious that some observers feared the reappearance of the dust bowls of the 1930s. Particularly in the West, legal and legislative battles were fought over how limited water supplies should be allocated among such competing uses as urbanization, agriculture, and energy production. And President Carter created substantial political controversy by attempting to change the federal government's traditional approach to water supply problems.

Ten years ago, with the passage of the 1972 amendments to the Federal Water Pollution Control Act (now called the Clean Water Act), we embarked on the most ambitious program ever undertaken to improve water quality. The goal for 1983 was to clean all waters until they were satisfactory for swimming, and for fish and wildlife, and then, by 1985, to eliminate pollution discharges completely.[1] This effort was soon supplemented by attempts to protect drinking water supplies and to control serious pollution sources, such as hazardous waste dumps, that may not have been addressed adequately in the original legislation.

As we move into the 1980s, many of our water policies are being reconsidered. The Clean Water Act and the Safe Drinking Water Act[2] are being reviewed as they come up for reauthorization; the Environmental Protection Agency (EPA) appears to be considering substantial changes in the way it attempts to implement some of the other programs controlling sources of water pollution; and the Reagan Administration has substantially reduced the size and influence of the Federal Water Resources Council, the group responsible for analyzing, formulating, and coordinating federal policies and programs affecting water resources. It is a period of great uncertainty.

TRENDS IN WATER RESOURCES

The United States is a diverse country, physically and climatically. Some parts of the United States receive an abundance of precipitation, and water shortages are rare. Other parts receive very little rainfall, and water shortages are almost a permanent condition, leading people to use virtually every drop of water available. Industrial dischargers are the major pollution sources in some parts of the United States; agricultural and other nonpoint sources are more important in other places. Because of this diversity, it is difficult to generalize about the seriousness of national trends in either the availability or quality of our water resources.

Water Use

Nationally, we have continually, throughout this century, increased the amount of water we use.* Our rate of water withdrawal rose 35 percent between 1965 and 1975 (figure 3.1). Our fastest-growing uses have been for public water supplies (covering most residential and commercial uses) and for generating electricity, the latter having passed irrigation as the largest use in the 1960s (figure 3.2). In 1950, we used, on average, 1,317 gallons of water per person per day; by 1975, this had grown to 1,972 gallons per person per day.

Most of the water withdrawn is returned to surface water or groundwater supplies soon after its use. For example, out of 100 gallons withdrawn from a river for cooling steam electric utilities, over 99 gallons are usually returned almost immediately to the river; less than 1 gallon is consumed through evaporation. Overall, only 23 percent of total withdrawals are "consumed."

Between 1965 and 1975, consumption of water in the United

---

*The two common measures of water use are "withdrawal" and "consumption." Water is *withdrawn* when it is taken from a ground or surface source and is conveyed to the place of use. Water is *consumed* when it is no longer available for use because it has been removed from available supplies by evaporation, by transpiration, by use in agriculture or manufacturing, or for food and drinking.

Figure 3.1
Water Use in the United States, 1900-1975

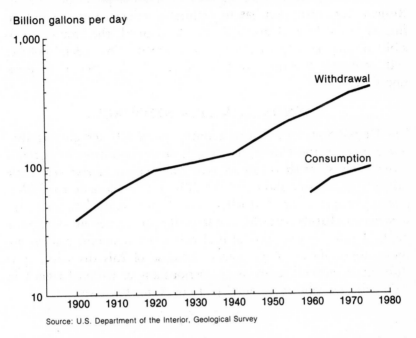

Billion gallons per day

Source: U.S. Department of the Interior, Geological Survey

States grew by about 23 percent (figure 3.1). In absolute terms, most of the increase came as a result of growth in the use of water for irrigation—although the amount consumed in generating electricity grew at the fastest rate (figure 3.3). By the mid-1970s, about 45 million acres of agricultural lands were irrigated. Most of these lands are in the West.[3] The western states, in fact, consumed more than 12 times more water per capita than the eastern states, largely because of irrigation.[4]

Rapid development in the West has resulted in excessive water withdrawals from rivers and streams in such areas as the Rio Grande Basin, Lower Colorado Basin, and California (figure 3.4). These areas have to rely on importing water from great distances or on depleting groundwater reservoirs for their supplies. In the Southwest and Great Plains states, 70 percent or more of the streamflow is consumed in an average year in 14 of 45 subregions, leaving little instream water for navigation, hydropower, recreation, and fish and wildlife. In a dry year, 9 additional subregions have inadequate streamflows.

To overcome this lack of surface water, wells have been dug to

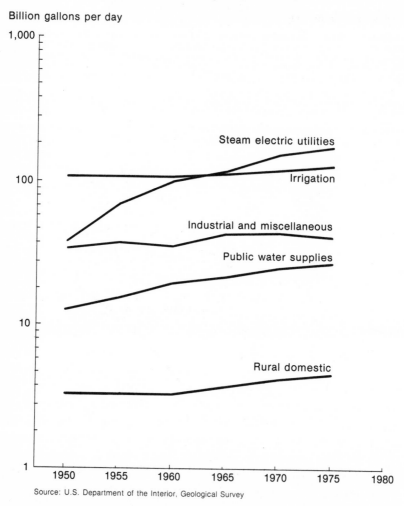

Figure 3.2
Water Withdrawal by Use, 1950-1975

Billion gallons per day

Source: U.S. Department of the Interior, Geological Survey

tap groundwater supplies. But groundwater, too, is being used up. Groundwater "overdraft" is occurring in 27 of 45 Southwest and Great Plains subregions (figure 3.5). (This means that groundwater is being withdrawn from sources more rapidly than the sources are being recharged.)

Although the severest water shortages are focused generally in the Southwest (our fastest-growing region), periodic droughts (a normal climatic variation) create local and regional shortages in almost every part of the United States. For example, parts of the

Figure 3.3
Water Consumption by Use, 1960-1975

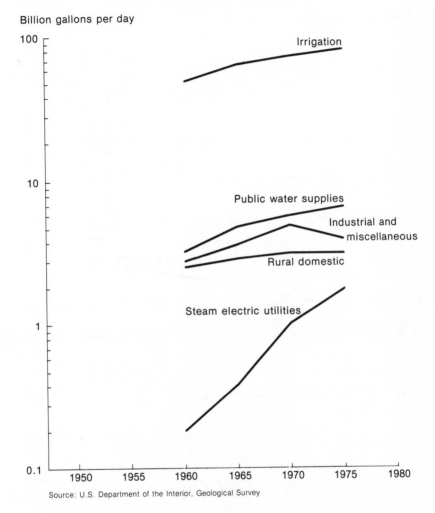

Billion gallons per day

Source: U.S. Department of the Interior, Geological Survey

Atlantic Coast experience chronic groundwater overdrafts, and the 1980 drought forced many communities in the normally water rich Mid-Atlantic region to ration water to reduce consumption.[5]

Stresses on available water supplies are likely to lead to water quality problems. Deteriorating water quality, in turn, will limit the amount of available water that is suitable for many uses. Irrigation practices along the Colorado River, for instance, have not only diminished the amount of water in the river but have increased its salinity to such an extent that the water in the river's lower

Figure 3.4
Surface Water Depletion by Region, 1975

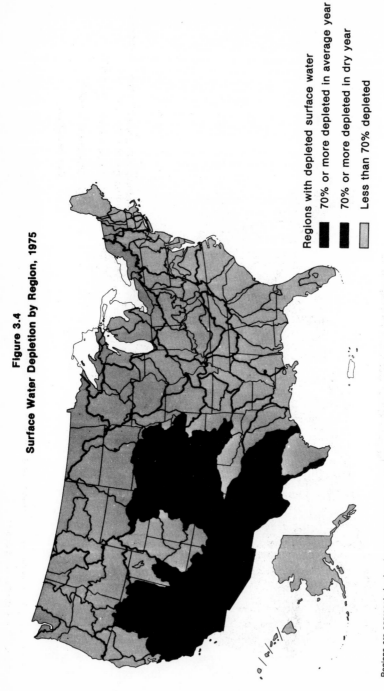

Regions with depleted surface water

70% or more depleted in average year

70% or more depleted in dry year

Less than 70% depleted

Regions are aggregated subregions as defined by the U.S. Water Resources Council.

Source: U.S. Water Resources Council

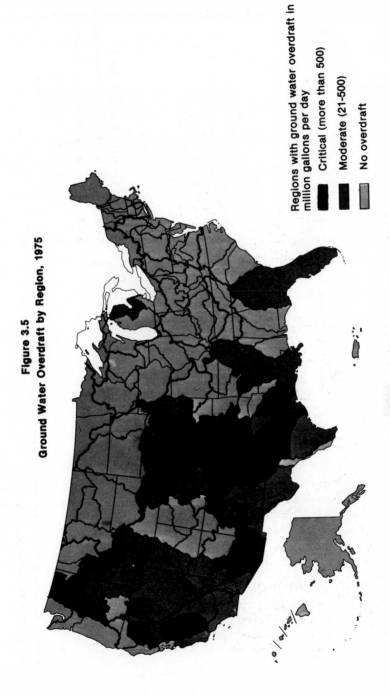

Figure 3.5
Ground Water Overdraft by Region, 1975

Regions with ground water overdraft in
million gallons per day

Critical (more than 500)

Moderate (21–500)

No overdraft

Regions are aggregated subregions as defined by the U.S. Water Resources Council.

Source: U.S. Water Resources Council

reaches is no longer suitable for irrigation.[6] In many parts of the United States, groundwater contamination has forced people to close their wells and shift to other, sometimes already tight, water supplies.[7]

Water Quality

The only coherent nationwide information on water quality is provided by an ambient monitoring system established by the United States Geological Survey (USGS) over the past seven years. The National Stream Quality Accounting Network (NASQAN) is an assemblage of monitoring stations located in different river basins and subbasins. The size of the network has increased steadily; it is now composed of over 500 stations.[8] The same data have been collected on the same pollutants for up to seven years.

Because they were initially established for another purpose—to measure the amount of surface water flowing out of a watershed—the NASQAN stations are often not located where people use water. In some cases, the watersheds that the stations were established to monitor are located upstream of major pollution sources; in other cases, the station is located substantially downstream of such sources. For those pollutants that do not degrade or otherwise change in the water, the downstream monitoring locations may be adequate. However, some water pollution problems are quite localized—for example, the rapid depletion of oxygen in a stream near the point where municipal sewage flows into it—and a river may well have "cleansed" itself by the time it reaches the NASQAN station.* The stations do not measure all pollutants (for instance, most potentially toxic organic chemicals are not measured). And, in many cases, monitoring equipment may not be able to measure low concentrations of pollutants which nonetheless may have a significant effect on water quality.

Additional information on water quality is collected by state water pollution authorities. The usefulness of much of this information, however, is limited because of variations in state programs and monitoring procedures and because the data often cannot be easily obtained. One useful source of state-generated information is the set of reports that state authorities are required to submit to EPA

---

*Cleansing takes place primarily as a result of oxidation of organic contaminants. Although a pollutant may not show up at a downstream location, that does not mean it had no effect upstream. For example, although dissolved oxygen levels at NASQAN stations may be adequate, levels at the point of discharge may have caused fish kills.

every two years under section 305(b) of the Clean Water Act.[9] These reports look at violations of water quality criteria for specific pollutants and provide an indication of the extent and seriousness of water quality problems.

Given the data limitations, and recognizing that many important pollutants are monitored imperfectly or not at all, conclusions about the condition of the nation's waters must be made very cautiously. On the basis of available information, it appears that, nationally, there has been little change in water quality over the past seven years—at least with respect to the "conventional" pollutants.* For three out of five pollution indicators, a small majority of NASQAN stations show improving trends (figure 3.6). However, for two of those apparent improvements, the small majority disappears when the monitoring data are adjusted to take account of variations in streamflow.** Furthermore, for individual pollutants, at only 17 to 22 percent of the NASQAN stations are the trends statistically significant.†

There is, however, scattered evidence all over the United States that some of the worst pollution problems may be abating. Salmon have reappeared in the Connecticut and Penobscot Rivers in New England. The acceleration of the natural aging process of Lakes Ontario and Erie has slowed; less of their water now contains large amounts of algae; fish populations are increasing. Controls imposed on industrial and municipal dischargers are returning the ecological productivity of such sensitive estuaries as those of Pensacola, Florida (Escambia Bay, East Bay, and Pensacola Bay) to previous levels.[11] These cases, and others like them, are encouraging and important.

---

*This analysis will focus on five conventional pollution indicators: dissolved oxygen, fecal coliform bacteria, suspended solids, total dissolved solids, and phosphorous.

**Conditions of water quality are often significantly affected by climatic variations. For example, since suspended sediments are discharged during storms, dry years and fewer storms produce improving trends and lower amounts of suspended sediments. On the other hand, lower flow levels in dry years may produce lower levels of dissolved oxygen. U.S.G.S. scientists have recently developed a technique that adjusts pollutant trends for variations in flow, and may more accurately reflect trends in man's contribution to pollution.[10]

†Only if a site shows a statistically significant trend can any conclusion be reached concerning what is actually happening to the water quality at that particular location. However, the aggregation of all trends, whether statistically significant or not, can be used to indicate whether, on the whole, things are getting better or worse. In this chapter, conclusions about overall water quality based on aggregate trends were made only if there was a statistically significant difference between the numbers of trends showing improvements and deterioration.

Figure 3.6
Water Quality Trends at NASQAN Monitoring Stations, 1974-1980

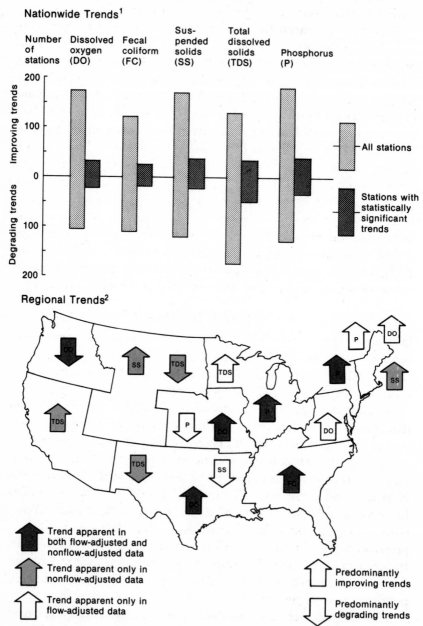

Nationwide Trends[1]

Regional Trends[2]

Trend apparent in both flow-adjusted and nonflow-adjusted data

Trend apparent only in nonflow-adjusted data

Trend apparent only in flow-adjusted data

Predominantly improving trends

Predominantly degrading trends

[1] Nationwide trends are for nonflow-adjusted data only.

[2] Regions are U.S. Environmental Protection Agency regions. Alaska (not pictured) is in the Northwestern region. If the regional trend for a particular pollutant was not statistically significant, no arrow appears.

Source: U.S. Department of the Interior, Geological Survey

Nevertheless, in aggregate, there has been very little net change, and state water pollution authorities report that violations of water quality criteria continue to be extensive (figure 3.7).

This does not mean that our water pollution control programs have been a failure. As chapter 1 points out, our gross national product has grown in real terms by about 40 percent since 1970. And the manufacturing sector, responsible for much of our pollution, has grown even faster. In addition, 57 million acres of new cropland are being farmed (see chapter 6), and 20 to 30 million acres of land have been converted to urban uses over the past decade. Both types of shifts result in increased amounts of pollution. Thus, in the absence of water pollution control programs, water quality might have become much worse; holding our own is, in itself, an accomplishment. This is all the more noteworthy because no serious attempt has yet been made to deal with such major pollution sources as agricultural runoff, urban runoff, and sanitary and storm sewers.

The following analysis covers trends for each of five conventional pollution indicators—dissolved oxygen, bacteria, suspended solids, dissolved solids, and phosphorus—as well as for toxic pollutants.

Dissolved Oxygen

Dissolved oxygen, which is present in clean water at levels of five parts per million, is necessary for fish and other aquatic life to survive. The amount of dissolved oxygen in a stream is depleted by organic pollutants such as municipal sewage.

Analysis of dissolved oxygen trends at NASQAN stations indicates that, nationally, a majority of stations are showing improvements—that is, more dissolved oxygen is present (figure 3.6). These results apply to both flow-adjusted and nonflow-adjusted data. The most frequent improvements appear to be occurring in some areas of the Northeast and in the South Central and Great Plains states. In New England and the South Central states, many of the trends are statistically significant. The Northwest, on the other hand, shows a preponderance of trends toward degradation, but few of these are statistically significant. The improving trends may indicate that we are beginning to see the benefits of our municipal as well as industrial pollution control programs.

State officials perceive dissolved oxygen violations as a frequent problem (figure 3.7). Particularly widespread or serious violations are reported along the Atlantic and Gulf Coasts, the lower Mississippi, the Tennessee River, and the Ohio River Basin. State reports

Figure 3.7
Water Quality Conditions as Reported by State Authorities, 1980

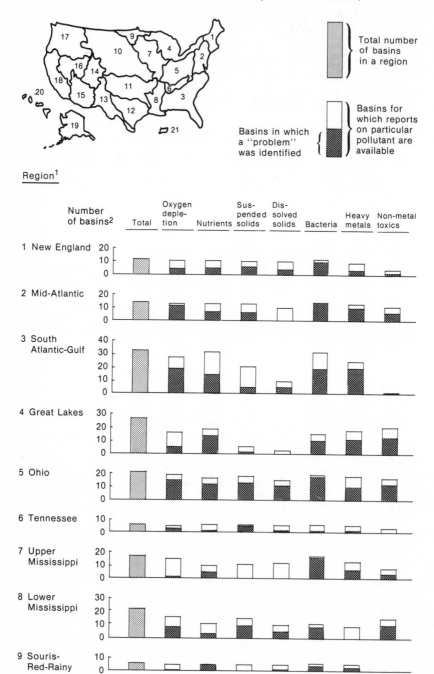

Region[1]

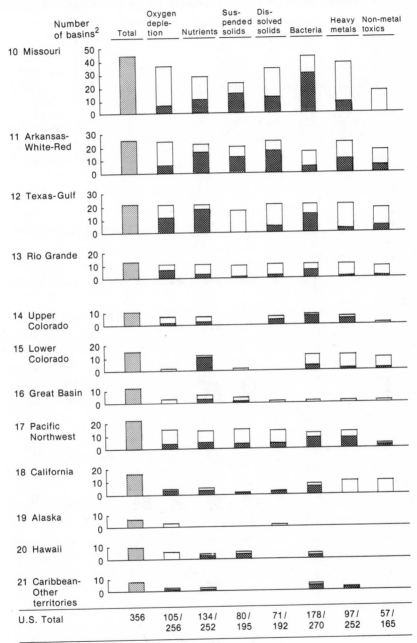

	Number of basins[2]	Total	Oxygen depletion	Nutrients	Suspended solids	Dissolved solids	Bacteria	Heavy metals	Non-metal toxics
U.S. Total		356	105/ 256	134/ 252	80/ 195	71/ 192	178/ 270	97/ 252	57/ 165

[1] Water resources regions as defined by the U.S. Water Resources Council.

[2] Basins are U.S. Geological Survey accounting units.

Source: U.S. Environmental Protection Agency

of trends in dissolved oxygen violations support NASQAN's trend information. Of the basins for which states reported trends, 29 percent showed improving trends and 17 percent deteriorating trends.[12]

Bacteria

The last seven years appear to have seen virtually no change in the extent to which surface waters suffer from bacterial pollution.* A major source of these bacteria is household and municipal waste, although they also can come from animal waste. The presence of bacteria may indicate a potential for infection and disease; high bacteria counts usually force officials to prohibit swimming and certain other recreational uses of water.

Analysis of trends at NASQAN stations shows that, nationally, there are about as many stations showing decreases in fecal coliform counts as are showing increases. However, when the monitoring results are adjusted to take account of changes in streamflow from year to year, a majority of stations do show improvement. In all regions except the Southeast, the number of stations showing improvement is roughly equal to the number of stations experiencing degradation; in the Southeast, more stations are showing improvement.

State water quality officials continue to see bacterial pollution as a significant problem (figure 3.7). In some regions, the problem was considered to be very extensive, affecting 75 percent or more of the drainage basins. Generally, these basins lie in the Northeast and North Central states.

Suspended Solids

Suspended solids include soil and other solid particles which, in addition to turning rivers brown, can significantly affect aquatic life. Sediment can also carry bacteria, nutrients, pesticides, and other harmful substances and can interfere with the proper operation of water purification plants.

Analysis of trends in suspended solids at individual NASQAN stations shows improvement at a majority of the stations—that is, suspended solids are decreasing (figure 3.6). However, adjusting the actual measurements to take account of the fact that the amount of streamflow varies from year to year leads to a different assessment.

---

*The actual measurements are made of fecal coliform which is taken as an indicator of the presence of other disease-causing bacteria.

For the statistically significant trends, the data not adjusted for flow show more basins improving than degrading. When the data are adjusted for flow, the opposite is true, particularly for larger rivers.

Improvements predominate in New England and the Northern Mountain states. Deteriorating conditions predominate in the South Central states, which probably reflects serious soil erosion problems (see chapter 6). The available summaries of reports by state authorities do not contain information adequate for reporting on problems caused by suspended solids.

Total Dissolved Solids (TDS)

TDS is a measure of the total of inorganic salts and other substances that are dissolved in water. High levels of dissolved solids can make water unfit to drink, adversely affect fish and other freshwater aquatic life, accelerate corrosion in water systems and equipment that uses water, create problems of salinization, and depress crop yields when water with high TDS content is used for irrigation.

Trends at a majority of NASQAN stations show increases in TDS (figure 3.6). However, when the original data are adjusted to take account of variations in streamflow, the number of trends showing improvement is about equal to the number showing deterioration, indicating that the situation is not as bad as it appears to be. The preponderance of the trends that are statistically significant shows that there has been improvement, but the rate of improvement is usually very small—less than 1 percent per year. The Great Lakes states and the far Southwest show general improvements, but the South and the Northern Mountain states show deterioration. Again, however, many of the latter trends disappear when data are adjusted for variations in streamflow.

Many state officials of states with the worst TDS problems have not submitted reports on TDS. Where reports were submitted, the officials generally did not see total dissolved solids as being a serious problem—the Arkansas and Ohio River Basins excepted (figure 3.7).

Nutrients

Nutrients such as phosphorus and nitrogen, though essential to aquatic life in small amounts, at higher levels can stimulate the growth of algae and seaweed, tending to accelerate eutrophication (the aging of lakes and reservoirs) and problems of oxygen depletion.

A majority of NASQAN stations seem to indicate that phosphorus concentrations are decreasing (figure 3.6).* However, adjusting the data to take account of variations in streamflow equalizes the number of trends in each direction. For those trends that are statistically significant, there is a slight preponderance of trends showing improvement, but some trends are very strong in either direction at individual monitoring stations.

The parts of the United States showing the most improvement are the Great Lakes and North Central states; nutrient pollution in the Plains states seems to be increasing (particularly when the data are adjusted for variations in streamflow).

Pollution by nutrients is seen as being a relatively widespread problem by state officials (figure 3.7). The problem appears most extensive in the South, particularly in the Red River basin (Texas) and the Texas-Gulf and Lower Colorado regions. It was also identified as a common problem in the Mid-Atlantic region.

Toxics

There continues to be widespread concern about other, potentially toxic, pollutants in water, although there is little information about the extent or severity of this problem, and no data that can be used to determine whether it is getting better or worse.

NASQAN does not monitor most toxic chemicals, and relatively few state officials have reported on them. Many of those who did saw problems involving metals and other toxics as fairly commonplace, particularly in the Atlantic coastal states, and, more generally, throughout the Northeast (except for New England) (figure 3.7).

PROSPECTS AND ISSUES

The available data thus indicate that we have made little progress in solving the problems of water scarcity and water pollution that existed 10 years ago, in spite of having undertaken some major programs to deal with these problems. (It is worth repeating, however, that just holding our own is a significant accomplishment, given the growth in economic activity and water use that has occurred over the past decade.)

The lack of substantial progress in the past does not necessarily mean that there will not be progress in the future. For example, EPA has invested a substantial amount of effort in research and

---

*Although both nitrogen and phosphorous are important nutrients, this analysis focuses on the latter because it is usually considered to be the "limiting" nutrient, which means that changes in its prevalence will have the greatest impact on eutrophication.

Flooding

Roughly 7 percent of the land in the United States—some 178 million acres—is floodplain.[1]* (That is, it can expect to be flooded at least once every 100 years.) An estimated 3.5 to 5.5 million acres of floodplains are in urban use; between 75 and 100 million acres are used for agriculture; and between 40 and 90 million acres are forest, rangeland, and other undeveloped areas.[2] The urban and built-up areas include more than 6,000 places with populations of 2,500 or more.[3] The largest floodplain areas are in the South, but the most populous are in the North Atlantic and Great Lakes regions and California.

Throughout history, Americans have found floodplains attractive locations for development. Floodplains contain some of the richest soils for agriculture, level land with access to fresh water and transportation, and easy routes for the construction of railroads and highways. Given these advantages, it is not surprising that risks to life and property from flooding often seemed acceptable.

The floodplain is the heart of many cities in the United States. In a review of 26 cities, ranging in size from 50,000 to 7 million people, the U.S. Geological Survey found that, on the average, 53 percent of the floodplain in these cities was developed, ranging from 11 percent in Lorain-Elyria, Ohio, to 97 percent in Great Falls, Montana.[4] Some cities have converted their floodplains to low risk uses such as parks, golf courses, and recreation areas. However, urbanization of floodplains continues. Although data from the 1980 Census are not yet available, surveys taken during the 1970s suggest that urban population growth within floodplain areas was between 1.5 percent and 2.5 percent per year, roughly twice the rate of population growth for the country as a whole.[5]

For all other major geophysical hazards—earthquakes, hurricanes, tornadoes—loss of life and property

has been declining in recent decades. Not so for floods. The average number of lives lost in floods annually during the 1970s was 176 (varying from a low of 74 in 1971 to a high of 540 in 1972,[6] the latter due in large part to a disastrous flood in Rapid City, South Dakota). The annual average for the 1960s was 72; for the 1950s, 79.[7] Property damage from flood losses of homes, household goods, roads, bridges, businesses, crops, and so forth is estimated to average about $3.8 billion per year (in 1979 dollars).[8]

Building new houses, roads, and other structures in floodplains not only adds to the property and lives at risk, it also reduces the amount of land available to dissipate and absorb the volume and velocity of flood waters. Natural vegetation and permeable soils moderate flood conditions. Removing that vegetation and paving with an impermeable surface, such as asphalt or concrete, increases the volume of runoff and intensifies flooding.

Development on floodplains has come increasingly under the scrutiny of public authorities. As the federal government, through flood insurance and relief payments, has taken on a larger role in assisting flood victims, it has also begun to require that state and local governments pay greater attention to what is built on floodplains.[9] In addition, a 1977 Executive Order prohibits federal agencies from supporting construction activities on floodplains unless no other alternative is feasible.[10]

Twenty-four states have adopted regulations or standard-setting for floodway areas, and 17 have programs for flood fringe areas as well.[11] Some state floodplain programs provide for direct state regulation through permitting procedures for activities such as flood control works, subdivision proposals, and large structural uses. Others provide state standards for local regulations.

*See figure references at end of chapter.

development to identify toxic constituents of industrial effluents, technological controls for such effluents, risks in hazardous waste disposal, and alternative approaches to land and subsurface disposal of hazardous substances. Having completed this work, the agency could now begin to implement a program to control those substances.

In other areas, less progress has been made. Problems of water scarcity have remained basically unaddressed at the national level except for continued congressional pressure for traditional water resource projects. Very little has been accomplished in dealing with "nonpoint" sources of surface water pollution, such as runoff from agricultural fields and urban streets.

Clearly, much of the job remains to be done. It is less clear whether there is the will to do it. This is an important period in the nation's efforts to solve its water resource problems. The federal government is substantially reducing support for this effort (see chapter 9). And Congress must review and reauthorize two of the most important statutes dealing with water—the Clean Water Act and the Safe Drinking Water Act. The result of the deliberations will have a significant impact on the quality of our water in the future. Among the specific issues of debate are:

- implementation of a pretreatment program aimed at reducing industrial discharges of toxic pollutants into municipal sewer systems;
- variances from technology-based effluent controls on toxic chemicals for industries that discharge their effluents directly into streams and rivers;
- variances from uniform treatment requirements for municipalities;
- extensions of permit deadlines for industrial dischargers;
- revisions in the jurisdiction and scope of the Clean Water Act's provisions for controlling the dredging and filling of wetlands (Section 404);
- reduction of the federal role in setting drinking water standards; and
- the type of public notice that should be required when drinking water standards are violated.

The basic question in each case is whether the nation should continue with its present programs or whether it should back off because of their cost. There is little attention being given to taking on new problems—for instance, developing a workable nonpoint source pollution control program—or to achieving existing goals faster and more efficiently. The two issues addressed in this chapter are what can be done to prevent depletion and degradation of groundwater resources, and what should be done about toxic pollutants entering the nation's surface water and groundwater. In the following discussion, the issues of groundwater degradation and toxic pollutants are addressed primarily from the federal perspective, because EPA has the initial responsibility under the applicable federal statutes for setting national policies. Although the Reagan Administration has emphasized shifting more responsibility to state authorities, many states are waiting to see what the federal policies will be before they attempt to implement their own programs.

Protecting Groundwater

There are vast quantities of groundwater underlying the United States. The amount estimated to lie within 2,500 feet of the surface is 33 to 59 quadrillion gallons, or enough to supply withdrawals at current rates for 200 to 300 years (even if there were no recharge to the aquifers).[13] Only one-fourth of this groundwater is usable with present technology, but even this amount is equivalent to total U.S. surface water runoff for 35 years.[14] Of our total water withdrawals, 22 percent come from groundwater.[15] Approximately half the U.S. population depends on groundwater for its domestic water supply.[16]

Both groundwater depletion and groundwater pollution may be essentially irreversible—that is, once they occur there may be no way of correcting them. Groundwater depletion, for instance, can cause an aquifer to consolidate, diminishing its storage capacity. Near the coast, groundwater withdrawals may draw saltwater into an aquifer, which could render the aquifer permanently useless. And in many cases, groundwater contamination is irreversible, because water moves through an aquifer so slowly that the contamination will remain for a very long time, even after the source of the pollution has been stopped. Also, pollutants do not degrade through oxidation in groundwater as they do in surface water.

Many regions of the country that have faced problems of groundwater overdraft—taking more out of groundwater reservoirs than normally goes into them—have been concerned for some time about the manner in which we use and abuse our groundwater resources. Concern has become more widespread because of a rising national demand for groundwater withdrawals and an increasing number of incidents of groundwater contamination and well closures. Much of this concern has focused on what states can do to manage their groundwater more effectively. At the same time, the federal government has been considering a national strategy to coordinate its activities in preventing groundwater contamination.

Groundwater Depletion

In many areas, the amount of water withdrawn from an aquifer is in balance with the natural recharge. As a result, there has been no long-term increase or decrease in the water level, although it may fluctuate up and down, depending on the rate of withdrawal and the amount of rainfall. Many parts of the country, however, are depleting their groundwater.

The rate of groundwater withdrawals in the United States has risen, on average, at 3.8 percent a year since 1950, almost twice the rate of increase in the use of surface water (figure 3.8). Much of this increase has been for irrigation in the water-short areas of the West. Irrigation now accounts for about 68 percent of groundwater use, compared to 13 percent for the next highest use, public

Figure 3.8

Groundwater Withdrawals by Use, 1950-75

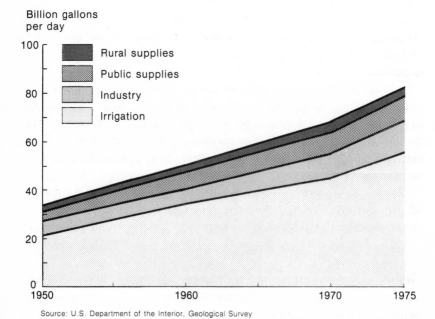

Source: U.S. Department of the Interior, Geological Survey

water supplies. Groundwater withdrawals account for 40 percent or more of the total fresh water withdrawn in almost a fifth of the Water Resources Council (WRC) water resource subregions in the United States.[17] Many of these withdrawals represent "overdrafts." Nationally, 25.4 percent of the amount of groundwater withdrawn is not replenished.[18] In the Texas-Gulf region, this percentage rises as high as 77.2 percent.[19] In 1975, two-thirds of WRC's water resource regions were experiencing overdrafts. The water table is declining an average of 0.5 to 6.6 feet per year under 15 million acres of land irrigated by groundwater (out of a total irrigated acreage of 32.3 million acres).[20]

In the Gila River Basin in Arizona, a net depletion of groundwater exceeding 8 trillion gallons over the current decade is expected to cause substantially higher pumping costs, as well as land subsidence. Each additional foot of pumping requires an estimated 6 million kilowatt hours of electricity.[21] In some parts of the basin, land subsidence because of overdrafts has already been large—for example, 7.5 feet near Elroy, Arizona, between 1948 and 1967.[22]

From the Rio Grande to Nebraska and in California's San Joaquin Valley, rapidly falling groundwater levels may make the costs of pumping irrigation water out of the ground prohibitive, potentially threatening farming practices in two of the United States' most productive agricultural regions. In New York and Pennsylvania, depletion of the Upper Susquehanna River Basin is not only increasing pumping costs, but reducing streamflows during periods of low rainfall. In southeast Georgia, high rates of groundwater depletion are drawing saltwater into aquifers. And groundwater overdrafts in the Houston/Galveston area are causing surface subsidence that is damaging structures, interfering with the drainage of streams and sewers, and increasing the threat of flooding from rainfall and high tides. This surface subsidence cost (as of 1975) an estimated $31.7 million or more per year, and the economic viability of 600 thousand acres of agriculture is in jeopardy.[23]

Rapid rates of groundwater exploitation can also affect the quality of groundwater. In general, the more an aquifer is pumped, the faster pollutants will spread through it.

Groundwater Contamination

Groundwater contamination is becoming a serious problem throughout the United States. Although there is no systematic, comprehensive monitoring of groundwater quality, there are increasing instances of groundwater contamination from saltwater, micro-biological contaminants, and toxic organic and inorganic chemicals (figure 3.9).

Irrigation practices in the West and Southwest have increased groundwater salinity, as have groundwater overdrafts along the Atlantic, Pacific, and Gulf Coasts. In the West, saline ground and surface waters are creating new deserts in some areas.[24] Between 1971 and 1978, contaminated groundwater was reported as a cause of 32 percent of the waterborne disease outbreaks recorded by the Center for Disease Control.[25] Groundwater contamination from organic chemicals may still be relatively infrequent, but nevertheless serious, for pollutant concentrations have been found to be relatively high, particularly compared to surface water concentrations.[26] Over the past few years, in areas from Maine to Hawaii, there have been hundreds of episodes (affecting millions of people) of well closures because of contamination from toxic organic chemicals.[27]

One of the major sources of groundwater pollution—including both toxic and nontoxic pollutants—is waste disposal. For instance, there are an estimated 16.6 million septic tanks in the United States, receiving an estimated 800 billion gallons of waste a year.[28] All of this seeps into the ground, potentially contaminating groundwater. Municipal landfills and hazardous waste disposal facilities are also potential sources of contamination. But the most serious source appears to be impoundments and landfills used for the disposal of industrial wastes.

A joint EPA/state survey of waste disposal sites (called the Surface Impoundment Assessment), underway since 1976, has located over 77,000 waste impoundment sites containing over 176,000 separate impoundments (including waste pits) for industrial, municipal, agricultural, and mining wastes, and brines from oil and gas extraction.[29] An estimated 82 billion gallons per day of wastewater—equivalent to 350 gallons for each person in the United States—flows into these impoundments.

Almost 11,000 of the sites, containing about 26,000 impoundments, are used for disposing of industrial wastes (figure 3.10). Those impoundments covered 430,000 acres and received an estimated 54 billion gallons of wastewater per day.* Of the 8,163

---

*These estimates, however, may be too high since the U.S. Geological Survey estimated that total water withdrawals by the category "industry and miscellaneous" was only 40 to 50 billion gallons a day in 1975, and the rate of withdrawal was not increasing then (see figure 3.2).

Figure 3.9

Actual and Anticipated Groundwater Quality Problems by Region, 1980

● Actual problem   ○ Anticipated problem

Source of problem	1	2	3	4	5	6	7	8	9	10	11	12	13	14	15	16	17	18	19	20	21
Waste disposal																					
Industrial impoundments	●	●	●	●	●			●	●	●				●			●				
Industrial and municipal landfills	●	●	●	●	●			●	●	●	●				●		●	●		○	
Illegal hazardous waste disposal	●	●			●		○														
Wastewater treatment	●		●	●	●	●	●		●	●	●	●		●	●		●		●		●
Septic tanks	●	●	●	●	●	●	●														●
Radioactive waste disposal			○			○								○							
Deepwell injection			●	●	○	○		●	●		●	●									○
Oil and gas field brines			●		●			●			●										
Other pollution sources																					
Accidental spills	●	●	●	●	●			●		●									●		
Storage tank leaks		●	○	●	●					○			○	○			●				
Acid mine drainage		●	○	●	●	○		○					○			●	●				
Other mining					○	○			●				●		●	●	●				
Salinity from saltwater intrusion & irrigation	●	●	●									●				●	●	●	●	●	●
Pesticides and other agricultural runoff	●	●	●		●		○		●	●					●		●	●		○	●
Synfuels development														○							
Roadsalt and other	●			●																	

[1] Water resources regions as defined by the U.S. Water Resources Council.

Source: U.S. Water Resources Council and the Conservation Foundation

Figure 3.10

**Groundwater Contamination Potential of Impoundments
by Waste Generator, 1980**

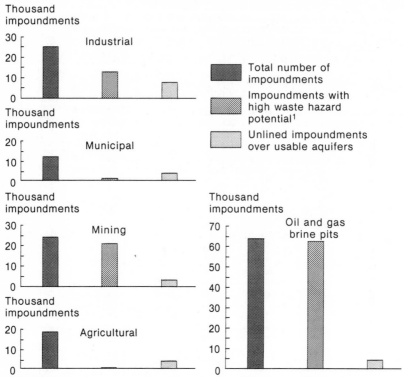

[1] Waste hazard potential was assessed on an industry-wide basis using the following criteria: toxicity, persistence, mobility, and intensity of application.

Source: U.S. Environmental Protection Agency

industrial impoundments that were actually examined, over 70 percent were found to be unlined; approximately 30 percent were also found to be located in permeable materials and to overlie usable aquifers; and, in turn, one-third of these sites are within one mile of a water-supply well. Less than 10 percent of the sites have any groundwater monitoring, and only half of these are regularly sampled. It is not clear how many of these impoundments contain hazardous wastes (see chapter 4), but many of them pose a risk of some kind of groundwater contamination.

Groundwater pollutants can come from a variety of other sources as well. In some cases, wastes are injected directly into the ground. Pollution in lakes or streams that are recharging aquifers can spread into the groundwater. Pesticides and fertilizers used on cropland may eventually seep into groundwater. Salts washing off roads in winter can contaminate nearby wells. In short, any pollutant reaching the ground—whether dumped there intentionally, washed off roads, or deposited from the air—may eventually reach groundwater.

It is difficult to predict or monitor what happens to pollutants after they enter groundwater. They tend to spread in a plume. But the shape of the plume and the rate at which it spreads depends on the permeability and slope of the confining materials and the location of wells and the amount of water being pumped from them. The faster the rate of pumping, the faster the pollution will move toward the wells. A plume of groundwater contamination may move very slowly, or it may move rapidly. One area may be contaminated, and an area only 100 feet away may not. As pollutants travel from land surface to aquifer, soil may act as a natural filter. Once in the groundwater, however, contamination is likely to stay for many years.[30]

It is usually impractical, if not impossible, to remove contaminants from water that is still in the ground. Purification can, in theory, take place after water is extracted, but even this is often prohibitively expensive. Removing salts or toxics, for example, usually requires expensive purification equipment that is probably not within the economic reach of most municipalities that depend on groundwater, much less the large number of individuals who rely on private wells.

Current Government Roles

Public control over the quantity and quality of groundwater is exercised principally at the state level.[31] The predominant state approach to management of groundwater withdrawal is the common law rule of reasonable use. This allows withdrawals of water that are necessary to use and enjoy the land, with restrictions that the water be applied to some "beneficial purpose" and that it not be transported away from the land overlying the point of withdrawal. In the 13 western states, a doctrine of prior appropriation (first in time, first in right) similar to that used in surface water management is the predominating principle for managing groundwater. Groundwater withdrawals are managed through a permitting process in at least 31 states.[32] This process may be either statewide, or apply only to designated areas. Of the 19 states with no permit procedures, most are in the historically water-rich areas of the East and Midwest.

Because water allocation has historically been a state prerogative, the federal government's involvement in groundwater depletion issues principally has been to study and present information on aquifer location and on groundwater availability and use, and to provide financial assistance for such projects as installing recharge wells or drainage systems.

Most states have some minimum regulatory program designed to address groundwater contamination problems. Many have statutory authority to do so under their general water quality acts, which cover all "waters of the state." This definition includes groundwater in all but a few instances. Aquifer classification systems have been established in at least 15 states, and are under development in 3 more.[33]

Implementation of state programs to prevent groundwater contamination has been uneven. In many instances, these efforts have been delayed while state authorities await EPA's implementation of relevant sections of various federal statutes.

The 1972 Amendments to the Federal Water Pollution Control Act (the Clean Water Act) refer in several places to protection of groundwater resources, but the regulatory scheme of this act is clearly directed toward surface water.[34] Legislation adopted subsequent to the Clean Water Act has addressed groundwater contamination from selected sources, principally hazardous waste sites. But this legislation (the Resource Conservation and Recovery Act, or RCRA, and the Comprehensive Environmental Response and Liability Act, or "Superfund" program) lacks clearly stated groundwater quality objectives.[35]

The Safe Drinking Water Act contains a provision that allows the federal government to attempt to prevent pollution of specific aquifers designated as the sole source of drinking water supplies.[36] This program prohibits any federal financial assistance (loans, grants, and so on) that would be detrimental to an aquifer designated as a sole source of drinking water. In the seven years since passage of the act, nine aquifers have been designated as sole-source aquifers.[37] About a dozen aquifers are in various stages of investigation. The Safe Drinking Water Act also contains a program to control underground injection as a method of waste disposal.[38] Final regulations to implement and enforce this program had been not issued by the end of 1981.

The Safe Drinking Water Act provides for the establishment of Maximum Contaminant Levels (MCLs) for a variety of organic and inorganic contaminants of drinking water.[39] MCLs for drinking water are to be designed to protect public health. In fact, the MCLs are set not only on the basis of what numerical level will protect the public health, but also take into account a variety of technical and economic factors. The lack of information on the precise health impacts of likely exposure levels, and lack of information on actual exposure levels, has resulted in EPA's adopting standards for only a few drinking water contaminants.*[40]

In 1979, EPA began to integrate its various legislative authorities addressing groundwater quality problems into a coherent groundwater protection strategy. A draft of this strategy was published in November 1980.[41] In it, the agency proposed water quality goals for groundwater and alternative means of achieving those goals. The draft contained some specific proposals for groundwater protection and for controlling pollution from hazardous waste facilities, and invited public comment on these proposals and the alternative approaches that were considered.

The agency also is considering other actions that could affect groundwater pollution, such as promulgating the final environmental criteria for hazardous waste sites, establishing cleanup standards for abandoned hazardous waste sites, revising the "interim final" drinking water standards, and promulgating the final regulations to control underground injections. Each of these decisions would benefit from a coherent and coordinated groundwater strategy.

Options for Groundwater Management

With a problem as complicated and multifaceted as groundwater, there are a number of different issues that are worthy of consideration and a number of options for dealing with each of these issues. The situation is further complicated by the fact that different local, state, regional, and federal authorities are dealing with different types of problems.

Although many states, particularly in the West, have adopted legislation that allows them to exert more control over the use of groundwater than they have in the past, clearly many problems still exist. The major questions facing these states are how much control they will actually exert, the extent to which they will protect some

---

*In contrast, water quality criteria under the Clean Water Act are established solely on the basis of a pollutant's impact on the desired use of the body of water. Economic and technical factors only come into play when water quality criteria are converted into effluent standards.

users (for instance, communities and individuals depending upon extracting groundwater from shallow wells for their drinking water supplies) by limiting withdrawals by others, and the extent to which they (with the support of the federal government) will integrate their management of groundwater and surface water.

Principles for Controlling Pollution. What should the underlying philosophy be for protecting groundwater quality? One possibility is protecting current or projected uses. A second is adopting a uniform standard that would protect all possible uses. And a third is to prevent any further deterioration of groundwater quality regardless of what use it may be put to.

Under the current or projected use approach, each aquifer or part of an aquifer would be classified (probably by a state authority) according to its primary use, and groundwater pollution would be controlled to preclude interference with this use. For instance, if the aquifer were a major source of drinking water, pollution control standards would be sufficiently tight to prevent contamination that would exceed safe drinking water standards. If the primary use were agriculture, the standards could be lower, as long as contamination did not become so great that crop yields were depressed (for instance, by high salinity) or that the uptake of contaminants made crops unfit as food. For other designated uses—for instance, for mining—water quality might be allowed to deteriorate substantially.

Under a "current use" approach, the amount of contamination allowed would be the maximum amount that would not create an unreasonable risk to any of the existing users. Determining these levels would involve balancing the risks to the different users of the aquifer, a very difficult task, particularly when there is insufficient information on either the potential health risk or the other types of costs that can be associated with many groundwater pollutants. Because, as pointed out earlier, groundwater pollution is essentially irreversible, there is a potential for making very costly errors if contamination is allowed.

The current use approach has the apparent advantage of "economic efficiency," since it would avoid excessive economic costs associated with imposing stricter controls than are necessary to protect the existing uses of the water. This advantage, however, might only exist in the short run, and could become very expensive if the desired primary use were to change to one requiring better water quality. In this case, the new use might have to be satisfied by some alternative, much more expensive source, or extremely costly efforts would have to be undertaken to make a source fit for the new use. For instance, if agriculture were the primary current use, anyone wishing to use the aquifer for a drinking water supply in the future would probably have to treat the water following its extraction. Small municipalities and individuals might, as a result, face serious financial problems, because such treatment is typically very costly. It might be both less costly and more equitable to prevent ground-water contamination than to force future users to remove the con-taminants after an aquifer has been polluted. As in many other instances, prevention may be much less expensive than attempting to cure a problem subsequently.

As an alternative to managing groundwater on the basis of current use, the aquifer could be managed to satisfy likely future uses. This "projected use" approach would avoid some of the most obvious problems of a current use approach, but not all of them. It is very difficult to project exactly what sorts of developments will occur and what the relative social value of the alternative uses will be in the future. The process of balancing risks would be even more problematic because of the uncertainty about who future users would be. And even with the most sophisticated projections, often irre-versible and potentially very expensive mistakes can be made.

Because of the very difficult problems of balancing risks in a current or projected use approach, the National Governors' Asso-ciation suggested that all aquifers be required to meet drinking water standards.[42]

Establishing a uniform standard for all aquifers has the advantage of administrative simplicity and would avoid unexpected future costs. A uniform drinking water standard would not mean that all degradation of water quality would be prohibited. The drinking water standards, which are based on economic and technical achiev-ability as well as the protection of public health, would allow some pollution to occur in the more pristine aquifers.

Adopting a uniform drinking water standard for all aquifers has the disadvantage of imposing greater, and perhaps unnecessary, costs on current users, because it would treat all groundwater as drinking water when, in fact, this is not the largest use of groundwater and may never be the use in some cases. It also creates three significant management problems. One is how the authority responsible for groundwater management can devise a plan that will allow the groundwater to degrade to a certain level and then degrade no further. The second is that drinking water standards currently exist for only a relatively small number of potential pollutants, and the authority would have to determine how much contamination it could allow for pollutants that are not now covered by these standards. The third is the problem of what should be done with aquifers that are already contaminated beyond the drinking water standards. Should they be allowed to degrade further? Should they be kept at their current level of contamination? Or should they be cleaned up, probably at very high cost?

A third alternative for managing groundwater, a "nondegradation" approach, has some obvious administrative advantages. The authority responsible for groundwater management would not have to project expected uses of the aquifers and undertake complicated analyses of the relative social value of these different uses and of the relative risks to the users. This approach would also avoid the problem of creating possibly serious and expensive problems in the future if, on the basis of mistaken projections, the management authorities were to allow more groundwater pollution than is compatible with the uses that do actually develop.

However, in some cases, this approach might impose very high and perhaps unreasonable costs. Waters do not need to be preserved in a pristine state for all uses, although this would be the result of a nondegradation approach for some aquifers. And in some areas, such as oil fields, the value of the product produced (and the production of which results in some contamination) is likely to be much greater than the likely value of undegraded groundwater.

There are also some significant problems in implementing a nondegradation approach. It might require prohibiting all development in aquifer recharge areas and, if so, could have very substantial indirect economic impacts. In recharge areas that have already experienced development, it would be almost impossible to prevent any additional contamination from reaching the groundwater.

As mentioned earlier, the "sole source" provisions of the Safe Drinking Water Act adopt a nondegradation approach to protecting an aquifer that is the only source of drinking water for the people who use it. However, this designation has been applied to only a few aquifers so far, and its success has yet to be determined.

Conclusions. In its 1980 draft of a strategy to protect groundwater, EPA proposed adopting a "projected use" classification scheme and a groundwater quality goal that was to protect and enhance groundwater quality to the degree necessary for current and projected future uses and "for the protection of the public health and significant ecological systems."[43]

The proposed strategy relied on the states' ability to classify groundwater according to use, with all supplies that were currently of drinking water quality or better presumed classified for drinking water use (although the state could establish a different use classification after public review). The agency also proposed using drinking water standards as the basis for limiting contamination from hazardous waste landfills, unless variances from these standards would not endanger the public health.[44]

However, EPA is currently reconsidering this whole approach, and it is unclear whether the agency intends to adopt any comprehensive groundwater strategy as a means of coordinating and integrating its various statutory authorities related to groundwater protection. For the time being, most states are awaiting EPA's decision. If it is too delayed, however, individual states may increasingly conclude they will have to take action to protect themselves, and will in turn have to choose among the policy options discussed above.

Controlling Toxic Pollutants*

Across the United States, over 55,000 chemicals are being manufactured, imported, marketed; yet only a small fraction of these have been tested for their long-term effects on the environment and human health.[45] Little is known about the potential toxicity of most of these chemicals, about precisely how they are used, whether and how they enter aquifers and other environments, the manner in which they are transported and transformed in water, and their ultimate fate in water bodies and on aquatic plants and species. What to do about toxic pollutants is one of the major issues in the current debates on reauthorizing the Clean Water Act and the Safe Drinking Water Act.

Effects of Toxic Pollutants

The types of toxic substances found in water can cause a wide variety of health and environmental effects. Figure 3.11 summarizes some

---

*The substances described here as "toxic" pollutants are in many cases exactly the same as those described as "hazardous" in chapters 2 and 4. The use of the different terminology results from the statutory language in the applicable legislation. This discussion, however, is not limited to the specific substances that are listed as "toxic" pollutants in the Clean Water Act.

Figure 3.11
**Selected Human Health and Environmental Effects of
Twenty-Five Toxic Chemicals**

| Chemical | Human health effects | | | Environmental effects |
	Carcin-ogen	Terato-gen	Other effects	
Aldrin/dieldrin	●		tremors, convulsions, kidney damage	toxic to aquatic organisms, reproductive failure in birds and fish, bioaccumulates in aquatic organisms
Arsenic	●	●	vomiting, poisoning, liver and kidney damage	toxic to legume crops
Benzene	●		anemia, bone marrow damage	toxic to some fish and aquatic invertebrates
Bis (2-ethylhexyl) phthalate	●	●	central nervous system damage	eggshell thinning in birds, toxic to fish
Cadmium	●	●	suspected causal factor in many human pathologies: tumors, renal dysfunction, hypertension, arterio-sclerosis; Itai-itai disease (weakened bones)	toxic to fish, bioaccumulates in aquatic organisms
Carbon tetrachloride	●		kidney and liver damage, heart failure	
Chloroform	●		kidney and liver damage	
Chromium	●		kidney and gastro-intestinal damage, res-piratory complications	toxic to some aquatic invertebrates
Copper			gastrointestinal irritant, liver damage	toxic to juvenile fish
Cyanide			acutely toxic	kills fish, reduces growth and development of fish
DDT	●	●	tremors, convulsions, kidney damage	reproductive failure of birds and fish, bioac-cumulates in aquatic organisms, biomagnifies in food chain
Di-n-butyl phthalate			central nervous system damage	eggshell thinning in birds, toxic to fish
Dioxin	●	●	acute skin rashes	bioaccumulates
Ethylbenzene[1]				
Lead	●	●	convulsions, anemia, kidney and brain damage	toxic to domestic plants and animals, biomagnifies in food chain

| Chemical | Human health effects | | | Environmental effects |
	Carcin-ogen	Terato-gen	Other effects	
Mercury		●	irritability, depression, kidney and liver damage, Minamata disease	reproductive failure in fish species, inhibits growth and kills fish, methylmercury biomagnifies
Methylene chloride[1] (dichloromethane)				
Nickel	●		gastrointestinal and central nervous system effects	impairs reproduction of aquatic species
PCBs	●	●	vomiting, abdominal pain, temporary blindness	liver damage in mammals, kidney damage and eggshell thinning in birds, suspected reproductive failure in fish
Phenol				reproductive effects in aquatic organisms, toxic to fish
Silver				toxic to aquatic organisms
Tetrachloro-ethylene	●		central nervous system effects	
Toluene	●			toxic to aquatic organisms at high concentrations
Toxaphene	●	●		decreased productivity of phytoplankton communities, birth defects in fish and birds

[1]The absence of commentary means only that no adverse effects were described in selected sources, and not that the possibility of such effects can be excluded.

In many cases human health effects are based on the results of animal tests.

If a substance is identified as a carcinogen, there is evidence that it has the potential for causing cancer in humans. If it is identified as a teratogen, it has the potential for causing birth defects in humans.

Source: National Academy of Sciences, *et al.*

of the potential effects for 25 of the 129 "priority pollutants" identified for regulatory action under the Clean Water Act.*

*The act lists 65 substances or categories of substances as priority pollutants.[46] The list of 129 results from identifying the individual substances that are included within the several chemical categories in the original list of 65.[47]

Whether a substance actually produces adverse effects indicated in figure 3.11 depends on the duration and intensity of exposure, the form of the exposure (whether it is inhaled, ingested, and so on), the susceptibility of the individual exposed, and other factors. The simple presence in the environment of one of the chemicals listed in the table does not mean that the listed adverse effects will necessarily occur, and, in fact, most of the chemicals are rarely present in water at sufficiently high concentrations to cause the acute effects indicated.

"Acute" effects on human health from these pollutants—for instance, chemical burns, nausea, poisoning—are rare because, except in cases of chemical spills, toxic contaminants generally occur in low concentrations in surface water supplies. Acute effects on the environment may be more common, although the only nationwide system for reporting such effects indicates that there are many fish kills that result from other types of pollution. Measured concentrations of toxic substances in groundwater supplies have been within the known limits for acute human effects, and many wells have been closed for this reason.[48]

For some "chronic" effects, such as cancer, any level of exposure to these chemicals is thought to increase risk. For other types of chronic health problems—for instance, birth defects and genetic damage—there is less information on the effects of low levels of exposure.

People are exposed to so many different compounds during their lives (and the latency period of some effects, such as cancer, can be as long as 40 years) that it is practically impossible in most cases to associate health problems with exposure to a specific chemical that may have occurred years before. At least for surface water, the amount of direct human exposure is thought to be small—both in terms of frequency and intensity. (The major exception, discussed below, may be the class of compounds known as trihalomethanes, which are created, often in relatively high concentrations, in the process of chlorinating drinking water.)

People may be exposed indirectly to higher concentrations of these substances. Some chemicals bioaccumulate in fish and other aquatic species, and in animals that feed on these species. Eating either the former or the latter can expose humans to much higher toxic concentrations than exist in the aquatic environment.

Thus, although there is little direct evidence of human health problems caused by toxic substances in water, there are good reasons for being concerned about the risks that these contaminants may be creating. And, as in other environmental areas, important, and potentially very costly, decisions must be made under conditions of substantial uncertainty.

Sources of Toxic Pollutants

Although much attention has been focused on industrial sources of toxic pollutants found in water, many other sources of these pollutants, including waste disposal facilities, agricultural and urban runoff, airborne deposition, and even water treatment processes, have also been documented (figure 3.12).*

The frequency with which toxic pollutants are released varies from industry to industry (figure 3.13). Some chemicals (for example, benzene) are likely to be found in the effluents of some—though not necessarily a high proportion of—plants in every industry. Other chemicals (for example, copper) were not found in several industries, but were present in a high proportion of plants in others. And the electrical, nonferrous metals, iron and steel, and pulp and paper industries, for example, have a large proportion of plants releasing many of the 25 substances.

Figure 3.14 shows the amount of all 129 "priority pollutants" estimated to be produced and discharged by major industrial categories.** Some plants, after treating their wastes, discharge the effluent directly to streams, rivers, or other bodies of water. Other plants discharge their wastes into a municipal sewer; the wastes are subsequently treated in a municipal treatment plant before being discharged. Many of the "indirect dischargers" are relatively small establishments, but the aggregate of their discharges is almost two-thirds as high as the aggregate amount of raw wasteloads produced by direct dischargers.

Direct dischargers shown in this figure have over 70 percent more toxics in their untreated wastewater than indirect dischargers. However, these direct dischargers remove an estimated 81 percent of their toxic pollutants. Only 47 percent of the toxics generated by indirect dischargers shown in the figure is removed (even after treatment in municipal treatment plants). The net effect is that direct dischargers put 40 percent less toxics into the environment than do indirect dischargers.†

According to the EPA estimates in figure 3.14, the organic chemical and plastics industries are the largest sources of organic

---

*Figures 3.12 and 3.13 cover only the particular 25 substances listed in Figure 3.11. Many other potentially toxic substances have been found coming from these different sources, and could have been listed as well.

**The actual discharge of potentially toxic pollutants is probably much larger than figure 3.14 indicates. There are many other industrial categories. The figure covers only a subgroup of all discharged chemicals; at least 100 additional organic substances discharged by the organic chemical industry, for instance, are not included in these estimates. Finally, the estimates are based on discharges from a small sample of relatively well-operated plants that had already installed pollution control devices.

†These percentages represent an average of all "priority pollutants" removed; individual chemicals may be removed at either a higher or lower percentage.

Figure 3.12
Sources of Selected Toxic Chemicals in Water

Chemical	Industrial discharge (point)[1]	Landfill/ surface impoundment (non-point)[2]	Other non-point	Airborne deposition	Drinking water treatment
Aldrin/Dieldrin	●	●	●	●	
Arsenic	●	●	●		
Benzene	●	●			
Bis (2-ethylhexyl) phthalate	●	●			
Cadmium	●	●	●		
Carbon tetrachloride	●	●			
Chloroform	●	●			●
Chromium	●	●	●		
Copper	●	●	●		
Cyanide	●	●	●		
DDT	●	●	●	●	
Di-n-butyl-phthalate	●	●			
Dioxin	●	●	●	●	
Ethylbenzene	●	●			
Lead	●	●	●		
Methylene chloride (dichloromethane)	●	●			●
Mercury	●	●	●	●	
Nickel	●	●	●		
PCBs	●	●	●	●	
Phenol	●	●			
Silver	●	●			
Tetrachloroethylene	●	●			●
Toluene	●	●			
Toxaphene	●	●			

[1]Some of the chemicals found in industrial discharge are no longer produced or are only produced inadvertently as a byproduct of other manufacturing processes.

[2]Some chemicals (for example, copper, nickel, and phthalates), although present in landfills and impoundments, may not be leached in significant amounts from those disposal sites.

Source: U.S. Environmental Protection Agency, *et al.*

Figure 3.13

Discharge of Selected Toxic Chemicals to Surface Water, by Industry, 1980

Percent of firms within an industry found discharging a particular chemical:

- ● More than 50%
- ● 11% to 50%
- · 1% to 10%
- [ ] Less than 1%
- uk Unknown[1]

Industry	Aldrin/Dieldrin	Arsenic	Benzene	Bis (2-ethylhexyl) phthalate	Cadmium	Carbon tetrachloride	Chloroform	Chromium	Copper	Cyanide	DDT	Di-n-butyl-phthalate	Dioxin	Ethylbenzene	Lead	Methylene chloride (dichloromethane)	Mercury	Nickel	PCBs	Phenol	Silver	Tetrachloroethylene	Toluene	Toxaphene
Car washes and other laundries	·	●	●	·	·	●	●	●	●	·	·	·	·	·	●	●	●			·	·	●	●	·
Electrical	●	·	●	●	·	·	●	●	●	●			·	●	●	●	●	●		●	●	●	●	
Foundries	●	·	●	●	·	·	●	●	●	·			·	●	●	●	●	·		●	●	·	·	
Iron and steel	●	●	●	●	·	·	●	●	●	·			·	●	·	●	·	●		●	●	·	·	
Mechanical products	uk	·	●	uk	●	uk	uk	uk	uk	●		·	●	uk	●	uk	uk	●		●	uk	●	●	·
Non-ferrous metals	●	●	●	●	·	●	●	●	●	·			·	●	●	●	●	●		●	·	●	·	
Organics and plastics	·	·	●	●	·	·	●	●	●	·		·	●	●	●	●	·	·	·	●	·	●	·	
Pesticides	·	·	●	●	·	·	●	●	·	·	●	●		●	●	●	●			●	·	●	·	●
Petroleum refining	·	·	●	·	·	●	●	●	·	·	·	●	·	●	●	●	·	·		●	·	·	·	
Publicly owned wastewater treatment works	uk	●	●	uk	●	·	●	uk	uk	●		·	●	uk	●	uk	uk	●		●	uk	●	·	
Pulp and paper	●	●	●	●	·	●	●	●	●			·	●	●	●	●	●	·	●	●	●	·	●	
Timber products	●	·	●	●	·	●	●	·	·			·	●	●	●	●	·	·	·	●	·	·	●	·

[1] Unknown because no samples for heavy metals were taken.

Source: U.S. Environmental Protection Agency

Figure 3.14

Generation and Discharge of Toxic Chemicals by Industry, 1981

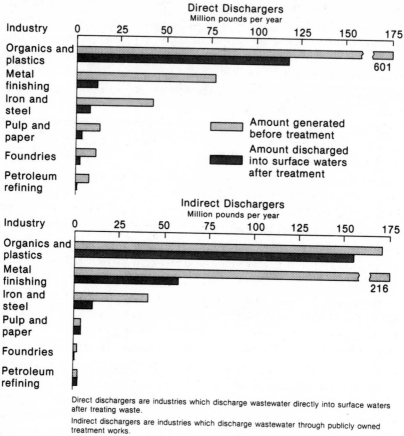

Direct dischargers are industries which discharge wastewater directly into surface waters after treating waste.

Indirect dischargers are industries which discharge wastewater through publicly owned treatment works.

Source: JRB Associates

toxics; the metal finishing industry is the largest source of toxic metals. Most of the effluent from metal finishing plants is discharged into municipal treatment systems. Chemical plants are concentrated in the Northeast, on the Gulf Coast, and in California. The largest concentration of metal finishing plants is in the eastern United States, particularly in the Northeast. The fastest growth in both industries tends to be occurring in the South and West.

Hazardous waste disposal is another major source of toxic pollutants. Of the 115 sites EPA has identified as being of highest priority for cleanup (see chapter 4), almost three-fourths pose actual or potential groundwater problems, and 65 percent pose surface water problems.[49] Figure 3.15 summarizes the specific problems associated with the 30 highest-priority sites.

Not all toxic pollutants found in water come from specific sources such as sewers or disposal sites. Some come from "nonpoint" sources, including runoff from farms and urban areas. Agricultural runoff, in addition to containing large amounts of sediment, may contain pesticides, which are being used in increasing amounts on American farms (see chapter 6). Urban runoff (from streets, parking lots) not only carries litter, but such heavy metals as lead and cadmium as well as other toxic pollutants.

Other nonpoint sources may be less important nationally, but may be significant contributors to local pollution problems. Runoff from mining activities may contain acid and carry a wide range of metals such as lead, copper, cadmium, and chromium. Septic tank cleaners containing trichloroethylene have caused the closing of wells in Long Island, New York.[50] Street de-icing chemicals, containing cyanide, and herbicides used in forests are also potential sources of pollution. An even more diffuse source is deposition of hazardous air pollutants, which is becoming increasingly recognized as a major source of toxic chemicals in the aquatic environment (see chapter 2).

Ironically, we also create some toxic contaminants by our efforts to clean up the water. Chlorine used to treat industrial and municipal wastewaters and to purify drinking water can react with other organic contaminants (both synthetic and natural) to create potentially toxic, chlorinated organic compounds, such as chlorinated phenols and trihalomethane compounds (for example, chloroform, bromodichloromethane, dibromochloromethane, and bromoform.)[51] Chloroform is a known animal carcinogen and a suspected human carcinogen. The carcinogenic properties of many of the other chlorinated compounds are unknown.

When chlorinated organic compounds are formed in plant effluents which are then discharged into surface waters, the chemicals tend to diffuse and degrade, resulting in their being found in relatively low concentrations. When formed by the addition of chlorine to drinking water, however, the concentrations can be relatively high and result in direct human exposure.[52] Trihalomethane compounds seem to be found more commonly in drinking water taken from surface water supplies than from groundwater supplies.[53] This is probably because surface water is more likely to be chlorinated before being put in drinking water systems and because it contains more of the natural and synthetic organics with which the chlorine reacts.

Figure 3.15
Groundwater and Surface Water Pollution at 30 Superfund Sites,[1] 1981

Site	Ground-water problem	Surface water problem	Chemical nature of problem
1 Commencement Bay, Takoma, Washington	●	●	Heavy metals, synthetic organics, chlorinated hydrocarbons
2 Keefe Environmental Services, Epping, New Hampshire	●	●	Solvents, acids, caustics, metals, pesticides
3 Lipari Landfill, Pitman, New Jersey	●	●	Methanol, benzene, toluene, xylene, isopropanol, butanol, bis(2-chloroethyl) ether, beryllium, mercury
4 Mark Phillip Trust, Woburn, Massachusetts	uk	uk	Arsenic, chromium, lead, other metals
5 McAdoo Associates, McAdoo, Pennsylvania	●	●	Toluene, benzene, xylene, naphthalene, nitrobenzene, trichloroethylene, cyanide
6 Nyanza Chemical Waste Dump, Ashland, Massachusetts	●	●	Mercury dyes, other chemicals
7 Pollution Abatement Services, Oswego, New York	●	●	Polymer gels, plating wastes, metal sludges, paint wastes, laboratory chemicals, picric acid crystals and boron hydride
8 Price Landfill, Pleasantville, New Jersey	●		Benzene, chloroform, trichloroethylene
9 Tar Creek Ottawa County, Oklahoma	●	●	Acid mine drainage, lead, zinc
10 Tybouts Corner, New Castle, Delaware	●	●	Trichloroethylene, vinyl chloride, 1,2-dichloroethane, benzene
11 Northwest 58th Street Landfill, Hialeah, Florida	●		Arsenic, cadmium, chromium, lead, selenium, phenols, halogenated volatile organic compounds
12 Miami Drum Services, Miami, Florida	●		Corrosives, solvents, phenols, toxic metals
13 Varsol Spill Site, Miami, Florida	●		Varsol (petroleum distillates)
14 Bruin Lagoon, Bruin, Pennsylvania		●	Sulfuric acid, heavy metals, pesticides and waste residuals
15 Burnt Fly Bog, Middlesex County, New Jersey	●	●	PCBs, lead, benzene, chloroform, trichloroethylene
16 Delaware Sand and Gravel — Llangollen Army Creek Landfills, New Castle, Delaware	●	●	Tetrachloroethylene (TCE) 1,2-dichloroethane (EDC), trichlorofluoromethane, trans 1,2-dichloroethylene
17 Goose Farm, Ocean County, New Jersey	●	●	Methylene chloride, dichloroethane, trichloroethane, benzene toluene, xylene

Site	Ground-water problem	Surface water problem	Chemical nature of problem
18 Lone Pine Landfill, Freehold Township, New Jersey	●[2]	●	Benzene, toluene, vinyl chloride, lead, zinc
19 MOTCO, La Marque, Texas	●	●	Vinyl chloride, heavy metals
20 Pijack Farm, Ocean County, New Jersey	●	●	Metals, organic solvents, pesticides, PCBs, phenolic compounds, oil sludges
21 VERTAC, Inc., Jacksonville, Arkansas		●	Dioxin
22 Bridgeport Rental and Oil Services, Bridgeport, New Jersey	●	●	Vinyl chloride, methylene chloride, trichloroethylene, toluene, benzene
23 Spence Farm, Plumsted Township, New Jersey	●	●	Halogenated hydrocarbons, PCBs, phenolic compounds
24 D'Imperio Property, Atlantic County, New Jersey	●		Trichloroethylene, toluene, xylene, hexane
25 French Limited Disposal Site, Crosby, Texas		●	Unspecified
26 Love Canal, Niagara Falls, New York	●	●	22,800 tons of waste chemicals, including dodecyl mercaptans, hexachloro-cyclohexanes
27 Old Bethpage Landfill, Oyster Bay, New York	●		Toluene, urethene, waste alcohol, PVCs, PCBs
28 Pickettville Road Landfill, Jacksonville, Florida	●[2]	●	Unspecified
29 Reeves Southeastern Corporation, Tampa, Florida	●	●	Iron, zinc, chromium
30 Seymour Recycling Corporation, Seymour, Indiana	●	●	Toxic, flammable, corrosive chemicals

uk = unknown

[1]The top 30 of the first 115 Superfund sites designated for cleanup by EPA. Sites were ranked according to the severity of groundwater, surface water, and air pollution; size and proximity of the population at risk; distance from sensitive areas such as wetlands and floodplains; and various administrative factors.

[2]Potential problem.

Source: U.S. Environmental Protection Agency

The Existing Legal Framework

Over the past decade, the federal government has enacted a series of statutes containing provisions to limit the amount of toxic pollutants entering surface water and groundwater. In 1972, the Clean Water Act established a "national policy that the discharge of toxic pollutants in toxic amounts be prohibited."[54] However, the provision of the act dealing specifically with toxic pollutants (Section 307) proved very difficult to implement. This provision required that effluent limitations be set for specific substances at a level that would prevent, with an adequate margin of safety, any "toxic" effects, taking into account the substance's toxicity, persistence, degradability, and impact on organisms found in the aquatic environment.

The process of implementing this part of the act broke down because of the difficulty of defining a toxic substance within the context of the act. Many substances may be toxic at high concentrations but relatively innocuous, or even necessary to the maintenance of good health, at low concentrations. Another problem was that effluent limitations were to be based solely on avoiding adverse health and environmental effects, with no consideration of the economic or technical feasibility of implementing controls. As of 1976, EPA had identified only six chemicals as "toxic" according to this section of the act.[55]

As a result of a suit by the Natural Resources Defense Council (NRDC), EPA agreed, in a 1976 consent decree, to name 65 substances and categories of chemicals as toxic chemicals, and to establish effluent standards for them under another section of the Clean Water Act (Section 301) on the basis of the "best available technology economically achievable" (commonly referred to as BAT), which allows consideration of both the availability and the cost of controls.[56] Congress incorporated this agreement into the statute in 1977, requiring EPA to develop effluent limitations for direct discharges of 21 major industries, covering 65 "priority pollutants."* Based on BAT, the controls are to be in place by July 1, 1984. Controls for other "nonconventional" pollutants were to be based on the same technology standard and are to be in place no later than July 1, 1987.

The Clean Water Act also requires controls on toxic pollutants from industrial facilities that discharge into municipal sewers and treatment plants. These "pretreatment" provisions (Section 307) were designed to control pollutants that might contaminate sludge, interfere with the efficient operation of the treatment facility, or pass through the facility and cause water quality problems. EPA failed to implement these requirements. Following the NRDC suit and the 1976 consent decree, Congress in the 1977 amendments called for EPA to issue pretreatment standards for each of the 65 priority pollutants and the 21 listed major industrial categories by

---

*The number of industrial sectors was increased to 34 by a 1979 modification of the NRDC consent decree.[57]

July 1, 1983.* However, recognizing that municipal treatment plants can remove some toxic contaminants, the amendments allowed firms discharging into a municipal facility to be credited with the treatment that the municipal facility provided.

Both the direct discharge and the pretreatment effluent standards were to be supported by ambient water quality standards. If the technology-based effluent standards were not adequate to protect the designated use of a stream (for example, for recreation or drinking water), then stricter controls would be required.

There has been very limited progress in implementing the toxic controls mandated in 1977. Only one final industrial BAT effluent limitation had been promulgated by the end of 1981, although 12 BAT standards were proposed.[58] EPA did promulgate general regulations for the pretreatment program in 1978. These regulations were revised and repromulgated in 1981, and then rescinded pending a Regulatory Impact Analysis (see chapter 9). The agency has issued industry-specific requirements for only two industrial pretreatment categories—timber processing and electroplating.[59]

The second major federal law dealing with toxic pollutants in water is the Safe Drinking Water Act, enacted in 1974.[60] EPA was instructed to promulgate primary drinking water standards, establishing maximum levels for contaminants that could affect public health. In response, the agency repromulgated the old Public Health Service drinking water standards that had been in place since the mid-1960s.[61] These only addressed a few inorganic contaminants and pesticides and conventional contaminants such as bacteria and turbidity. Although the act requires the standards to be reviewed and, if appropriate, revised every three years, these "interim" standards still stand essentially unmodified except for the addition of a trihalomethanes standard.[62]

The trihalomethanes standard, based on a balancing of public health considerations and "feasibility of achievement," could result in somewhere between 30 and 300 additional cases of cancer a year if all drinking water supplies had the allowable concentration of the group of pollutants.**[63]

---

*Again, the number of industrial categories was increased to 34 in a 1979 modification of the NRDC consent decree.

**The standard actually applies only to water supply systems serving more than 75,000 people, which were estimated to cover 390 communities containing 52 percent of the population. The level in other systems can legally be above the standard, causing increased levels of risk.

A third federal law controlling potential pollution sources is the Resource Conservation and Recovery Act (RCRA), enacted in 1976 (see chapter 4).[64] This law addresses ground and surface water pollution resulting from inadequate hazardous waste disposal practices and adopts a technological control strategy similar to the Clean Water Act. However, the law failed to state clear objectives for water quality, leaving some doubt about what disposal standards are appropriate, particularly when groundwater pollution may occur (existing water quality standards may suffice for surface water, but no such standards exist for groundwater). The implementation of this act has also been substantially delayed, with only some of the required regulations having been promulgated on an interim basis— and even these are under review.

A fourth major piece of legislation, the Comprehensive Environmental Response and Liability Act (known as "Superfund") was passed in late 1980 and included a $1.6 billion trust fund to be used for the cleanup of abandoned hazardous waste sites.[65] EPA has taken some initial steps to implement this program (see chapter 4), but reductions in EPA's budget and staff appear likely to slow the effort.

Although these are the four major federal laws that most directly relate to toxic pollutants in surface water and groundwater, several other statutes are also relevant. These include the Federal Insecticide, Fungicide, and Rodenticide Act,[66] which restricts the use of pesticides; the Toxic Substances Control Act,[67] which could be used to control commercial sources of toxic chemicals not adequately limited under other legislation; the National Environmental Policy Act,[68] which could limit federal activities that might result in the discharge of toxic pollutants; and the Clean Air Act,[69] which could be used to restrict airborne substances that might eventually contaminate water (see chapter 2).

State and local governments also play significant roles in the implementation of the Clean Water Act. In fact, the act declares that "it is the policy of the Congress to recognize, preserve and protect the primary responsibilities and rights of the States to prevent, reduce and eliminate pollution."[70] The federal government has the primary responsibility for establishing minimum effluent standards, but the states are expected to establish water quality standards and to issue permits to individual dischargers and enforce the various state and federal requirements. The federal government exercises these responsibilities only when the state authority is unwilling to (33 states were implementing the permitting program by the end of 1981). The states can also receive financial assistance from the federal government to support basic program needs for such activities as monitoring and enforcement, managing the pretreatment program, and overseeing the federal program that provides grants for the construction of publicly owned sewage treatment facilities. In addition, the states may have primary responsibility for enforcing drinking water standards and implementing the underground injection program established by the Safe Drinking Water Act.

Alternative Approaches

The question of what to do about toxic pollutants is probably the major substantive issue Congress is addressing in its reauthorization of the Clean Water Act this year. There seems to be little disagreement about the legitimacy of the basic goal established in 1972—to prohibit "the discharge of toxic pollutants in toxic amounts."[71] But there is substantial debate on how quickly this should be done, and whether the basic regulatory approach should be changed. That is, should we shift to an approach that depends more on ambient standards, or should we continue with the current approach, which focuses on technology-based effluent standards?

Ambient Standards. An ambient standard approach would involve three separate steps. The responsibility for implementation probably would lie primarily with the state water pollution control authority.

The first step is to designate an intended use for each water body, stream, or stream segment. This designated use would determine the overall water quality standard. Streams designated as drinking water sources would have to be maintained at a very high quality; streams designated for agricultural use would have a lower standard; and streams designated for industrial use would have an even lower standard.

The authority responsible for implementation (using water quality criteria developed by EPA), as a second step, would have to establish limits on the allowable concentration of individual pollutants consistent with the designated uses. For drinking water sources, these allowable concentrations would usually be very low; for agricultural uses, they would usually be higher; and for industrial uses, they would usually be higher still.

The third step would be for the implementing authority to impose limitations on the amount of each pollutant that individual sources could discharge. These discharge limitations would be set so that the combined discharges of all sources would not cause the ambient standards to be exceeded anywhere in the water body.

As an alternative to the first step in this sequence—designating different uses for different water bodies—all water bodies could be classified for the same use. For instance, all water bodies could be required to meet drinking water standards. This alternative is implicit in the Clean Water Act, which established the goal of making all waters suitable for fishing and swimming by 1981. However, the act does not establish this goal as a uniform national standard.

Either approach leaves the implementing authorities with a number of problems. The first is how the allowable ambient concentration limits for the individual pollutant are to be set. Is this to be done by a careful balancing of the risks created by the pollutant against the benefits of allowing the pollutant to continue to be discharged?* If so, the appropriate balance would be different for every stream in the nation—and, in fact, for every reach of every stream—for the number and type of downstream users will vary from location to location, as will the cost of pollution abatement to dischargers. Implementing such a finely tuned program would be practically impossible.

Limits might be set so as to eliminate risk (or impose a minimal level of risk) on any downstream users. This would be administratively simpler, for it would require the implementing authority to establish only one set of ambient concentration limitations for each type of use, and then to classify each stream or each stream segment according to the use to be made of it. But even this would not be easy, given limited knowledge about what pollutants are actually discharged, how hazardous many of these pollutants are (even by themselves, much less in combination with other chemicals), and what happens to them after they enter a stream.

Finally, the implementing authority still has the problem of converting the ambient limitations into effluent limitations for individual dischargers. When many sources discharge the same pollutant, how much should each be forced to clean up to achieve the ambient standard?**

---

*The benefits in this case would be primarily the cost savings accruing to dischargers because they do not have to clean up their effluents.

**Another question is how individual dischargers should be controlled. This could be done by a regulation prohibiting them from discharging more than a certain amount of the pollutant, or by an "effluent charge," which would force them to pay for the amount

Clearly, an ambient standard approach creates a number of implementation difficulties. Also, it was found to be generally unsuccessful in improving water quality when it was used prior to 1972. The approach was abandoned because the difficulty of establishing a legally defensible cause-and-effect relationship between individual polluters and stream quality made the law unenforceable. Our ability to establish such cause-and-effect relationships has not significantly improved since 1972, and it is even more difficult to establish such relationships for toxic substances than for the "conventional" pollutants that were of primary concern at that time.

The ambient standard approach continues to serve as a backup to the technological control strategy currently being used. EPA has issued quantitative criteria for a wide range of conventional pollutants and for 64 of the 65 priority toxic pollutants, but most states have failed to adopt criteria for other than conventional pollutants in their water quality standards program.[72] Most states have classified streams for "fishable/swimmable" uses but have not adopted the criteria and standards that would actually make the streams usable for these purposes.

The advantage of the ambient standard approach is that it would theoretically be more "efficient," in that no discharger would have to spend more to clean up effluent than would be necessary to make the receiving water suitable for its designated use. However, switching to an ambient approach would probably greatly increase the administrative costs of pollution control efforts. It would largely render useless much of the work done over the past five years and would require a substantial investment of time and resources to collect the information required for implementation. Much larger government programs would probably be required to implement the system, and there would be even further delay in achieving improved water quality.

Technology Standards. Problems similar to some of those just dis-

---

of pollution they discharge without placing any limit on this amount, with the level of the charge depending on how much cleanup we wanted to accomplish. Whatever the merits of a charge system for conventional pollutants, the approach does not seem workable as a way of dealing with toxics. The difficulty of accurately measuring discharges of toxics is a major problem for any control system but would be even more of an obstacle for a charge system. Also, a charge system to some extent involves trading off a gain in economic efficiency for a higher degree of uncertainty about the level to which a particular pollutant will be controlled. It can be argued that the greater uncertainty is acceptable for some conventional pollutants, but it is not likely to be acceptable when public health is at stake.

cussed, and the lack of progress prior to 1972, caused Congress to adopt an approach to controlling toxic pollutants based on technology standards rather than ambient standards. Under the technology standard approach, each type of discharger (for instance, a particular type of manufacturing facility) has to satisfy an effluent standard that is established on the basis of the amount of pollution control that can be achieved using abatement technologies suitable for that type of discharger. Thus, the standard is based on the availability of abatement technologies without regard to the ambient quality of the receiving waters, or what those waters are used for.

As adopted, the technology standard approach takes into account not only the availability of the technology but the costs of adopting it and the likely economic impact of these expenditures. In addition, an individual firm can get a variance from the industry standard for all but "priority" pollutants if the costs are too great for it to bear.

The technology-based standards of the Clean Water Act are supplemented by the use of an approach based on ambient water quality standards. If the effluent limitations established on a technology basis are inadequate to achieve water quality goals (the designated use of the stream), then more stringent controls may be required.

A major problem with technology standards is that they may impose excessive costs on dischargers by requiring more cleanup than is necessary to achieve the desired ambient water quality. Opponents also argue that this approach may, because it focuses on available technologies for treating effluents, discourage innovations that could provide less costly means of pollution abatement. There is, however, no evidence one way or the other on this issue.

The advantages of the technology standard approach are that it is easier to implement than the ambient approach (although EPA has been very slow in issuing second-stage—BAT—standards); it ensures that each standard is, in fact, technically and economically achievable; and it is compatible with the way in which firms actually go about reducing pollution. Typically, to deal with a number of different pollutants in its discharge, a firm will not adopt a series of different treatment systems each dealing with a specific pollutant, but will install one system that treats all pollutants together. Thus, it is more logical to establish aggregate cleanup requirements that are achievable by an available treatment technology than to establish a series of individual, and perhaps inconsistent, standards for each individual pollutant.

Most industries and many municipalities have already installed "best practicable technology," the first stage of technological requirements under the Clean Water Act. A major controversy in 1982 is whether industry should have to comply with the second stage of technological control for toxic pollutants, based on the "best available technology economically achievable." The controversy involves the question of whether the first-stage controls have reduced toxic effluents to such an extent that the second-stage BAT controls would not produce any additional water quality benefits. If this is the case, then imposition of BAT would involve major additional costs for industry and produce no significant improvement in water quality. A closely associated issue is whether indirect dischargers should be required to remove toxic chemicals before discharging their effluents into municipal sewers, or whether the municipal sewage treatment facilities remove enough of these pollutants to make such a requirement unnecessary. Thus, even within the framework of technology-based controls, there are major questions of the degree of control.

If the first-stage technology controls do not provide adequate protection from the adverse effects of toxic pollutants, then the policy choice returns to the question of whether to revert to some kind of standards-based approach. Proponents of technology-based controls argue that such a reversion would be equivalent to deciding to do nothing for the foreseeable future and that the real choice is between acting now or deciding not to act at all.

FURTHER READING

A particularly good introduction to the general subject of water resources is provided by Luna B. Leopold in *Water: A Primer* (San Francisco, Calif.:, W.H. Freeman, 1974). It provides a clear and concise explanation of many of the scientific, technical, and policy issues affecting resources development and use. The most recent comprehensive assessment of America's water resources, covering both surface water and groundwater, water pollution, and water availability is the Second National Assessment conducted by the federal Water Resources Council, *The Nation's Water Resources, 1975-2000* (Washington, D.C.: U.S. Government Printing Office, 1978). This report contains a substantial amount of water resources data, and attempts to project regional demands and supplies of water through the year 2000.

The most complete analysis of the implementation of the Clean

Water Act is the Final Report of the National Commission on Water Quality (Springfield, Va.: National Technical Information Service, 1976). The commission, established by Congress, examined what was known about water quality, the technological alternatives available to industrial and municipal dischargers, and the economic costs of meeting the goals of the act. Four volumes, which are particularly informative, provide the background research for the commission report: *Water Pollution Control Act of 1972, Economic Impacts*; *Technology Assessment; Water Quality Analyses and Environmental Impact Assessment*; and *Public Law 92-500, Assessment of Regional Impacts*. These documents were completed in April 1976, and all are available from the National Technical Information Service, Springfield, Va.

A more recent attempt by the Environmental Protection Agency to summarize information on surface water quality and to project likely pollutant loads in the future is presented in *Environmental Outlook 1980*, published by EPA's Office of Research and Development.

The most comprehensive summary of national groundwater information is contained in the Water Resources Council's Second National Assessment, mentioned earlier. The *Conservation Foundation Letter* (June 1981) presents a brief summary of current groundwater quality issues. Three useful publications prepared by EPA to provide background information for its efforts to develop a groundwater strategy are: *Planning Workshops to Develop Recommendations for a Groundwater Protection Strategy* (June 1980); *Planning Workshops to Develop Recommendations for a Groundwater Protection Strategy, Appendices* (June 1980); and *Proposed Groundwater Protection Strategy* (November 1980). All are available from the National Technical Information Service, Springfield, Va.

The Environmental Protection Agency's *Quality Criteria for Water*, published in 1976, summarizes information on the health and environmental effects of different pollutants; a supplement covering 64 of the 65 priority pollutants was published in 45 *Federal Register* 79318 (November 28, 1980). The problem of toxic pollutants in water supplies was addressed in a series of reports (issued consecutively from 1977 through 1981) prepared by the Safe Drinking Water Committee of the National Research Council: *Drinking Water and Health* (Washington: National Academy Press), vols. 1-4.

To keep current in water-related topics, it is useful to scan *Selected Water Resources Abstracts*, a monthly journal coordinated by the Department of the Interior and available, by subscription, from the

National Technical Information Service. A computerized counterpart, "Water Resources Abstracts," is commercially available on the Lockheed *Dialog* System. Abstracts from journals, monographs, reports, conference proceedings, court cases, and federal and state agencies can be searched by key word in this data base. Subject coverage includes the life, physical, and social sciences as well as the engineering and legal aspects of the conservation, control, use, and management of water.

TEXT REFERENCES

1. Federal Water Pollution Control Act Amendments of 1972, 33 U.S.C., sec. 1251(a)(1) (1981).

2. Safe Drinking Water Act, 42 U.S.C., sec. 300f *et. seq.* (1981).

3. U.S. Water Resources Council, *Second National Water Assessment, The Nation's Water Resources, 1975-2000,* Vol. 1, Summary (Washington, D.C.: U.S. Government Printing Office, 1978), p. 36.

4. Council on Environmental Quality, *Environmental Trends* (Washington, D.C.: U.S. Government Printing Office, 1981), p. 221.

5. "Drought in the Northeast," *Newsweek,* January 5, 1981, p. 20.

6. David Sheridan, *Desertification of the United States* (Washington, D.C.: U.S. Government Printing Office, 1981) p. 54.

7. Council on Environmental Quality, *Contamination of Groundwater by Toxic Organic Chemicals* (Washington, D.C.: U.S. Government Printing Office, 1981), p. 10.

8. Council on Environmental Quality, *Environmental Quality—1980* (Washington, D.C.: U.S. Government Printing Office, 1980), p. 101.

9. 33 U.S.C., sec. 1315(b) (1981).

10. Richard Smith, et al., "A Study of Trends in Total Phosphorous Measurements at Stations in the NASQAN Network," Geological Survey Water-Supply Paper No. 2190 (Reston, Va.: U.S. Geological Survey, Water Resources Division, undated), pp. 13-19.

11. U.S. Environmental Protection Agency, Office of Planning and Management, *National Accomplishments in Pollution Control, 1970-1980* (Washington, D.C.: U.S. Environmental Protection Agency, 1980), pp. 13-14, 29-31, 53-55.

12. U.S. Environmental Protection Agency, Office of Water and Waste Management, Monitoring and Data Branch, Monitoring and Data Support Division, "Assessment of Ambient Conditions, Water Quality Portion 1980" (unpublished) (Washington, D.C.: U.S. Environmental Protection Agency, February 10, 1981), p. 20.

13. U.S. Water Resources Council, *Second National Water Assessment, The Nations Water Resources, 1975-2000,* Vol. 1, p. 20.

14. National Commission on Water Quality, *Water Policies for the Future, Final Report to the President and Congress,* (Washington, D.C.: U.S. Government Printing Office, 1973), p. 230.

15. *Ibid.*

16. Council on Environmental Quality, *Environmental Quality—1980,* p. 230.

17. U.S. Water Resources Council, *The Nations Water Resources, 1975-2000,* Vol. I, p. 20.

18. *Ibid.,* p.18.

19. *Ibid.*

20. Gordon Sloggett, *Prospects for Groundwater Irrigation: Declining Levels and Rising Energy Costs*, Agricultural Economic Report Number 478 (Washington, D.C.: U.S. Department of Agriculture, 1981), p. 8.

21. U.S. Water Resources Council, *The Nations Water Resources, 1975-2000*, Vol. II, Part II, p. 15.

22. *Ibid.*

23. U.S. Water Resources Council, *The Nation's Water Resources, 1975-2000*, Vol. II, Part II, p. 17.

24. David Sheridan, *Desertification of the United States*, p. 31.

25. This reporting reflects the number of outbreaks, not necessarily the population affected. The actual population affected by such outbreaks may be more or less, as an outbreak can include two people or 5,000 people. U.S. Department of Health and Welfare, Center for Disease Control, *Water Related Disease Outbreaks, Surveillance, Annual Summary 1978* (Atlanta, Ga.: Center for Disease Control, 1980), p. 19.

26. Council on Environmental Quality, *Contamination of Groundwater by Toxic Organic Chemicals*, pp. 36-37.

27. *Ibid.*, pp. 16-38.

28. U.S. Environmental Protection Agency, *The Report to Congress: Waste Disposal Practices and Their Effects on Groundwater*, Executive Summary (Washington, D.C.: U.S. Environmental Protection Agency, 1977).

29. Lyle R. Silka and Francoise Brasier, "The National Assessment of Groundwater Contamination Potential of Waste Impoundments" (Washington, D.C.: U.S. Environmental Protection Agency, 1980), pp. 4-6.

30. U.S. Environmental Protection Agency, *The Report to Congress: Waste Disposal Practices and Their Effects on Groundwater*, p. 12.

31. This discussion is based on U.S. Water Resource Council, *State of the States: Water Resources Planning and Management, Groundwater Supplement* (Washington, D.C.: U.S. Government Printing Office, 1981), p. III, 2-3.

32. *Ibid.*, p. IV, 1.

33. *Ibid.*, p. IV, 1.

34. 33 U.S.C., sec. 1251-1376 (1981).

35. Resource Conservation and Recovery Act, 42 U.S.C., sec. 6901 *et. seq.* (1981); and Comprehensive Emergency Response and Liability Act of 1980, 42 U.S.C., sec. 9601 (1981).

36. 42 U.S.C., sec. 1424(e) (1981).

37. 47 Fed. Reg. 14779 (1982).

38. 42 U.S.C., sec. 300(h) (1981).

39. 42 U.S.C., sec. 300(g-l) (1981).

40. 40 C.F.R., sec. 141 (1981).

41. U.S. Environmental Protection Agency, Office of Drinking Water, *Proposed Groundwater Protection Strategy* (Washington, D.C.: U.S. Environmental Protection Agency, 1980)

42. "NGA Calls for New Land Disposal Rules to Protect All Underlying Aquifers," *Inside E.P.A. Weekly Report*, October 16, 1981.

43. U.S. Environmental Protection Agency, "Proposed Groundwater Protection Strategy," p. VI, 1.

44. 46 Fed. Reg. 11126-11177 (1981).

45. A register of "chemicals in commerce" is maintained by EPA Office of Toxic Substances pursuant to section 8(b) of the Toxic Substances Control Act. This register has over 55,000 substances listed, but does not include chemicals that are only used as drugs, pesticides, food additives, or cosmetics.

46. U.S., Congress, House Committee on Public Works and Transportation, *Data Relating to H.R. 3199, Clean Water Act of 1977*, Committee Print, 95th Cong., 2nd sess., 1977, pp. 3-4.

47. Memo from William A. Tellinard, Chief, Energy and Mining Branch, U.S. Environmental Protection Agency, to Robert Schaffer, Director, Effluent Guidelines Division, U.S. Environmental Protection Agency, "Rationale for the Development of BAT Priority Pollutant Parameters," May 24, 1977.

48. U.S. Environmental Protection Agency, Office of Solid Waste, "The National Potential for Damage from Industrial Waste Disposal" (Washington, D.C.: U.S. Environmental Protection Agency, Open File Report, 1977).

49. Undated summary reports on individual Superfund priority sites, released by EPA with October 23, 1981, press statement.

50. Council on Environmental Quality, *Contamination of Groundwater by Toxic Organic Chemicals*, p. 13.

51. The National Research Council, *Chloroform, Carbon Tetrachloride, and Other Halomethanes: An Environmental Assessment* (Washington, D.C.: National Academy of Sciences, 1978), p. 109.

52. *Ibid.*, p. 103.

53. *Ibid.*, p. 103.

54. 33 U.S.C., sec. 1251(a)(3) (1981).

55. 40 C.F.R., 129 (1975).

56. Natural Resources Defense Council v. Train, No. 75-172, 8 ERC 2120, (D.D.C. June, 1976)

57. Natural Resources Defense Council v. Costle, No.75-1267, 12 ERC 1833, (D.D.C. March, 1979).

58. 46 Fed. Reg. 8285 (1981).

59. 46 Fed. Reg. 8285 (1981), 46 Fed. Reg. 9461 (1981).

60. 42 U.S.C., sec. 300f *et. seq.* (1981).

61. 40 Fed. Reg. 11990 (1975).

62. 40 C.F.R., sec. 141 (1980).

63. U.S. Environmental Protection Agency, Office of Water Monitoring and Data Support Division, *Exposure Assessment Document*, draft (Washington, D.C.: U.S. Environmental Protection Agency, 1981) p. 2.

64. 42 U.S.C., sec. 6901 *et. seq.* (1981).

65. 42 U.S.C., sec 9601 (1981).

66. Federal Insecticide, Fungicide and Rodenticide Act, as amended, 7 U.S.C., sec. 135-135k (1981).

67. Toxic Substances Control Act, 15 U.S.C., sec. 2601-2629 (1981).

68. National Environmental Policy Act of 1969, as amended, 42 U.S.C., sec. 4321-4361 (1981).

69. Clean Air Act, as amended, 42 U.S.C., sec. 7401-7642 (1981).

70. 42 U.S.C., sec. 300f *et. seq.* (1981).

71. 33 U.S.C., sec. 1251(a)(3) (1981).

72. 45 Fed. Reg. 79318 (1980).

FIGURE REFERENCES

Figure 3.1

Council on Environmental Quality, *Environmental Statistics* (Springfield, Va.: National Technical Information Service, 1978), p. 212.

Figure 3.2

Council on Environmental Quality, *Environmental Statistics* (Springfield, Va.: National Technical Information Service, 1978), p. 213.

Figure 3.3

Council on Environmental Quality, *Environmental Statistics* (Springfield, Va.: National Technical Information Service, 1978), p. 214.

Figure 3.4

Council on Environmental Quality, *Environmental Trends* (Washington, D.C.: U.S. Government Printing Office, 1981), Figure 10-8, p. 217.

Figure 3.5

Council on Environmental Quality, *Environmental Trends* (Washington, D.C.: U.S. Government Printing Office, 1981), Figure 10-6, p. 215. Estimates of groundwater overdraft are averaged over the entire subregion, and may not reflect local conditions.

Figure 3.6

Based on analysis by The Conservation Foundation of unpublished data provided by the U.S. Department of the Interior, Geological Survey, Water Resources Division, (Reston, Va.: U.S. Geological Survey).

Figure 3.7

Based on analysis by The Conservation Foundation of data provided by the U.S. Environmental Protection Agency, Office of Water and Waste Management, Monitoring and Data Branch, *Assessment of Ambient Conditions—Water Quality Portion, 1980* (Washington, D.C.: U.S. Environmental Protection Agency, February 10, 1981), Appendix C.

Figure 3.8

U.S. Water Resources Council, *Second National Water Assessment, The Nation's Water Resources: 1975-2000* (Washington, D.C.: U.S. Government Printing Office, December, 1978), Vol. 2, Part IV, p. 19. U.S. Environmental Protection Agency, Office of Drinking Water, *Planning Workshops to Develop Recommendations for a Ground Water Protection Strategy, Appendices* (Washington, D.C.: U.S. Environmental Protection Agency, June 1980), Table 1, 2, pp. II 3-4.

Figure 3.9

U.S. Water Resources Council, *A Summary of Groundwater Problems* (Washington, D.C.: U.S. Water Resources Council, September 1981).

Figure 3.10

Lyle R. Silka and Francoise Brasier, "The National Assessment of Groundwater Contamination Potential of Waste Impoundments," (unpublished) (Washington, D.C.: U.S. Environmental Protection Agency, 1980), pp. 4-6.

Figure 3.11

U.S. Environmental Protection Agency, *EPA Chemical Activities Status Report*, 1st ed. (Washington, D.C.: U.S. Environmental Protection Agency, Toxic Information Services, April 1979); U.S. Environmental Protection Agency, Office of Toxic Substances *A Study of Industrial Data on Chemical Candidates for Testing* (Washington, D.C.: U.S. Environmental Protection Agency, June 1978); National Academy of Sciences, *Contemporary Pest Control*

Practices and Prospects, vol. 1 (Washington, D.C.: National Academy of Sciences, 1975); International Agency for Research on Cancer, *IARC Monograph in the Evaluation of the Carcinogenic Risk of Chemicals to Humans* (Lyon, France: IARC, September 1979); National Research Council, Safe Drinking Water Committee, *Drinking Water and Health*, vols. 1-4 (Washington, D.C.: National Academy Press, 1981); Council on Environmental Quality, *Chemical Hazards to Reproduction* (Washington, D.C.: U.S. Government Printing Office, 1981); U.S. Environmental Protection Agency, internal memorandum, prepared for risk assessments of 56 priority pollutants (Washington, D.C.: U.S. Environmental Protection Agency, undated); National Research Council, *Nonfluorinated Halomethanes in the Environment* (Washington, D.C.: National Academy of Sciences, 1978); U.S. Environmental Protection Agency, *Quality Criteria for Water* (Washington, D.C.: U.S. Government Printing Office, 1975); U.S. Department of the Interior, Bureau of Mines, *Mineral Facts and Problems*, Bull. 667 (Washington, D.C.: U.S. Government Printing Office, 1976); and U.S. Environmental Protection Agency, *Summary Characteristics of Selected Chemicals of Near-Term Interest* (Washington, D.C.: U.S. Government Printing Office, 1976).

Figure 3.12

U.S. Environmental Protection Agency, Office of Water, Monitoring and Data Support Division, Draft Exposure Documents on 56 priority pollutants, Fall, 1981; Council on Environmental Quality, *Contamination of Groundwater by Toxic Organic Chemicals*, (Washington, D.C.: U.S. Government Printing Office, 1980); Steven J. Eisenreich, et al, "Airborne Organic Contaminants in the Great Lakes Ecosystem; *Environmental Science and Technology*, 15(1):30-38 (1981); Undated summary reports on individual superfund priority sites, released by U.S. Environmental Protection Agency with October 23, 1981 press statement.

Figure 3.13

U.S. Environmental Protection Agency, memorandum from Dean Neptune, Chief, Office of Analytical Support, to Robert Schaeffer, Director, Effluent Guidelines Division, "Priority Pollutant Frequency Listing Tabulations and Descriptive Statistics," November 4, 1980.

Figure 3.14

JRB Associates, "Assessment of the Impacts of Industrial Discharges on Publicly Owned Treatment Works - Final Report" prepared for U.S. Environmental Protection Agency, (McLean, Va.: JRB Associates, November 20 1981), p. 1-3. Amounts of discharged toxic substances shown include whichever of the 129 priority pollutants were present in the industrial wasteloads.

Figure 3.15

Undated summary reports on individual superfund priority sites, released by EPA with October 23, 1981 press statement.

FLOODING

1. U.S. Water Resources Council, *Estimated Flood Damages: Appendix B, Nationwide Analysis Report*, (Washington, D.C.: U.S. Government Printing Office, January 1977), p. 26.
2. *Ibid.*, p. 27.
3. *Ibid.*, p. 22.
4. U.S. Department of the Interior, Geological Survey, *Extent and Development of Urban*

Flood Plains, Circular 601-J (Washington, D.C.: U.S. Geological Survey, 1974), pp. J-5, J-12, J-13.

5. Gilbert F. White, *Flood Hazard in the United States: A Research Assessment* (Boulder, Colo.: University of Colorado, Institute of Behavioral Science, 1975), p. xviii.

6. U.S. Department of Commerce, Bureau of the Census, *Statistical Abstract of the United States: 1980*, 101st ed. (Washington, D.C.: U.S. Government Printing Office, 1980), p. 219, no. 380.

7. U.S. Department of Commerce, National Oceanic and Atmospheric Administration, *Climatological Data: National Summary*, Annual Summary, Volume 28, no. 13 (Asheville, N.C.: National Oceanic and Atmospheric Administration, National Climatic Center, 1977), p. 117.

8. The Conservation Foundation, "Flood Hazard Management and Natural Resource Protection," Training Institute Background Papers (Washington, D.C.: The Conservation Foundation, April 1980), p. 15. The Water Resources Council projects that if present trends continue, 1985 annual flood losses will rise to $5 billion (in 1979 dollars). *Ibid.*

9. The National Flood Insurance Act of 1968, as amended, 42 U.S.C., sec. A001, *et. seq.* (1980).

10. Executive Order No. 11,988, 3 C.F.R., sec. 117-120 (1978).

11. Department of the Army, Office of the Chief of Engineers, *A Perspective on Flood Plain Regulations for Flood Plain Management* (Washington, D.C.: Department of the Army, June 1976), p. 95.

Chapter 4

Hazardous Wastes

Probably the most important, controversial, and difficult environmental problem to emerge over the past few years has been what to do with hazardous wastes—those that are being generated, those that will be generated, and those that are already sitting in tens of thousands of sites around the country. Major federal programs to deal with this problem were initiated by statutes passed in 1974 (the Safe Drinking Water Act),[1] 1976 (the Resource Conservation and Recovery Act),[2] and 1980 (the Comprehensive Environmental Response, Compensation, and Liability Act, popularly known as "Superfund").[3]

Hazardous wastes can create potentially very serious health and environmental problems. However, much of the information needed to define these problems adequately and determine what to do about them is lacking. Groundwater contamination appears to be the most widespread problem. But little is known about hazards associated with exposure over a long period to small amounts and combinations of chemicals in groundwater—or elsewhere. Nor is it known how many people are or will be exposed to such hazards.

These uncertainties greatly complicate the difficult, but necessary, decisions to be made about hazardous wastes. Even with much better information, decisions would not be easy. But clearly they must be made. Hazardous wastes are being generated, and they are being disposed of. If not properly managed, these activities can impose unreasonable risks on us and generations to come.

HAZARDOUS WASTE TRENDS

There are almost no data on trends in the amount of hazardous waste that has been generated or disposed of, or on the health and environmental problems that these wastes may have caused. Relatively little is known even about the current status of hazardous waste management. Most of the available information is based on special studies undertaken at different times by different people for different purposes. There is little consistency in definitions or methodology. The conclusions of most of the studies either are based on surveys of a limited number of facilities handling hazardous waste or are crude national estimates based on such surveys in combination with professional judgments.

The quality of information should improve as the Environmental Protection Agency (EPA) implements the Resource Conservation and Recovery Act (RCRA). This statute requires record keeping and reporting by all facilities generating, storing, treating, disposing of, or otherwise handling hazardous wastes, and requires those firms that store, treat, or dispose of such wastes to obtain operating permits from EPA or an authorized state agency. As of early 1982, facilities were operating with "interim" permits.

There are a number of problems with the information that has been collected in EPA's efforts to implement this program. EPA identified about 400,000 firms that, because of the nature of their business, could be involved with handling hazardous wastes.[4] The agency sent a letter to each of these firms, notifying them of the law's requirements and asking them to respond if they believed they were subject to regulation under RCRA. Approximately 67,000 firms responded.[5] EPA judged that 44,000 of these firms were not required to obtain permits because they only generated or transported wastes, and did not store, treat, or dispose of them. The remaining 23,000 firms were sent permit applications. Only 14,659 of these firms responded. EPA is in the process of reviewing these applications and believes that approximately 11,000 of the facilities will require permits under the existing regulations.[6] A summary of all these numbers is presented in figure 4.1.

There are several legitimate reasons why a firm might not have applied for a permit. It might not be dealing with wastes included within the definition of *hazardous* finally adopted by EPA. It also might not have been involved in storing, treating, or disposing of wastes, as these activities were defined by EPA, or may have decided to stop engaging in such activities before the permitting requirements took effect. Or, finally, a firm may have handled less than an average of one metric ton of waste a month—EPA's arbitrary cutoff. However, EPA has made little effort to determine why, in fact, such a low percentage of firms responded to either of their notifications.[7]   Thus, there remains substantial uncertainty about how many firms are actually involved in hazardous waste manage-

Figure 4.1
Permitting of Hazardous Waste Facilities, 1980-1982

Item	Number of firms	Gn	Tp	St	Tr	Ds	Description
1	400,000	●	●	○	○	○	Number of industrial firms that EPA (1) identified as possibly involved in handling hazardous wastes and (2) sent letters, seeking responses from those considering themselves subject to RCRA.
2	67,000	●	●	○	○	○	Number of responses received by EPA to letters described in item 1. (Approximately 333,000 firms did not respond.)
3	23,000	○	○	●	●	●	Number of responses described in item 2 that EPA judged were from firms that might require a permit under RCRA. (EPA judged that some 44,000 responses were from firms involved only in generating or transporting wastes, and therefore they did not require a permit under RCRA.) EPA sent permit applications to the 23,000 firms thought to require a permit.
4	14,659	○	○	●	●	●	Number of permit applications received by EPA in response to item 3. (Approximately 9,400 firms did not return their permit applications.)
5	11,000	○	○	●	●	●	EPA's estimate of the number of applicants included in item 4 that actually require a permit. (In reviewing the permit applications, EPA has estimated thus far that about 3,600 of the applicants will not require a permit under present rules.)
6	9,600	○	○	●	●		EPA's estimate of the total number of firms included in item 5 that only store or treat wastes (including incinerators).
7	1,400	○	○	○	○	●	EPA's estimate of the total number of firms included in item 5 that dispose of wastes as well as possibly store or treat them.

Activities

● Activities that are primary focus of estimate
○ Other activities in which firms included in estimate could also be engaged

Gn — generation
Tp — transportation
St — storage
Tr — treatment
Ds — disposal

Source: U.S. Environmental Protection Agency

ment. For the time being, the information from the permit application process appears to be the best available. This is the information used below, along with the results of some special studies that have been undertaken over the past several years.

Waste Generation

It is often difficult to determine whether a particular substance presents a hazard to human health. This problem is even more complicated with respect to hazardous wastes, which vary widely in composition and concentration. Thus, the definition of what constitutes hazardous waste varies from study to study. The hazardous waste provisions of RCRA cover any wastes that are ignitable, corrosive, reactive, or toxic.[8] EPA has developed a more detailed definition.[9]

A study conducted for EPA estimates that about 41 million metric tons of industrial hazardous waste were generated in the United States during 1980 (figure 4.2).[10]* This is equivalent to approximately 400 pounds per person. The estimate does not include wastes from many sources—such as mining, nuclear generators, government facilities, or small generators—that, in total, produce substantial amounts of potentially hazardous waste. For instance, the study did not cover some 700,000 establishments that produce less than a metric ton of wastes per month.[12] The two largest hazardous waste producers covered were the chemical industry (producing 62 percent of the total) and the primary metals industry (10 percent).[13] The four regions of the country generating the most waste—over three-fourths of the total—were the Middle Atlantic, Great Lakes, Southeast, and South Central (figure 4.3).

The amount of hazardous waste being generated is probably increasing, but no one knows how fast. With the implementation of air and water pollution control programs, there has been a rapid increase in sludges created by such pollution control devices as wastewater treatment plants and stack scrubbers. Many of these sludges contain hazardous substances. During the past decade, the largest producer of hazardous wastes, the chemical industry, grew significantly faster than the average growth rate of the rest of U.S. industry. It should also be noted, however, that two factors may

---

*EPA often uses a figure of 57 million metric tons (over 550 pounds per person) as the amount of industrial hazardous waste generated in 1980.[11] The authors of the study cited could not be confident that the correct number was 41 million metric tons, but were very confident that it fell between 27 and 54 million metric tons.

Figure 4.2
Hazardous Waste Generation by Industry, 1980

Standard Industrial Classification (SIC)	Industry	Quantity (wet weight in thousand metric tons)	Percent[2]
28	Chemicals and allied products	25,509	61.9
33	Primary metal industries	4,061	9.8
29	Petroleum and coal products	2,119	5.1
34	Fabricated metal products	1,997	4.8
—	Non-manufacturing industries[1]	1,971	4.8
26	Paper and allied products	1,295	3.1
37	Transportation equipment	1,240	3.0
36	Electrical and electronic equipment	1,093	2.7
31	Leather and leather tanning	474	1.1
35	Machinery, except electrical	322	0.8
39	Miscellaneous manufacturing industries	318	0.8
30	Rubber and miscellaneous plastic products	249	0.6
22	Textile mill products	203	0.5
27	Printing and publishing	154	0.4
38	Instruments and related products	90	0.2
24	Lumber and food products	87	0.2
25	Furniture and fixtures	36	0.09
32	Stone, clay and glass products	17	0.04
Total		41,235	100.0

[1]SIC 5085-Drum reconditioners, SIC 07-Agricultural services, SIC 5161-Chemical warehouses, SIC 40-Railroad transportation, SIC 55-Automotive dealers and gasoline service stations, SIC 72-Personal services, SIC 73-Business services, SIC 76-Miscellaneous repair services, SIC 80-Health services, SIC 82-Educational services.

[2]Figures do not add to total because of rounding.

Source: U.S. Environmental Protection Agency

be slowing the increase: many individual firms have reduced their generation of hazardous waste; some of the major waste-producing industries have grown relatively slowly (see chapter 1).

Treatment and Disposal Practices

EPA estimates that from 1973 through 1975 over 80 percent of the hazardous waste generated by industry was disposed of on land; another 15 percent was incinerated.[14]

Land disposal includes landfills (in which wastes are covered with earth), impoundments (in which solids are allowed to settle out of a predominantly liquid waste stream, and some natural decomposition of the waste may occur), underground injection (in which liquid wastes are pumped deep into the ground, where they are less likely to contaminate usable groundwater supplies), and land treatment (where the waste is mixed with a layer of soil, allowing natural decomposition to occur).

Many impoundments are apparently used primarily for storing and treating wastes, with the wastes subsequently being removed for disposal. Wastes can be treated by a variety of physical (settle-

Figure 4.3

Industrial Hazardous Waste Generation, by EPA Region, 1980
(in thousand metric tons, wet weight)

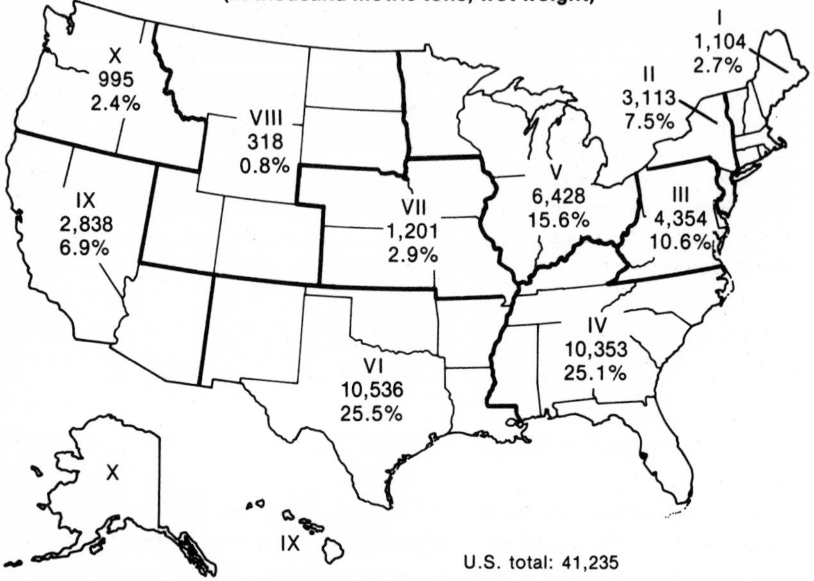

X
995
2.4%

VIII
318
0.8%

I
1,104
2.7%

II
3,113
7.5%

V
6,428
15.6%

III
4,354
10.6%

IX
2,838
6.9%

VII
1,201
2.9%

IV
10,353
25.1%

VI
10,536
25.5%

X

IX

U.S. total: 41,235

Due to rounding, the sum of individual state totals exceeds the estimated U.S. total.
Source: U.S. Environmental Protection Agency

ment, filtration, evaporation), chemical, or biological methods to reduce their bulk or toxicity. Incineration, which attempts to destroy wastes by subjecting them to very high temperatures in a controlled manner for a specified length of time, can also be considered a form of waste treatment. Wastes may be stored not only in impoundments, but in cans (for very small amounts of waste), drums, barrels, tanks, or waste piles.

More than three-fourths of industrial hazardous waste is estimated to be treated or disposed of by generators on their own property.[15] Much of this waste probably goes into surface impoundments—one study estimates that about half of the potentially hazardous industrial waste generated is put into surface impoundments[16]—although there are no national data on techniques used by generators who dispose of their own waste.

A 1980 report does describe the practices of commercial facilities, which handle just under a fourth of the volume of industrial hazardous waste. The largest amount of this waste is landfilled. A third of the total undergoes some type of chemical, biological, or physical treatment before being disposed of[17] (figure 4.4). The report esti-

Figure 4.4

Commercial Disposal Methods for Industrial Hazardous Waste, 1980

Disposal method	Estimated quantity (wet weight in thousand metric tons)	Percent
Landfill	2,699	37.5
Chemical, biological, and physical treatment[1]	2,346	32.6
Deep well injection	788	11.0
Land treatment/solar evaporation	537	7.5
Resource recovery	424	5.9
Incineration	398	5.5
Total	7,192	100.0

[1] This estimate includes a 10 percent residue which requires further processing, usually by landfill.

Source: U.S. Environmental Protection Agency

mated that the capacity of commercial facilities in 1981 would be about twice the national demand for commercial treatment and disposal, but noted several difficulties with making such a projection.[18] In the first place, the capacity is not evenly distributed throughout the United States: there are already shortages in five regions—New England, the Great Lakes area, the Plains states, the Northern Mountain states, and the Northwest. Transportation costs make it difficult to shift waste to areas with excess capacity, such as the South. Second, the demand estimates do not cover some wastes—sludges from pollution control devices, for example, or cleanup from spills—that might be placed in commercial sites. Third, the amount of waste going to commercial facilities may change if firms generating waste modify their production processes or decide to dispose of more or less of their wastes in their own facilities. In addition, EPA can affect the amount of demand by changing its definition of what wastes are hazardous and by the criteria it adopts for determining whether disposal facilities are adequate.

Each of the different waste disposal methods creates health and environmental risks. Landfills and impoundments can contaminate groundwater and surface water (see chapter 3) and may create air pollutants. Incinerators can emit hazardous air pollutants (see chapter 2). One EPA report found that over 90 percent of potentially hazardous industrial waste was disposed of with inadequate environmental protection.[19]

The Number of Sites

Until the passage of the Resource Conservation and Recovery Act (RCRA), there was no nationwide attempt to keep track of sites used for hazardous waste disposal. There is no way of knowing how many sites there were—or are—though estimates in one study place the number at 32,000 to 50,000 (figure 4.5).[20] EPA has identified 9,000 to 11,000 inactive sites, in addition to the 11,000 active sites listed in figure 4.1.[21]

Of the active facilities that will require permits, EPA estimates that about four-fifths are involved only in treating or storing wastes

Figure 4.5

Estimates of Hazardous Waste Sites in the United States

Item	Number of sites	Status of sites — Operating	Status of sites — Inactive	Description
1	32,000 to 50,000	●	●	Estimates of the number of hazardous waste disposal sites in a 1979 EPA sponsored study.
2	1,200 to 2,000 22,000 to 34,000	●	●	Two estimates of the number of sites in item 1 which may pose significant health and/or environmental problems.
3	1,400	●		EPA's estimate of the total number of disposal facilities that have applied for and require permits under current rules implementing RCRA (see figure 4.1).
4	5,000 to 6,000	●		Number of industrial impoundment sites that may contain potentially hazardous wastes identified in a study conducted by EPA in association with state authorities.
5	127	●		Number of commercial disposal sites identified in a 1980 EPA sponsored study.
6	9,000 to 11,000		●	Number of inactive sites that EPA had identified as of April, 1982.
7	400		●	Number of sites that can be given a top priority designation for cleanup under Superfund between 1981 and 1985.
8	115		●	Number of sites EPA has designated as being of highest priority for cleanup under Superfund as of March, 1982.

Source: U.S. Environmental Protection Agency, *et al.*

(for more than 90 days), and the remaining one-fifth in disposing of them (many in addition to treating or storing waste).[22] Most of these facilities are owned and operated by the waste generators. An independent study conducted for EPA identified only 127 commercial facilities.[23]

The applications for permits under RCRA are beginning to indicate the types of facilities that plan to operate in the future. Although the figures are still not complete, EPA estimated in April 1982 that, among the facilities requiring RCRA permits, woulc be at least 400 incinerators, 530 landfills, and 150 injection wells.[24] The great majority of these facilities are run by waste generators. The independent study of commercial facilities found 25 incinerators, 44 landfills, and 9 injection wells.[25]

Firms have applied for RCRA interim permits for 1,850 impoundment sites, but, according to the applications, more than 80 percent of these sites are used solely to store and treat wastes; only about 350 impoundment sites are used for waste disposal.[26] The results of an EPA study of waste impoundments suggest that these numbers may be low. That study, using a broader definition of hazardous, identified 5,000 to 6,000 impoundments that may contain potentially hazardous industrial wastes.[27]

Many disposal sites may be creating serious risks. One study attempting to estimate the number of sites that may pose "a significant threat to public health and/or the environment" concluded that this number could be anywhere from 1,200 to 34,000,[28] depending on the estimation technique used. The lower estimates, 1,200 to 2,000, were based on an assumption that 4 percent of all sites may pose a problem.* The higher estimates, 22,000 to 34,000, were derived using EPA estimates that 90 percent of all sites had inadequate environmental protection, and 75 percent of landfill sites are located on or near wetlands, major aquifers, or floodplains. Many of the sites, like Love Canal, were used for waste disposal many years ago. EPA has identified 115 sites as being of highest priority for remedial action under its "Superfund" program because of the risk of air, surface water, or groundwater contamination, the toxicity of the wastes, and the potential for human exposure (figure 4.6).

Very little is known about the environmental controls being used at generator-owned sites, although a study of impoundments found that "over 70 percent of the industrial impoundments are unlined,

---

*The 4 percent figure was apparently based on estimates provided by EPA regional offices.

Figure 4.6

Hazardous Waste Sites With Highest Priority for Remedial Action Under Superfund Program, 1981

Washington
Tacoma

California
Glen Avon
Keswick
Rancho
Cordova

Utah
Salt Lake City

Arizona
Phoenix

Colorado
Denver

New Mexico
Church Rock
Clovis
Milan

North Dakota
Rural south-
eastern corner

South Dakota
Deadwood

Kansas
Arkansas City

Oklahoma
Criner
Ottawa County

Texas
Crosby
Grand Prairie
La Marque

Minnesota
Andover
Oakdale
St. Louis Park
St. Paul

Iowa
Council Bluffs

Missouri
Ellisville
Springfield

Arkansas
Ft. Smith
Jacksonville
Mena
Walnut Ridge

Michigan
St. Louis

Illinois
Waukegan

Kentucky
Brooks

Tennessee
Memphis

Mississippi
Greenville

Indiana
Bloomington
Seymour

Alabama
Triana

Ohio
Ashtabula
Cleveland
Deerfield
Hamilton

Georgia
Athens

Maine
Winthrop

New Hampshire
Epping
Kingston
Nashua

Vermont
Burlington

Massachusetts
Ashland
North
Dartmouth
Tyngsborough
Woburn

Rhode Island
Burrillville
Coventry
Smithfield

Connecticut
Naugatuck

New York
Batavia
Elmira
Niagara Falls
Olean
Oswego
Oyster Bay
Philipstown
Wheatfield

Delaware
Delaware City
New Castle
Red Lion

Maryland
Baltimore

Washington, D.C.

Pennsylvania
Bruin
Buffalo
Chester
Girard
McAdoo
Natrona
Heights
Old Forge
Pittston

New Jersey
Bridgeport
Edison
Elizabeth
Freehold
Hamilton
Marlboro
Monmouth
County
Pitman
Pleasantville
Plumsted

Virginia
West of Salem
York County

West Virginia
Point Pleasant

North Carolina
Highway
dumping in
fourteen
counties

South Carolina
South of
Columbia

Florida
Between
Alford and
Cottondale
Clermont
Davie
Ft. Lauderdale
Galloway
Hialeah
Jacksonville
Miami
Pensacola
Tampa
Warrington
Whitehouse
Zellwood

States not included in survey: Alaska, Hawaii, Idaho, Louisiana, Montana, Nebraska, Nevada, Oregon, Wisconsin, Wyoming

Source: U.S. Environmental Protection Agency

potentially allowing contaminants to infiltrate unimpeded into the subsurface," and "nearly 95 percent of the sites are virtually un-monitored as to possible ground-water contamination."[29] A review conducted by the General Accounting Office (GAO) of 230 interim status permit applications showed that many sites were probably not in compliance with EPA's interim regulations, and GAO inspection of 38 operating sites found that over three-fourths of the facilities "had violations of the interim status regulations and/or significant operating problems."[30]

PROSPECTS AND ISSUES

There are several reasons why we should begin to see improvements in the hazardous waste situation. Broad public recognition of the problem has resulted in legislative authority to control all aspects of hazardous waste management, from creation to disposal. The federal government and many states have taken steps to identify the wastes being produced and the facilities that are handling them, and are planning for future needs. Many larger companies and some smaller ones have assessed their hazardous waste management practices and begun to improve them. The chemical industry alone plans to spend $10 billion to improve its overall waste management practices in the next five years.[31]

However, the federal government has been very slow in implementing programs to deal effectively with hazardous waste problems. Some of the basic regulations to control hazardous wastes have not been completed. It is not clear to what extent private initiatives will continue to change the prevailing practice from "dumping" to "managing" hazardous wastes, given the lack of an effective federal program.

The following discussion considers three basic issues. What are we going to do about existing disposal sites? Where are we going to locate new sites to manage and dispose of hazardous waste? How rapidly can we adopt alternatives to leaving wastes in landfills or lagoons for future generations to deal with?

The issues are closely interrelated. The more aggressively we attempt to control risks from existing sites, the more pressure there is likely to be for new sites. And the more successful we are in developing new technologies for detoxifying or destroying hazardous waste, the less need there will be for special disposal sites. The issues are also closely linked because of budgetary constraints. EPA and state hazardous waste authorities have to operate with severely limited budgets, in terms of both money and staff. The more attention EPA and the states pay to existing sites, the less they will be able to focus on solving problems related to creating new sites. But, if focus is put principally on new sites, the risks associated with current and past disposal practices will continue to grow.

Existing Facilities

There are limited resources available to clean up hazardous waste sites that are no longer being used and to upgrade facilities still in operation. A GAO study has noted examples of the kinds of problems that can be found at currently operating sites.[32] At one site, for example, it noted chromium lead sludge being dumped into a wetland and at another facility an incinerator burning PCBs without adequate monitoring and control over disposal of the residue.

Identifying and correcting problems can be very difficult and expensive. A review of 180 remedial actions taken to correct problems at 169 different sites indicated that almost half of these actions resulted in no improvement. About 38 percent of the actions resulted in some improvement. But only 16 percent of all the actions were rated effective in solving the problem. Insufficient funds and inadequate corrective measures apparently explain most of the failures.[33]

A couple of examples dramatically illustrate the magnitude of the expenditures that may be required to correct hazardous waste problems. One company spent $7 million to remove and burn wastes it had placed in unlined pits and continues to spend $95,000 a year to operate barrier wells to prevent further groundwater contamination.[34] The estimated costs of correcting a mercury pollution problem at a now-closed chlorine manufacturing plant are $23 million.[35]

Impoundments, used to store nearly half the potentially hazardous wastes generated by the largest waste-producing industries in the United States, present a major problem.[36] To reduce releases to the environment, many of these facilities would have to be retrofitted with impermeable liners and a comprehensive system to detect and remove leachate.* These steps would be expensive and might cause additional damage as wastes were being moved. In some cases, plants might have to close during retrofitting because the impoundments

---

*Leachate is water that has percolated through the wastes and may have become contaminated as a result.

are an integral part of the plant. Without liners, however, ground-water contamination may occur, and it is essentially impossible to eliminate that contamination thereafter.

Landfills present similar difficulties. Although new sections of a landfill can be lined, older sections that have had no clay or synthetic liners will continue to pose problems. The owners can attempt to remove the waste and dispose of it elsewhere, create some form of barrier to contain the waste at the existing site, or install seepage collection systems to make sure that contaminants do not migrate from the site. There is some potential for treating existing landfills using biological or chemical techniques, but only if the chemicals already in the landfills are known. If there is room for expansion at a site, liners and leachate collection systems can be installed in the new sections and the inadequately contained wastes transferred there. Engineering measures usually cannot overcome the problems presented by a site located in a marsh or otherwise directly connected to groundwater.

Incinerators may in many cases be upgraded more easily by such means as adding suitable emission control equipment and moni-toring to assure proper temperatures and mixing, and lowered emis-sions. However, if the incinerator is located near a heavily populated area, the types of wastes burned need to be carefully considered.

The Role of Government

Two laws provide authority for the federal government to require cleanup of sites that are no longer being used or upgrading of currently operating facilities. The Comprehensive Environmental Response, Compensation, and Liability Act (known as the "Super-fund") focuses primarily on remedial action at sites no longer in use, while the Resource Conservation and Recovery Act (RCRA) addresses improvement at currently operating facilities.

The Superfund was passed to allow broad governmental response to actual or threatened release of hazardous substances.* The law creates a Hazardous Substances Response Fund which, in the absence of a responsible site owner or waste generator, pays for the costs of cleaning up. Otherwise, the site owner or waste generator must clean up the site or reimburse the fund for doing so. The $1.6 billion fund is financed mainly by a tax on oil and chemicals.

---

*The Superfund Act covers accidental spills of hazardous substances as well as inactive storage, treatment, and disposal sites.

Although costs of monitoring and restoring the site and damage to public natural resources are covered by the Superfund, the law does not provide a basis to collect claims for private injuries to health or property. These must still be litigated under common law. The Superfund also includes a Post Closure Fund, which assumes liability for hazardous waste sites closed in accordance with RCRA procedures. This $200 million fund is financed by a tax on hazardous wastes received at permitted facilities.

Under RCRA, the federal government is setting standards for all phases of handling hazardous waste: generation, storage, transport, treatment, and disposal. The authority to run the RCRA program can be delegated to the states, and more than half the states have received some delegation of that authority. The original waste generator must get a permit to treat or dispose of its hazardous wastes or, alternatively, can ship them with a manifest identifying the substances, the company of origin, and their destination. Anyone transporting the waste must deliver it to the designated site, keep records, and report spills. The only sites where the wastes can be handled are those that meet the standards set by EPA and that hold a permit issued by EPA or a state agency.

So far, EPA has defined which wastes are hazardous and, with the Department of Transportation, has set up a manifest system that tracks waste from generator to facility operator. The manifest system covers about 60,000 generators and 14,000 transporters.[37] It does not apply to the 700,000 or so generators that produce less than one metric ton a month of hazardous waste. Nor do these smaller generators need to put their waste in a permitted facility. They may use a municipal landfill, unless either the state defines "small" more narrowly than EPA does or the firm generates one of the few wastes designated as acutely toxic.

RCRA requires that EPA regard all applicants for hazardous waste facility permits—whether commercial disposal facilities or firms handling their own waste—as though they have a permit until their application is reviewed. Under this "interim status," applicants may continue to operate, on the presumption that they are adhering to the agency's management requirements, which involve analysis of wastes, security precautions, inspection for and prevention of environmental or health hazards, plans to deal with emergencies, personnel training, maintenance records of wastes handled, and the development of plans for closing the facility.[38]

Additional regulations—covering technical operating, design, and construction standards—have been developed very slowly. Standards for storage of hazardous waste in containers, certain types of treatment, and incinerators were promulgated in January 1981. However, their implementation was deferred for existing surface impoundments and incinerators.[39] Interim regulations for land disposal have already missed several court-ordered deadlines.

More than half the states have laws allowing them to control existing hazardous waste facilities.[40] Most of these laws were passed after the enactment of RCRA, and in many cases the state laws and regulations are tied to federal law and regulations. (Thus, some states are awaiting EPA action.) Other states had active programs before RCRA was passed and have continued to implement these programs. All states with the necessary legislation, and ability to implement it, will have the primary authority for implementing RCRA regulations within their borders. They may also adopt more stringent rules if they desire.

State laws increasingly preempt local governments from regulating existing facilities. However, particularly in states that have no hazardous waste laws, localities can use their zoning authorities and health and nuisance laws to exert some control. In Illinois, one community has won a suit in the state supreme court allowing it to close a facility approved by the state and by EPA and to force removal of wastes brought into the site from outside the town's borders.[41]

The issue of what should be done about existing sites has two major components. The first is what to do about sites that are no longer in use. The second is what to do about sites that continue to be used. To a large extent, these components can be resolved independently of each other. However, they come into conflict in terms of how government resources should be allocated. With current budget constraints, there are neither sufficient people nor dollars available at the federal, state, or local level to deal with all existing hazardous waste sites as quickly or as thoroughly as might be desired.

Inactive Sites

As has been noted, there is no comprehensive list of all existing hazardous waste sites, and abandoned sites will probably continue to be found. The experience with Love Canal has demonstrated that, although it is extremely difficult to determine the actual health and environmental risks associated with sites no longer in use, many such sites clearly present serious potential risks. EPA has slowly begun to implement the Superfund statute directed at cleaning up these inactive sites, but has listed only 115 high priority sites for remedial action, far short of the 400 the statute calls for (see figure 4.5). EPA estimates that it may be able to deal only with about 15 percent of possibly 2,000 high-risk sites before the Superfund program is now scheduled to end (in 1986).[42]

What can be done to accelerate the effort to clean up inactive sites? First of all, EPA or state authorities could devote more resources to identifying and evaluating high-risk sites. This would require assembling all the information available on the 9,000 to 11,000 inactive sites that have already been identified (see figure 4.5), making field surveys to collect additional information when too little is known about the possible problems that may be associated with a site, and then evaluating the sites according to criteria such as probable toxicity of wastes, the likely intensity and extent of possible human or environmental exposures to those wastes, the extent to which any contamination caused by the sites is likely to be irreversible, and so forth. Undertaking a comprehensive assessment would be expensive in terms of staff resources, travel funds, and field and laboratory analyses, and might interfere with getting to work on the sites that have already been identified. But, without such an effort, some very serious problems may be missed, and cleanup efforts may be focused on sites that are not creating the greatest health and environmental problems.

As an alternative to this comprehensive approach, EPA could focus its full efforts initially on cleaning up the 115 sites it already has listed for priority action and, when this work has been completed, begin to address additional sites that it already knows about and that, on the basis of whatever information is available, appear to present potential risks. At its present level of activity, EPA is unlikely to be able to deal with more than 300 sites over the next five years, and spending substantial resources to evaluate the risk associated with more than 9,000 other inactive sites already identified by EPA is unlikely to speed things up.[43]

Another important question is what strategy to use in cleaning up inactive sites. One strategy is to concentrate government resources on identifying the facility owner or other responsible party in as many cases as possible and then attempt, through negotiation or legal action, to force these parties to clean the sites up. EPA would begin cleaning up a site only if no responsible party could be found. As an alternative, EPA could use some of its resources to begin cleaning up high-risk sites, while simultaneously searching for the responsible party in order to obtain reimbursement for the cleanup expenses incurred. The third option is for the government to undertake the cleanup action itself, without devoting substantial resources and efforts to identifying and seeking reimbursement from the private parties.

The first of these strategic options would result in the least depletion of the Hazardous Substances Response Fund, the special fund established to clean up old sites. However, it would probably have a larger impact on EPA's normal operating budget, and would likely delay—sometimes substantially—the initiation of remedial actions. The second option would result in a faster depletion of the response fund, but would presumably result in its subsequently being reimbursed. The third option would result in fast depletion without subsequent reimbursement.

Under the first option, the sites creating the greatest risks might not be the ones cleaned up first. EPA's cleanup efforts would be concentrated only on the sites for which no responsible party could be found, and these sites might or might not be creating the greatest risks. As to those sites for which responsible parties are identified, it is unclear how quickly cleanup would proceed. One problem is that EPA has been unwilling or unable to establish cleanup standards. The lack of such standards could well result in extended negotiations on cleanup plans and leave these plans vulnerable to court suits.

The second option would probably result in faster action on the most serious sites, with action on the less serious sites delayed until the response fund is replenished. This option would avoid the problem of delaying the initiation of the cleanup efforts until the cleanup standard could be agreed to, because the agency could establish appropriate standards on a case-by-case basis. However, the responsible parties might subsequently contest these standards and attempt to avoid reimbursing the trust fund for the full cleanup costs.

The third option would have the same benefit of speed as the second, but would result in less overall cleanup over the longer run, since the Superfund would be quickly depleted without subsequent reimbursement.

There are some major obstacles to taking swift action on cleaning up sites that are no longer used. Defining the degree of risk presented by a site can be very difficult and expensive. So is deciding both what type of action to take to remedy the problem and what is adequate cleanup. Because sites differ so greatly, setting a standard for "how clean is clean" is not easy. These obstacles argue for moving more slowly in trying to clean up old sites.

However, there are probably greater costs associated with proceeding too slowly. People will continue to be exposed to potentially very risky situations. Some of the contamination that is allowed to occur may be impossible to correct; when subsequent correction is possible, it may be substantially more expensive than containing the problem in the first place. Excessive delay is also likely to result in substantial political pressure, and possibly court suits, as the public becomes frustrated with the government's apparent inability to respond in a reasonable way to situations like Love Canal.

Currently Operating Facilities

Under the RCRA permitting program, EPA is identifying currently operating disposal facilities and the parties responsible for them. As the process continues, more will be learned about which of these sites are creating the greater potential risks and about what remedial action should be undertaken.

However, there is no special response fund established to deal with currently operating facilities. This means that any government activity has to be paid for out of very tight normal operating budgets. Moreover, aggressively regulating these facilities could, in some localities or regions, result in insufficient treatment and disposal capacity. These capacity problems could, in turn, lead to increased uncontrolled dumping or create serious problems for waste generators.

EPA has not completed regulations that establish environmental standards for currently operating facilities. Facilities are being operated on the basis of "interim permits." Should attention be focused on developing and implementing final regulations? Or should a more gradual approach to upgrading be pursued?

Focusing immediately on final regulations would entail devoting substantial resources to research, analyses, and other activities required to support development of such regulations. Until these regulations took effect, little would be done to upgrade currently operating facilities, and, given the budget constraints facing all levels of government, there would be limited ability to enforce even the minimal operating requirements already in place.

Adopting a more gradual approach would involve tightening

existing requirements in stages over a period of years. Under this approach, fewer resources would initially have to be devoted to developing regulations, and more could be devoted to enforcing existing regulations.

The approach emphasizing development of final regulations might result in all operating facilities achieving a uniformly high level of control sooner than they would under the gradual approach. The gradual approach would eliminate the most risky sites early on, allowing sites of intermediate risk to continue to operate longer.

The gradual approach offers several advantages: regulatory activity would not outstrip the ability of regulatory authorities to implement and enforce the rules; there would be less of a risk that the regulations do not have an adequate scientific or technical basis; and the final regulations could be fully sensitive to the diversity of situations and conditions that actually exist. Attempting to develop more rigorous final standards too quickly can create problems in all these respects.

No matter which approach is taken, sites will have to be dealt with according to some kind of priority. Priority could be given to sites that handle the greatest volume of wastes, to sites that handle the most dangerous wastes, to sites located near large population centers or above groundwater used for drinking. The difficulty of using any one of these criteria is that no single factor is a good indication of the risk from a site. And any extensive effort to assess combinations of these factors can be difficult, expensive, and time consuming.

An alternative might be to issue permits to the safer sites first. For instance, landfills using liners, collecting leachate, and monitoring groundwater that were located away from environmentally sensitive areas could be issued permits fairly quickly. This approach would probably speed up the issuance of permits at the beginning of the process, ensure that relatively safe disposal capacity was available, reduce uncertainty for operators about how permitting would be handled, and might stimulate more rapid upgrading of facilities. Steps could then be taken to close facilities providing less environmental protection, thus encouraging use of safer facilities.* It would be important to involve local citizens extensively in the permitting process to ensure that their concerns were taken into account.

---

*Incentives might also be offered to encourage the use of the safer sites as soon as they are issued final permits.

Conclusions

At the present time, many states are waiting for the federal government to issue standards for existing hazardous waste facilities before implementing their own program. Clearly, however, the problem is bigger than EPA can handle alone, particularly with its current stringent budget constraints. Thus, one set of questions the agency must address is which actions can best be undertaken at the federal level and which can be delegated to the states or to the private sector. The implementation of Superfund cannot be delegated, because this is a federal trust fund and because the delegation would require some necessarily arbitrary allocation of available funds among the states. It is unlikely that any such allocation formulas would be directly proportional to need. The states can, however, help substantially in identifying and evaluating sites that are no longer in use.

States could also take over many of the responsibilities of dealing with currently operating sites, allowing EPA to focus on regulatory development, research, and technical assistance. Some of this responsibility could also be placed directly on the private sector. For instance, currently operating facilities could be required to collect information and conduct analyses that would help to identify serious problems. The Reagan Administration is attempting to minimize such burdens on the private sector (see chapter 9). However, given the potential seriousness of the problems and the limited resources available to deal with them, it may be only reasonable and equitable to ask the private sector to pick up a larger share of the costs and responsibilities.

Siting New Facilities

We now know how to build much safer hazardous waste facilities than were built in the past. But widespread public recognition of the potential dangers of hazardous waste and of the often poor practices at many old facilities have created widespread fear and strong public opposition to most proposals for locating new sites. While this opposition may encourage efforts to reduce or recycle wastes, some wastes will continue to be generated and have to be disposed of. If we do not develop enough additional well-designed sites to handle hazardous wastes, we may provoke uncontrolled dumping. Some manufacturers also fear that a lack of sites could close down some of their plants.

The Demand for New Sites

As indicated earlier, there already appears to be a shortage of commercial hazardous waste disposal capacity in some regions, and transportation costs and the differences in types of waste make it difficult to shift waste to areas with excess capacity.

The next few years may see an increased demand for new commercial facilities. Many currently operating sites (both commercial and generator owned) might not meet strict environmental protection standards. As the Resource Conservation and Recovery Act is implemented, some of these sites may be required to close, and nearby facilities will be needed to replace them. Similarly, implementing and enforcing RCRA's permit/manifest system should reduce the amount of "illegal" dumping that has occurred, adding additional demands for new commercial disposal capacity. And, finally, cleaning up abandoned sites under the Superfund program will, in some cases, involve removing hazardous materials from the old site and disposing of them safely elsewhere, increasing the demand for new sites even further.

Industry's response to tougher disposal requirements is a major factor affecting demand. Firms can sometimes substantially reduce the amount of wastes generated by modifying manufacturing processes, using different, less hazardous materials, or by finding beneficial uses for some of the materials they formerly discarded. Another factor affecting the number of new sites is the rate of growth in industrial production. The method used for disposal is also important: some methods reduce the volume of waste; others can sufficiently reduce toxicity to allow the waste to be disposed of in normal landfills. If large facilities are developed, fewer sites will be needed. California, for example, estimates it would need only three sites for large regional facilities to handle high priority wastes. Alternatively, perhaps seven new sites and some expansion of existing sites would be needed if smaller, more localized facilities were built—or if sites specialized in specific types of waste.[44] The distance wastes need to be transported must also be considered.

Desirable Site Characteristics

With hundreds of millions of acres of vacant land in the United States, there would seem to be plenty of opportunities for siting new hazardous waste facilities. However, several factors can severely limit the number of potential sites.

One of these is proximity to people. The potential health risks associated with hazardous waste disposal—from explosion, spillage, seepage into drinking water supplies—are reduced if sites are not located near where people live, work, or spend their leisure time. For the same reasons, the risk is reduced if major transportation routes to commercial facilities avoid residential and commercial neighborhoods as well as roads not built for heavy vehicles.

On the other hand, transportation costs and the possibility of accidents in transit argue for not siting facilities at great distances from the sources of the wastes. Transportation can account for 20 to 80 percent of disposal costs.[45] Thus, the best locations for facilities would be areas that are far enough away from people to provide relatively little risk, but close enough to the waste generators to keep the transportation costs low.

The environmental characteristics of the site are also important. To avoid groundwater contamination, landfills should be located away from areas where the groundwater aquifer is near the surface, and there should be a layer of soil with low permeability, such as clay, between the disposal site and the groundwater. To lessen the possibility of surface water contamination, the site should not be located in a floodplain, and runoff from rainfall should not flow through the site. To minimize risks associated with air pollution, particularly with incinerators, care must be taken that prevailing winds will not carry emissions toward population concentrations.

Public Opposition

Beyond these technical criteria, public opposition is probably the primary obstacle to establishing new hazardous waste facilities or expanding existing ones. The possible health problems associated with living near the Love Canal and other such sites have created a strong fear among much of the general public. This fear is commonly expressed by aggressive citizen action opposing proposed sites, by court suits, and by enactment of local or state laws prohibiting the establishment of new sites. Banning wastes imported from other states has been ruled unconstitutional, but a state-run facility may be able to refuse to handle these wastes.[46]

Much of the public's fear probably stems from uncertainty. To reiterate, there is a real paucity of information available about hazardous waste. While there is some information about the frequency of groundwater contamination and about the effects of long-term exposure to individual chemicals, little is known about the risks associated with the mixtures found in industrial wastes. And, too many times in the past, no one has known exactly what substances were being disposed of, so there was no way of determining how much of a hazard they presented. It can be very difficult for individuals to find out how much they, their families, or their descendants might actually be exposed, and to what substances. All of these factors, combined with the fact that by the time some of the more serious potential health effects are observed it is too late to take any corrective action, combine to make hazardous waste facilities appear very frightening, and to inhibit the kind of dialogue that would lead to informed choices of sites designed and operated to prevent environmental and health problems.

Nor are the risks of living near a site necessarily offset by any economic benefits, unless the facility is operated by the waste generator. Hazardous waste facilities seldom provide many jobs directly. Taxes derived from these facilities may not cover the heavy demands put on roads and emergency services. If the site is a commercial facility taking wastes from a broad area, it may not even be seen as supporting local industries or encouraging development of new industries that would employ residents and pay substantial taxes. In such cases, the community may strongly resent the prospect of becoming the "dump" for other people's wastes. Fear spills over into concern about residential property values.

A recent public opinion poll found that only 5 percent of the respondents did not care how close a hazardous waste disposal site was to their home. The remaining 95 percent responded that they would "want to move to another place or to actively protest" such a site.[47] A study of 21 operating or planned hazardous waste facilities reported public opposition at all but one.[48] There are few issues that can generate such a depth and breadth of public concern.

Strong laws are now on the books, but given the many reported problems, citizens do not have confidence that these laws will, in fact, result in sites near their homes being operated in a way that protects their community's health and environment.

The Role of Government

While the federal government focuses on the conditions for acceptable sites and the standards they must meet, state governments have taken the lead in determining how sites are to be selected. At least 20 states have enacted statutes dealing with the siting of new hazardous waste facilities. These statutes typically require a state hazardous waste plan, a means of providing public participation, a way of resolving disagreement about a site, and may provide some assistance to private facility owners.[49]

The state hazardous waste plans usually include inventories of the amounts and types of wastes being generated, a survey of the facilities available to handle the wastes, an estimate of the number and type of facilities likely to be needed in the future, and, in some cases, a list of areas that may be technically suited for new facilities. In most states, these plans are being prepared by existing environmental or health protection agencies, but several states (for instance, Michigan, Minnesota, and Utah) have established special boards or committees for this purpose.

Different states have adopted a variety of measures for ensuring adequate public participation in the siting decision. Over 18 states require that a public hearing be held near the proposed site. Some states include local representatives on the state siting board, and a few (for instance, Florida, Massachusetts, and Nebraska) require a local board to review the proposal and make recommendations on the site.

Even with thorough planning and substantial public participation, strong disagreements can arise about the desirability of a proposed facility and the suitability of a proposed site. In 17 states, the state has the final authority for making these decisions. Eight states (for instance, Colorado, Kentucky, and New York) allow local authorities a veto power. A few states also explicitly provide for citizen suits, though the courts will often become involved even in the absence of such a provision.

Most of the state laws are concerned primarily with regulating the siting of hazardous wastes facilities; few provide financial assistance to owners of facilities. Where such assistance is provided, it can take the form of making use of eminent domain authority or allowing access to tax-free financing. Some states (for instance, Florida and Ohio) have special assistance provisions for facilities involved in resource recovery. And 13 states provide for state ownership of waste-handling facilities.

Possible Approaches

Most states currently leave actual siting problems to the private sector. A company selects a site that meets its needs—one it already owns or can buy at a good price, has adequate transportation, and is convenient to potential users—and then obtains the necessary permits and informs local officials. The state or federal role is limited to reviewing information provided by the firm to insure that it satisfies state and federal requirements. There is usually no independent collection or analysis of information. This approach puts few demands on government resources, but it also limits the state's ability to assist the firm attempting to find a site, or to help a local community assess potential problems. Until recently, this approach has worked reasonably well (at least in locating new sites, if not in providing environmental protection). Because of increased public concern, it may work less well in the future.

Some states play a role in planning and facilitating the development of hazardous waste facilities through such actions as making detailed inventories of the wastes produced and of the availability and quality of potential disposal sites in the region. This information, along with siting criteria, is then incorporated into a state plan. When a firm proposes a site, the state may check the firm's previous record and gather its own data on the suitability of the site. The state may go further and provide assistance to the firm through public financing or bonding authority, by streamlining the permit process, or by using its power of eminent domain to make the appropriate site available.

State planning has the advantage of allowing state officials to evaluate proposed facilities independently in relation to the state's needs for a site and the availability of alternative sites. This kind of active state role obviously requires more resources than would a passive role, and may create conflicts between the state and communities, and, within the state government, between the dual roles of promoting and regulating facilities.

In other countries, hazardous waste facilities are publicly owned and operated. This approach is commonly also used in the United States for other solid waste disposal sites. Locating facilities on existing public lands may avoid some of the conflicts with local landowners and communities. The public might conceivably be more trusting of a publicly owned and operated facility than of one under private ownership, because, in the former, long-term ownership is assumed. If private operation is more efficient, the government may be able to have a private company operate the facility under government supervision.

Any level of government—federal, state, regional, or local—could take this approach, although the high risks and sometimes complicated technologies involved would probably exclude all but the larger local governments. Thirteen states already have laws providing for state ownership and control. Government ownership can be self-supporting by charging for the services it provides and avoid the net budgetary impacts of closely regulating private disposal. On the other hand, public ownership can accentuate the conflict-of-interest problems that arise when government is both promoter and regulator. It can also result in having many primarily technical issues resolved in a political forum.

Alternatives to Land Disposal

The primary method of handling hazardous waste in the United States has been land disposal—that is, putting the waste into surface impoundments or landfills or injecting it into deep wells. But this method of disposal does not solve the problem. It only stores and, it is hoped, contains it. The wastes usually retain their toxicity, and future site disturbances, although they should be less likely with RCRA in force, may result in significant human or environmental exposure. The sites receiving the most public attention, like Love Canal, have usually involved land disposal methods of handling waste.

There are three general alternatives to simple land disposal: (1) reduction and reuse; (2) physical, chemical, and biological treatment; and (3) incineration. They are not disposal methods, but rather methods of treating hazardous waste to reduce its volume or toxicity before the residue is put in a landfill.

Waste reduction can take several forms. Different raw materials can be substituted for those that create a serious hazardous waste problem. For example, one company developed a chloride metal-plating process that eliminates the need for cyanide baths.[50] Or the manufacturing process can be modified to use less of a material or to reuse materials. A Baltimore plant, which has generated over 200,000 tons of chrome wastes annually, is installing a process change that is expected to reduce these wastes by 40 percent.[51]

With higher disposal costs, recycling both within a plant and after the waste leaves a plant may become more attractive. Sometimes this potential is very high; for example, an estimated 95 percent of wastes in pharmaceuticals and 40 percent in paints and allied products can be recycled.[52] Solvent recycling is expected to grow from a $200 million to a $1 billion a year business in the next five years.[53] Around 30 waste exchanges, clearinghouses that operate on the principle that one firm's waste may be another's raw material, are now in operation in the United States. They exchange about 10 percent of the wastes listed as available. European exchanges are transferring 30 to 40 percent of their listed wastes.[54]

One assessment lists at least 30 different physical, chemical, and biological processes for treating hazardous wastes.[55] Many of these are still in the development stage, but others are already widely used. About 30 percent of the hazardous waste handled at commercial facilities receives physical, chemical, or biological treatment.[56]

Physical processes separate hazardous materials from the rest of the waste, which can then be more readily disposed of. For instance, activated carbon adsorption can be used to remove pesticides; sedimentation or filtration, to remove suspended particles; flotation, to remove oils; and distillation, to remove other fluids from waste process water. Evaporation ponds are used to concentrate brines and sludges.

Some chemical processes can change the structure of a substance to make it less toxic or to aid other treatment or disposal methods. For example, adding precipitants to electroplating wastes hastens sedimentation. A neutralizing agent may be added to acids or alkaline wastes to adjust the pH level. Adding oxidants or catalysts to other types of wastes can promote detoxifying reactions.

Biological processes employing microorganisms can sometimes be used to decompose organic wastes into natural nontoxic substances such as water and carbon dioxide. This is the most common way of treating normal municipal sewage wastes and can be effective with some forms of organic hazardous wastes as well, such as those from textile mills and refineries. Scientists are developing special bacteria strains that can decompose not only wastes from pulp mills and refineries but even potentially highly toxic wastes associated with the manufacture of certain pesticides.

Incineration, which uses very high temperatures to decompose waste materials, is the third major alternative to simply using land for dumping waste. Of the approximately 15 percent of industrial hazardous wastes incinerated, only about a third are burned in "environmentally adequate" facilities.[57] EPA estimates about 60 percent of all U.S. hazardous wastes could be incinerated.[58] (The Netherlands incinerates half of its hazardous waste.[59]) To be effective, hazardous waste incineration requires a careful mixture of waste, oxygen, and supplemental fuel (if needed) to ensure continuous temperatures of 750^0 to $3,000^0$ F (different temperatures are required for different types of waste). Special incinerator ships can burn particularly dangerous wastes offshore, away from populated areas. A single ship may be able to dispose of as much as 200 thousand tons of liquid wastes a year.[60] And, in some cases, cement kilns can burn chemical wastes for fuels (EPA estimates that some states could destroy all of their chlorinated wastes in cement kilns).[61]

Figure 4.7 provides approximate costs for various waste management techniques. Specific costs will vary from situation to situation, but simple methods, such as land treatment and solar evaporation, are relatively inexpensive, while incineration and sophisticated chemical treatments are costly.

Alternative disposal techniques are generally more expensive than traditional methods. Considering only the direct costs may be misleading, however, for there may be offsetting savings. Methods that detoxify waste will allow the waste to be disposed of much less expensively and permanently eliminate its hazards—something that straight landfilling is unable to do. Changing raw materials or manufacturing processes may reduce manufacturing costs. Recycling can turn cost streams into revenue streams.

Alternative disposal techniques not only differ in cost, but sometimes in their health and environmental impacts as well. Very little is known about the potential risks associated with some of the newer

Figure 4.7
Reported Prices for Hazardous Waste Management Services, 1980

Waste management method	Dollars per metric ton
Landfill	
Wastes which are not acutely hazardous, including sludges	20-90
Highly toxic, explosive, or reactive wastes	100-400
Deep-well injection	
Oily wastewaters	15-40
Dilute toxic rinse waters	50-100
Resource recovery	50-200
Land treatment	5-25
Chemical treatment	
Acids, alkalines	15-80
Cyanides, heavy metals, highly toxic wastes	100-500
Incineration	
Wastes with high BTU value, presenting no acute hazard	50-300
Highly toxic, heavy metal wastes	300-1000

Prices are exclusive of transportation costs, which may represent 20-80% of the total costs of off-site disposal depending on the method of hauling and distance shipped.

Source: U.S. Environmental Protection Agency

techniques, such as biological treatment with special microorganisms. The main difficulty with the more traditional biological treatment is making sure sludge is disposed of properly. Several of the physical methods of separating wastes could cause air pollution—for example, if volatile substances are present in open ponds. Again, these techniques leave a residual sludge that must be disposed of. Chemical processes are also likely to have residues requiring further treatment or disposal, and some processes employ other highly toxic substances, such as chlorine gas, that must be handled carefully. Air pollution is a primary concern with incineration. Although some incinerators have succeeded in destroying 99.9999 percent of wastes, there may still be trace contaminants in the incinerator emissions.[62] (EPA's current standard is 99.99.)[63] Thus, all the alternative techniques require careful management. Under proper circumstances, however, most can significantly reduce the residual risks associated with waste after its disposal.

The Role of Government

The federal government has done little directly to encourage the adoption of alternative disposal techniques, except for sponsoring some research. EPA budgeted $3.4 million in 1980 to study technologies for managing waste streams, but this included work done on land disposal as well as other techniques.[64] If stringent federal disposal regulations are adopted, they should stimulate additional research and development by the private sector as it attempts to find cheaper or more effective alternatives. Widespread local opposition to landfills may also stimulate the search for alternatives.

Several of the states are taking a more active role than the federal government. California, for example, has developed a proposal to discourage use of landfills and to encourage other methods of dealing with hazardous wastes. After completing a study that found there was a suitable alternative to land disposal for three-fourths of the hazardous wastes generated in the state, California prepared a broad-ranging plan using regulations and various types of incentives to encourage use of these alternatives.[65] It is too early to determine how successful this effort will be.

Should other states or the federal government also attempt to do more? Their options range from simply depending on existing incentives to requiring that alternative methods be used for disposal of specific types of waste.

One option, of course, is to assume that RCRA regulations,

together with public opposition to landfills, will provide the incentive for private companies to develop new techniques. This seems to be the approach currently favored by all levels of government—state, local, and federal. Implementing the statutes may indirectly stimulate the private sector to develop and adopt alternative techniques by increasing the cost of land disposal. However, regulatory programs could slow the adoption of some alternatives, because these alternatives, too, would have to be approved. This approach has the advantage of requiring no government resources for developing new techniques, but it may be more costly in the longer run if government assistance could have substantially accelerated the use of less expensive disposal methods (in terms of their economic and health and environmental impacts).

Another option would be for the government to sponsor research on the potential health and environmental risks associated with different techniques, so that they could be adopted more quickly and more widely when their development is completed. An Office of Science and Technology panel report[66] has recommended, among other alternatives, working with small companies and companies that produce large amounts of waste or particularly toxic wastes to develop new waste reduction processes, conducting bench and field testing of the most promising new treatment techniques; and studying the operating characteristics required for the successful incineration of different types of wastes, developing safer air pollution control technology for incinerators, and evaluating the effectiveness of different types of incinerators.

Although this kind of research program might significantly speed up the development and adoption of safer and potentially lower cost disposal techniques, it would require a greater expenditure of government resources than would the first option. If not carefully planned, it could also discourage private sector research. There is also the danger that government research would not focus on problems of concern to particular companies, since waste problems differ significantly.

A third option is for the government to provide incentives that would encourage private firms—whether the generators themselves or commercial firms—to develop and use alternative treatment facilities. Administrative incentives might include streamlining permitting procedures for alternative facilities. Direct financial incentives might include low-interest loans, assistance in obtaining tax-exempt bonds, rapid amortization of equipment, providing low cost sites, and income guarantees. Landfill fees can be adjusted to provide indirect incentives. California, for instance, plans to establish higher landfill fees for highly toxic, persistent, or mobile wastes and for wastes that can be recycled.[67] Kentucky has initiated a tax on waste generators, with rates that give preference to use of incineration and chemical treatment.[68] All of these incentives could speed the process of adopting alternative treatment technologies, thereby saving landfill space for residues and wastes for which no alternatives exist.

Given public opposition to landfills, the incentive to develop other methods is already strong, so further incentives may not be necessary. There is also some dispute about how effective financial incentives really are in accomplishing their goals. Programs that reduce red tape, speed up the siting approval process, and otherwise provide administrative assistance are less costly, and may, in some instances, be as effective.

A fourth option would be for government to require the adoption of new techniques. An indirect regulatory approach would be to prohibit land disposal of specific wastes that are better handled using alternative techniques. California, for instance, is considering prohibiting land disposal of some highly toxic wastes, including various pesticides, PCBs, cyanides, toxic metals, halogenated organics, and nonhalogenated volatile organics.[69]

A direct regulatory approach would require that specific types of wastes be disposed of in specific ways. Using this approach, the regulatory authority could require solvents to be recycled, specific types of organic wastes to be detoxified with biological treatment, other specific types of wastes to be treated chemically, certain particularly toxic substances to be incinerated, and so forth. EPA has used this approach for the disposal of highly toxic polychlorinated biphenyls (PCBs). Materials containing high concentrations of PCBs can only be incinerated in specially approved facilities or treated in some other manner that accomplishes a like degree of destruction.[70] The stringency of these regulations may have helped stimulate private companies to develop several innovative chemical destruction techniques that are now coming into use.

The regulatory approach would likely stimulate more rapid adoption of the designated alternative technologies, although there is substantial controversy about whether it would stimulate or discourage the development of new technologies. To the extent that it does result in more rapid adoption of safer techniques, it can significantly lower the residual health and environmental risks, avoid potential future cleanup and liability costs, and conserve resources, including secure landfill capacity. That capacity will still be required, since some wastes cannot be treated by alternative techniques, and some can be handled with little risk and less cost in landfills.

A major disadvantage of the approach is that, being relatively insensitive to the subtleties of individual situations, the regulatory requirements cannot always be met, at least not without imposing large, and possibly excessive, costs on the waste generator. California estimates that using alternative treatment techniques for all high priority wastes may cost firms in that state an additional $20 to $30 million a year.[71] In such cases, this approach can actually increase risks if the generator decides to dispose of the waste illegally in order to save money. But it may also encourage a manufacturer to change his processes so that less waste is produced.

FURTHER READING

Hazardous waste information is just beginning to emerge from newspaper clippings and government reports into more easily digested form and more accessible publications.

An introduction to the overall hazardous waste problem is found in Selim M. Senkan and Nancy W. Stauffer, "What to Do with Hazardous Waste," *Technology Review*, vol. 84, no. 2 (November-December 1981), pp. 34-47. This article draws on EPA publications and other references to describe the types of wastes and the sources as well as the alternative methods of management and disposal.

The discovery of problems at hazardous waste disposal sites has been documented by newspaper reporters across the country. A series that appeared in the Buffalo *Courier-Express* describing numerous problem sites in the eastern part of the country is reprinted in U.S. Congress, House, Committee on Interstate and Foreign Commerce, *Oversight-Resource Conservation and Recovery Act*, Committee Print, 95th Cong., 2d sess., 1978, pp. 1-65. Michael Brown, who reported the story about Love Canal, describes problems with chemicals in seven other states in his *Laying Waste: The Poisoning of America by Toxic Chemicals* (New York: Pantheon, 1979). Lois Gibbs, former president of the Love Canal Homeowners' Association, has also written an account *Love Canal—My Story* (Albany, N.Y.: State University of New York Press, 1982).

Our limited knowledge about how to measure the effects of hazardous waste on people's health explains some of the difficulties in dealing with the problems at sites such as Love Canal. Thomas Maugh II describes the state of the art of assessing health effects from exposure to hazardous waste in "Just How Hazardous Are Dumps?" *Science*, vol. 215 (January 29, 1982), p. 490, and "Biological Markers for Chemical Exposure," *Science*, vol. 215 (February 5, 1982), p. 643. This series draws on a symposium report edited by William W. Lowrance, *Assessment of Health Effects at Chemical Disposal Sites* (New York: The Rockefeller University, 1981), which notes areas of agreement and controversy among scientists and the implications for research and policymaking.

Maugh also outlined the state of the art in methods of treating and disposing of hazardous waste in several articles: "Toxic Waste Disposal—A Growing Problem," *Science*, vol. 204 (May 25, 1979), p. 819; "Hazardous Waste Technology Is Available," *Science*, vol. 204 (June 1, 1979), p. 930; "Incineration, Deep Wells Gain New Importance," *Science*, vol. 204 (June 15, 1979), p. 1188; and "Burial is Last Resort for Hazardous Wastes," *Science*, vol. 204 (June 22, 1979), p. 1295.

Perhaps the most extensive literature is available on siting of hazardous waste facilities. The goal of much of this material is to encourage effective participation by the public. Three examples are: Jeff Belfiglio, Tom Lippe, and Steve Franklin, *Hazardous Waste Disposal Sites: A Handbook for Public Input and Review* (Stanford, Cal.: Stanford Environmental Law Society, 1981); Keystone Center, "Siting Non-Radioactive Hazardous Waste Management Facilities: An Overview" (Keystone, Col.: Keystone Center, 1980); and four handbooks prepared for the New England Regional Commission by Clark-McGlennon Associates (Boston, Mass.: New England Regional Commission, November, 1980). The handbook titles are *An Introduction to Facilities for Hazardous Waste Management, Criteria for Evaluating Sites for Hazardous Waste Management, A Decision Guide for Siting Acceptable Hazardous Waste Facilities in New England*, and *Negotiating to Protect Your Interests*. A group representing environmental organizations, the chemical industry, and the waste industry is preparing a publication that outlines the questions a community and the operator of a site should address. It is expected to be published by The Conservation Foundation this fall.

David Morrell and Christopher Magorian analyze the politics of siting in their forthcoming *Siting Hazardous Waste Facilities: Local Opposition and the Myth of Preemption* (Cambridge, Mass.: Ballinger, 1982). Centaur Associates prepared *Siting of Hazardous Waste Man-*

agement Facilities and Public Opposition (Washington, D.C.: Environmental Protection Agency, Office of Water and Waste Management, November 1979). The latter describes the relationship between 21 sites and their surrounding communities.

Much of the information about the generation and handling of hazardous waste continues to appear in government reports. One of the most useful consultant reports prepared in the past year is *Hazardous Waste Generation and Commercial Hazardous Waste Management Capacity: An Assessment* (Washington, D.C.: Environmental Protection Agency, Office of Water and Waste Management, December 1980). It provides the most recent accurate information about the amounts of waste being produced and how they are handled. Earlier reports are summarized in the Annual Reports of the Council on Environmental Quality, particularly those published in the years 1977 through 1980.

Hazardous Waste Report is one of several newsletters following regulatory action as well as other issues in the field on a regular basis (Aspen Systems Corporation, 1600 Research Blvd., Rockville, Md. 20850).

Although this chapter does not discuss the issue of compensation for injury from damage from hazardous waste dumping, the literature in this field has increased rapidly in the past several years. Examples of how compensation is handled at the state level are analyzed in a report prepared for the U.S. Senate, Committee on Environment and Public Works, *Six Case Studies of Compensation for Toxic Substances Pollution: Alabama, California, Michigan, Missouri, New Jersey, and Texas* (Congressional Research Service, June 1980). Jeffrey Trauberman explains the Comprehensive Environmental Response, Compensation and Liability Act in "Superfund: a Legal Update," *Environment*, vol. 23 (March 1981), p. 25. Superfund and RCRA issues are analyzed in "Hazardous Substances in the Environment," *Ecology Law Quarterly*, vol. 9, no. 3 (1981), p. 519. A useful bibliography has been prepared by the U.S. Department of Justice, Land and Natural Resources Division Library, *Nuclear/Hazardous Wastes—A Selected Bibliography*, Bibliography Series No. 2 (Washington, D.C.: U.S. Department of Justice, July 1981).

TEXT REFERENCES

1. Safe Drinking Water Act, 21 U.S.C., sec. 349 (1981).

2. Resource Conservation and Recovery Act of 1976, 42 U.S.C., sec. 6901 (1981).

3. Comprehensive Environmental Response, Compensation, and Liability Act of 1980, 42 U.S.C., sec. 9601, (1981).

4. U.S. Comptroller General, *Hazardous Waste Facilities with Interim Status May Be Endangering Public Health and the Environment* (Washington, D.C.: General Accounting Office, 1981), p. 11.

5. *Ibid.*

6. Information provided by U.S. Environmental Protection Agency, Office of Solid Waste, April 21, 1982.

7. U.S. Comptroller General, *Hazardous Waste Facilities with Interim Status May Be Endangering Public Health and the Environment*, p. 11.

8. U.S. Environmental Protection Agency, Office of Solid Waste and Emergency Response, *Hazardous Waste Regulations Under RCRA: A Summary*, series SW-939 (Washington, D.C.: U.S. Environmental Protection Agency, 1981), pp. 4-5.

9. 45 Fed. Reg. 33119 (1980).

10. Booz-Allen & Hamilton, Inc., and Putnam, Hayes, & Bartlett, Inc., *Hazardous Waste Generation and Commercial Hazardous Waste Management Capacity: An Assessment*, prepared for U.S. Environmental Protection Agency, Office of Water and Waste Management, series SW-894 (Washington, D.C.: U.S. Environmental Protection Agency, 1980), pp. III-2,3.

11. U.S. Comptroller General, *Hazardous Waste Facilities with Interim Status May Be Endangering Public Health and the Environment*, p. 11.

12. U.S. Environmental Protection Agency, Office of Solid Waste and Emergency Response, *Hazardous Waste Regulations Under RCRA: A Summary*, p. 8.

13. Booz-Allen and Hamilton, Inc., and Putnam, Hayes, & Bartlett, Inc., *Hazardous Waste Generation and Commercial Hazardous Waste Management Capacity*, p. III-3.

14. U.S. Environmental Protection Agency, Office of Solid Waste, *The National Potential for Damage from Industrial Waste Disposal* (Washington, D.C.: U.S. Environmental Protection Agency, Open File Report, 1977), Table 3.

15. Booz-Allen and Hamiliton, Inc., and Putnam, Hayes, & Bartlett, Inc., *Hazardous Waste Generation and Commercial Hazardous Waste Management Capacity*, pp. III-4,6,7.

16. U.S. Environmental Protection Agency, *The National Potential for Damage from Industrial Waste Disposal*, Table 3.

17. Booz-Allen and Hamiliton, Inc., and Putnam, Hayes, & Bartlett, Inc., *Hazardous Waste Generation and Commercial Hazardous Waste Management Capacity*, pp. viii, IX-1.

18. *Ibid.*, pp. IX-3, II-3,4.

19. U.S. Environmental Protection Agency, *The National Potential for Damage from Industrial Waste Disposal*, Table 3.

20. Fred C. Hart Associates, *Preliminary Assessment of Cleanup Costs for National Hazardous Waste Problems*, prepared for the U.S. Environmental Protection Agency, 1979, p. 25 (cited in Council on Environmental Quality, *Environmental Quality—1979*, p. 181).

21. Information provided by U.S. Environmental Protection Agency.

22. *Ibid.*

23. Booz-Allen and Hamilton, Inc., and Putnam, Hayes, & Bartlett, Inc., *Hazardous Waste Generation and Commercial Hazardous Waste Management Capacity*, pp. V-9-17.

24. Information provided by U.S. Environmental Protection Agency.

25. Booz-Allen and Hamilton, Inc., and Putnam, Hayes, & Bartlett, Inc., *Hazardous Waste Generation and Commercial Hazardous Waste Management Capacity*, p. V-18.

26. Information provided by U.S. Environmental Protection Agency.

27. Lyle R. Silka and Francoise M. Brasier, U.S. Environmental Protection Agency,

Office of Solid Waste, "The National Assessment of the Ground-Water Contamination Potential of Waste Impoundments," paper presented at The Symposium on Surface-Water Impoundments, Minneapolis, Minn., June 2-5, 1980, p. 8.

28. Fred C. Hart Associates, *Preliminary Assessment of Cleanup Costs for National Hazardous Waste Problems*, pp. 1, 25.

29. Lyle R. Silka and Francoise M. Brasier, "The National Assessment of the Ground-Water Contamination Potential of Waste Impoundments," p. 5.

30. U.S. Comptroller General, *Hazardous Waste Facilities with Interim Status May Be Endangering Public Health and the Environment*, pp. ii-iii.

31. Chemical Manufacturers Association, *The Chemical Balance: Benefiting People, Minimizing Risks* (Washington, D.C.: Chemical Manufacturers Association, 1982), p. 17.

32. U.S. Comptroller General, *Hazardous Waste Facilities with Interim Status May Be Endangering Public Health and the Environment*, pp. 11-13.

33. U.S. Environmental Protection Agency, Office of Water and Waste Management, *Remedial Actions at Hazardous Waste Sites: Survey and Case Studies* (Washington, D.C.: U.S. Environmental Protection Agency, 1981), p. 7.

34. *Ibid.*, p. 197.

35. *Ibid.*, p. 8.

36. U.S. Environmental Protection Agency, *The National Potential for Damage from Industrial Waste Disposal*, Table 3, p. 12.

37. U.S. Environmental Protection Agency, *Hazardous Waste Regulations Under RCRA: A Summary*, pp. 8, 11.

38. 45 Fed. Reg. 33066 (1980).

39. 46 Fed. Reg. 2802 (1981); and U.S. Environmental Protection Agency, *Hazardous Waste Regulations Under RCRA: A Summary*, pp. 17-18.

40. "Update on RCRA State Plan Authorizations," *Hazardous Waste Report* 3(13):8-11 (1982).

41. "Illinois Wins Cleanup Efforts at SCA and U.S. Ecology Sites," *Hazardous Waste Report* 3(17):7 (1982).

42. *Chemical Regulation Reporter* 5(42):1111-12 (1982).

43. Information provided by U.S. Environmental Protection Agency.

44. State of California, Governor's Office of Appropriate Technology, Toxic Waste Assessment Group, *Alternatives to the Land Disposal of Hazardous Wastes: An Assessment for California* (Sacramento, Calif.: Office of Appropriate Technology, 1981), pp. 168-169.

45. Booz-Allen and Hamilton, Inc., and Hayes, Putnam, & Bartlett, Inc., *Hazardous Waste Generation and Commerical Hazardous Waste Management Capacity*, p. V-35.

46. *City of Philadelphia v. New Jersey*, 11 ERC 1770 (1978). For additional discussion, see Final Report of the National Governors' Association, Subcommittee on the Environment, *Siting Hazardous Waste Facilities* (Washington, D.C., National Governor's Association, 1981), Appendix A.

47. Council on Environmental Quality, *Public Opinion on Environmental Issues: Results of a National Public Opinion Survey* (Washington, D.C.: U.S. Government Printing Office, 1980), pp. 30-31.

48. Centaur Associates, *Siting of Hazardous Waste Management Facilities and Public Opposition*, prepared for U.S. Environmental Protection Agency, Office of Solid Waste (Washington, D.C.: U.S. Environmental Protection Agency, 1979), p. 9.

49. This discussion is based on surveys by the Council of State Governments, *Waste Management in the States* (Lexington, Ky., 1982); the National Conference of State Legislatures, et. al., *Abstracts of State Hazardous Waste Siting Laws* (Denver, Colo.: 1981) While it provides an idea of the types of approaches states are taking to siting, the exact numbers are already out-of-date in this rapidly changing area.

50. David L. Brunner, Will Miller, and Nan Stockholm, eds., *Corporations and the Environment: How Should Decisions be Made?* (Los Altos, Calif.: Stanford University Graduate School of Business, 1981), p. 101.

51. Baltimore Environmental Center, Hazardous Waste Project. Fact Sheet No. 1: "Chrome Wastes" (Baltimore, Md.: Baltimore Environmental Center, undated).

52. State of California, Governor's Office of Appropriate Technology, *Alternatives to the Land Disposal of Hazardous Wastes: An Assessment for California*, p. 163.

53. Selim M. Senkan and Nancy W. Stauffer, "What to do with Hazardous Waste", *Technology Review* 84(2):39 (1981).

54. *Ibid.*

55. Eugene P. Crumpler, U. S. Environmental Protection Agency, "Status of Chemical, Physical and Biological Treatment Processes in Hazardous Waste Management," paper presented at NATO-CCMS International Symposium on Hazardous Waste, October 1981.

56. Booz-Allen, and Hamilton, Inc., and Hayes, Putnam, & Bartlett, Inc., *Hazardous Waste Generation and Commercial Hazardous Waste Management Capacity*, p. V-19.

57. U.S. Environmental Protection Agency, *The National Potential for Damage from Industrial Waste Disposal*, Table 3.

58. U.S. Environmental Protection Agency, Region V, "Incineration: The Ultimate Disposal," in *Environment Midwest: Managing the Waste Problem* (Chicago, Ill.: U.S. Environmental Protection Agency, 1981), p. 8.

59. Christian Nels, Federal Environmental Agency, West Berlin, Federal Republic of Germany, "Hazardous Waste Incineration," paper presented at NATO-CCMS International Symposium on Hazardous Waste, October 1981, p. 4.

60. U.S. Environmental Protection Agency, Region V, "Incineration: The Ultimate Disposal," p. 9.

61. State of California, Governor's Office of Appropriate Technology, *Alternatives to the Land Disposal of Hazardous Wastes: An Assessment for California,* p. 225.

62. U.S. Environmental Protection Agency, Region V, "Incineration: The Ultimate Disposal," p. 8.

63. 46 Fed. Reg. 7666 (1981).

64. Executive Office of the President, Office of Science and Technology Policy, *Scientific and Technical Needs for Hazardous Waste Management* (Washington, D.C.: Office of Science and Technology Policy, 1979), p. 4.

65. State of California, Governor's Office of Appropriate Technology, *Alternatives to the Land Disposal of Hazardous Wastes: An Assessment for California*, p. 183; see also, State of California, *Managing Hazardous Wastes for a Non-Toxic Tomorrow: 1981-82 Implementation Program* (Sacramento, Calif.: Office of the Governor, 1981).

66. Executive Office of the President, Office of Science and Technology Policy, *Scientific and Technical Needs for Hazardous Waste Management*, Appendix V.

67. State of California, *Managing Hazardous Wastes for a Non-Toxic Tomorrow: 1981-82 Implementation Program*, pp. 2-3.

68. Ky. Rev. Stat., sec. 224.862 (1980).

69. State of California, *Managing Hazardous Wastes for a Non-Toxic Tomorrow: 1981-82 Implementation Program*, p. 4.

70. 43 Fed. Reg. 7150 (1978); and 44 Fed. Reg. 31514 (1979).

71. State of California, Governor's Office of Appropriate Technology, *Alternatives to the Land Disposal of Hazardous Wastes: An Assessment for California*, p. 7.

FIGURE REFERENCES

Figure 4.1

(1-4)—U.S. Comptroller General, *Hazardous Waste Facilities with Interim Status May Be Endangering Public Health and the Environment* (Washington, D.C.: General Accounting Office, 1981), p. 11. (5-7)—Information provided by U.S. Environmental Protection Agency, Office of Solid Waste, April 21, 1982.

Figure 4.2

Booz-Allen and Hamilton, Inc. and Putnam, Hayes and Barlett, Inc., *Hazardous Waste Generation and Commercial Hazardous Waste Management Capacity: An Assessment*, prepared for the U.S. Environmental Protection Agency, Office of Water and Waste Management (Washington, D.C.: U.S. Environmental Protection Agency, 1980), p. III-2.

Figure 4.3

Booz-Allen and Hamilton, Inc. and Putnam, Hayes and Barlett, Inc., *Hazardous Waste Generation and Commercial Hazardous Waste Management Capacity: An Assessment*, prepared for the U.S. Environmental Protection Agency, Office of Water and Waste Management (Washington, D.C.: U.S. Environmental Protection Agency, 1980), p. III-6.

Figure 4.4

Booz-Allen and Hamilton, Inc. and Putnam, Hayes and Barlett, Inc., *Hazardous Waste Generation and Commercial Hazardous Waste Management Capacity: An Assessment*, prepared for the U.S. Environmental Protection Agency, Office of Water and Waste Management (Washington, D.C.: U.S. Environmental Protection Agency, 1980), p. V-25.

Figure 4.5

(1 and 2)—Fred C. Hart Associates, *Preliminary Assessment of Clean-Up Costs for National Hazardous Waste Problems*, prepared for the U.S. Environmental Protection Agency (Washington, D.C.: U.S. Environmental Protection Agency, 1979), p. 25 (cited in Council on Environmental Quality, *Environmental Quality—1979*, p. 181). (3, 6, 8)—Information provided by U.S. Environmental Protection Agency, Office of Solid Waste, April 21, 1982. (4)—Lyle R. Silka and Francoise M. Brasier, U.S. Environmental Protection Agency, Office of Solid Waste, "The National Assessment of the Ground-Water Contamination Potential of Waste Impoundments," paper presented at The Symposium on Surface - Water Impoundments, Minneapolis, MN., June 2-5, 1980, p. 8. (5)—Booz-Allen & Hamilton, Inc., and Putnam, Hayes & Bartlett, Inc., *Hazardous Waste Generation and Commercial Hazardous Waste Management Capacity: An Assessment*, prepared for U.S. Environmental Protection Agency, Office of Water and Waste Management, (series SW-894) (Washington, D.C.: Environmental Protection Agency, 1980), pp. V-9-17. (7)—Comprehensive Environmental Response, Compensation, and Liability Act of 1980, 42 U.S.C., sec. 9601 (1981).

Figure 4.6

U.S. Environmental Protection Agency, Office of Emergency and Remedial Response, unpublished data.

Figure 4.7

Booz-Allen and Hamilton, Inc. and Putnam, Hayes and Barlett, Inc., *Hazardous Waste Generation and Commercial Hazardous Waste Management Capacity: An Assessment*, prepared for the U.S. Environmental Protection Agency, Office of Water and Waste Management (Washington, D.C.: U.S. Environmental Protection Agency, 1980), p. V-36.

Chapter 5

Energy

During the 1970s, Americans had to deal with gasoline shortages, sharp energy price increases, and shifting government policies on energy. In response, the nation adjusted its patterns of energy use and supply, though sometimes at substantial cost to individuals and companies alike.

The past couple of years have been calmer, leading some people to believe that the crisis is over and that the federal government should reduce its presence in the energy field. But these opinions are not universally shared, and it remains unclear whether the adjustments that have already taken place are sufficient to resolve our long-term energy problems or whether we are yet adequately prepared to deal with disruptions in energy supplies.

ENERGY TRENDS

Since 1973, the United States has substantially shifted its patterns of energy consumption and production. Until the 1970s, we experienced steadily increasing domestic production and consumption as well as falling real energy prices. In 1970, however, domestic production (particularly of petroleum) began to level off. Consumption continued to increase at its historical rate of 3.3 percent annually until the oil embargo of 1973-74. Since then, consumption has actually fallen in four out of eight years; in 1981, consumption was 0.3 percent lower than it had been in 1973. Domestic production drifted slowly downward until the mid-1970s, then rose slightly as coal production increased and Alaskan oil became available (figure 5.1).

Energy Consumption

The shifts in patterns of energy consumption during the 1970s were particularly significant in terms of oil consumption, which dropped 6 percent from 1973 to 1975, and 15 percent between 1978 and

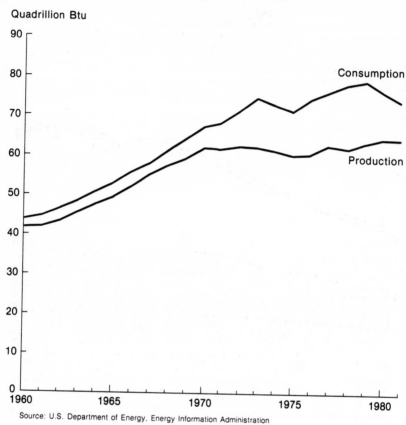

Figure 5.1
Production and Consumption of Energy
in the United States, 1960-1981

Source: U.S. Department of Energy, Energy Information Administration

1981, after hitting a historical peak in 1978 (figure 5.2). Fluctuations in other types of energy consumption were less dramatic, but nonetheless significant. The consumption of natural gas remains 11 percent below its historical peak of 1972, while the consumption of coal has increased 29 percent in the same period. Consumption shifts occurred in every energy-consuming sector (figure 5.3).

Two fundamental factors contributed to the changes in the rate at which Americans use energy. First, the American economy grew at a slower rate, causing lower growth in energy consumption (see chapter 1). Second, higher energy prices (and, in some cases, temporary shortages) had the twin effects of causing people to forego some activities and to carry on other activities more efficiently.

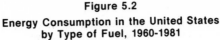

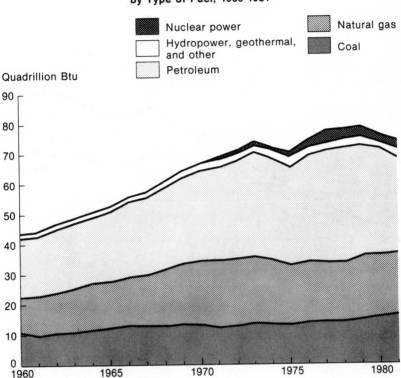

Figure 5.2
Energy Consumption in the United States by Type of Fuel, 1960-1981

Nuclear power · Natural gas · Hydropower, geothermal, and other · Coal · Petroleum

Quadrillion Btu

This figure excludes many important types of energy—wood used for home heating, passive solar building designs, windmills, and energy self-generated by industry from waste products. Taken together, these and similar noncommercial sources may be a significant component of energy production.

Source: U.S. Department of Energy, Energy Information Administration

Energy now is being consumed more efficiently in all parts of the economy (figure 5.4). Energy consumption in the average residence dropped 11 percent from 1972 to 1980. Over the same period, energy consumption per square foot in commercial buildings dropped 9 percent; industrial energy use per unit of output fell by more than 11 percent; and, for automobiles, fuel consumption per mile dropped 11 percent. New cars routinely do better than meet the annual federal fuel-efficiency standards, and the 50-mile-per-gallon car, available in a few models already, may soon begin having a significant impact on overall gasoline consumption.[1]

All of these changes are reflected in the aggregate relationship between energy consumption and economic growth. Before 1970,

Figure 5.3
Energy Consumption by Sector, 1950-1981

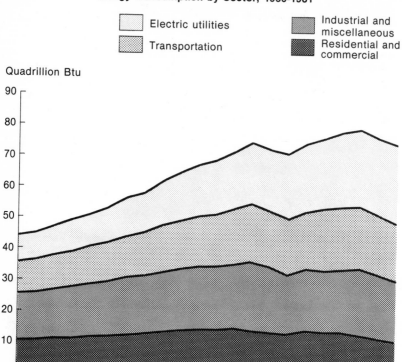

☐ Electric utilities   ▨ Industrial and
                                miscellaneous
▨ Transportation   ▨ Residential and
                                commercial

Quadrillion Btu

Electric utilities, shown in this figure as a separate sector, supply energy to the other sectors. In 1981, with electricity distributed, the transportation sector used 18.7 Quads; industrial and miscellaneous, 29.3 Quads; and residential and commercial, 26.4 Quads.

Source: U.S. Department of Energy, Energy Information Administration

few analysts believed that energy use would ever show an absolute decline. In fact, during the late 1960s, the average amount of energy consumed per dollar of Gross National Product (GNP) was increasing rapidly (figure 5.5). Many expected this trend to continue, but, since 1973, a 20.3 percent growth in real GNP was matched by a slight drop in total energy consumption. This decoupling of consumption from the GNP continues: energy consumption in 1981 was 2.5 percent below that of 1980, while real GNP rose 2 percent. Thus, the trends of the past decade have demonstrated that there is much greater flexibility in the relationship between GNP and energy consumption than the high-growth period of the 1960s may have suggested. This flexibility is an indication of the ability of the economy to shift among inputs in response to their relative prices.

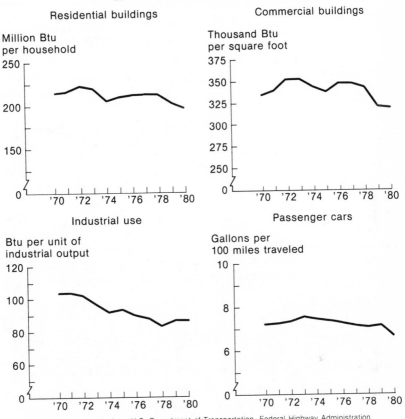

Figure 5.4
Energy Use Intensity by Sector, 1970-1980

Residential buildings

Commercial buildings

Industrial use

Passenger cars

Source: Motor vehicle data: U.S. Department of Transportation. Federal Highway Administration.
All other data: Oak Ridge National Laboratory. Energy Division.

Energy Supplies

Compared with the rest of the industrialized world, the United States has always been blessed with large supplies of domestic energy. Reserves of some fuels—notably, coal and uranium—are very large compared to current levels of use.[2] Even our reserves of natural gas and petroleum are plentiful compared to those in most industrialized countries. The United States led the world in the production of crude oil until 1974, when the Soviet Union became the leading producer. During 1980, America was the world's largest producer of energy when supplies of all types are included.[3]

Domestic energy production in 1981 totaled 64.9 Quads, or 87.8 percent of consumption (figure 5.6). This represented a 3.8 percent increase in production over 1970 and a 7.8 percent increase over

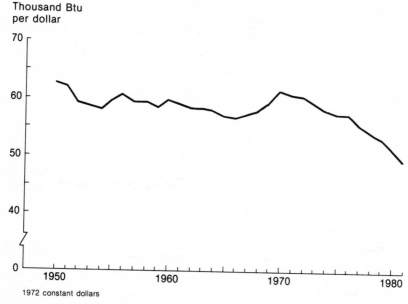

Figure 5.5

Energy Consumption per Dollar of GNP, 1950-1981

Thousand Btu
per dollar

1972 constant dollars

Source: U.S. Department of Energy, Energy Information Administration

1975, the year with the lowest total domestic production during the 1970s. The trend toward reduced oil imports that began in 1978 continued in 1981 (figure 5.7). The United States imported 35.6 percent of its petroleum (1.96 billion barrels) in 1981, compared to 49.1 percent (3.13 billion barrels) in 1977, the year of highest imports. Only 11.3 percent of oil consumed in the United States in 1981 came from the Middle East, down from 17.8 percent in 1977.

There has been a dramatic growth of coal production in the western states (figure 5.8). While overall coal production increased 47.9 percent between 1971 and 1980, production in the West jumped 394.2 percent. In 1971, western coal accounted for only 7.5 percent of American coal production; in 1980, it accounted for 25.2 percent. Strip mining accounted for 89.7 percent of production in 1980 in the West, for 41.4 percent of production in Appalachia, and for 68.6 percent in the Midwest. These changes in location and extraction technology have had major effects on the physical environment.

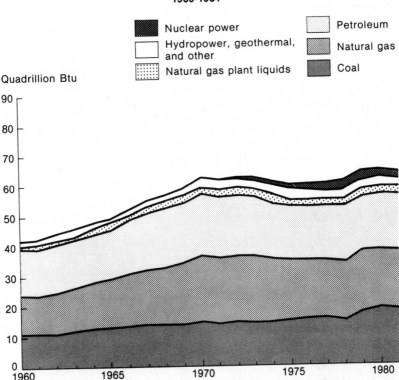

Figure 5.6
Production of Energy by Type,
1960-1981

- Nuclear power
- Hydropower, geothermal, and other
- Natural gas plant liquids
- Petroleum
- Natural gas
- Coal

Quadrillion Btu

This figure excludes many important types of energy—wood used for home heating, passive solar building designs, windmills, and energy self-generated by industry from waste products. Taken together, these and similar noncommercial sources may be a significant component of energy production.

Source: U.S. Department of Energy, Energy Information Administration

Energy Prices

During the 1970s, much attention was paid to the large and sudden increases in the price of energy and the effects these increases might have on the stability of the world's economic structure and political arrangements. In real terms, the price rise for most forms of energy sold in America has been less than consumers might think (figure 5.9). For instance, when adjusted for the general rate of inflation, the real price of gasoline increased 39 percent from 1974 to 1980, compared to a 124 percent increase in the unadjusted price. The real price of electricity increased 7 percent, and is still below prices that prevailed before 1965. However, the real price of residential heating oil increased almost 70 percent over the same period (and

Figure 5.7
Foreign Trade in Energy Resources, 1950-1981

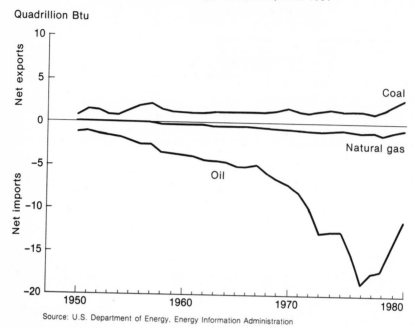

Source: U.S. Department of Energy, Energy Information Administration

might have increased even more in the absence of price controls on petroleum products, which continued until January 1981).

It can be argued that these price data are misleading because some of the higher energy costs occurred in the form of long gas lines and closed factories. Moreover, the effects of price increases were intensified since the changes did not occur smoothly. Large jumps occurred between 1972 and 1974 (26.6 percent for gasoline) and particularly from 1978 to 1980 (56 percent for gasoline). From 1980 to 1981, the real price of heating oil increased 12.5 percent, electricity 5.4 percent, and natural gas 4.8 percent, while gasoline prices fell 0.4 percent.

These price increases resulted in slower economic growth and an inflationary spiral. Wage earners and companies tried to catch up by demanding higher wages and prices to maintain their position. The impact of the higher prices fell unevenly across the country, affecting regions differently, according to the predominant kind of heating fuels and electricity-generating plants, and also affecting income groups differently. Lower-income Americans generally suffered the most, because they spend a higher portion of their income

Figure 5.8
Coal Production in the United States by
Coal Producing Region, 1971-1980

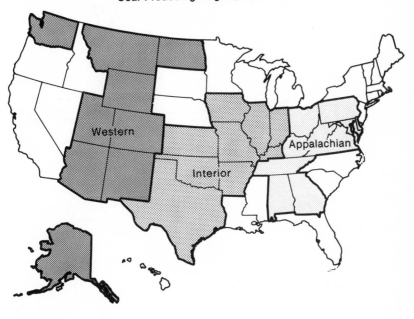

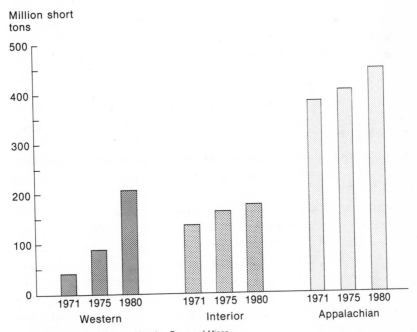

Million short
tons

Source: U.S. Department of Interior, Bureau of Mines

Figure 5.9
Cost of Fuels to End Users, 1960-1981
(in 1972 constant dollars)

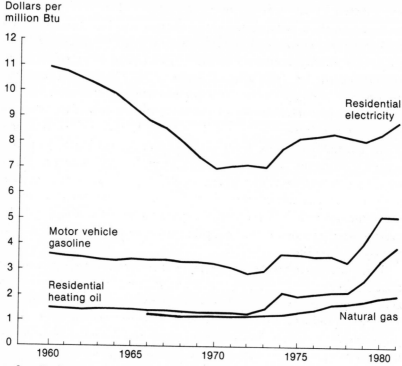

One million Btu is the energy contained in approximately 8 gallons of gasoline. 6.7 gallons of heating oil. 293 kilowatt hours of electricity. or 981 cubic feet of natural gas.

Price deflator: Consumer Price Index for all items less energy

Source: U.S. Department of Energy. Energy Information Administration

on direct energy purchases. One study calculates that, at the beginning of 1981, those earning below 125 percent of the official poverty level were suffering losses of some $5 billion per year (compared to their pre-embargo position) simply because higher energy prices had outstripped their income (including growth in welfare payments) by that amount.[4]

The United States and the world adapted well to higher energy prices. The dollar did not collapse; the international financial system made the necessary adjustments, although at some cost to poor nations and risk to lender nations;[5] the superpowers avoided armed conflict over energy. But future international events might well present discontinuities and shifts in supply, price, and consumption that will be much more difficult to manage than those of the 1970s.

PROSPECTS AND ISSUES

Major government attention to energy problems in the last decade was spurred by the fear of the consequences of dependence on oil from the Middle East. But events during the last year, with its slackening in world oil demand and the highly publicized disagreements among members of the Organization of Petroleum Exporting Countries, are seen by some as a reason to reduce the importance of energy as an issue for government attention.

Is this wise? The supply of oil from the Middle East, though diminished in importance, is still a major factor in the economies of the United States and its trading partners. Even barring a major supply disruption, a return to faster growth rates in the economy would add to pressures on energy supplies and prices. About half of the energy that we conserved in 1981 can be attributed to slower economic growth.[6] If economic expansion returns, there will be greater need to ensure that supplies are available and used as efficiently as possible.

Thus, there are reasons for government to continue to be concerned about energy. And, in fact, it is not possible for government to avoid having an energy policy, at least for the foreseeable future. Energy is produced from government lands (see box on pages 196, 197); public agencies control many energy prices and license many types of energy production facilities; the nuclear-generating industry depends on federal assistance for activities ranging from basic research to providing means for disposing of waste fuel; and, in many other ways, all levels of government continue to have substantial influence on the demand for and supply of different energy forms.

The question, then, is not whether government should have an energy policy—it must. The question is what that policy should be. The three components of our energy policy addressed in the following pages are whether government should actively promote energy conservation, whether current policies used in setting electricity rates should be modified, and what steps should be taken to avoid the severe disruptions that could be caused by future energy emergencies.

Federal Energy Conservation Programs

Until the 1970s, all levels of government were almost exclusively concerned with influencing the price and availability of energy—not with influencing the efficiency of its use. But following the

Oil and Gas Leasing
in Wilderness Areas

To increase domestic energy production, the Reagan Administration has taken various initiatives on oil and gas leasing policies for wilderness areas.[1*] These proposals have stirred intense environmental controversy during the past year.

To date, 257 areas have been set aside in the National Wilderness Preservation System, which contains a total of some 80 million acres, including nearly 57 million acres in Alaska.[2] About another 39 million acres have been recommended or are under study for inclusion in the system.[3**]

Wilderness is "an area where the earth and its community of life are untrammeled by man, where man himself is a visitor who does not remain."[4] The Wilderness Act made one exception to the primacy of natural and primitive qualities of the areas: mineral exploration is permitted in national forest and Bureau of Land Management (BLM) wilderness areas, but only until the end of 1983.[5] Thereafter, wilderness areas are foreclosed to mineral development unless previously existing leases have been granted.

Even before the Reagan Administration took office, applications had been submitted to explore wilderness areas for fuel and nonfuel minerals.[6] The focus of attention has been the oil-rich Overthrust Belt that runs along the Rocky Mountains from Canada to Mexico. Applications for oil and gas leases have been filed for several wilderness areas in the region—some 350 in the Bob Marshall Wilderness alone[7]—and in a number of additional areas recommended or being studied for wilderness designation. Prior to 1981, no federal leases were granted on any of these applications.[8]

The 40,000-acre Capitan Wilderness in southwestern New Mexico was the first wilderness area in which leases were granted; three oil and gas leases, covering 1,700 acres, were issued in November 1981.[9] While the surface cannot be disturbed until an environmental assessment is completed, the lessees can begin "slant drilling" by boring under the wilderness from adjacent land. Tentative approval was also given on several lease applications for an 89,000-acre area of the 687,000-acre Washakie Wilderness in northwestern Wyoming,[10] and the Interior Department indicated it was reviewing mineral lease applications for

1973-74 oil embargo, with its disruptions of supply, spot shortages, and price increases, a host of new initiatives, depending heavily on information programs, regulatory pressures, and research, emerged at the federal, state, and local levels.

At the federal level, the Energy Policy and Conservation Act of 1975 mandated the development of energy-consumption information labels for furnaces, hot water heaters, refrigerators, and other appliances.[7] The act also instructed the government to study industrial energy use, to fund state energy offices to develop energy conservation goals and plans, and to establish a program to audit and retrofit public schools and hospitals. The next year Congress enacted the Energy Conservation and Production Act of 1976, which called for energy conservation performance standards for new buildings (BEPS) and provided conservation assistance to low-income consumers.[8] Two years later, two more statutes, the Energy Tax

many other wilderness areas, including the Santa Lucia in California.[11]

These actions generated enormous public concern and controversy. The debate over mineral leasing in wilderness areas stirs the passions of numerous Americans, involving as it does some fundamental, emotion-laden issues. Energy company lease applications to explore by seismic testing within the 950,000 acre Bob Marshall wilderness in northwestern Montana intensified congressional interest.[12]

In response to public and congressional concern, Secretary of the Interior James Watt proposed revamping wilderness leasing policies.[13] He initiated legislation to bar surface mineral leasing of all designated wilderness areas, as well as of Forest Service lands recommended for wilderness and of lands under study by BLM, through the end of the century. Controversy has arisen, however, over two other provisions that would allow for mineral exploration and drilling in these areas. Under one section, the Forest Service "recommended" areas and BLM "study" areas could be released administratively to mineral development unless Congress designated them as wilderness within a specified period.[14] Moreover, the President could permit mineral leasing in an existing wilderness area if he found an "urgent national need" for the resources that outweighed other public values and the environmental impacts that mineral leasing would cause. Congress would have 60 days to reject the President's finding, though the President, in turn, might veto such a decision by Congress.

The Watt-initiated legislation, along with legislation offering opposite views (extending current mineral leasing provisions until 1993, prohibiting leasing immediately and altogether), is now before Congress.[15] Because of a moratorium put into effect by Secretary Watt, no wilderness leasing or exploration is permitted until January 1983.[16] Regardless of the outcome in Congress, the issue is likely to continue provoking environmental controversy.

*See figure references at end of chapter.
**Management responsibility for wilderness rests with one of four different federal agencies, depending on which has jurisdiction over the particular area; the Department of the Interior's Bureau of Land Management (BLM), however, has ultimate authority over mineral activity in these areas.

Act of 1978[9] (establishing a tax on low-efficiency automobiles and providing an energy conservation tax credit for residences) and the National Energy Conservation Policy Act of 1978[10] (creating a mandatory program for utility company audits of homes) were added. Many states enacted similar statutes, and many local governments began to provide technical assistance to homeowners to assist them in reducing their energy consumption.

This growth in programs was accompanied by an equivalent growth in the amount of budget resources devoted to energy conservation, research, regulatory programs, and information and outreach activities (figure 5.10).

The Reagan Administration has completely reversed this trend. The proposed 1983 budget would eliminate many conservation programs entirely, and reduce the total amount spent on conservation by 97 percent (see chapter 9). The Building Energy Performance

Figure 5.10

Energy Conservation Expenditures of the U.S. Department of Energy and Its Predecessor Agencies,[1] 1970-1981 (in 1972 constant dollars)

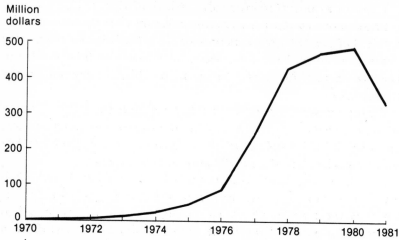

[1] Predecessor agencies from 1974 through 1977 were the Federal Energy Administration (FEA) and the Energy Research and Development Administration (ERDA). The National Science Foundation, which funded energy conservation research before FEA and ERDA were created, provided budget estimates for fiscal years 1970 through 1973.

Source: Oak Ridge National Laboratory, Energy Division

Standards (BEPS) program has been eliminated. No energy efficiency standards are being issued for new appliances such as furnaces and water heaters, even though that failure to act serves to overturn standards now imposed by some states. The Residential Conservation Service, the program providing utility-conducted energy audits for homes, has been weakened by new regulations and has been called unnecessary by the secretary of energy.[11] Proposals have been considered that will reduce the funding available for Low Income Weatherization, a program to upgrade the efficiency of the homes of poor people.[12] Research has been cut back, and the consumer conservation information program has, for all intents and purposes, been terminated.

The justification for this shift is the belief that the marketplace, not a government agency, should determine the nation's energy policy—that a freely operating market will stimulate the right amount of conservation as well as the right amount of production.

Higher Prices and Conservation

The market, with its higher energy prices, has clearly played a major role in producing much of the energy conservation that has taken

place over the past decade.[13] But does the market, by itself, sufficiently promote conservation—or should government have a supporting role? Several arguments can be advanced for the latter.

There are a number of instances in which markets fail, in practice,
to bring about as much energy conservation as is theoretically desirable. For example, markets provide little incentive for the private
sector to invest in developing better information on how people can
conserve energy, for it is difficult to sell this information in the
marketplace.

Energy conservation benefits can reach well beyond the person
saving the energy. Everyone benefits if energy conservation reduces
the price of oil because of reduced demand, or if it results in less
pollution related to the provision of energy supplies.

Sometimes the incentives provided by the market do not reach
the right person. For instance, landlords may pay the utility bill,
but it is the tenants who open windows in the winter or fail to
defrost refrigerators. Even if the higher utility bill is passed on in
higher rents, the tenant will see little benefit from individual actions,
because the cost savings are shared equally by all the tenants. Conversely, if tenants must pay their own energy bills, the landlord
has little incentive to install storm windows, purchase efficient air
conditioners, or plug leaky window frames.

Markets often do not provide all the information needed to make
efficient decisions. For example, the buyer of a new house may know
that the price of the home is higher because of extra insulation, but
not what the associated savings in utility bills will be.

Finally, consumers (and companies) often do not have the financial
resources to undertake conservation expenditures, even if such expenditures would pay for themselves in a very short time.

Thus, there are a number of instances in which, even with a
perfectly operating energy market, less energy conservation would
occur than might be desirable. Government can help to fill this
gap.

Government Aids to Energy Suppliers

The philosophy of the free market does not seem to have been
applied to energy supplies with the same fervor as it has to energy
conservation. The Reagan Administration is continuing, and in
many instances expanding, the traditional support given to energy
suppliers by federal, state, and local governments. The Administration's emphasis is demonstrated by the fiscal year 1982 budget,

which increased research and development funding for electric-related (and particularly nuclear) supply programs by 14 percent, while severely reducing funding for energy conservation.[14] (See also chapter 9, figures 9.3 and 9.5.) Figure 5.11, which lists tax expenditures for energy supply investments, further illustrates the Administration's support for energy suppliers. The Economic Recovery Tax Act of 1981 provided $1.966 billion (14 percent of the tax expenditures created by the act) to the electric utility industry alone. And both the Carter and Reagan Administrations have provided large subsidies for synthetic fuels.

Subsidies are not the only government measures that favor production of energy over conservation. Public regulation of natural gas and electricity prices holds these forms of energy at below-market prices for their users.[15] Building codes serve to make some energy-conserving innovations difficult. Land-use planning practices usually do not take passive solar energy design needs into account.[16] The Internal Revenue Code permits direct expensing of energy purchases for business (immediately lowering this year's taxes), while capital invested in equipment to save energy must be depreciated over time.[17]

Thus, there are a number of ways in which government continues to encourage energy supplies, and discourage energy conservation.

Figure 5.11

Tax Expenditures for the Energy Supply Industries, 1981 and 1982 (billion dollars)

Industry	1981	1982
Oil and gas	0.824	2.040
Oil and gas drilling	(0.046)	(0.112)
Oil and gas production	(0.253)	(0.655)
Oil and gas pipelines	(0.029)	(0.088)
Petroleum refining	(0.471)	(1.115)
Petroleum marketing	(0.025)	(0.070)
Gas utilities	0.147	0.480
Electric utilities	0.603	1.966
Total, energy supply industries	1.574	4.486
Energy supply share of total expenditures	28%	33%
Electric utility share	(11%)	(14%)

These figures are Congress's estimates of the tax expenditures for energy supply industries implicit in the Reagan Administration's tax bill, as originally proposed.

Source: U.S. Congress Joint Committee on Taxation

The Effectiveness of Energy Conservation Programs

Government energy conservation programs would be hard to defend, even in view of market failures and subsidies to supply, if they did not work or if they cost more than they saved. A number of studies in recent years have suggested that improvements in energy efficency are extremely cost-effective, often with payback periods ranging from a few months to six years.[18] In many cases, conservation costs only a few dollars per barrel of oil saved, in contrast to new subsidized production facilities that produce oil at well above its market price. Expensive supply options are being favored over more cost-effective conservation options, even in a period of smaller federal budgets.

Two recent studies from the Oak Ridge National Laboratory analyze the effectiveness of some of the existing conservation programs. In one, the analysts concluded that about 10 percent of energy "saved" may have resulted from federal government conservation programs.[19] The second study, which was a specific analysis of the role of such programs, suggests that as much as 23 percent of the savings can be attributed to them. The savings would thus amount to 5 Quads of energy saved in 1981.[20]

There are also resource and environmental differences between government programs that increase supply and those that increase efficiency. For every Quad of electricity that is not consumed, almost three Quads of fuel used to produce electricity are saved.[21] In this sense, energy conservation has high payoffs indeed. Not only are the initial savings in consumption returned with interest in terms of the reduced energy production, but the health, safety, and environmental costs associated with both production and consumption are avoided. When viewed from this perspective, energy conservation may be one of the best investments that we can make.

The Cost of Electricity

Economics teaches us that a market system allocates resources best when those who use a resource pay what it costs to provide. Price serves to prevent consumers from wasting what they really do not want or need, and signals producers to make more or less of a product as demand rises and falls. But a number of influences can interfere with the smooth working of such an economic system, and, as noted above, many of those influences may be found in energy markets. Monopolies, where consumers can buy from only one supplier, are the rule for electricity and natural gas. Price controls were the rule in petroleum products until early 1981 and are still a feature of natural gas pricing policy.[22] But where markets have been tried, notably for oil, they have served to moderate demand when prices rose too high and to call forth more supply when consumers were willing to pay the price.

From this perspective, electricity should not be sold for less than it costs to provide: consumers should pay for what they get. If they do not, they will tend to use more electricity than they might otherwise. As a result, other energy forms will be underused. Perhaps more importantly, more energy overall will be consumed, as consumers fail to conserve energy in the face of inexpensive electricity. And, as electricity is generated, social costs resulting from mining, air pollution, and water use accumulate.

Two long-established elements of electricity regulation tend to lower the price of electricity below what it would cost if its price were set by the free market. First, the system of public rate regulation underprices electricity by using historic costs as the basis for current prices.[23] Second, special government subsidies are given to producers of electricity, subsidies that are not given to other businesses.[24]

Electricity plays an important part in the national energy picture. About one-third of all energy used in the United States is converted into electricity.[25] About two-thirds of the nation's coal is consumed in electric power plants.[26] The impact of this use on the physical environment is large. To the extent that pricing policies can provide better information to consumers about the effects of their decisions to consume or save electricity, those decisions will likely translate into a better environment.

Regulating Electricity Rates

The history of electricity generation and public regulation in the United States is barely 100 years old. During most of this period, economies of scale made possible by the construction of larger power plants permitted dramatic cost reductions. The result was that the addition of new plants lowered the real cost of electricity to users. Public utility commissions routinely ordered lower rates as a means of sharing at least part of these savings with customers.

The period of growth in the industry was also the time during which utility rate regulation practices were being formulated into legal principles.[27] Since many of the principles were developed during an extended period of stability in power plant construction costs, the accounting conventions then established assumed that construction costs would not escalate over time. The assumption was that the value of a plant carried on the utility company's books (plus accumulated depreciation) would be sufficient to reproduce the plant.

In more recent times, however, a number of factors have coalesced to put strains on utility companies and on traditional public regulatory practices. Four of the most important factors have been (1) the increase in the price of fuel used to produce electricity; (2) the rapid rise in the cost of constructing new electric power plants; (3) the slowing down of efficiencies proceeding from larger plants; and (4) uncertainty about forecasts of future electricity demand.

The first factor, rapidly increasing fuel prices, was a large problem for many utilities following the rapid energy price increases of the early 1970s. Utilities had traditionally been able to estimate their fuel costs well in advance. But rapidly escalating prices made it impossible to estimate accurately a year or two in advance the price that companies would have to pay for the oil, natural gas, or coal required to generate electricity. During the last 10 years, virtually every public regulatory body has permitted the use of the "automatic fuel adjustment clause" as a means of passing through higher (or lower) primary energy costs to users.[28] The effect of fuel adjustment clauses is to pass directly and almost immediately onto customers the higher price that the utility company itself pays. As energy prices have escalated in the past decade, these clauses have served to raise the fuel component of the price of electricity quickly. These price increases have probably induced electricity users to cut back on their consumption.

But fuel costs are only one component of the price of electricity. The fuel must be burned in a large, expensive generating plant that takes a decade or more to plan and build. The capital costs of building electric power plants skyrocketed during the 1970s, rising faster than the general rate of inflation.[29] Moreover, high costs of borrowing money have had a particularly harsh effect on generating facilities.

At the same time, the economies of scale that formerly were associated with construction of ever-larger power plants appear to have ended. Bigger plants no longer produce power less expensively than smaller, older plants. In fact, because a new power plant commands large capital resources and must be planned and built even though costs and demands are both highly uncertain, it is possible that newer plants actually raise costs for consumers rather than lower them.[30]

Finally, and most fundamentally, regulators and utility companies alike are faced with a very uncertain future insofar as the possible growth in demand for electricity is concerned. The decade just past, when demand growth dropped sharply with little warning, has served to undermine the assumption that electricity growth would forever increase at 7.8 percent annually, as it used to prior to the 1970s.[31] Utility company planners fear both overbuilding (which would saddle the company with expensive, underused generating capacity) and underbuilding (which would lead to brownouts and perhaps slower economic growth in the service territory). Large errors in either direction could have serious economic consequences for a region. The long planning horizons that generating plants require complicate an already obscure future.

Thus, the last 10 years have been a period in which many of the basic assumptions about utility rates, public regulation, and future demand have been overtaken by rapid change. Reaction has been painful for the industry; for many companies, revenues have been so low that raising capital is difficult, while bonds sell at unprecedented interest rates.[32] Given the important role that electricity plays in the economy, there have been various attempts to find solutions to the problems facing the industry.

Policy Options

At least three possible policy options might be adopted in the face of these difficulties: "business as usual," increased subsidies, and market pricing.

Business as Usual. The business-as-usual option would essentially be a continuation of current policies, which include providing assistance through the tax code for new construction, delaying or denying rate increases, and basing rates on the traditional methods of calculating costs, looking to the past rather than to the present.

Traditional utility accounting practices (imposed by state utility regulators) operate to the disadvantage of electric utility companies during times when new construction costs are rising. For instance, if a plant is expected to last 30 years, the company may be allowed to put aside only one-thirtieth of the original cost of each plant each year. Yet that amount falls substantially short of what is needed to replace a plant at today's prices. This problem is likely to become more acute as the many plants built during the 1950s and 1960s need to be replaced during the 1980s and beyond.

The financial health of many utility companies has also been complicated by the actions of at least some public regulators, who have in theory permitted adequate rates of return but in practice have made earning those returns impossible.[33]

If the business-as-usual option is pursued, whether by deliberate choice or by inaction, most of the difficulties faced by many utility companies would continue. Electricity prices would continue to be less than current costs, thus encouraging electricity use, discouraging energy conservation investments, and eroding the financial health of utility companies (perhaps leading to more special rescue efforts for individual utilities). Although this option could lead to relatively lower prices for consumers (at least in the short run), it would be unpopular in the longer run if it led to significant disruption in electrical service.

Subsidies. A number of federal initiatives already undertaken or proposed would have the effect of subsidizing electricity generation (principally through the use of tax incentives), thus lowering the price of electricity to its users. In addition to direct subsidies, many utility companies are seeking permission to charge for new plant construction before it is finished and before the plant is operating, and to change other accounting and rate-making conventions in order to produce greater cash flows.[34]

One major argument frequently advanced for subsidizing electricity is that coal and nuclear power plants can help the United States decrease its dependence on imported oil in favor of increased reliance on abundant domestic coal and uranium. For this argument to be valid, however, oil must be displaced in significant amounts by the contemplated fuel-switching.

It is far from clear that subsidizing electricity will substantially reduce oil use. In 1981, only 9.0 percent of the electricity generated came from oil-fired plants, and these plants consumed only 6.9 percent of the oil used in the United States.[35] Much of the oil used for power generation is residual oil, which is in relatively abundant supply and is unusable for transportation purposes.

Furthermore, it is not likely in the short run that electricity will replace other major uses of petroleum. Electric automobiles and the use of electric heat pumps for home heating, the two innovations that could result in large-scale substitution of electricity for oil, are not likely to be adopted on a large enough scale in the next decade to have a significant effect on petroleum consumption. Both would require not only large investments in power plants, but also massive investments by energy consumers. Moreover, studies suggest that, with currently available production technology, the costs to the consumer of internal combustion engine vehicles are still below those of the electric-powered vehicle.[36]

Increased electricity generation thus appears unlikely to play a major role in reducing U.S. oil imports. But reducing imports is not the only argument advanced for subsidizing the industry. Some observers, concerned about the vital role that electricity plays in the modern economy, fear the consequences of a possible shortfall in supplies or the collapse of a major utility. And subsidies are seen as a means of promoting the basic health of the industry.

Subsidies might well have the effect of making investments in the utility industry more attractive to the financial market than they now are. But the attractiveness would be based on provisions of the tax law or regulatory policies, not on any real underlying improvement in the health of the industry. To that extent, although additional investment might ease the financial condition of some utilities, it would only by accident serve the public goal of promoting efficient use of resources. There are also many unanswered questions: How much subsidy is enough? Are the particular activities being subsidized (generally new construction, particularly of nuclear plants) the correct response to the problems facing individual utilities? Unless care is taken, there is a risk that broadly designed subsidies of this type may help some utility companies that do not need it, help others in the wrong way, and not help deserving ones at all.

Market Pricing. An alternative to "business as usual" and increased subsidies is to modify the way in which electricity prices are set, so that they are more in tune with normal market forces and with the costs of production. Although the regulated public utility is the classic example of the "natural monopoly," there are at least two approaches that might move prices closer to market-determined levels. These are time-sensitive pricing and marginal cost pricing.

Time-sensitive pricing (usually called time-of-day or time-of-use pricing in the context of electric rates) is familiar to most consumers, since it is the system used to charge for long-distance telephone calls. In the case of the telephone system, adding new capacity is extremely expensive. Therefore, the telephone company encourages callers to make more calls when the system is less busy (nights and weekends) and fewer calls during peak hours (the business day). More precisely, the marginal cost of calls made during the day is high, since to serve more calls would require additional capital investment, while the marginal cost is low during the night, since idle equipment is readily available.

The situation is exactly analogous for electricity sales. Utility companies traditionally have built enough generating capacity to meet all demands made on the system during the peak time (plus a reserve margin to allow for repairs and unexpected contingencies). But, unlike the telephone long-distance network, almost all electricity is sold to customers at the same price, whether used during peak times or during the middle of a winter night. The case for time-of-use pricing of electricity is especially compelling, since electricity supplied during peak periods is often produced by putting into service either inefficient plants or those consuming very expensive fuels. Thus, it would be to the advantage of the utility and its customers if electricity could be sold inexpensively when it is relatively cheap to supply and at a higher price when it costs the most to produce.

Time-of-use pricing for electricity requires electric meters that can record when electricity is used as well as how much is consumed. Clock-driven, twin-dial meters are now available, but a more versatile meter—perhaps read telemetrically—would make future rate changes easier to accomplish. Meters of this kind are more expensive than conventional ones, and it would be economically rational to introduce them for large customers first. (The savings that accrue from time-sensitive pricing come faster from larger users, and the expense of replacing all meters in a system could be absorbed more gradually.)[37] Moreover, the utility and its customers would have to gain experience concerning the correct duration and pricing structure for peak and off-peak power. But the empirical and econometric studies of time-of-use pricing indicate that large electricity users do respond by reducing their peak consumption and increasing their off-peak consumption of electricity.[38]

Marginal cost pricing of electricity is a further innovation. It would require experimentation to introduce, but could bring many of the benefits of market pricing to the supply and use of electricity. To understand the argument for marginal cost pricing, it is helpful to recall how electricity rates are now set. Electricity is produced from a large number of plants built over a period of many years, at various costs, and with possibly quite different efficiencies of operation. Older plants may be somewhat less efficient in an engineering sense, but, because they were built at a time when construction costs were low and interest rates in the single-digit range, their cost of operation may be lower than that of newer plants. Traditionally, electricity rates have *averaged* the cost of electricity from all of the plants in a system, spreading the costs more or less evenly over all kilowatt-hours sold. This means that electricity from the highest cost plants is sold for less than the cost of replacing the power made in those plants; the lower-cost electricity from older plants lowers the average. Yet, from a resource point of view, it is a mistake to sell energy for less than it costs to replace it, since users cannot properly compare the economic benefits of conserving that energy with the benefits of consuming it.

Marginal cost pricing would not average the costs of producing power from different plants but would, instead, price all electricity at the cost of producing it in the newest plant, which is most likely the most expensive.

The consequences of marginal cost pricing have already been accepted in the case of crude oil. It is this system of pricing that was adopted in 1978 when the decision was made to permit domestic oil prices to rise to world levels and to terminate the allocation system (which served to average prices).[39] Marginal cost pricing is also the justification for decontrol of natural gas producer prices.[40] For each of these energy forms, marginal cost pricing conveys to ultimate users more accurate information (in the form of prices) about what it will cost to buy or produce the next unit of energy.

Marginal cost and time-of-use pricing of electricity would be a major departure from traditional electricity pricing, however, and would lead to large price increases, at least during peak demand hours. In addition, because electricity from older (less costly) plants would be sold for more than it costs to produce, the electric utility would collect more total revenue from all its customers as a group than it now does.[41] A variety of methods might be used to deal with this problem of "excess" revenues. The system adopted in the case of crude oil, for example, was to tax away the extra revenues that decontrol provided. Perhaps an analogous system might be devised in the case of electric utilities.

Why consider applying these market-like pricing strategies to electricity? Energy is a resource that is not in limitless supply, at least in forms that are immediately usable in a modern industrial society. Only if electricity is priced at its replacement value will users know the true value, both to themselves and to society, of using electricity more efficiently. A change to marginal cost pricing principles for electricity is not without its problems, however. Market-like prices would, under current conditions, be higher than those now charged. This would place an additional burden on the poor and on those who found themselves unable to make their residences more efficient in the use of electricity (tenants, for example). Higher prices have the desirable effect of providing information about the cost of resources being consumed, but attention needs to be paid to the burdens they impose.

Nor can major rate changes be effected by a single action. Public regulation is divided among levels of government. Even within a single state, experimentation with the rates charged for electricity will be difficult. Such changes, if they take place at all, are conducted in an atmosphere of hostility and distrust, through adversarial procedures in which the rewards for experimentation are almost nonexistent and the uncertainties very great.

Preparing for Oil Emergencies

The world has experienced three oil shocks in the past decade: the 1973-74 embargo, the 1979 Iranian revolution, and the 1980 Iraq-Iran war. In each case, the amount of oil denied to worldwide commerce has been relatively small. For example, only about 2.7 million barrels of oil per day were withheld during the first quarter of 1974, which was 13.4 percent of the United States demand in September 1973.[42] The relative scale of the more recent shortfalls has been even smaller. Yet, in each case, the effects on the economies of the importing nations have been large. Because of the 1979 shortfall, prices increased 133 percent from 1978 to 1980, causing the United States to spend an average of about $100 million dollars per day more on imported oil during 1980.[43]

The initial domestic reaction to the 1973-74 oil embargo was to declare that the United States should embark on policies designed to make it "independent" of all energy imports.[44] That goal was almost immediately rejected not only because of its technical difficulty, but also because it would have been enormously expensive and environmentally damaging. The Synthetic Fuels Corporation is perhaps the only remnant of that early thinking about dropping oil imports to zero.[45]

A more sustained reaction has been the development of the Strategic Petroleum Reserve (SPR), created by the Energy Policy and Conservation Act of 1975 to develop storage for publicly owned oil to be held and used in case of oil emergencies.[46] The SPR was originally planned to hold one billion barrels, with 150 million to be in storage by the end of 1979. However, by April 5, 1982, there were only 250 million barrels in reserve, an 83-day supply.* Furthermore, the salt caverns used for storage of the SPR are likely to be filled sometime during 1982. No more oil can be added to the reserve until the salt caverns being prepared for storage are drained of 50 percent of their brine, which may take several years. And should we decide to increase the planned capacity, creating new salt-dome storage capacity can take as long as eight years from the planning stage.[48]

Concern about inadequate amounts of oil in public storage was somewhat muted during 1981, because private companies had built up their own stockpiles in response to fears of shortfalls arising from the Iraq-Iran war.[49] This led to some interest in the possibility of transferring part of the burden of holding oil to industry, perhaps following the German example, in which a government/private corporation is responsible. However, private companies in the United States drew down their reserves during 1981, as they found the carrying costs too high in view of the relative slack in the world oil market.

A second reaction to the oil shocks has been less salutary than the creation of the SPR. There have been those who have urged that the United States relax its environmental controls to permit more domestic energy production. It is quite likely that, in the case of another world oil shortage, an early reaction would include pressure to open protected federal lands to exploration and extraction, to switch electric power production from oil to coal (under eased emission regulations), and to add lead to gasoline.

Yet any relaxation of environmental regulations might have no timely effect on energy supplies: even removing controls quickly would not produce more energy during the time the crisis existed. The experience of the past decade suggests that plans made during emergencies are not likely to endure after the panic has subsided. Careful weighing of environmental quality against increased domestic production takes time, data, and political balancing, resources that are frequently in short supply during an emergency.

It is against this background that the subject of emergency energy planning can be understood as an environmental issue. Emergency planning often serves to prevent a crisis from occurring by making

---

* The supply period is based on a usage level equal to the current 3 million barrel per day import level. However, the drawdown rate of the salt-dome storage is only 1.7 million barrels per day, requiring 147 days to empty the SPR during a crisis.[47]

supply disruptions a less potent weapon of political blackmail. More importantly, planning ahead for a possible emergency gives more time for assessing choices when an emergency actually happens. Stockpiles provide time to think; more realistic trade-offs between wilderness drilling and energy conservation can be made. Thus, decisions are more likely to be sound ones, reflecting more accurate cost-benefit analysis.

The key issues that policymakers need to address in selecting a strategy to deal with stockpiling are: (1) how much stockpiled oil is "enough," given the fact that storing oil costs money; (2) where to store the oil; and (3) how to release the oil in a time of emergency.

The Size of the SPR

In some respects, a reserve may be likened to a large standing army during peacetime: its very existence serves to deter those who might otherwise consider a hostile act. However, if a disruption does occur, the stockpile plays its other important role: providing emergency supplies to carry the nation while it responds to the cause of the disruption. Not the least important function a stockpile might play in the early days of a disruption would be to calm the market so that prices did not shoot up for all buyers because of the panic of some.

There is no way to determine what size stockpile is "enough." It is impossible to predict the timing, extent, and duration of an emergency. Nor is it clear how long a given stockpile would last. Simply dividing our current daily imported oil consumption into the amount of stockpiled oil ignores both the sharp increases in purchases that would occur at the beginning of an emergency, as individual buyers attempted to provide a stockpile for themselves, and the decrease in oil consumption that would result from the higher oil prices associated with shortfalls. A long oil shortage would also slow economic growth worldwide, further curtailing consumption; if the cutoff precipitated war, normal civilian market-determined consumption patterns could be altered by war planning efforts. Most observers argue that a billion-barrel reserve is sufficient to deter a threat from a rational opponent.[50]

The larger the size of the stockpile, the greater the impact its accumulation will have on the federal budget and on world prices. America's slow rate of stockpiling probably reflects both of these concerns, as well as the natural tendency to put off preparing for emergencies that do not seem imminent.

Where to Store Oil

Even if a decision were made to increase dramatically the rate at which the SPR is filled, the problem of storage space would remain. Salt-dome caverns are the least expensive form of storage. But, as noted above, the salt domes that are currently prepared for use will soon be filled, and many obstacles could delay the preparation and filling of the additional 500 million barrels of storage capacity planned for 1990.[51] An alternative is to develop but not pump oil from known fields. However, these fields could not be pumped out quickly in an emergency. Other options include having industry store oil in unused tanks (with government paying storage charges) or, to follow the practice of the Japanese government, leasing large crude oil tankers (which are currently underused), filling them, and anchoring them offshore. The larger tankers can hold in the range of 1.8 to 3.6 million barrels each.[52] These options would allow the country to continue to purchase and store crude oil during the current period of soft prices while additional permanent storage facilities were being prepared.

Private stockpiling, as an alternative to public stockpiles, is another possibility. Such reserves could be required by statute, with companies paying all the associated costs (and passing those on to their consumers), or could be stimulated by government subsidies (for instance, by allowing private entities to hold oil in the SPR at a discounted storage cost), or by strong assurances that, unlike the experience in the 1973-74 embargo, private stockpiles would not be subject to price and allocation controls, allowing stockpilers to enjoy the "windfall" profits that their investments earn. But each of these initiatives suffers from severe difficulties. Requiring private stockpiling would be politically unpopular because of its cost to the companies and their current consumers. Direct subsidies would be a large, and probably unpopular budget item. Private holdings in the SPR would reduce the direct public cost of the SPR, but this plan depends on the existence of publicly owned storage space, a current problem. And, given the history of changes in national energy policies, private companies might be suspicious of the durability of any assurance that emergency allocation schemes would not be implemented during hard times. Moreover, before any private stockpiling program is undertaken, it would be wise to compare its costs with those of operating the SPR.

Emergency Allocation

There is a good deal to be said for an emergency plan that is not too explicit. An extremely detailed plan would provide valuable information to potentially hostile suppliers without corresponding benefits to the public, and would reduce any incentive for domestic users of oil to stockpile for their own benefit if they were assured that the government stockpile would go to the imprudent. If different users are uncertain whether government will protect them, then some degree of private stockpiling is in everyone's self-interest, although the exact amount stockpiled will differ from company to company, depending on perceptions of risk and ability to tie up capital in stockpiles.

According to the Energy Policy and Conservation Act of 1975, the secretary of energy must prepare a plan for use of the SPR and submit it to Congress. The plan now in effect was transmitted in October 1979.[53] It is properly unspecific, giving the federal government wide latitude in when and how to release from the stockpile. But public reports of deliberations of the Cabinet Council on Environment and Natural Resources during mid-1981 make it appear likely that, in the event of an emergency, the government would withhold the SPR from the market during the early weeks to avoid dampening the price rise that would follow a cutoff.[54]

This intention not to intervene early to stabilize prices may be shortsighted. Following each of the three preceding shortfalls, the spot market prices for oil began to rise almost immediately; those high spot market prices later became the basis for contract prices. Releasing oil at the beginning of an emergency might moderate such price increases, reduce panic buying, and give government more freedom to deal with the emergency without the intense political pressures that extremely high oil price increases create.

In spite of the desirability of having a vague public plan, government still must have some well-considered scheme for actually allocating supply during a shortage. In the aftermath of the 1973-74 oil embargo, price controls were maintained on petroleum products and an elaborate system of allocations and entitlements was developed to share the additional cost among various companies. There is considerable evidence that the rationing system thus developed contributed to the gasoline lines during the 1973-74 emergency.[55] The Emergency Petroleum Allocation Act, which created that rationing system, was permitted to expire on September 30, 1981, and President Reagan actively opposed any substitute, vetoing extension legislation in early 1982.[56]

If no rationing scheme is implemented during an emergency, prices of all oil—domestic and imported—would be expected to rise to the world spot market price, and such a price increase could create significant economic problems. Oil companies would initially receive enormous windfall profits, particularly on domestically produced oil, although a large portion would eventually be captured by government through the windfall profits tax and normal corporate income taxes (after a time lag that is important, given the size of the extra revenues). Of more concern is the impact that these price increases could have on the economy. A price increase of a penny a gallon is equivalent to an annual cost to the nation of about $2.5 billion; a price rise of 50 cents a gallon would cost the nation approximately $123 billion.[57]

Markets can do an important part of the job following an oil emergency in allocating petroleum products to those users who are willing to pay enough. But this process may result in draining large amounts of income away from all sectors except suppliers of oil. The effects would be heaviest on the poor. The United States may well want to have some system ready for offsetting these effects and reducing the total impact of the price rise on the economy.

FURTHER READINGS

A decade of shortfalls in energy supplies produced no corresponding shortage of literature on the subject.

A number of books are classics. The Ford Foundation sponsored three major energy policy studies. Two of them, *A Time to Choose* (Cambridge, Mass.: Ballinger Publishing Company, 1974), and Hans H. Landsberg, et. al., *Energy: The Next Twenty Years* (Cambridge, Mass: Ballinger Publishing Company, 1979), rank among the handful of most important general readings. The third, *Nuclear Power: Issues and Choices* (Cambridge, Mass: Ballinger Publishing Company, 1977), is valuable for those interested in this aspect of energy.

Amory B. Lovins' article in the October 1976 issue of *Foreign Affairs* 55(1), "Energy Strategy: The Road Not Taken?" helped structure much of the debate during the second part of the decade. The article urges conservation and renewable energy sources as the most appropriate responses to higher-priced energy. A longer exposition of Lovins' views is contained in *Soft Energy Paths: Toward a Durable Peace* (Cambridge, Mass.: Ballinger Publishing Company, 1977). In 1977, National Economic Research Associates, Inc., a firm of consulting economists (80 Broad Street, New York, N.Y. 10004), published one critique of Lovins' work, *Multiple Paths for Energy Policy: A Critique of Lovins' Energy Strategy*, by Harry Perry and Sally H. Streiter. The Edison Electric Institute (EEI), representatives of the investor-owned electric utility companies, devoted an entire issue of *Electric Perspectives*, its bimonthly publication, to a series of critical essays on Lovins (1977, Number 3, EEI, 1111 19th Street, N.W., Washington, D.C. 20036).

Two other classics are: Sam H. Schurr, ed., *Energy In America's Future: The Choices Before Us* (Baltimore, Md.: Johns Hopkins University Press for Resources for the Future, 1979), and Roger Stobaugh and Daniel S. Yergin, eds., *Energy Futures: Report of the Energy Project at the Harvard Business School* (New York, N.Y.: Random House, 1979). The latter is one of the most readable books on energy policy.

Other studies include *Energy in Transition, 1985-2010*, Final Report of the Committee on Nuclear and Alternative Energy Systems of the National Academy of Sciences (Washington, D.C.: National Academy of Sciences, 1979) and *A New Prosperity: Building a Sustainable Energy Future* (Andover, Mass.: Brick House Publishing, 1981). *A New Propserity* is the report of a study undertaken at the federal Solar Energy Research Institute, setting out the technical and economic potential for energy conservation in the United States.

Electricity pricing policy is heavy-going for the concerned lay person. A lucid description of how electricity rates are set is contained in the early chapters of *Rate Design and Load Control: Issues and Directions* (November 1977), an interim report of the Electric Utility Rate Design Study requested by the National Association of Regulatory Utility Commissioners (available from Electric Power Research Institute, 3412 Hillview Avenue, Palo Alto, Calif. 94303). The volumes of studies and reports that were commissioned for the Electric Utility Rate Design Study, although not always easy, are important resources. Bridger M. Mitchell and Willard G. Manning, *Peak-Load Pricing: European Lessons for U.S. Energy Policy* (Cambridge, Mass.: Ballinger Publishing Co., 1978) is an empircal study of the effects of various pricing strategies. Those interested in keeping current with the electricity rate debate should examine the index to the journal *Public Utility Fortnightly*. William Ramsay's *Unpaid*

Costs of Electrical Energy: Health and Environmental Impacts from Coal and Nuclear Power (Baltimore, Md.: Johns Hopkins University Press for Resources for the Future, 1979) is a balanced account of environmental impacts of electricity production.

Energy security and stockpiling are subjects of a number of studies. David Deese and Joseph Nye, eds., *Energy and Security* (Cambridge, Mass.: Ballinger Publishing Co., 1981) is useful and comprehensive. The National Petroleum Council has prepared a report on stockpiling, *Emergency Preparedness for Interruption of Petroleum Imports into the United States* (Washington, D.C.: National Petroleum Council, 1981).

Several institutions have been notable for the quality of their studies on energy. U.S. Congress, Office of Technology Assessment, has released *Energy Efficiency of Buildings in Cities* (1982) and *Residential Energy Conservation* (1979); these publications are available from the U.S. Government Printing Office.

The General Accounting Office has prepared a number of studies over the past few years that are critical of the implementation of particular energy programs, but are generally supportive of the potential for conservation. A list of studies is available from their Energy and Minerals Division, Washington, D.C. 20548.

Finally, Oak Ridge National Laboratory (Post Office Box Y, Oak Ridge, Tenn. 37830) and Lawrence Berkeley Laboratory (University of California, Berkeley, Calif. 94720) have both been the source of excellent studies on energy conservation. A list of their publications is available from the Publications Department of each laboratory.

Energy data is collected and distributed by the U.S. Department of Energy's Energy Information Administration (EIA), Washington, D.C. 20585. EIA staff are helpful on the telephone; a list of people and areas of specialty may be obtained by writing to EIA and asking for their "Energy Data Contacts Finder." Also valuable is the *1980 EIA Publications Directory: A User's Guide* (June 1981).

The energy policies of the Reagan Administration have been unpopular with a wide spectrum of groups, ranging from promoters of synthetic fuels to members of the scientific community. An energy coalition has published a statement of its concerns with the Administration's policies, drawing on the work of 14 organizations. The critique, *The Reagan Energy Plan: A Major Power Failure* (March 24, 1982), is available from a number of national groups, including Solar Lobby (1001 Connecticut Avenue, N.W., Suite 510, Washington, D.C. 20036) and Natural Resources Defense Council (1725 I Street, N.W., Washington, D.C. 20036).

TEXT REFERENCES

1. Charles L. Gray, Jr. and Frank Von Hippel, "The Fuel Economy of Light Vehicles," *Scientific American* 244(5):48-59 (May 1981).

2. Hans H. Lansberg, ed., *Energy: The Next Twenty Years* (Cambridge, Mass.: Ballinger Publishing Co., 1979), pp. 228-238.

3. *Energy Users Report*, No. 430, p. 1563 (November 5, 1981).

4. Committee for Economic Development and The Conservation Foundation, *Energy Prices and Public Policy*, draft (Washington, D.C.: The Conservation Foundation, November 18, 1981), p. 16-21.

5. Hans H. Landsberg, ed., *Energy: The Next Twenty Years*, pp. 170-176.

6. Eric Hirst, et al., *Energy Use From 1973 to 1980: The Role of Improved Energy Efficiency* (Springfield, Va.: National Technical Information Service, 19081), p.5.

7. Energy Policy and Conservation Act of 1975, 42 U.S.C., sec 6201 *et. seq.* (1981).

8. Energy Conservation and Production Act of 1976, 42 U.S.C., sec. 6801 *et. seq.* (1981).

9. Energy Tax Act of 1978, codified in scattered sections of U.S.C., Title 23 and Title 26.

10. National Energy Conservation Policy Act of 1978, 42 U.S.C., sec. 8201 *et. seq.* (1981).

11. *Energy User Report*, No. 431, p. 1579 (November 12, 1981).

12. *Energy User Report*, No. 414, p. 1104 (July 16, 1981).

13. Eric Hirst, et al., *Energy Use From 1973 to 1980: The Role of Improved Energy Efficiency*, pp. 1-10.

14. Energy Research Advisory Board, Research and Development Panel, *Federal Energy R&D Priorities*, (unpublished) (Washington, D.C.: Energy Research Advisory Board, 1981) Appendix B., p. 5.

15. Peter Navarro, "Our Stake in the Electric Utility's Dilemma," *Harvard Business Review*, 60(3):94 (1982); and L. A. Nieves and J. R. Lemon, *Estimation of the Social Costs of Natural Gas* (Springfield, Va.: National Technical Information Service, 1979), pp. 11-18.

16. Martin Jaffe and Duncan Erley, *Protecting Solar Access for Residential Development: A Guidebook for Planning Officials* (Washington, D.C.: U.S. Government Printing Office, 1979), pp. 1-154; and Gail Boyer Hayes, *Solar Access Laws: Protecting Access to Sunlight for Solar Energy Systems* (Cambridge, Mass.: Ballinger Publishing Company, 1979).

17. Information provided by U.S., Congress, Joint Committee on Taxation, May 1982.

18. John C. Sawhill, ed., *Energy Conservation and Public Policy* (Englewood Cliffs, N.J.: Prentice-Hall, Inc., 1979), pp. 104-107.

19. Eric Hirst, et al., *Energy Use From 1973 to 1980: The Role of Improved Energy Efficiency*, p. 7.

20. Eric Hirst, et al., *Energy Use from 1973 to 1980: The Role of Federal Conservation Programs*, draft (Washington, D.C.: U.S. Department of Energy, Office of Conservation and Renewable Energy, 1982), pp. 38-40.

21. U.S. Department of Energy, Energy Information Administration, *Monthly Energy Review*, March 1982 (Washington, D.C.: U.S. Government Printing Office, 1982), pp. 25,65.

22. Executive Order 12287, "Decontrol of Crude Oil and Refined Petroleum Products," January 28, 1981, see 46 Fed. Reg. 9909 (1981).

23. Alfred E. Kahn, *The Economics of Regulation: Principles and Institutions*, Vol. I (New York, N.Y.: John Wiley and Sons, Inc., 1970), pp. 37-41.

24. U.S., Congress, Joint Committee on Taxation, *Proposed Depreciation and Investment Tax Credit Revisions, Part II: Present Law and Description of Proposals* (Washington, D.C.: U.S. Government Printing Office, 1981), p.203.

25. Energy Information Administration, *Monthly Energy Review*, March 1982, pp. 20,25.

26. *Ibid.* pp. 6, 25.

27. Alfred E. Kahn, *The Economics of Regulation: Principles and Institutions*, pp. 37-41.

28. Charles J. Hitch, "Utilities in Trouble," *Public Utilities Forthnightly*, 109(3):18-20 (1982).

29. Committee for Economic Development and The Conservation Foundation, *Energy Prices and Public Policy*, p. 35.

30. *Ibid.*, p. 35.

31. U.S. Department of Energy, Energy Information Administration, *1980 Annual Report to Congress, Vol. II: Data* (Washington, D.C.: U.S. Government Printing Office, 1981), p. 153.

32. Peter Navarro, *Our Stake in Electric Utility's Dilemma*, p. 59.

33. *Ibid.*, p. 89.

34. Charles S. Hitch, *Utilities in Trouble*, p. 3.

35. Energy Information Administration, *Monthly Energy Review*, March 1982, pp. 6,25,64.

36. The Aerospace Corporation, Electric and Hybrid Vehicle Directorate, *Performance and Cost Assessment of the Electric Vehicle Project: Electric and Hybrid Vehicle Program* (Washington, D.C.: U.S. Department of Energy, Office of Transportation Programs, March 1981), p. vii.

37. Bridger M. Mitchell, et al., *Peak-Load Pricing* (Cambridge, Mass.: Ballinger Publishing Company, 1978), pp. 206-207.

38. Jan Paul Acton, et al., *Promoting Energy Efficiency Through Improved Electricity Pricing: A Mid-Project Report* (Santa Monica, Calif.: The Rand Corporation, 1982) pp. 25-26.

39. Richard Corrigan, "Carter's Latest Energy Plan-Fill in the Blanks," *National Journal*, 11(15):608 (1979).

40. Committee on Economic Development and The Conservation Foundation, *Energy Prices and Public Policy*, pp. 58-67.

41. *Ibid.*, p. 37.

42. *Petroleum Intelligence Weekly*, (March 11, 1974), p. 6.

43. *Energy Information Administration, Monthly Energy Review*, p. 32, 76.

44. President Richard M. Nixon, Message to Congress, January 23, 1974, reprinted in Council on Environmental Quality, *Environmental Quality: 1974* (Washington, D.C.: U.S. Government Printing Office, 1974), pp. 551-563.

45. The Synthetic Fuels Corporation was created by The Energy Security Act of 1980, 42 U.S.C., sec. 8711-8719 (1981).

46. The Energy Policy and Conservation Act of 1975, 42 U.S.C., sec. 6247 (1981).

47. Information provided by U.S. Department of Energy, Strategic Petroleum Reserve, May 1982.

48. National Petroleum Council, Committee on Emergency Preparedness, *Emergency Preparedness for Interruption of Petroleum Imports into the United States* (Washington, D.C.: National Petroleum Council, 1981), p. 112.

49. Energy Information Administration, *Monthly Energy Review: March 1982*, p. 30.

50. Committee on Energy Preparedness, *Emergency Preparedness for Interruption of Petroleum Imports into the United States*, pp. 107-109.

51. Information provided by U.S. Department of Energy, Strategic Petroleum Reserve, May 1982.

52. U.S. Comptroller General, *Strategic Petroleum Reserve: Substantial Progress Made But Capacity and Oil Quality Concerns Remain* (Washington, D.C.: General Accounting Office, 1981), p. 30.

53. U.S. Department of Energy, Resource Applications, *Strategic Petroleum Reserve Plan: Distribution Plan for the Strategic Petroleum Reserve*, Amendment No. 3 (Springfield, Va.:

National Technical Information Service, 1979).

54. Information provided by the U.S. Department of Energy, 1982.

55. Paul W. MacAvoy, *Federal Energy Administration: Regulatory Report of the Presidential Task Force* (Washington, D.C.: American Enterprise Institute, 1977), pp. 1-195.

56. "Senate Fails to Override Reagan's Veto on Bill," *Wall Street Journal*, March 25, 1982, p. 2.

57. Energy Information Administration, *Monthly Energy Review*, March 1982, p. 6.

FIGURE REFERENCES

Figure 5.1

(1950-1979)—U.S. Department of Energy, Energy Information Administration, *1980 Annual Report to Congress, Volume Two: Data* (Washington: U.S. Government Printing Office, April, 1981), pp. 5, 7. (1980-1981)—U.S. Department of Energy, Energy Information Administration, *Monthly Energy Review*, February 1982 (Washington: U.S. Government Printing Office, 1982), p. 4.

Figure 5.2

(1960-1979)—U.S. Department of Energy, Energy Information Administration, *1980 Annual Report to Congress, Volume Two: Data* (Washington: U.S. Government Printing Office, 1981), pp. 6-7. (1980-1981)—U.S. Department of Energy, Energy Information Administration, *Monthly Energy Review*, March 1982 (Washington: U.S. Government Printing Office, 1982), p. 8.

Figure 5.3

1960-1979: U.S. Department of Energy, Energy Information Administration, *1980 Annual Report to Congress, Volume Two: Data*, (Washington: U.S. Government Printing Office, 1981), pp. 8-9. (1980-1981)—U.S. Department of Energy, Energy Information Administration, *Monthly Energy Review*, February 1982, (Washington: U.S. Government Printing Office, 1982), p. 21.

Figure 5.4

For Residential, Industrial & Commercial Sectors: Eric Hirst, Coordinator, *Energy Use from 1973 to 1980: The Role of Improved Energy Efficiency*, Energy Division, Oak Ridge National Laboratory, ORNL CON-79, Draft, (Oak Ridge, Tenn.: Oak Ridge National Laboratory, 1979). For Motor Vehicles: U.S. Department of Transportation, Federal Highway Administration, Federal Highway Statistics Division, *Highway Statistics* (Washington: U.S. Government Printing Office, 1980), Table VM-1. The Federal Reserve Board index of industrial output was used as the measure in calculating industrial energy use intensity.

Figure 5.5

Energy Consumption: U.S. Department of Energy, Energy Information Administration, *1980 Annual Report to Congress, Volume Two: Data* (Washington: U.S. Government Printing Office, April, 1981). p.7. GNP: Executive Office of the President, Council of Economic Advisors, *Economic Report of the President* (Washington: U.S. Government Printing Office, 1981), p. 234.

Figure 5.6

(1960-1979)—U.S. Department of Energy, Energy Information Administration, *1980 Annual Report to Congress, Volume Two: Data* (Washington: U.S. Government Printing Office, 1981), pp. 4-5. (1980-1981)—U.S. Department of Energy, Energy Information Administration, *Monthly Energy Review*, February, 1982, (Washington: U.S. Government Printing Office, 1982), p. 6.

Figure 5.7

(1950-1979)—U.S. Department of Energy, Energy Information Administration, *1980 Annual Report to Congress, Volume Two: Data* (Washington: U.S. Government Printing Office, 1981), p. 15. (1980-1981)—U.S. Department of Energy, Energy Information Administration, *Monthly Energy Review*, February 1982 (Washington: U.S. Government Printing Office, 1982), p. 10.

Figure 5.8

(1971)—U.S. Department of the Interior, Bureau of Mines, *Minerals Yearbook* (Washington: U.S. Government Printing Office, 1971), p. 334. (1975)—U.S. Department of the Interior, Bureau of Mines, *Coal Bituminous and Lignite Annual* (Washington, D.C.: Bureau of Mines, 1975), Table 8, p. 11. (1980)—U.S. Department of Energy, Energy Information Administration, *Weekly Coal Production*, Report No. 212 (Washington: U.S. Department of Energy, 1981), Table 5, p. 6. The Bureau of Mines only provides production data for twenty-six coal-producing states.

Figure 5.9

(1960-1980)—U.S. Department of Energy, Energy Information Administration, *1980 Annual Report to Congress, Volume Two: Data* (Washington: U.S. Government Printing Office, 1981), p. 95 (motor gasoline & residential heating oil), p. 171 (residential electricity), p. 119 (natural gas). (1981)—U.S. Department of Energy, Energy Information Administration, *Monthly Energy Review*, April 1982, (Washington: U.S. Government Printing Office, 1982), p. 4.

Consumer Price Index, all items less energy (1972 = 100): Executive Office of the President, Council of Economic Advisors, *Economic Report of the President* (Washington, D.C.: U.S. Government Printing Office, 1982), Table B-54, p. 294.

Motor gasoline prices are for leaded regular. They are calculated from a sample of service stations providing all types of service (i.e., full-, mini-, and self-service) in 85 urban areas.

Residential heating oil (No. 2 fuel oil) prices are derived by dividing the sum of the estimated national value of retail sales by the estimated volume of retail sales for residential heating only.

Residential natural gas average prices were calculated by dividing the total value of the gas consumed by the residential sector by the total quantity consumed.

Residential electricity is that sold by Classes A and B privately-owned electric utilities only.

Figure 5.10

Eric Hirst, Richard Goeltz, and John Trimble, "Energy Use from 1973 to 1980: The Role of Federal Conservation Programs," Draft (Oak Ridge, Tenn.: Oak Ridge National Laboratory, Energy Division, April 1982), p. 14.

Figure 5.11

U.S., Congress, Joint Committee on Taxation, "Proposed Depreciation and Investment Tax Credit Revisions, Part II: Present Law and Description of Proposals" (Washington, D.C.: U.S., Congress, May 1981), Table B.1.

OIL AND GAS LEASING IN WILDERNESS AREAS

1. In the spring of 1981, Secretary of Interior Watt stated that the goals of the Interior Department included increasing energy and minerals production and opening up wilderness areas. *Environmental Reporter*, "Current Developments," Vol. 12, no. 4, p. 128 (May 22, 1981).

2. U.S. Department of Agriculture, Forest Service, Recreation Management Staff "National Wilderness Preservation System, designated and proposed areas, 1964-1980" (1980).

3. Communication from U.S. Department of Agriculture, Forest Service, Recreation Management staff and U.S. Department of the Interior, Bureau of Land Management, Division of Recreation, Cultural and Wilderness Resources, May 1982.

4. 16 U.S.C., Section 1131(c) (1980).

5. 16 U.S.C., Section 1133(d)(3) (1980); 43 U.S.C. Section 1782(c) (1980).

6. "District Court's Approval of Bob Marshall upstaged by Watt's Proposed Wilderness Legislation," 12 *ELR* 10023, 10024 (1982).

7. *Ibid.*

8. *Ibid.*

9. "Unique Mineral Leases for Wilderness Surprise and Anger Environmentalists," *Washington Post*, November 14, 1981, p. A24.

10. William E. Schmidt, "Forest Office Backs Drilling in Second Wilderness Area," *New York Times*, November 14, 1981. See also, William E. Schmidt, "U.S. Considers Drilling Leases in a Wilderness," *New York Times*, August 30, 1981.

11. See, Wallace Turner, "U.S. Forest Aides Ponder Oil and Gas Leases," *New York Times*, October 24, 1981; "Oil and Gas Leasing commended in Los Padres Wilderness Areas," *Public Land News*, 6(21):5 (1981), p. 5.

12. See, "District Court's Approval of Bob Marshall Upstaged by Watt's Proposed Wilderness Legislation," 12 *ELR* 10023 (1982).

13. *Ibid.*, p. 10026. See also, H.R. 5603 (Feb. 24, 1982).

14. Additionally, BLM study areas may be recommended for non-wilderness status by the President and be opened by the Secretary of the Interior for immediate development. *Ibid.*, p. 10026.

15. The "National Minerals Security Act," proposed by Rep. Santini (R-N.M.), H.R. 3364 would allow mineral leasing in wilderness areas until the end of 1993. *Ibid.* See also, H.R. 5282, to withdraw the National Wilderness Preservation System from appropriation under the mining and mineral leasing laws, 97th Cong., 1st sess., 1982.

16. "Watt's One-Year Halt on Oil, Gas Leases in Wilderness Areas Called Win For Critics," *Wall Street Journal*, Feb. 1, 1982, p. 1.

Chapter 6

Agriculture and Forestry

Agriculture and forestry employ 3.5 percent of the U.S. work force,[1] use over 50 percent of our land,[2] and account for four times as much consumption of fresh water as all other uses combined.[3] These two sectors of the economy intentionally put toxic chemicals into the environment, can be major sources of water pollution and, to a lesser extent, air pollution, and are of fundamental and perhaps growing importance to the economy in general and to maintenance of the overall quality of life we have come to expect in the United States.

The agricultural sector, in particular, is going through very difficult times. Although crop and livestock production are reaching new highs, net farm income, adjusted for inflation, is the lowest it has been since 1933.[4] Farmers are more in debt than ever before; bankruptcies among farmers are expected to increase in 1982.[5] These economic conditions divert attention from many of the environmental issues associated with agriculture. The farmer's primary interest is to make enough money to get through the year. But the environmental issues involved in agriculture as well as in forestry also demand attention.

TRENDS IN AGRICULTURE AND FORESTRY

There are perhaps more statistics collected about agriculture than about any other economic sector. The statistics, however, are predominantly oriented toward commodity production and do not reflect the environmental effects of this production. Thus, there is information available on the use of resources, but little or none on how much pollution is generated by agriculture. The many statistics available about forestry are similar—that is, they are oriented toward factors relating to production of commercial forest products and not toward environmental effects associated with this production.

Agriculture

Our total agricultural production has continued to increase over the years (figure 6.1). This trend has occurred in all major crops, but most notably in corn and soybeans, which rose 60 percent and 61 percent, respectively, from 1970 to 1980.[6] Most of the increased production has been for export. Food consumption in the United States has risen slowly, with per capita consumption rising less than 1 percent from 1970 to 1980.*[7]

Agricultural exports have grown rapidly (figure 6.2). In 1980, 39 percent of our cropland was devoted to production for export, and agricultural products accounted for 19 percent of all U.S. exports.[8] Agricultural exports would likely have increased rapidly even without the spurts caused by major purchases in the world grain market by the Soviet Union in 1973 and 1981. Rising incomes in many less-developed countries have led to greater consumption of

Figure 6.1
Agricultural Production in the United States, 1967-1981

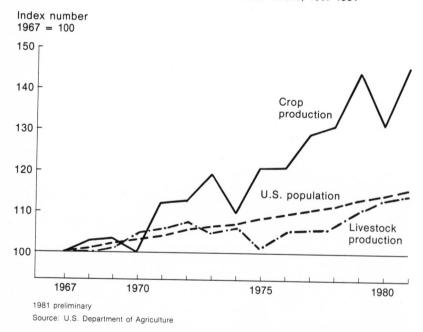

1981 preliminary
Source: U.S. Department of Agriculture

*The per capita consumption of meat is almost the same as it was in 1967, and is less than it was in 1971 and 1972. The per capita consumption of crops increased 7.1 percent between 1967 and 1980.

Figure 6.2
Exports of Agricultural Products, 1967-1980

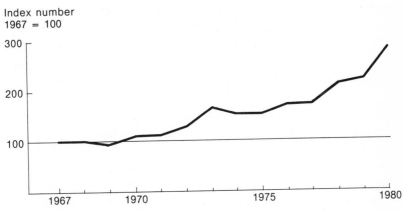

Index number
1967 = 100

Source: U.S. Department of Agriculture

beef and other animals, which are fed with grain exported from the United States. We can expect these demands to continue to increase.

The growth in agricultural production has been achieved by using more resources—more water, land, fertilizer, pesticides—and by improving the productivity of these resources. Figure 6.3 shows how resource use has increased. We farmed 57 million more acres of land in 1980 than we did in 1970, an increase of 19.7 percent. Over the same period, use of irrigation water rose 13.2 percent, and use of fertilizer 42.6 percent. Pesticide use has risen even faster— almost 100 percent from 1966 to 1976.* The only resource for which use is decreasing is labor.

In some areas of the United States, the resource limits of land and water are being severely tested. Many acres of lower-quality land have been brought into production, causing serious problems of erosion and water pollution. Groundwater supplies have been "mined" extensively for irrigation. The level of groundwater is declining beneath about half the lands where it is used for irrigation, at rates varying from 0.5 to over 6 feet per year (see chapter 3).[9] Since 1940, the groundwater level in the Ogallala Aquifer, where it underlies the Texas High Plains, has fallen about 200 feet.[10] In

---

*1976 is the last year for which there are data showing pesticide use on farms. Herbicide use, in particular, has grown rapidly (and now accounts for approximately 60 percent of total agricultural pesticide use) as the cost of other forms of weed control becomes relatively more expensive and as farmers adopt "low-till" farming techniques to reduce erosion. (See discussion of soil erosion below.)

Figure 6.3
Resources Used in Agricultural Production, 1960-1980

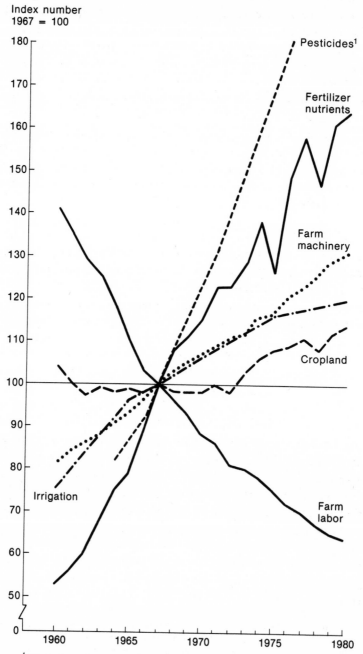

Source: U.S. Department of Agriculture

parts of Oklahoma, water levels in the same aquifer have dropped as much as 40 feet in 4 years.[11] Groundwater levels in Trans-Pecos County, Texas, are declining an average of 4 feet per year; those in Tulare County, California, an average of 6.6 feet per year.[12]

Figure 6.4 provides information on the distribution of U.S. cropland and indicates the areas where the increase in the amount of land under crops has been the greatest. The South (Southeast, Delta, and Appalachian states) has generally shown the largest advance in percentage terms over the past decade—as much as 44 percent in the Southeast—although the Northern Plains and Corn Belt states have the largest amount of land under crops. In the Corn Belt, as well in as in the Great Lakes states, most of the increase has been in row crops such as corn and soybeans, which make the land particularly subject to erosion.

In the future, because of potential shortages of some key resources, more emphasis will have to be put on productivity—that is, increasing the amount of production per unit of input—than on using more resources. Productivity improvements in agriculture have already been significant. Figure 6.5 shows the rate at which productivity has increased for land (yield per acre) as well as for all resources used in agriculture. In recent years, yields have fluctuated widely: rising 7 percent in 1979, decreasing 10 percent in 1980, and rising 12 percent in 1981. Some observers see the rate of productivity increase falling off in the future.[13]

Forestry

As indicated in chapter 7 (figure 7.2), the amount of forestland in the United States decreased slightly from 1969 to 1978. Between 1970 and 1977, the amount of commercial forestland decreased by about 2.8 percent;*[14] since 1977, as more land has been used for crop production, the rate of decline may have accelerated. Nonetheless, forests still cover nearly one-third of the United States, and the question of how we manage these lands is clearly of major environmental importance. It is also of major economic importance, for although the United States is a major producer of timber, and grows more wood than is cut each year, we are a net importer of timber products.

---

*Commercial forestland includes all forested land that produces over 20 cubic feet a year of timber and is not reserved for purposes other than timber production. Of the total of the more than 730 million acres of forest in the United States, approximately 480 million acres are considered commercial forest.

Figure 6.4
Cropland Used for Crops by Region and Type of Crop, 1969-1980

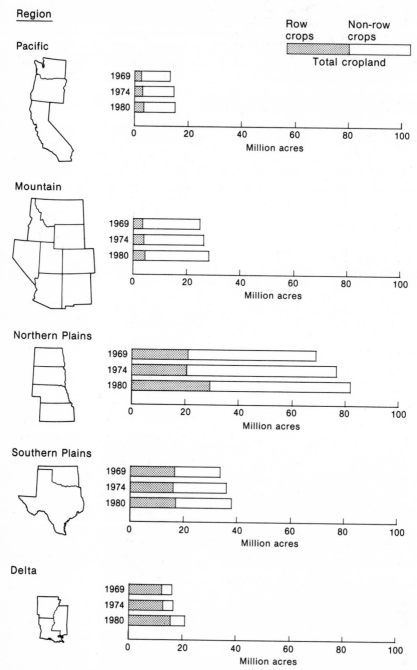

Lake

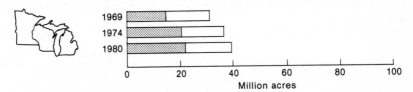

Corn Belt

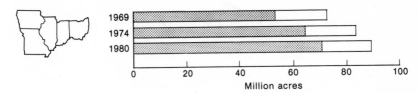

Northeast

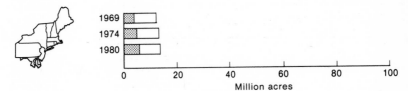

Appalachian

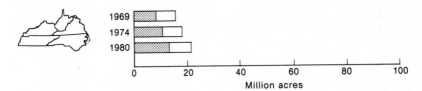

Southeast

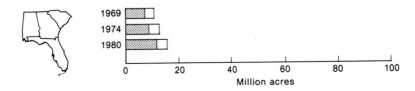

Row crops include planted acreage for corn, sorghum, soybeans, flaxseed, peanuts, sunflowers, cotton, drybeans, sugar beets, potatoes, and harvested acreage of tobacco.

Non-row crops include planted acreage of oats, barley, wheat, rice, rye, and harvested acreage of hay.

Regions are U.S. Department of Agriculture farm production regions.

Source: U.S. Department of Agriculture

Figure 6.5
Agricultural Productivity, 1967-1981

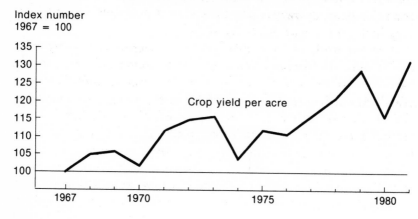

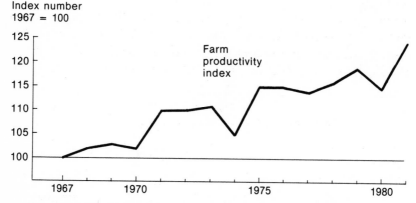

The farm productivity index is the ratio of total farm output to total farm input, measured in constant dollar values of each. Farm inputs include labor and such items and services as land, machinery, agricultural chemicals, and feed, seed, and livestock purchases. Farm outputs include crop and livestock production.

Source: U.S. Department of Agriculture

The federal government owns more than a third of our total forestland, and there are numerous statutes determining how this federal forestland is to be used. (For example, some of it is allocated to special uses, like wilderness, and cannot be used for commercial production.) The two other major holders of forestland are large corporations and "nonindustrial" private owners. The federal government, by law, must manage its lands to satisfy a number of different uses, including timber production, mining, recreation, wildlife habitat, and so forth. Large industrial owners may also practice such multiple uses, but their main focus is on timber production. Private, nonindustrial owners hold 58 percent of the commercial forestland.[15] This group includes a wide range of farmers and miscellaneous owners who have various goals and frequently do very little in the way of management.

A recent study of forest management, covering the period 1976 to 1978 in 25 timber-producing states, found that timber was harvested on about 1.3 percent of the commercial forestland each year.[16] About 36 percent of the area harvested was planted or seeded, and another 6 percent received site preparation for natural regeneration. Less than 1 percent of the total forest area received some form of intermediate stand management such as thinning. Harvesting and management activities were more intensive on forest industry lands than on government or privately owned lands.

Growth and Removal. The most recent assessment of the U.S. commercial timber situation, issued in 1980, shows that total net timber growth increased 9.6 percent between 1970 and 1976—a rate of 1.5 percent per year. The net growth of softwood timber rose 9.3 percent, and exceeded removals by roughly 22 percent in 1976 (figure 6.6). The net growth of hardwood timber was up 10

Figure 6.6
Timber Production: Growth and Harvest, 1952-1976

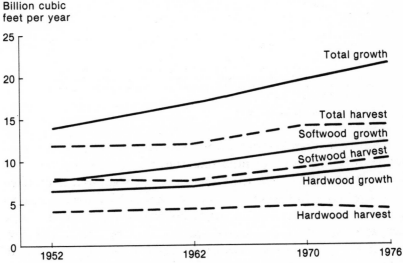

Hardwoods are usually broadleafed and deciduous trees such as oak, hickory, and maple.

Softwoods are conifers, usually evergreens, with needles or scale-like leaves, such as spruces, firs, cedars, and pines.

Source: U.S. Department of Agriculture, Forest Service

Figure 6.7
Exports and Imports of Forest Products, 1950-1980

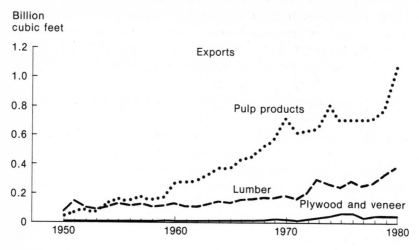

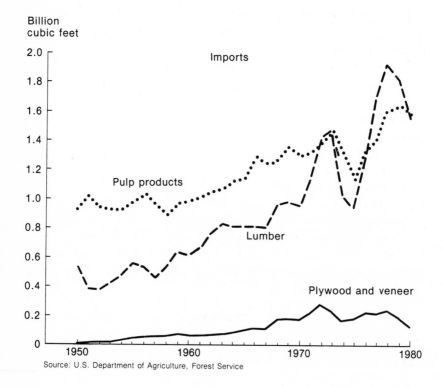

Source: U.S. Department of Agriculture, Forest Service

percent, and exceeded removals in 1976 by 124 percent.[17] These data suggest that the situation has improved substantially since 1952, when growth and removals of softwoods were about equal, while growth of hardwoods was about 52 percent greater than removals. However, as pointed out later in this chapter, this optimistic conclusion does not uniformly apply to all areas of the country or to all types of timber.

Exports and Imports. The United States has long been a net importer of timber and timber products (figure 6.7), despite the size and accessibility of our timber resources. Canada is the major supplier. Newsprint and wood pulp were the major imports from Canada for many years; during the 1970s, imports of softwood lumber greatly expanded.[18]

In volume, pulp products account for the largest category of U.S. exports, having risen 291 percent between 1960 and 1980 (equivalent to 7.1 percent per year). Log exports have also increased rapidly, primarily from the West Coast to Japan, although a surprisingly large volume also goes from New England to Canada.[19] It appears that log exports to Japan have peaked, and they are projected to decline after 1990.[20]

Exports of pulp products have been rising steadily since 1950. But we continue to import approximately 50 percent more pulp products than we export. In volume, the United States now imports about as much lumber as wood pulp, but the value of the lumber products is significantly greater.

Consumption. The net effect of changes in production, exports, and imports has been a relatively stable per capita consumption of forest products in the United States. Trends in consumption follow the general trend of economic conditions, and particularly trends in housing starts. In 1976, new houses accounted for 39 percent of our total consumption of lumber and 40 percent of plywood.[21] The consumption of wood for energy production has grown rapidly, particularly in the Northeast, but it still accounts for a very small percentage of total consumption.*

SELECTED ISSUES

Demands for increased production in our agricultural and forestry sectors are creating and exacerbating a number of resource and

---

*The statistics on fuel wood are very uncertain, and are thought by many to be substantially underestimated.

environmental problems. The following pages deal with four issues: increased erosion from agricultural lands, the loss of prime farmland to nonagricultural uses, the prospects for improving the productivity of our forestlands, and the conflicts between timber production and wildlife habitat in our forests.

These issues are interrelated. If we cannot maintain high agricultural productivity on our best cropland, we will probably have to bring other lands into crop production. In addition to forestlands, these will include wetlands (see box, page 249), lands having a high potential for erosion, and less fertile lands requiring large fertilizer, pesticide, and energy inputs that can create serious environmental impacts. Increasing productivity on prime farmlands will also require the additional use of such inputs, but the resulting environmental impacts are likely to be much less than those associated with new lands brought into production.

Similar interrelationships exist in the forestry sector. Lower rates of productivity improvement will increase the pressure to harvest more fragile lands, more erodible lands, and areas providing wilderness, recreation, undisturbed wildlife habitat, and other valuable functions. In areas where tree growth is particularly rapid—for instance, the Southeast—lower forest productivity may also result in conversion of agricultural and grazing lands into forests. As with farmland, there will inevitably be adverse environmental impacts associated with improving the productivity of our best forestland, but these impacts are likely to be less than those associated with harvesting large areas of less desirable land.

Soil Erosion

In spite of the estimated \$15 to \$30 billion devoted to controlling soil erosion over the past 40 years,[22] recently tabulated information from the 1977 National Resources Inventory indicates that the problem remains extremely serious. In 1977, for each ton of corn raised by an Iowa farmer, 5 tons of soil eroded from that state's land. Nationally, over 6.4 billion tons of soil a year are lost in water and wind erosion. Eighty-three percent of this (5.3 billion tons) is from agricultural land (including cropland, pasture, grazing lands, and forestland), and more than half of this, equivalent to 89 tons per second, is from cropland (figure 6.8).

The rate of erosion depends on how land is being used and on the characteristics of the land itself. Lands permanently covered with vegetation have lower erosion rates than croplands. On cropland,

Figure 6.8
Soil Erosion by Land Use, 1977

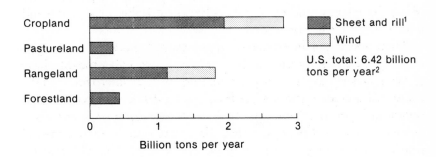

Billion tons per year

[1] Sheet erosion occurs when beating rain and flowing water remove layers of soil from the land. Rill erosion occurs as the flowing water carves out small channels.

[2] U.S. total includes an additional 1.10 billion tons per year of soil eroded from streambanks, gullies, roads and roadsides, and construction sites.

Source: U.S. Department of Agriculture, Soil Conservation Service

the rate of erosion ranges from a national average of 2.8 tons per acre per year on the best land, to an average, in some states, of over 50 tons per acre per year on the poorest.[23] Because so much of the cropland in the United States is high quality, over 75 percent of the total cropland erosion comes from the three best classes of land (which account for 85 percent of all cropland).[24] The inverse of this statistic is that a quarter of our total cropland erosion comes from the 15 percent of land not in these top three classes.

Although soil erosion occurs everywhere in the United States, the most serious problems tend to be concentrated in specific areas. Almost a third of our agricultural land is experiencing very little erosion (less than one ton per acre per year), accounting for a little over 2 percent of total erosion. At the other extreme, slightly less than 3 percent of our land (including some of our best cropland) is eroding at a rate of more than 25 tons per acre per year, but this amounts to almost a third of total erosion.[25]

As indicated in figure 6.9, over half the cropland erosion occurs in the Corn Belt and the Northern Plains. However, Hawaii and the Caribbean Islands, as well as the Appalachian states, have higher erosion rates per acre of land. The erosion in the Corn Belt is of particular concern because this is one of the most productive agricultural areas in the world. Its intense cultivation in row crops (such as corn and soybeans) results in over a third of the cropland

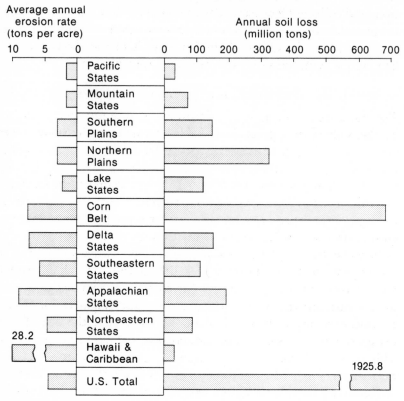

Figure 6.9
Cropland Erosion by Region, 1977

Includes sheet and rill erosion only.
Regions are U.S. Department of Agriculture farm production regions (see figure 6.4).
Source: U.S. Department of Agriculture, Soil Conservation Service

eroding at an annual rate of 5 tons per acre or more.*[26]

There are serious local erosion problems in other regions. For instance, in Washington, Oregon, and Idaho, the combination of steep slopes and easily erodible soil produces erosion rates of 50 to 100 tons per acre annually in some cropped areas. And in some parts of Maine, the intense cultivation used in growing potatoes over the past decade or two has resulted in a loss of up to 24 inches of topsoil.[28]

Even these data on soil erosion do not tell the whole story. The

---

*Five tons is roughly considered to be a tolerable erosion rate, although, in fact, the "tolerable rate" may be lower, depending on the depth of topsoil and the rate at which new topsoil forms. The depth varies widely; thus, the loss of an inch of topsoil may mean a significant portion of the topsoil is lost or that only a very small fraction of it is lost.[27]

1977 National Resources Inventory, though the most extensive survey to date, produced incomplete information on rangeland erosion, and collected few useful data on wind erosion. The information it did collect on wind erosion indicates that over 27.7 million acres of cropland in the Great Plains (two-thirds of the total cropland) had annual wind erosion rates of over 5 tons per acre.[29]

Impacts of Soil Erosion

The statistics on the amount of erosion, though impressive, do not by themselves say a great deal. Serious erosion problems have been occurring for many years, yet agricultural production continues to increase.

Soil erosion poses two problems, one that occurs on the farm and one that occurs off the farm. The on-farm problem is predominantly lost agricultural productivity. The off-farm problem is the effect of erosion on the environment downstream (or downwind).

On-Farm Impacts. Under natural conditions, it takes from 300 to 1,000 years to form one inch of soil;[30] at the "tolerable" erosion rate of five tons per acre per year, it takes only 33 years to lose an inch. Thus, for the most part, U.S. cropland soil is being eroded significantly faster than it is being formed. And the soil that is being eroded is the soil that is most productive for farming—topsoil. This is the soil that usually is highest in organic content, has the most nutrients, and is best at holding the water needed by crops.

Relatively little information exists on the extent to which erosion decreases soil productivity. Average productivity nationally has continued to increase at a rapid rate. In the absence of soil erosion, productivity might have risen faster, or required fewer inputs, such as fertilizer, to achieve the same level. A farmer can usually compensate for the loss of natural productivity by applying more fertilizer—at least until erosion becomes so severe that the soil's capacity to hold water is substantially affected. Because of new crop varieties and increased fertilizer use, crop yields generally have not declined despite erosion. However, there is also evidence that, at some point, productivity can drop suddenly and substantially—by as much as 40 to 60 percent.[31] Moreover, even if farmers compensate for losses in natural productivity for a time, they do so only by increasing their costs of production.

Off-Farm Impacts. Off the farm, much eroded soil ends up in streams, rivers, lakes, and reservoirs. (See box, page 238.) The sediment entering streams and rivers can increase flood damage,

The Illinois River:
An Ecological Disaster

The effects of the cycle of sedimentation and ruin can be seen most vividly along the Illinois River. What has happened to the Illinois system—the river plus backwater lakes, sloughs and flood plains which originally totaled roughly 400,000 acres—since the turn of the century is an ecological catastrophe. Seventy-five years ago the lower Illinois attracted swimmers and boaters from across the state. Summer resorts flourished, and each fall hunters swarmed into the Illinois valley from many states in search of migratory waterfowl so numerous that even a mediocre shot could bag up to 100 ducks a day. Fishing was equally good, and not just for the sportsman. In the early 1900s the 15 million pounds of fish, mussel and turtle taken from the river made it the second richest commercial fresh water fishery in the U.S. after the Great Lakes.

Within a generation, however, half the backwater lakes along the river were drained and put under the plow. Pollution from cities upstream (mainly Chicago) turned the Illinois into a sewer; by 1920 the river was dead, devoid of dissolved oxygen, as far south as Chillicothe.

Improved sewage treatment upstream gradually cleaned the water, and the river ecosystem revived through the 1940s and 50s, only to fall victim to a second enemy—sediment. The Illinois is truly a "river gently flowing," as the state song says; its vertical drop from source to mouth is very modest, and flow is further slowed by a series of navigation dams. Since the ability of moving water to carry sediment varies with its speed, the lethargic Illinois drops most of its sediment in and (when its waters overflow in flood) along its channel.

Soil pollution, in the opinion of Frank Bellrose of the Illinois Natural History Survey, has proved to be even worse than sewage or chemical pollution because "it's more insidious and it's more persistent." The backwater lakes that were not already drained have been gradually strangled by sediment from the farms of the rich Illinois valley.

The effects of sedimentation on the river's ecosystem are dire. Except for carp and buffalo, most of the fish are gone, as are the mussels. Waterfowl populations have survived somewhat better, but even the migratory flocks are finding the valley a less congenial stopover; the weedy biomass of the river's backwater lakes—a sizable proportion of which is duck food—averaged more than a ton per acre in the 1920s but by the 60s many of them yielded none at all. They are half to three-fourths filled with mud, and in the worst of them it is hard to find enough water to float a canoe.

Researchers from the Illinois Natural History Survey and its predecessor agencies have been studying the Illinois system since 1890. Their investigation has taken on the nature of an autopsy. They have learned that the rate of sedimentation has been increasing in recent years, going from an average of 0.67 inches per year prior to 1965 to 1.21 inches per year since then. A study by the state's Water Survey reveals that 25 million tons of soil pour into the Illinois each year. Of this, 14 million tons remain in the river as sediment—a statistic Bellrose characterizes as "startling."

Peoria Lake will be a mud flat in 50 years; the 3,000-acre Lake Chautauqua federal wildlife preserve will disappear in a century. The average depth of the remaining 70,000 acres of backwater lakes is now only two feet, and scientists fear that because heavy rains kept river waters in the lakes for long periods, 1981 may prove to be one of the worst years on record for sedimentation. In time the lakes will become mosquito-ridden bottomland forests populated by willows, cottonwoods and soft maples.

— by James Krohe, Jr.
   Reprinted from Illinois Issues, November, 1981. Published by Sangamon State University, Springfield, Illinois 62708.

hinder inland waterway traffic, and destroy valuable fish spawning beds and other wildlife habitat. As sediment enters lakes and reservoirs, it settles to the bottom, reducing their capacity to prevent floods or to store water for municipal supplies and irrigation. Irreplaceable reservoir storage capacity is continually being silted up. Where this is occurring, the reservoirs may some day be little more than long flat plains.

Other, perhaps more serious problems arise because erosion from cropland not only includes natural soil but also fertilizers and pesticides. Pesticides can be toxic to fish, and potentially to humans. Fertilizers cause algae to grow, accelerating the eutrophication of lakes and reservoirs. As algae die and decay, they use up oxygen, sometimes reducing oxygen levels so much that some fish species can no longer survive. These off-site pollution problems are exacerbated when farmers try to compensate for lost productivity by using more fertilizers, pesticides, and other inputs, without reducing the amount of erosion.

Both on-farm and off-farm problems from soil erosion are, at least potentially, very serious. The off-farm problems may be more serious in areas like the Appalachian Mountains, where increased sediment loads can contribute to the size of floods, and in the West, where reserviors are vital in maintaining the water supply. The on-farm problems may be more serious in areas like Maine, where important potato-growing lands are losing productivity rapidly, and in the Corn Belt, which produces large amounts of food for America and the rest of the world.

Why Soil Erosion Continues

Government has promoted soil conservation since at least the mid-1930s, and most farmers and landowners are probably well aware of appropriate soil conservation practices. For all but the most extreme cases, there are well-proved technologies for reducing erosion to tolerable rates, and these technologies are not only widely advertised, but often subsidized. Why, then, do we still have a problem?

The reason for the continuing problem lies principally in the economics of soil conservation. Measures to control erosion almost always impose some cost on the farmer (one important exception is discussed below). Careful contour plowing is more expensive—particularly given the large size of new machinery—than plowing long, straight rows. Constructing terraces requires an often substantial up-front investment. Many plans to control soil erosion require leaving hedgerows to reduce wind erosion, and stream banks and other lands uncropped to reduce water erosion, thereby reducing the amount of land in production, with a corresponding loss of potential revenues. These immediate costs may well seem to be larger to the farmer than the costs of allowing soil erosion to continue.

Furthermore, a farmer weighing the pros and cons of implementing soil conservation practices will probably not consider all of the pros and may underestimate some of those that are considered. Off-farm costs, for example, are likely to be ignored—someone else must pay them. But these costs are real, and should be included in the social calculus. Even when it comes to on-farm costs, expectations regarding productivity loss are likely to be based on past experience—experience that may not be a good guide for the future.

Three other factors that can precipitate a decision against erosion control include interest rates, conditions of farm tenure, and short-term profitability. The high interest rates over the past few years have discouraged many investments, particularly those that pay off as slowly as erosion control.

Farm tenure may also have an impact. An owner-operator can expect to reap the benefits of erosion control investments over many years. A tenant, renting land on an annual basis, may not, and thus would be less likely to make an investment. A landlord, not actually working the farm, may not be aware of the seriousness of the erosion problem. Several studies have shown that there is likely to be more conservation on land that is farmed by the owner than on land that is farmed by a tenant.*[32]

Short-term profitability in farming may also be a factor weighing against erosion control. Although there are no sufficiently detailed data on annual rates of erosion to document sharp changes from one year to the next, the rate of erosion appears to have begun to rise during the early 1970s.[34] This was when the rapid increase in foreign demand for U.S. agricultural exports stimulated farmers to intensify cultivation, and to begin cultivating more land by removing acreage from the "land banks" established to support agricultural prices. In periods of weak demand, farmers tend to idle those lands that are the most difficult to farm or that are the least productive. These

---

*Other studies, however, have found no clear relationship between farm tenure and erosion control.[33]

lands (steeply sloped lands, for example) are also the ones that are likely to be most susceptible to serious soil erosion.

A relative decline in livestock prices may also affect land use and contribute to erosion problems. As cattle prices fall, farmers may decrease the size of their herds, and shift land out of pasture and hay into row crops. Pasture and hay produce less soil erosion than such row crops as corn and soybeans. There are signs that this occurred during the 1970s. From the beginning of 1975 to the end of 1977, cattle prices received by farmers were essentially constant (which, because of increased costs, means that real prices were declining).[35] Between 1974 and 1978, the proportion of farms with livestock declined from 65 percent to 59 percent.[36] Among smaller farms, and in many states experiencing particularly high erosion rates, the decline was even greater. For instance, during this period, the proportion of smaller farms in Iowa with livestock declined from 51 percent to 37 percent.[37] This kind of shift can be difficult to reverse, because the farmer tends to remove fences surrounding pasture and allow livestock buildings to fall into disrepair. Livestock prices would probably have to increase substantially to stimulate a return to raising livestock once such disinvestment has occurred.

Government Efforts to Promote Conservation

The U.S. Department of Agriculture has at least 30 different programs dealing with soil and water conservation.[38] The most important of these programs are the Agricultural Conservation Program (administered by the Agricultural Stabilization and Conservation Service, ASCS), which provides financial assistance to farmers for soil conservation investments, and several technical assistance programs (administered by the Soil Conservation Service, SCS) that prepare soil erosion control plans and provide other technical advice for farmers, primarily through local conservation districts. The ASCS and SCS also have a number of other, more limited, cost-sharing, technical assistance, data collection, and data analysis programs. In addition, the Farmers Home Administration, the Agricultural Research Service, the Cooperative State Research Service, the Extension Service, and the Forest Service have complementary research, financial assistance, and technical assistance programs.

There is no way of knowing how much erosion has been prevented by these programs. One study, covering about 24,000 erosion control measures adopted by farmers in 171 counties, found that sheet and rill erosion had been reduced by 4.1 million tons a year, or 61 percent of the amount of erosion occurring prior to the adoption of the measures.[39] However, this study, as well as previous studies, concluded that much of the federal assistance had gone to lands having relatively minor erosion problems, and that in many cases the farmer seemed more interested in increasing productivity than in reducing soil erosion.[40]

Nor have the continuing expenditures resulted in steady progress in installing erosion control measures. To the contrary, the net investment in erosion control measures appears to have decreased since the mid-1950s. Since then, the cost of control measures installed has been less than the replacement cost of control measures that have been removed or allowed to deteriorate.[41]

Other government programs, some of which are implemented for quite unrelated reasons, can have an important—and sometimes greater—impact on soil conservation than do the soil conservation programs themselves. For instance, stabilization and price support programs, though directed at supporting agricultural prices, can have important ancillary benefits in controlling soil erosion. Under these programs, the government pays farmers to take land out of production to reduce agricultural output and thus generate higher commodity prices. As pointed out above, the idled lands are, in many cases, precisely the lands most susceptible to erosion when cultivated. However, the effect of these programs almost disappeared during the 1970s, as farmers brought their idled lands back into production in response to high export demand for agricultural goods.

Government research and extension agencies are providing substantial support for new "conservation tillage" techniques that can reduce erosion rates substantially. Under the most extreme form, "no-till," the farmer does not plow, but controls weeds with herbicides, and plants crops through the crop stubble and dead weeds with a special heavy-duty seed drill. The major incentives favoring the adoption of such techniques are their savings in fuel and labor costs. But, because the fields are not stripped and cultivated, there is also substantially less erosion. One potential concern with this technique is that increased herbicide use may cause serious pollution problems. There is as yet, however, too little information to allow this risk to be evaluated.

It is not clear how much more our traditional soil conservation programs can accomplish. Development of significant new conservation technologies through additional research is unlikely. Still, it would be very useful to have a better understanding of the on-farm and off-farm impacts of soil erosion, and of the most efficient methods of soil conservation under current economic conditions and farming practices. Most farmers are generally familiar with erosion control techniques. Yet many still depend on the site-specific plans and technical assistance provided by the diminishing cadre of SCS field representatives. Financial assistance programs may still have an important role. But if the programs continue to be operated as they have in the past, the budgetary impacts are potentially very large.

There do appear to be opportunities for spending government funds much more effectively. A Department of Agriculture evaluation of past soil erosion investments found that over half of the activities studied were undertaken on lands eroding at less than five tons per acre per year (that is, within the "tolerable" range), whereas only a fifth were on highly eroding lands (more than 14 tons per acre), which were, in aggregate, responsible for 86 percent of the erosion.[42] The evaluation concluded that targeting the funds to achieve maximum erosion reduction "could more than triple the amount of soil saved through the program."*[43]

Policy Options

Soil erosion seems to be an almost intractable problem. Each farmer is an independent decision maker; most do not have the proper incentives for controlling erosion; some may lack adequate information. Certainly, the government has been actively trying to deal with this problem for a longer period than it has spent on practically any other environmental problem, but with only limited success. How, then, can soil conservation be promoted?

More Research. One option is to continue to conduct research on soil erosion and its control in the hope that there may be a technological breakthrough or that additional information on the impact of erosion on farm productivity will convince more farmers that it would be profitable for them to adopt soil conservation measures. This approach might help, and is a relatively low-cost option, although the results are very uncertain because there is no direct link between such research and reduced erosion. This approach also does not directly modify the often adverse economic incentives facing the farmer.

---

*The Department of Agriculture has announced that it will begin a limited targeting program in 1982, involving $9 million of agricultural conservation funds in 15 states.[44]

Making Conservation Cheaper. A more direct approach to controlling soil erosion is to attempt to modify economic incentives for farmers so that conservation investments look profitable. This approach is the basis of most existing programs, which have focused on making conservation cheaper either by providing free technical assistance or by subsidizing the conservation investments themselves. The programs have obvious political appeal, but can be very expensive and, as noted, often have not been focused on the most serious erosion problems.[45] The likelihood of additional funds being allocated to these programs, given current budget policies, is slim.

Available funds could be spent more effectively by "targeting" the most serious problems. However, there are several difficulties involved in doing this. First, a broader distribution of funds is more attractive politically. Second, it can be difficult to identify the precise lands that create the most serious erosion problems, much less those lands where erosion control expenditures would be most "cost effective."* Third, the owners of targeted lands may not be receptive to assistance. (Existing programs give help primarily to the farmers who want it, which means that improvements have been made faster and with fewer difficulties than might be involved in targeting.) An effective targeting program would probably require more teeth than existing programs.

Finally, in targeting the most serious problems, the government would have to make judgments about the relative seriousness of, and public interest in, the two types of problems associated with soil erosion—the on-farm productivity problem and the off-farm environmental problems. Determining how serious each really is would be difficult. And even this information would not, in itself, define an appropriate targeting strategy. For instance, even if the total cost of lost productivity were greater than the total cost of off-farm environmental problems, that would not necessarily mean that government should focus its efforts on areas where productivity losses are greatest. The farmer already has some incentive to solve on-farm problems, but little or none to solve off-farm problems. The most efficient government program might well be one that only attempts to inform the farmer of the on-farm costs, and focuses any financial assistance on providing the farmer with an incentive

---

*That is to say, it is difficult to identify the lands that would provide the most erosion control benefits per dollar spent. These are not necessarily those lands having the worst erosion problems; control measures there may be too expensive and the benefits of enhanced productivity too low to be "cost effective."

to solve the off-site problems. Clearly, a substantial amount of analysis, in addition to a good measure of political courage, is needed before an effective targeting program can be implemented. However, given the severe limitations on funds available for subsidies, can we afford not to be spending funds more efficiently?

Making Erosion More Expensive. An alternative way of providing the farmer with stronger incentives to practice soil conservation would be to make it more expensive for him not to adopt such measures where they are needed. This might be done through adopting laws that require that conservation efforts be adopted on land with serious erosion problems. It could also be accomplished by charging farmers for the amount of soil that erodes from their land. Or farmers could be paid for the amount of soil that they prevent from eroding.

The first alternative has been adopted by some local governments, at least at construction sites, but would probably be politically difficult to apply to farmers—particularly from the federal level. The second approach, though perhaps theoretically attractive, has yet to be adopted as the primary approach in any environmental program and would present significant problems in determining exactly how much any specific farmer should be charged. Controlling soil erosion would scarcely seem to be a promising area for experimenting with a system of charges. The third approach would avoid some of the political opposition associated with the second, but would be even more difficult to implement because it is impossible to know precisely how much soil would have eroded if the farmer had not taken action.

An indirect way of making soil erosion more expensive would be to prohibit other government benefits, such as commodity loans, if farmers are not practicing adequate soil conservation. Called "cross-compliance," this approach was actively considered in the Carter Administration.[46] It would appear to involve fewer (though certainly not insignificant) logistic and political problems than the first three approaches. Cross-compliance may create some equity problems insofar as some farmers (those who own high-quality, nonsloping lands or who farm in areas of light rainfall) would receive other program benefits without much or any expenditure on soil conservation, whereas other farmers would have to spend significant amounts. If the latter tended to be poorer and have smaller farms—that is, if they tended to be precisely those people whom income-maintenance programs are intended to benefit—the cross-compliance ap-

246 STATE OF THE ENVIRONMENT 1982

proach might have to be coupled with a generous program subsidizing conservation expenditures. The cross-compliance approach also loses its effectiveness during periods, like the present, when farmers are relying very little on government income-support programs.

The Loss of Prime Agricultural Land

From 1967 to 1977, some 2 to 3 million acres of agricultural land (including cropland, pasture, rangeland, and forest) were converted each year to homes, roads, artificial lakes, or other uses:[47] 675,000 acres of this lost land were cropland,[48] and almost 1 million acres were "prime farmland."[49]

Over 30 percent (413 million acres) of the privately owned agricultural land (1,364 million acres) in the United States is currently classified as cropland, with another 10 percent (127 million acres) having a high or medium potential for conversion to that use.*[50] Almost half the potential cropland lies in the South, which currently accounts for roughly a fourth of existing cropland (figure 6.10). Between 1967 and 1975, more land was being shifted out of crops than into them; most of this land was converted to other agricultural uses (see discussion in chapter 7 and figure 7.3).

The amount of prime farmland being lost is a small percentage of total U.S. agricultural land—less than 0.1 percent annually. But there are two disturbing factors about this trend. First, the land base is fixed; it cannot be increased. Second, conversion to urban uses is essentially irreversible. Given these considerations, it is sobering to realize that we are losing "forever" approximately 8,000 acres of agricultural land per day; from 1967 to 1975, an area equivalent to 23.3 million acres of agricultural land was lost to urbanized uses.[51] If this is extrapolated linearly into the future, we will eventually be facing a very serious problem.

Moreover, the real loss in prime agricultural land may be much greater than indicated by the data showing the amount of land actually converted. In addition to soil erosion, other physical factors have contributed to reductions in the ability of land to grow crops—for example, excessive compaction of the soil from large farming machinery, the accumulation of crop-killing salts in topsoil because

---

*The definition of cropland is "land used to produce crops for harvest, either alone or in rotation with grasses and legumes. Cropland uses include row crops, close grown field crops, hay crops, rotation hay and pasture, nursery crops, orchard crops, other specialty crops, summer fallow, and other cropland temporarily idled or in conservation uses."

Figure 6.10
Potential New Cropland by Region, 1977

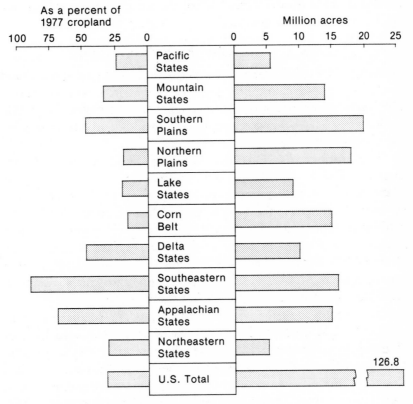

Regions are U.S. Department of Agriculture farm production regions (see figure 6.4)

Source: U.S. Department of Agriculture, Soil Conservation Service

of inadequate irrigation practices, and the depletion of available water supplies.

One study of rural land markets discovered a serious problem of "parcellation"—that is, a tendency to divide large parcels of land into smaller ones.[52] Smaller parcels may seriously interfere with the ability to use land productively for farming, since the economics of agriculture tend to make larger-scale operations more profitable. Parcellation is also frequently accompanied by low-density settlements, which create additional problems for neighboring farms.

The possibility of conversion, finally, has led to what has been called the "impermanence syndrome."[53] Particularly on the borders of metropolitan areas and in other locations where land conversion is occuring rapidly, farmers often tend not to maintain their farms adequately, assuming that the farms will soon be sold. Thus, land deteriorates and capital improvements are not made, with an inevitable loss in productivity.

There may be serious environmental impacts associated with the loss of prime cropland. If, in order to compensate for lost crop production, land has to be converted from other uses, the land brought into production is likely to be of a lower quality than the land that is removed. Thus, for every acre lost, more than an acre will be needed as a replacement. Lands of lower quality may well be more subject to erosion, may require more energy, more pesticides, more fertilizers, and generally involve higher costs of production. In addition, creating new cropland may involve draining wetlands and destroying other valuable wildlife habitats. These lands are already scarce, and their continued loss (likely to be irreversible) is of increasing concern.

The Demand for Cropland

Given reasonable assumptions about technological improvements and future growth in population and food consumption, we are unlikely for many decades to have a serious problem feeding ourselves because of the conversion of prime agricultural land to other uses.

However, projecting the demand for agricultural land is always risky. Such basic factors as the rate of population growth can vary significantly. And even if one has reasonable confidence in projections of demands for agricultural products (determined by population and income growth, and patterns of food consumption), turning these projections into their cropland equivalent requires making some very uncertain estimates of future trends in agricultural productivity. Will yields per acre continue to rise at past rates, or does the recent indication of a possible leveling off mean that we are reaching the limits of what can reasonably be expected in productivity increases?*

The demand on the U.S. agricultural sector, moreover, comes not only from domestic consumption. America is in the business of feeding the world. And U.S. agricultural exports, which are financing much of our petroleum imports, are important to main-

*This is probably the most important question. An average productivity increase of 1 percent a year on our existing cropland is equivalent to nearly 90 million acres of additional production in 20 years.

Wetlands

Wetlands now cover slightly more than 3 percent of the continental U.S. land area — about 70 million acres.[1] This is just over half the area originally occupied by wetlands.[2] In their natural state, wetlands perform several functions. They serve as food producers, spawning sites, and sanctuaries for many forms of fish and bird life. They produce timber, peat moss, and crops such as wild rice and cranberries. They serve as storage areas for storm and flood waters, reduce erosion, provide for groundwater retention, and at times purify polluted waters.[3]

Wetlands exist in both inland and coastal areas. More than 90 percent of all wetlands are freshwater marshes, swamps, bogs, wet meadows, fens, and potholes; the remainder are mainly coastal salt marshes and swamps, though salt marshes are also found as far inland as Utah and the Dakotas.[4] Twenty percent of the nation's wetlands are in Florida. Other extensive wetland areas are found in the Lower Mississippi River, Gulf and Southern Atlantic coasts, and in northern regions of Minnesota and Wisconsin.[5]

Throughout American history, inland wetlands have been drained by farmers seeking productive agricultural land, and coastal wetlands have become sites for industry, transportation corridors, houses, and ports. Other wetlands have been destroyed indirectly: construction of levees along the Mississippi River has prevented needed inflows of fresh water and sediment into wetlands;[6] cutting channels through coastal wetlands may allow saltwater to intrude into freshwater marshes, killing the vegetation.

Since the mid-1950s, wetland losses have averaged some 600,000 acres per year.[7] Losses have been particularly great in Arkansas, California, Connecticut, Florida, Missouri, Nebraska, and Wisconsin.[8] Between 1960 and 1975, bottomland hardwood forests, which cover more than half of all wetlands, decreased by about 431,000 acres annually.[9] About 80 percent of all riparian habitats found in wetlands along rivers, streams, and other water bodies have been destroyed.[10] No other ecosystem is considered more important to the survival of the nation's fish and wildlife.[11] If current loss rates continue, less than 40 percent of the continental United States' original wetlands may exist by the year 2000.

Several recent attempts have been made to decelerate the loss of valuable wetlands. States have established a variety of wetland protection and permitting programs. As of 1979, 31 coastal states and territories had wetland protection statutes.[12] Inland wetland areas have received less attention, but other laws governing critical areas, floodplains, pollution control, shorelands, and wild and scenic rivers offer additional protection.[13] Both coastal and inland programs provide either for local regulation in keeping with state standards or for direct state regulation.

At the federal level, most dredging and filling of wetlands is regulated by the U.S. Army Corps of Engineers under Section 404 of the federal Clean Water Act.[14] Federal government support of construction projects that could alter wetlands is limited by Executive Order.[15] The Fish and Wildlife Service of the Department of the Interior assesses the impacts of all federally funded or licensed wetland development projects on fish and wildlife and reports on adverse impacts and possible mitigation measures.[16] In addition, the federal Coastal Zone Management Act has given impetus to some of the state wetlands protection measures.[17]

taining the economic strength of the country. Estimating export demand is even more difficult than estimating domestic demand. Less is known about basic trends—population and income growth— and about the likely ability of developing countries to improve their own agricultural sectors. The export market fluctuates widely. A foreign country may, on the average, produce 95 percent of its own food and import 5 percent from the United States. A small fluctuation in that country's production can have a substantial impact on U.S. exports. For instance, a 5 percent change could either double U.S. exports to that country or eliminate them entirely.

Another possible demand on U.S. cropland relates directly to energy production. There has recently been substantial interest in the possibility of growing special crops that produce petroleum-like oils, grains that can be used to produce alcohol, or biomass that can be converted into methane. "Gasohol" has already appeared at local service stations. One study projects that some 7 to 11 million more acres of cropland might be needed to grow the corn necessary for a 1990 supply of 4 to 6 billion gallons of ethanol.*[54]

Finally, landowners are continually shifting land uses within the agricultural sector—for example, from cropland to pasture or forests, from grazing land to cropland, from forests back to cropland or grazing—depending on relative prices and productivity. If the demand for timber or meat, for instance, were to increase, there would be greater pressure to shift land into timber and meat production.**

All these factors—domestic consumption, exports, energy production, and shifts in land use within the agricultural sector—may make the loss of cropland of more concern in the future than it has been in the past. Projections made for the National Agricultural Lands Study indicate that under the most pessimistic assumptions about increased yields, and assuming that we do not change the amount of land used for crops other than "principal crops," by the year 2000 we will have had to convert into cropland most of the

---

*This is in addition to 8 to 12 million acres of existing cropland that would probably be converted into growing corn for energy.

**The shift to forests because of increased demand for timber products would probably be concentrated in the South. This is the only area in which the competition among different agricultural uses is very high and in which trees grow fast enough to warrant giving up the immediate profits from growing crops to gain the future profits from harvesting trees. In other areas of the country, particularly the East, large amounts of land have been converted from cropland or grazing land to forests, but this usually results from low agricultural profits which have forced the owner to give up farming, not from the high profits expected in forestry.

land that currently shows high or medium potential for conversion.*[55] Even reasonably optimistic assumptions about crop yield increases would leave a relatively small margin for error.

The Role of Government

Activities and policies pursued by all levels of government can either promote or hinder farmland conversion. There are many federal agricultural programs that provide technical assistance and income subsidies to farmers, and there are federal, state, and local taxation policies that favor agricultural land use over other land uses.

One comprehensive study of 131 federal programs (implemented by 37 agencies or bureaus) concluded that approximately 30 percent had characteristics fully supportive of maintaining agricultural land.[56] These included programs that promoted agricultural economic development, capital improvements for agriculture, housing for farmers, and improved agricultural land management, as well as agricultural technical assistance and income-support programs.

Still, 70 percent of the federal programs reviewed tended to reduce the availability of agricultural land (although a third of these had partially offsetting "secondary effects that helped maintain the availability of agricultural land").[57] Many federal investments in roads, sewers, and other infrastructure make it easier to locate homes and businesses in rural areas, thus accelerating the conversion of agricultural land to urbanized uses. Similarly, many economic development and natural resource development programs stimulate nonagricultural growth. It is impossible to quantify how much effect these programs have, but it appears that the 131 federal programs that were studied, on balance, promote conversion of agricultural lands to other uses.

It is more difficult to assess the net impact of state and local programs. In many cases, state and local governments participate in the federal programs, and thus can be said to be encouraging conversion of agricultural lands, although this is not the motive for participation. On the other hand, many states and localities have also adopted special programs focused directly on preserving agricultural lands. The most important of these are special tax and land-use policies.

As difficult as it is to determine what the net impact of all

---

*"Principal crops" include wheat, soybeans, and feed grains (corn, sorghum, oats, and barley). These projections apparently assumed no increase in real agricultural prices.

government programs is on the conversion of prime agricultural land, there is little question that they do have a substantial, though often unintended, impact. Thus, advocating that nothing else be done by the government is advocating that the current situation, with all its various pressures and incentives, continue.

Some Economic Considerations

Land plays a very special economic role in a farmer's financial situation. Land is, of course, the fundamental factor of production, but usually it also represents the farmer's major economic asset. The farmer probably depends on land for both retirement income and as a means of getting through any period of disability. Land is used to finance most of the other capital investments needed to operate a farm in a period of increasingly mechanized agriculture. Some policies for slowing agricultural conversion would substantially reduce the value of agricultural land, and thereby significantly affect the farmer's personal outlook.

Is conversion of agricultural land an issue that requires government involvement? Will such involvement improve the way in which the free market operates? There is, after all, a well-developed, active market for land. Particularly with recent improvements in market information, such as computerized multiple listing services, and the increased interest of a wide range of people in buying rural land, one has to question whether the market is not, in fact, already operating relatively efficiently. If so, there would be little to gain from government involvement. The main reasons, with respect to this particular issue, why the land market would not be operating efficiently are either that farming interests are not willing to pay as much for the land as society would like or that nonfarming interests are willing to pay more than society would like.

Undesirably low bids by farming interests could occur for several reasons. One is that farmland might provide benefits, such as wildlife habitat or pleasant scenery, that the farmer cannot sell in the market. A second is that the farmer may be quite concerned about the near-term financial situation and be unwilling to pay high prices for land in the hope of getting long-term profits. A third is that, because farming is a risky business for individuals, banks may be unwilling to lend money to make investments that a farmer considers desirable. Society probably sees a much smaller risk than banks do, because farming is much less risky when all farms are considered together and because one of the risks to the individual farmer is that crop prices will be too low—which is not nearly as unattractive a prospect for society as a whole.

In spite of these various problems, it is difficult to conclude that farmers are not willing to pay enough for prime farmland. The nonmarketable amenities are often quite limited. There is no reason to think that farmers are underestimating the future demand of farmland and the likely profits from farming. And, until very recently, most farmers were able to borrow substantial amounts of money to buy new land on the basis of the increased value of the land they already owned. The fact that the rate of return to farmers on new land purchases is very low indicates that they are not paying too little.

Are other buyers, then, willing to pay too much? Presumably they are willing to pay what the land is worth to them after deducting the costs of developing it for its intended use. However, because of the way mortgage interest and capital gains are treated under federal income tax codes, the buyer's purchase is subsidized by the government. There is also some reason to argue that the buyer's decision does not take into account all development costs. This is because some of these costs—for instance, the provision of roads, social services, and some other types of infrastructure—are distributed evenly over all taxpayers. Moreover, new development may be imposing costs on others—such as pollution and congestion—that the developer does not have to pay. There have been increased efforts to avoid these types of problems by making developers pay more of the costs associated with new developments, but in many cases there is still likely to be some subsidy.

On the other hand, there are a number of factors that tend to strengthen the ability of farmers to compete in the land market. One is the tendency to appraise agricultural land for tax purposes at less than its market value. A second is the collection of agricultural price and income maintenance programs that allows farmers to spend more for land than they could if they were completely at the mercy of the free market. Various state and local land-use controls also tend to make it more difficult to convert land to other purposes.

There is no way of knowing how these various pressures and counterpressures balance one another. There may still be a bias in favor of too much land conversion, but this bias is not obvious.

Policy Options

The recent movement of people and jobs out of urban areas, summarized in chapter 1, has been a prime reason for the increased pressures to convert agricultural land. Will this trend continue? Some factors suggest that conversion pressures will decrease: our rate of population growth is slowing; most of the interstate highway system in rural areas has been completed; and the rate at which we are building large dam projects has slowed substantially. Nonetheless, a review of recent projections concludes that between 10 and 20 million acres of current and potential cropland in the United States will be converted to urban and other built-up uses between 1978 and 2000.[58]

There is, at present, no coherent national program either to encourage or discourage the process of agricultural land conversion. Many states and localities have programs specifically designed to protect farmland, but their effectiveness cannot yet be determined. Clearly, we can leave federal programs as they are and let individual states and localities continue to attempt to protect farmland where they consider its continued conversion to pose serious problems. Assuming that state and local governments are sensitive to this issue, this approach might avoid the most serious conversion problems without adoption of new, wide-ranging programs that could have substantial unanticipated side effects. However, if prime farmland conversion is a serious national problem, this approach is unlikely to deal adequately with it.

An alternative would be to restrict government activities that appear to favor conversion. One of the most important of these activities is government investment in roads, sewers, and other such infrastructure in rural areas. The Carter Administration attempted to ensure that any planning for such investments (and other federal activities) would consider the impact on prime agricultural lands.[59] This effort has lost much of its momentum, and recent federal procedural changes that reduce the involvement of state and local governments in reviewing proposed federal decisions will probably result in less consideration being given to agricultural land conversion.

Reducing the impact of federal activities might be substantially aided by better and more comprehensive planning in rural areas. With good planning, government activities can be focused so that they work in concert to direct new development to where it will have the least detrimental impact on farmland as well as reduce other economic, environmental, and social costs. However, more planning will require more funds, which runs counter to current efforts to reduce budgets.

At least 16 states have adopted "right to farm" statutes.[60] These statutes have been developed to strengthen the farmer's position in the conflicts that often arise when city people move into rural areas and object to odors and other such "nuisances" associated with normal agricultural practices. The new residents may attempt to sue the farmer or enact local ordinances to prevent "objectionable" activities. The state "right-to-farm" statutes attempt to protect farmers by clarifying their right to engage in normal agricultural activities without restriction by courts or local government agencies.

An advantage of the various efforts to restrict government activities favoring land conversion is that such efforts can reduce inefficient and uncoordinated government expenditures, reinforce efforts to reduce government expenditures, and frequently claim general public support (although they are likely to be strongly opposed by the interest groups who would benefit from the government activities).

A more aggressive policy to discourage conversion of agricultural land would involve paying farmers not to convert it. This is most commonly done through preferential taxation schemes, which impose lower tax rates on land used for agriculture than on land used for other purposes. These schemes, however, may have limited effectiveness and, if not carefully designed, can actually make it cheaper for speculators to buy and hold agricultural land for future conversion.

Another approach is to pay the farmer for losses in land value. Landownership involves a whole package of different types of "rights"— water rights, mineral rights, and so forth—that can be sold separately from the land itself.* One of these is the right to develop, and landowners can sell their "development rights" in the same way any other rights are sold. Governments can purchase development rights directly, or private purchasers may be allowed to transfer the rights to other lands. In either case, payment is made for the loss in land value associated with giving up the right to develop the land sometime in the future.

There has not yet been sufficient experience with these kinds of schemes to determine how effective they are in discouraging agricultural land conversion. If the programs are not implemented in

---

*For years, the mineral rights associated with land have been sold separately, which creates a situation in which the apparent landowner no longer has the right to exploit any minerals that may lie under the land.

a well-planned and coherent fashion, they may actually exacerbate the problem by creating permanent but randomly placed pockets of protected agricultural lands, causing new development to be spread out more than it would have been otherwise. Programs that pay for development rights are likely to be politically popular, at least with farmers and other agricultural interests. However, because buying development rights may be as expensive as buying land outright, these approaches can make substantial drains on public treasuries.

Some states and localities have created legal barriers to conversion of prime agricultural land. Traditional zoning ordinances have been modified to establish "agricultural zones" in which intensive non-agricultural development is prohibited. Such zoning, however, usually allows "large lot" residential development (usually 5 to 10 acres per lot) and thus may actually increase the problem of "parcellation."

Agricultural zoning has been adopted primarily at the local level, although Hawaii has created agricultural zones at the state level and other states have provided strong incentives for local governments to establish such zones. Two states, Vermont and California, require developers to obtain a development permit from the state government for certain types of projects (in addition to any permission that might be required by the local zoning authority).[61]

Imposing legal barriers to development tends to diminish the value of farmland by restricting its potential uses, and is therefore likely to be unpopular with farmers. Again, most efforts of this sort are too new to determine how effective they really are.

Conclusions. There seem to be advantages and disadvantages associated with all the options currently available for discouraging conversion of prime agricultural land. Many programs have already been widely tried, with little clear impact on the rate of land conversion. The more aggressive options seem to be most suitable for states or localities that must deal with specific situations where the conversion problem is particularly serious. The federal government's role would seem to be limited to supporting better rural planning and taking care in its own efforts not to undertake programs and finance investments that unnecessarily increase pressure for farmland conversion.

Forest Productivity

Timber is a basic renewable resource that is of fundamental importance to the quality of American life. On the average, each

American consumes approximately 60 cubic feet of wood a year.[62] Rapid increases in prices and net imports over the past decade indicate that we are beginning to experience timber scarcities: our demand, were it not dampened by higher prices, would be exceeding the available supply. Nor can the rest of the world be depended on to satisfy U.S. shortfalls. The disappearance of forests in many countries is already creating a serious global problem.[63]

Overcutting forests creates not only economic problems, but serious environmental impacts. Forests catch rainfall, allowing it to seep into the ground and replenish groundwater aquifers. Deforestation allows this rainfall to run off the land quickly, eroding the soil and causing flooding and water pollution problems downstream, as well as reducing groundwater recharge. Forests provide valuable recreational and scenic amenities and habitat for much of our game and nongame wildlife. And forests are an important component of the biological system that converts carbon dioxide into the oxygen needed for most life forms to survive (see the discussion of carbon dioxide pollution in chapter 2).

How can America ensure that it produces enough timber without destroying its forests? As indicated in the discussion of prime farmland above, there is little prospect of resolving this issue by converting more land to forests. There is substantial pressure to do just the opposite. Thus, the solution must come through increasing productivity—raising timber growth rates closer to their biological and economic potential. And this requires substantial long-term planning. Every tree that is to be harvested at the beginning of the next century has to be growing now. Immediate and continued commitments are needed not only to solve existing problems, but to prevent them from becoming worse. And, as indicated below, a number of factors are making the job tougher by reducing the productive capacity of America's forestlands.

Demand for Forestland

The data on forest trends presented at the beginning of this chapter could be construed as indicating that there will be relatively little difficulty in maintaining a sufficient supply of forest products. After all, our rate of consumption has not been increasing rapidly, and, nationwide, we are growing more wood than we cut. But there are several signs of trouble ahead.

One is that the national statistics on rates of growth and harvest hide important variations among regions and among types of timber.

Although net annual growth exceeds annual harvest for softwoods in most of the United States, it does not in the Pacific Coast region (figure 6.11). Annual harvests in that region have exceeded annual growth since at least 1952.[64] The problem is particularly severe in the case of softwood "sawtimber"—that is, timber suitable for lumber. The Pacific Coast region contains 58.8 percent of the nation's total supply of such timber, and annual harvests exceeded annual growth by 65 percent in 1976 (down from 122 percent in 1952).[65] This excess harvest has occurred primarily on forest industry lands, leaving them understocked, and has put increasing pressure on the U.S. Forest Service to accelerate the harvesting of the old-growth timber in the national forests.[66]

A second sign of trouble is the rapid increase in the cost of forest products. From 1967 to 1980, the average wholesale price of lumber and wood products increased 28 percent more than the average of all industrial commodities (excluding energy).[67]

Moreover, studies by public and private organizations project that this situation will get worse.[68] Current reduced demand for softwood lumber and plywood, because of the recent slump in home building, does not change the long-range outlook substantially. The high rate of household formation, combined with a low rate of new housing starts (see chapter 1), may stimulate another building boom in the late 1980s. Markets for other forest products—such as wood pulp—have remained fairly strong. In addition, population and incomes continue to grow. There can be little doubt that the use of forest products will increase over the next several decades. The Forest Service projected that the demand for softwood products will increase at a rate of 1.3 percent per year through 2020, while supply of softwoods will increase only 0.6 percent per year.[69]

Finally, pressures for conversion in land use also affect forests. Even during the period 1967 to 1975, when the amount of cropland was declining, millions of acres of forestland were being converted to cropland. (See figure 7.3, chapter 7.) And the amount of forestland lost to homes, roads, and artificial lakes—all essentially irreversible losses—was greater than the amount of cropland lost. These conversion pressures may well continue.

Factors Reducing Productivity

Information collected by the U.S. Forest Service indicates that the average annual growth of commercial forests is only about 61 percent

Figure 6.11

Net Annual Growth and Removal of Timber by Region, 1952 and 1976

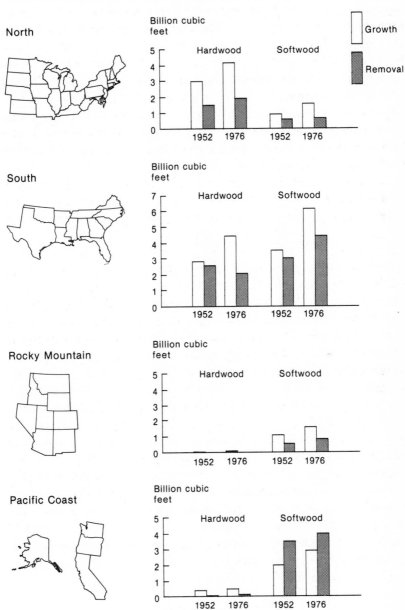

Regions are U.S. Forest Service Regions.

Source: U.S. Department of Agriculture, Forest Service

of "potential growth."*[70] Even this rate is often not met by the most valuable trees or on the most accessible sites. There are a number of factors—both technical and nontechnical—that have interfered with our ability to improve forest productivity. And it appears as if these problems are being joined by some newer ones.

Over half (58 percent) of the nation's commercial forestland is owned by "nonindustrial private owners" (figure 6.12). The Forest Industries Council identifies this land as having by far the lowest level of investment for forest regeneration.[71] Nonindustrial private owners frequently will not practice good forest management without financial or technical assistance. However, again, national statistics may be misleading. The largest amounts of nonindustrial private forests are in the North and South. Most of the timber grown in the North is hardwood, which is not currently in short supply (see figure 6.11). And in the South, the lands owned by the nonindustrial private owners are essentially as productive as forest industry lands (figure 6.13). Only in the Rocky Mountains do private, nonindustrial lands have an unusually low rate of productivity (compared to forest industry lands), but the amount of land involved is relatively small.

It is the low average productivity in the Pacific Coast region that is the greatest concern. In this region, the U.S. Forest Service is the largest owner (45 percent), with the rest of the land being divided about equally among the other ownership categories. Current growth in the Pacific Coast region's national forests is only a third of its potential, whereas that on forest industry lands is two-thirds of its potential. A major reason for the shortfall on the former is that national forests have a larger area in old, slow-growing timber. Many of these old-growth stands are inaccessible, in areas that might more suitably be designated as wilderness. There has been much debate about whether the government should make the investments necessary to provide access to the old-growth stands, and accelerate harvesting of this valuable timber.

"Acid rain" (see chapter 2) is one of the newer problems affecting forest productivity in some parts of the country—particularly the northeastern United States. The impact of acid rain on lakes in the

*"Potential growth" used in this and subsequent comparisons is the amount of growth that would occur with fully stocked natural stands of trees. Applying such agricultural practices as fertilization, thinning, stocking with faster-growing trees, and so forth, can raise the actual growth higher—sometimes substantially so—than these "potential growth" estimates.

Figure 6.12
Ownership of Commercial Forestland by Region, 1977

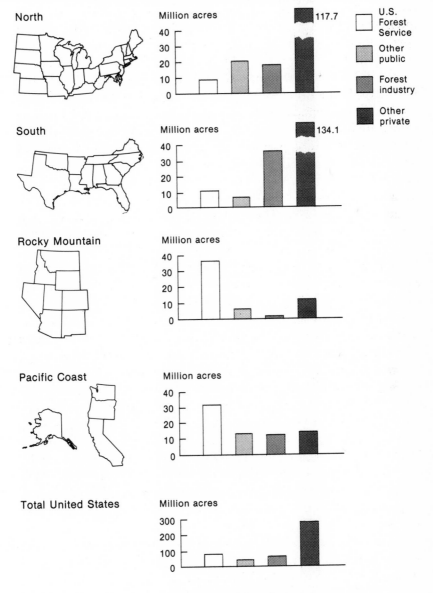

Regions are U.S. Forest Service regions.

"Other public" includes land owned by Indian tribes, state and local governments, and federal agencies other than the U.S. Forest Service.

"Other private" includes farmers and other private individuals.

Source: U.S. Department of Agriculture, Forest Service

Figure 6.13

Current and Potential Timber Growth in Commercial Forests by Region, 1977

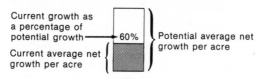

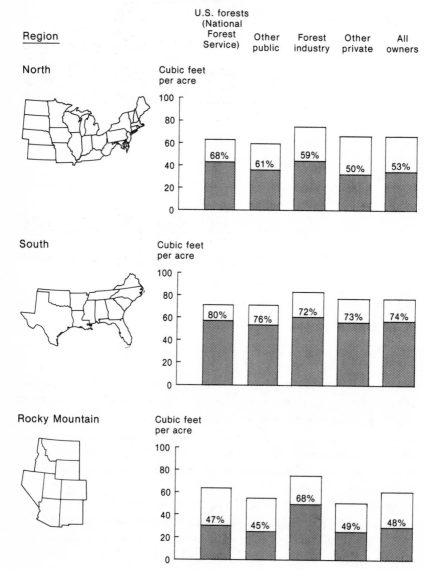

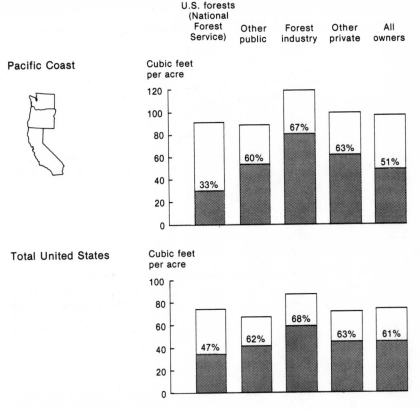

	U.S. forests (National Forest Service)	Other public	Forest industry	Other private	All owners

Pacific Coast

Cubic feet per acre

33% 60% 67% 63% 51%

Total United States

Cubic feet per acre

47% 62% 68% 63% 61%

Regions are U.S. Forest Service regions.

"Other public" includes land owned by Indian tribes, state and local governments, and federal agencies other than the U.S. Forest Service.

"Other private" includes farmers and other private individuals.

Net growth is average annual growth minus annual mortality.

Source: U.S. Department of Agriculture, Forest Service

Northeast is widely recognized, but there are other, less-recognized effects that may also be significant. One researcher, comparing impacts on forests to those on lakes, notes that pollutants from acid rain " . . . appear to be overriding normal ecosystem functioning in more subtle ways which may be long term in nature and which may compound adverse effects of intensive harvesting on forest ecosystems."[72]

What is known about acid rain and its effects at a few research sites does not lead easily to generalizations about an entire region. But, based on available evidence, another researcher suggests that some changes caused by acid rain and other pollutants are already underway in New England forests. These effects include reductions in photosynthesis, changes in the reproductive capacity of plants, and an increased predisposition of the forests to insect and fungus attacks.*[73] Thus, a loss of growth potential or productivity may already have occurred, although it is not evident in the general timber inventory statistics. Continued high levels of acid rain could further disrupt forest ecosystem processes and reduce productivity. By the time such adverse effects can be conclusively documented, remedial measures may be prohibitively expensive or technically impossible.

Improper logging and road-building practices can also reduce forest growth potential, as a result of soil erosion, soil compaction by heavy equipment, and the loss of soil nutrients. The effects of compaction, especially on skid trails that are used repeatedly, have lasted for as much as 16 years after logging.[74] The extent to which forest productivity has been lowered as a result of these impacts is not known. Some of these effects can be avoided by better planning of logging operations and the use of more appropriate equipment.

Another recent development, the large-scale use of wood for fuel, especially in industrial boilers, could have an impact on soil nutrients and carbon budgets—and, therefore, on productivity. Most logging in the past left behind enough woody matter, especially those parts with the highest concentrations of nutrients, so that nutrient depletion was not a significant problem. Whole-tree chipping, where everything, including leaves, is hauled away, may be a different matter.

Several major new wood-burning boilers are being installed in New England. One boiler can consume as much wood as a pulp mill, and much of the wood is expected to come from whole-tree chipping. Large areas will be affected. Use of wood for industrial fuel in New England may, or may not, expand beyond present plans. It also may, or may not, presage similar installations in other regions. The potential for affecting both productivity and the flow of timber into normal markets could be substantial.

Scope for Production Improvement

The fact that there is substantial scope for improvements in timber production has been demonstrated widely, both at forest research stations and, more importantly, in actual commercial operations.

---

*There are still, however, very few empirical data demonstrating how serious these impacts are.

The U.S. Forest Service and the Forest Industries Council conducted a a 25-state survey of opportunities for forest management investment for increasing forest productivity that could be met with current technology.[75] These states contain 83 percent of the nation's total commercial forestland. The Forest Industries Council analyzed these data to identify investments that would have a return of at least 10 percent per year after taxes.*[76] Making these investments would increase the nation's total annual growth by 50 percent, although only a third of the commercial forestland in the 25 states would be affected.[78] The greatest increase in growth rate would occur on the national forests, where the amount of increased growth would almost equal the total amount of timber harvested in 1976.[79] Making the recommended investments would allow the United States to become a net exporter of timber products.[80]

According to the council's estimates, 18 percent of the investments, accounting for 19 percent of the increased yield, should be made on national forests, predominantly in the Pacific Coast region. Private, nonindustrial owners should make 57 percent of the investment, accounting for 55 percent of the increased yield, primarily in the South. The forest industry should make 19 percent of the investment, accounting for 20 percent of the increased yield.[81]

The most common and generally most profitable improvement identified in the study is the regeneration of forestlands with faster-growing and more commercially valuable trees. This is recommended for 72 percent of the 139 million acres that were identified as benefiting from some form of treatment and would take 93 percent of the total required public and private investment of $10.3 billion.[82]

How likely is it that these investments will be made? Investments on federal lands are unlikely during the current period of tight budgets. Most investment opportunities on other public lands must deal with the same budgetary problems. And there are a number of factors that interfere with adoption of the recommended actions by nonindustrial private owners. There are a very large number of individuals involved in this category, many of whom have little interest in maximizing timber yield. They may, for example, own their land for recreational purposes or speculation. Others, who might be disposed to harvesting timber, may not have ready access

---

*The Forest Service also analyzed the data, identifying those opportunities that were not called for in current plans and that would return at least 4 percent a year after inflation. This analysis showed no "opportunities" on the national forests, because they were all already planned for, and substantially higher opportunities in other ownership categories.[77]

to the information or technical assistance they require, or are not in a financial situation to make heavy investments that do not pay off for decades.

The Role of Government

Government, especially the federal government, plays a very large direct market role in the forestry sector. The public owns 28 percent of America's commercial forest, much of it in the West, which is the region under greatest stress.* Of the publicly owned forests, the federal government, and particularly the U.S. Forest Service, owns 73 percent. (The national forests account for 89 percent of federally owned commercial forestland.) The rest is owned by Indian tribes (4 percent), state government (17 percent), and local government (5 percent).[83] The national forests are even more important than a simple comparison of acres indicates. Although national forests comprise only 18 percent of our commercial forestland, they contain 32 percent of the total volume of timber, and 51 percent of the softwood "sawtimber" (trees of suitable size and quality to be manufactured into lumber).[84] Thus, the way in which the federal government (particularly the Forest Service) manages its lands can have a substantial impact on the supply of timber products. Federal lands are predominantly managed according to two basic principles: "multiple use" and "sustained yield."

The principle of multiple-use management requires the government to attempt to satisfy simultaneously all of the diverse demands placed on the forest—production of forest products, protection of wildlife habitat and valuable natural amenities, provision of recreation opportunities, and so forth. For example, the better timber stands may be designated for harvest, unless they are used intensively for recreation, or the harvesting would cause serious pollution, scenic, or other problems. In these cases, the alternative uses may be protected by a small buffer of unharvested trees, or the harvest has to be carried out in a way that reduces impacts on other resources and uses. This multiple-use approach has frequently run into problems. Timber firms complain that the constraints on harvesting increase production costs excessively. Other users claim that non-timber uses are not adequately protected.

---

*Government also owns the great majority of the forestland that is not classfied as commercial either because the yield is too low (less than 20 cubic feet of timber per acre per year) or it is protected from lumbering by being classified as a park or wilderness area, or for some other reason.

The sustained-yield principle prohibits the government from allowing more timber to be harvested from its land than is being replaced by the natural growth of the remaining trees. Thus, the Forest Service is not allowed to deplete the national forests as some private owners have depleted the stock of timber on their lands. This is one of the major reasons why the amount of old-growth timber harvested from national forests is relatively limited. (Another reason is the high cost of providing environmentally acceptable access to old-growth stands; a third is that, as discussed later, these stands are particularly valuable for other forest uses under the multiple-use concept.) The growth rate of old-growth timber is much slower than that of younger trees, which, according to the sustained-yield principle, results in old-growth trees being harvested at a slower rate.* Thus, although the national forests contain over half of the nation's supply of softwood sawtimber, they account for only 22 percent of the annual growth in sawtimber, and provided only 23 percent of the sawtimber harvest in 1976.[85]

In addition to managing their own forests, federal and state governments also assist private forest owners. About 4 percent of the Forest Service's budget is allocated to cooperative forestry programs with the states. In 1976, state contributions to this program amounted to about four dollars for every dollar of federal funds.[86] The cooperative programs fund fire control, insect and disease control, and technical and financial assistance to private landowners.

The federal government and some state governments also provide various tax benefits to private forest owners to assist timber production. One benefit is to treat income from timber sales as capital gains rather than as ordinary income, allowing it to be taxed at a lower rate. Another, adopted by some states, is to assess forestland at its value for producing trees rather than at the price it could be sold for when calculating property taxes.** The federal government alone provides forest owners (particularly corporations) with $600 to $700 million a year in tax breaks.[88]

Policy Options

There are two basic parts to the question of how to increase timber

---

*The sustained-yield principle only interferes with the harvesting of old-growth trees as long as the principle is applied separately to these stands. If, for management purposes, the old-growth stands were combined with other stands of younger trees and the principle applied to the entire group, the more rapid growth of the younger trees would allow more rapid harvesting of the older ones.

**Forty states have tax laws that give some form of special consideration to forestland.[87]

productivity. First, how can production be increased on privately owned lands? Second, what should be done with publicly owned forests?

Focusing on Privately Owned Lands. Lands owned by the forest industry provide limited opportunities for increased production. In all likelihood, the firms that own this land have the information needed to make the investments required to realize these opportunities. They are also likely to have reasonable access to financing. Thus, the only public policies that might be useful, beyond continuing such technical assistance as forest-fire control, would involve increased production subsidies. But there is essentially no basis on which to justify such subsidies. Moreover, a subsidy program would probably be very expensive, particularly in relation to the amount of increased production.

The situation is quite different with respect to the private non-industrial owner. These owners have substantial opportunity to increase production, but apparently lack either the desire, the information, or the financing to do so. Public policies could be adopted to improve the availability of information and technical assistance. Having more information might convince some owners who currently have no desire to manage their forests for maximum timber production to begin to do so. Government could also provide funding for investments, as the federal government already does for farmers.

However, an aggressive program to increase the productivity on private nonindustrial lands could be very expensive, with no direct return to the government, and would involve greatly expanding the existing public information and technical assistance network. It is not clear how effective such a program might be. It would be risky, with high costs and uncertain returns. In the past, efforts to help private nonindustrial owners have been weakened by being fragmented and intermittent. Concentrating assistance on productive lands with responsive owners may be the key to more effective programs.

Increasing Production on Public Lands. Increasing production on public lands would involve, in some cases, substantial modifications of the current management principles of multiple use and sustained yield.

Probably the most pressing question is how quickly the old-growth stands in the Pacific Coast region should be harvested, if at all. Comparison of relative growth and removals, and analysis of which timber prices are increasing most rapidly, both indicate that the major current timber shortage is sawtimber in western states. And the major available source of this timber is the old-growth stands in the national forests. With no increase in the rate at which these stands are cut, lumber and plywood prices may well continue to rise rapidly.

Increased cutting in these areas will be costly. For example, expensive logging roads will have to be built to provide access to remote old-growth stands. In spite of current budget problems, the Reagan Administration apparently is willing to make these expenditures.*

There are other costs, however, that may be more important in the long run. Substantial lumbering activity in remote areas would probably, as discussed in the following section, have substantial adverse impacts on many forms of rare and valuable wildlife. It would eliminate the opportunity to reserve these areas as wilderness for future generations to enjoy. And, if combined with the construction of access roads, harvesting the old-growth timber might cause serious problems of erosion, water pollution, downstream flooding, and reduced groundwater recharge.

Whatever is done now with old-growth stands, the greater question is how our public lands are to be managed in the future. Should the principles of multiple use and sustained yield be modified?

A recent study for the Pacific Northwest analyzed possible effects of such changes.[89] In a typical scenario, timber harvests from public lands (especially the national forests) increased dramatically for the next several decades, while timber prices were much lower than with a continuation of current policies. At the same time, harvests on private lands fell, allowing these lands to recover from the heavy cutting they have been subjected to in recent decades. After three or four decades, harvests on public lands would fall to near current levels, and those on private lands would rise.

This scenario, resulting in significantly lower timber prices, would obviously benefit consumers. At the same time, it would lower the value of timber on private lands, and this, in turn, would discourage private investment in improved forest management. Thus, attempting to reduce timber shortages by more aggressively harvesting the public lands would discourage owners from taking actions on those lands that provide the largest potential for increased production.

---

*In its 1983 budget, the Administration proposed a more than 20 percent increase in funds allocated to road building at a time when most program budgets are being cut (see chapter 9).

Again, other uses of public forestland—recreation, wildlife habitat for certain species, water supply enhancement, erosion control, and so forth—would suffer under a policy of aggressive cutting. The losses incurred might be offset partially by the environmental benefits associated with allowing private lands to regenerate themselves. The benefits, however, would likely fall far short of compensating for the losses, particularly in wilderness areas and for wildlife species that require large amounts of natural habitat.

A compromise between continuing the existing management approach and extensive accelerated harvesting on public lands might be to manage selected lands intensively for timber production, while retaining current management approaches on the rest. The Pacific Northwest forest policy study considered this option. The study found that, if half of the national forestland in western Oregon and Washington were managed with the same criteria as used on forest industry lands, total timber harvests in the region could be sustained at current levels for the next several decades. Under current policies, timber harvests in this region will fall 10 to 15 percent below those in the 1970s. Timber prices under this "dedicated use" alternative would be lower than those under current policies.[90]

The "dedicated use" alternative would not eliminate environmental problems. However, the impact on wilderness and remote wildlife habitat would be lower. If the intensively lumbered areas were carefully chosen and managed to minimize adverse environmental effects, this option might provide the most reasonable compromise between the need for increased timber production and maintenance of environmental protection on public lands.

A quite different approach has also been suggested. Called "privatization," it would involve selling (or perhaps renting with long-term leases) public lands to private companies. If this were done in the Pacific Northwest, the result would probably be accelerated harvesting of the formerly public land, while current private lands were allowed to regenerate. There would undoubtedly be some immediate budgetary benefits, as the proceeds from sales or leases flowed into the U.S. Treasury. But this approach would probably create the most serious environmental problems. Because hunting and some other forms of outdoor recreation can generate income, they might be able to compete with timber production on private lands. The role of the forests in providing wildlife habitat, groundwater recharge, safeguards against erosion, and flood control probably could not.

If interest rates fall and stimulate a substantial rise in new housing starts, there will be even greater pressure to increase timber production on public lands. The question of how this pressure will be met and whether the government, especially the Reagan Administration, will do anything to help the private landowners to absorb it are important public policy issues that need to be dealt with soon.

Forests for Wildlife

There is potentially a sharp conflict between attempts to increase timber production and to preserve suitable wildlife habitat. Although the United States has enacted several laws protecting wildlife, too often inadequate attention has been given to preserving the habitat this wildlife depends on for its survival.[91] The effects of habitat modification have been clear for hundreds of years. Animals such as mountain lions, wolves, elk, and bison once ranged the deciduous forests of the eastern United States. By the end of the 19th century, as these forests were turned into cropland, many species largely disappeared east of the Mississippi. Habitat destruction is one of the reasons that the rate of species extinction in modern times has been unique in geological history.[92]

Forest management may have a major impact on habitat. Highly "productive" forests are often managed so that all of the trees are of the same type and age, are planted a constant distance apart, are harvested long before they reach their full maturity, and are replaced immediately with a new crop. Any dead trees are likely to be removed; herbicides, insecticides, and sometimes fertilizers may be used to increase yields.

These forest management practices affect the forest's ability to support diverse and stable wildlife populations. Some species, for instance, depend on dead trees for their food and nests. Others thrive best in the types of fields created after a fire or logging, but are eliminated by immediate reforestation and the use of herbicides. Still others depend on fully mature stands of trees.

In the Northwest, some 748 different species of vertebrates are known to depend, at least in part, on federal forestland for their habitat.[93] Some of these species—for instance, elk, whitetail deer, and mule deer—survive well in areas where timber has recently been harvested.[94] These species actually prefer the early and intermediate stages of forest growth, and their populations are likely to be higher in areas where logging is an on-going activity than in areas left in wilderness. Many other species, however, depend on natural, diverse, coniferous forest, 80 years old or older. These include mammals such as the marten and fisher, and birds such as Hammond's flycatcher and the pine grosbeak.[95]

Many species use a variety of habitats at different times and for different reasons. Deer, for example, browse in open meadows, but need dense thickets close to these areas for protective cover; in winter, they move into areas of dense, evergreen vegetation for warm shelter. Similarly, the grey timber wolf often builds its dens in mature forests, but requires nearby fields or younger forest to support its prey, such as deer.[96]

The amount of space a particular species needs varies tremendously. Many small mammals live out their lives within a radius of no more than a few hundred meters. The Kirtland's warbler needs at least 80 acres of jackpine forest to breed.[97] Large mammals range widely according to the seasons. The elk can cover hundreds of miles as it migrates from its summer home in the mountains to its lower elevation winter grounds, and its slender habitat chain along the way is as important to its survival as the primary summer and winter habitats. Migratory birds, such as plovers and peregrine falcons, may range nearly the length of the globe each year.

Biologists are reasonably successful in identifying what types of habitat specific species require—or at least prefer. However, it is very difficult to say how much of that habitat is needed. The minimum amount of habitat required to support one pair of a species depends on the particular species and the quality of the habitat. For example, a pair of northern spotted owls needs 300 to 600 acres of old-growth forest; the wood duck, 2 acres of marsh; and the river otter, some 50 miles of streams.[98] But a substantial number of individuals (or mated pairs) may be needed before there is a viable population. If the population falls below this minimum level, the species is likely to diminish and eventually become extinct.* The extinction of the passenger pigeon, for instance, may already have been assured, even while large numbers could still be seen, because of overhunting and the disappearance of their native habitat in the virgin beech and oak forests of the Midwest.[100] It is often impossible

---

*There are several reasons for such declines. There simply may not be enough young produced to replace those that die. The California condor, with a few dozen remaining individuals, many of which may be too old to reproduce, may be doomed for this very reason.[99] Small populations may suffer lethal genetic problems due to inbreeding. A minimum number of individuals may also be needed to stimulate reproductive behavior in a population.

to predict the size of a minimum viable population. We may know we have passed the minimum only when the population is in an irreversible decline.

Society may also want to maintain a larger number of individuals than that required solely for a population's survival. The species may be desirable because it is a predator of other species that can become pests if not controlled. It may be a valuable game species. Or it may—like the hummingbird—be highly prized for other reasons. Every species, from the grizzly bear to small insects and plants, performs some function in nature. Often, this function benefits humans, too. Some animals serve as the food for animals higher on the predatory chain. Others help decompose dead trees, aiding their return to the nutrient cycle. Eradicating any native species, no matter how seemingly insignificant, to some extent disturbs, and may disrupt, the ecological system.

The issue of habitat conservation raises very troublesome questions about the value of species and their natural communities. These are not easy questions to answer and, in particular, are not usually amenable to the kind of cost-benefit calculations currently being promoted for making public policy decisions.[101] There is no question that Americans value wildlife. In terms of recreation alone, for instance, the preliminary results of a 1980 survey by the Fish and Wildlife Service indicate that nearly 100 million Americans participated in some form of wildlife-related activity.[102] About 42 million fished; some 83 million people observed or photographed wildlife, or provided food or otherwise made their homesites attractive to birds and other wildlife. Approximately 17 million hunted, and many hunters also observed wildlife. In pursuing these activities, the American public spent $40 billion, $24.5 billion of this for equipment.

For some species, forests can be managed in a way that supports viable populations without seriously affecting timber productivity. With other species, particularly those requiring large areas of mature forest, conflicts may result. In the latter case, if the habitat is destroyed, restoration may take many years—or may, in fact, prove impossible—and the species may vanish.

Government Efforts to Conserve Habitat

The federal government is involved in managing wildlife resources through its responsibility for wildlife species that migrate or are traded internationally or between states, its responsibility for conserving endangered and threatened species, its policies controlling development and pollution, and its responsibilities for administering public lands.[103] Among other programs, the federal government undertakes wildlife surveys, undertakes research on wildlife habitat needs, provides technical assistance on wildlife conservation, and maintains samples of representative and unique ecosystems.

The U.S. Fish and Wildlife Service and the National Marine Fisheries Service are the two federal agencies that focus primarily on conserving wildlife resources. The Bureau of Land Management, the Forest Service, and the National Park Service, which together administer almost 90 percent of the federal lands, also have very important roles.[104] These agencies are required by law to administer their lands for the benefit of wildlife as well as for other uses.

The General Accounting Office (GAO) concluded in a 1981 report that the U.S. Fish and Wildlife service was unable to fulfill adequately its responsibilities under several federal statutes. For instance, in fiscal year 1980, the Service was able to respond to less than half (22,500 out of 47,000) of the requests it received for consultation on the impacts of federal activities on wildlife.[105] GAO concluded: "The Service (1) sometimes does not adequately study ways to lessen adverse impacts on fish and wildlife, (2) does not always respond in a timely manner, and (3) rarely follows up on its recommendations for conserving fish and wildlife."[106]

In reviewing the National Park Service's wildlife management program, GAO found that the agency's emphasis on preservation and recreation, varying interpretations of policy, and its reluctance to control wildlife populations were contributing to wildlife problems in several parks. For example, the elk population in Mount Rainier National Park is so large that it is damaging parkland.[107] The red-cockaded woodpecker, an endangered species, could disappear from the Great Smokey Mountains National Park unless suitable protective actions are taken.[108] The Park Service's chief for natural resources admitted that wildlife management has ranked low among park management objectives.[109]

A common attitude in the Bureau of Land Management was expressed by the agency's assistant director of renewable resources, whom GAO quoted as stating, "The best wildlife can do is not impede commodity oriented production."[110]

The GAO observed that the Forest Service tends consistently to favor timber production over wildlife protection.*[111] An example of this bias can be seen in the agency's management plan for its Northwest Region. The authors of the plan admit several problems in the plan, including (1) insufficient funds and expertise to meet fish and wildlife objectives, (2) lack of inventory information, and (3) a lack of quantifiable fish and wildlife management objectives.[112] The only quantified measure of wildlife habitat is "wildlife forage," a measure that reflects management consideration of only three vertebrate species—the elk, whitetail deer, and mule deer. These are the species most valued by big game hunters and most compatible with high levels of timber production. The plan includes some conservation measures for the northern spotted owl, which can be considered an "indicator species" for old-growth forests. But no specific plans are provided for maintaining more than the minimum amount of old-growth forest that this and other species require. In fact, most of the plan emphasizes the Forest Service's intention to replace old-growth with "more thrifty" younger stands. Management standards and guidelines for maintaining special habitats (for example, snags) are similarly left to the future. Although the Forest Service plans further research on some of these issues, and indicates that it will attempt to protect sufficient habitat to maintain the northern spotted owl and other species, it is not clear that the foresters and the wildlife biologists within the service agree with each other on what needs to be done.[113]

All of the states and many local governments have active wildlife conservation programs. Most states attempt to control the population of game species by regulating hunting and fishing, and by restocking.[114] Many also have adopted programs to protect endangered or threatened animal and plant species. State fish and wildlife agencies provide valuable assistance to both federal agencies and private landowners to help them maintain wildlife habitat and populations.

The Private Landowner

Although in some western states the federal government is the largest landowner, the great majority of wildlife habitat nationally is located on private lands.[115] The Fish and Wildlife Service's 1975 national

---

*GAO noted that the Forest Service has increased the amount of its budget devoted to wildlife management and is explicitly considering some wildlife needs in its regional forest management plans.

survey of hunting, fishing, and other wildlife-associated recreation found that 67.1 percent of all days spent hunting by residents within their state occurred on private lands; these lands also accounted for 55.3 percent of the hunting days spent outside of the state of residence.[116] Only 9.5 percent of the hunting days spent within the state and 23.2 percent of days outside the state were on federal land.

Many timber companies and other large private owners have active wildlife programs, and many smaller owners, such as farmers, also try to conserve wildlife habitat. However, local tax laws may assess land for the highest commercial potential and make it financially difficult for an owner to use his property for purposes that are inconsistent with high financial returns. To counter this effect, landowners in many states can take advantage of special tax provisions provided for agricultural land and forestland.[117]

Noncommercial private organizations also have played an important role in the conservation of wildlife habitat. Groups like Ducks Unlimited, the Nature Conservancy, the National Audubon Society, and others lease or acquire many tracts of important wildlife habitat that might be destroyed by commercial development. The Nature Conservancy, in cooperation with state conservation agencies, has initiated "heritage programs" in 27 states to identify rare species and natural communities, and to prepare recommendations about which areas should receive highest priority for protection in the states.[118]

Policy Options

Federal policy on wildlife habitat may not be explicit, and may not even be recognized as a policy. But the sum of the individual decisions made about different parcels of public land, combined with pollution control and other programs affecting land use, nonetheless constitutes a policy. A focus on timber production without protection of wildlife habitat is a policy to reduce the diversity of wildlife and to threaten more species with extinction. State and local governments own less land, and their actions affect smaller areas, but for specific species and specific areas they, too, must be concerned with the impact of their activities on wildlife.

Because the habitats of many species are not limited to an area of a few acres or even a few square miles, no one agency, or even one level of government, can approach the problem independently. The extensive migration of birds and many large animals, and their use of habitats distant from one another, often require coordination among many different land managers in both the public and private sector.

There are several different kinds of efforts that can be made to conserve wildlife habitat. Attempts by the federal government to improve the current multiple-use approach to public land management is one possibility. But it faces some serious political, technical, and managerial obstacles. Political pressures for commodity production frequently tend to override other values associated with public lands. In many cases, these pressures are difficult to resist because of the technical problem that, for most species, there is not sufficient information to specify exactly what type of habitat and how much of it is needed. Given the limited resources devoted to research on wildlife habitat and its management, this problem is not likely to be alleviated soon.* The lack of available information is compounded by the fact that most forest managers are primarily trained in timber production, and have relatively little training in wildlife-related subjects. This combination of factors reduces the likelihood that wildlife habitat needs will be adequately met when they are in competition with other forest uses, and increases the possibility that valuable wildlife habitat will be unnecessarily lost.

Further efforts might be made in training forest managers to recognize the impact of their actions on wildlife habitat and to anticipate shifting needs resulting from changes taking place on adjacent private lands. Multiple use of forestlands will always be an important component of efforts to provide adequate wildlife habitat. We may never be able to dedicate all the land we might wish to this purpose. But with careful planning and management, forestlands frequently can be used satisfactorily for timber production and other purposes, while retaining an important role in supporting wildlife habitat needs.

A supplementary approach is to focus on wildlife habitat needs directly, determine the amount and types of land required for them, and set this land aside. This is the philosophy that underlies, for example, the state and federal wildlife refuge programs. It is particularly appropriate for habitats that are extremely sensitive to modification.

Government can also stimulate increased conservation and maintenance of wildlife habitats on private lands. One way of doing this

---

*For instance, the draft environmental impact statement for the management plan for the Northwest Forest region makes quite clear that most of the problems and uncertainties associated with wildlife management are unlikely to be resolved soon.[119]

is to provide information and technical assistance to private land-owners to help them make decisions on which lands to preserve and how to manage them. A second is to provide some additional financial incentives (for example, property tax relief) to the private sector to provide such habitat. As part of its "water bank" program, the U.S. Department of Agriculture pays farmers to preserve wet-lands as waterfowl habitats. The Fish and Wildlife Service also buys fish and wildlife easements from private landowners in the upper Midwest to preserve valuable migratory waterfowl breeding areas. The General Accounting Office has endorsed this kind of approach as an alternative to outright purchase of land.[120]

Finally, regulations and permits might be used to discourage the conversion of valuable wildlife habitat to other uses. For instance, owners of wetlands must obtain permission from the Corps of En-gineers (under Section 404 of the Clean Water Act) before they can dredge or fill wetlands.) Similar permits could be required for particularly valuable forest wildlife habitat.

Many of these approaches are being employed at this time. But, with the increased emphasis on producing more timber products and other natural resources, additional attention to identifying and maintaining valuable wildlife habitats is needed. It is important to remember that the decision not to conserve such areas is, in many cases, irreversible. If we discover that we have too much of some habitat type, we can always convert some of it to another use. We cannot, however, quickly recreate a mature ecosystem out of a clear-cut forest.

FURTHER READING

As an entry point, R. Neil Sampson's book *Farmland or Wasteland: A Time to Choose* (Emmaus, Pa.: Rodale Press, 1981) is a readable, well-documented, broad discussion of the issues involved in the controversy over whether the U.S. will have enough land to meet the rising demand for food and fiber. Another overview is presented in The Conservation Foundation publication, *The Future of American Agriculture as a Strategic Resource*, edited by Sandra S. Batie and Robert G. Healy (1980). A study from the Office of Technology Assesment, *Impacts of Technology on the Productivity of U.S. Croplands and Rangelands* (Washington, D.C.: U.S. Government Printing Office, in press), promises to deliver more insight into the debate surrounding agricultural issues. A recent book that addresses the problem of forest resource planning to increase productivity is Charles

E. Hewett and Thomas E. Hamilton, eds., *Forests in Demand: Conflict and Solutions* (Boston, Mass.: Auburn House Publishing, 1982). A product of the annual Dartmouth Symposia on Renewable Resources, this volume includes authors' divergent viewpoints based on experience with the Resources Planning Act (RPA) and other planning processes.

As a standard reference to assess trends, the U.S. Department of Agriculture's *Agricultural Statistics* (Washington, D.C.: U.S. Government Printing Office) is published annually to meet diverse needs for data on agricultural production, supplies, consumption, facilities, costs, and returns. In addition, there is an annual companion volume, *Handbook of Agricultural Charts* (Washington, D.C.: U.S. Government Printing Office). For forestry, a recent reference is U.S. Department of Agriculture, Forest Service, *An Analysis of the Timber Situation in the United States, 1952-2030* (1980). For statistical data, see the U.S. Department of Agriculture, Forest Service, published in 1981, *U.S. Timber Production, Trade, Consumption, and Price Statistics 1950-80* (Miscellaneous publication 1408).

To fulfill statutory requirements, the Department of Agriculture, in 1980, issued a report in two parts. *Part I, RCA Appraisal, Soil, Water and Related Resources in the United States: Status, Condition, and Trends* presents data that local, state, and federal interests can use in evaluating existing soil and water conservation programs and policies. *Part II, RCA Appraisal, Soil, Water, and Related Resources in the United States: Analysis of Resource Trends* is the Agriculture Department's analysis of the data presented in Part I. The Forest Service, in January 1980, issued *An Assessment of the Forest and Range Land Situation in the United States*.

Since 1946, the Soil Conservation Society of America has consistently covered soil concerns in its bimonthly *Journal of Soil and Water Conservation*. The society's book *Soil Conservation Policies: An Assessment* (Ankeny, Iowa: 1979), *The Cropland Crisis: Myth or Reality*, edited by Pierre R. Crosson of Resources for the Future (Baltimore, Md.: The Johns Hopkins University Press, 1982), and Sandra S. Batie, *Soil Erosion: Crisis in America's Cropland?* (Washington, D.C.: The Conservation Foundation, forthcoming) are all recent noteworthy additions to the literature of soil conservation.

The U.S. Comptroller's office has issued several significant reports on soil erosion, including *To Protect Tomorrow's Food Supply, Soil Conservation Service Needs Priority Attention* (Washington, D.C.: General Accounting Office, 1977) and *A Framework and Checklist for*

Evaluating Soil and Water Conservation Programs (Washington, D.C.: General Accounting Office, 1980).

Farmland preservation issues were covered comprehensively in the landmark *National Agricultural Lands Study*, an 18-month effort commissioned by 12 federal agencies and departments and coordinated by the Council on Environmental Quality (Washington, D.C.: U.S. Government Printing Office, 1981). The study investigated six primary areas—agricultural lands in national and international perspective, America's agricultural land base, demands on and allocation of agricultural land, consequences of farmland conversion, state and local actions affecting land availability, and the influence of federal programs on the availability of agricultural land. Fifteen technical papers were prepared for the study and are listed in the final report.

Preservation of prime farmland is the focus of Charles E. Little's *Land and Food: The Preservation of U.S. Farmland* (Washington, D.C.: American Land Forum, 1980). The American Farmland Trust, established in 1980, serves as a clearinghouse for information on farmland preservation and publishes a bimonthly newsletter, *Farmland* (American Farmland Trust, 1717 Massachusetts Avenue, N.W., Suite 601, Washington, D.C. 20036).

Among the works that focus on forest productivity are two classics: Frank J. Convery and Charles W. Ralston, eds., *Forestry and Long Range Planning* (Durham, N.C.: Duke University School of Forestry and Environmental Studies, 1977), which is particularly vivid in detailing the historical and political context of forestry planning; and Marion Clawson's *Decision Making in Timber Production, Harvest and Marketing* (Washington, D.C.: Resources for the Future, Research Paper R-4, 1977). Clawson's report considers the decision-making process in timber management for small private forests, for large forest product companies, and for national forests. He focuses particularly on the practical economic problems, such as when to harvest timber, faced by landowners. The Conservation Foundation has published *Forest Land Use: An Annotated Bibliography of Policy, Economic, and Management Issues, 1970-1980* (Washington, D.C.: The Conservation Foundation, 1981). This volume presents information on significant academic conferences and research conducted on forest land use over the past decade.

The Forest Industries Council, in *Forest Productivity Report* (Washington, D.C.: National Forest Products Association, 1619 Massachusetts Avenue, NW, Washington, D.C. 20036, 1980), addresses the problem, from an industrial point of view, of how to increase forest productivity to satisfy government forecasts for a doubling in paper and wood products demand. Another study by the National Forest Products Association, Private Woodland Committee, *America Grows on Trees: The Promise of Private Nonindustrial Woodlands* (Washington, D.C.: National Forest Products Association, 1980) concentrates on how to stimulate productivity (an estimated 57 percent increase can be generated) among small landowners who typically do not regenerate their lands with softwood species.

An excellent primer on wildlife, edited by Howard P. Brokaw, is *Wildlife and America: Contributions to an Understanding of American Wildlife and Its Conservation* (Washington, D.C.: U.S. Government Printing Office, 1978).

Two books that address the forestry/wildlife management conflict are Jack Ward Thomas, tech. ed., *Wildlife Habitat in Managed Forest: The Blue Mountains of Oregon and Washington*, (Washington, D.C.: U.S. Government Printing Office, 1979) and the Society of American Foresters, *Choices in Silviculture for American Forests*, (Bethesda, Md.: Society of American Foresters, 1981). The first title classifies the types of wildlife found in the different forest habitats so that habitats can be considered simultaneously with timber management decisions. The latter book, written for landowners, discusses silviculture systems and identifies nine major forest types. Silvicultural choices can then be influenced by what the landowner wants to enhance or protect (aesthetic or recreation values, streamflow, or wildlife).

TEXT REFERENCES

1. U.S. Department of Commerce, Bureau of the Census, *Statistical Abstract of the United States: 1980* (Washington, D.C.: U.S. Government Printing Office, 1980), p. 406.

2. Thomas H. Frey, "Major Uses of Land in the United States: 1978" (Washington, D.C.: U.S. Department of Agriculture, Economic Research Service, 1982), p. 3.

3. See chapter 3—figure 3.3.

4. "U.S. Farmers Said to Face Worse Year Since 1930's," *The New York Times*, March 28, 1982.

5. *Ibid.*

6. U.S. Department of Agriculture, *Agricultural Statistics, 1981* (Washington, D.C.: U.S. Government Printing Office, 1981), pp. 31, 130.

7. *Ibid.*, Table 763, p. 551.

8. *Ibid.*, Table 626, p. 436; U.S. Department of Agriculture, Economics and Statistics Service, *U.S. Foreign Agricultural Trade Statistical Report, Calendar Year 1980: A Supplement to the Monthly Foreign Agricultural Trade of the United States* (Washington, D.C.: U.S. Department of Agriculture, 1981), Table 13, p. 31.

9. U.S. Department of Agriculture, Economic Research Service, *Prospects for Ground-Water Irrigation, Declining Levels and Rising Energy Costs*, Agricultural Economic Report 478 (Washington, D.C.: U.S. Department of Agriculture, 1981), p. 20.

10. Richard R. Luckey, Edwin D. Gutentag, and John B. Weeks, "Water-Level and Saturated-Thickness Changes, Predevelopment to 1980, in the High Plains Aquifer in Parts of Colorado, Kansas, Nebraska, New Mexico, Oklahoma, South Dakota, Texas, and Wyoming," *Hydrologic Investigations Atlas HA-652* (Washington, D.C.: U.S. Geological Survey, 1981).

11. "Ebbing of the Ogallala," *Time*, May 10, 1982, p. 98.

12. U.S. Department of Agriculture, Economic Research Service, *Prospects for Ground-Water Irrigation, Declining Levels and Rising Energy Costs*, pp. 32, 41.

13. Vernon W. Ruttan, "Agricultural Research and the Future of American Agriculture," in Sandra S. Batie and Robert G. Healy, eds., *The Future of American Agriculture as a Strategic Resource* (Washington, D.C.: The Conservation Foundation, 1980), p. 144.

14. U.S. Department of Agriculture, Forest Service, *An Analysis of the Timber Situation in the United States: 1952-2030* (Washington, D.C.: U.S. Department of Agriculture, 1980), pp. 244-46, and Appendix 3, Table 4, p. 25.

15. U.S. Department of Agriculture, Forest Service, *An Analysis of the Timber Situation in the United States*, p. 252, and Appendix 3, Table 4, p. 25.

16. Forest Industries Council, *Forest Productivity Report*, National Forest Products Association (Washington, D.C.: National Forest Products Association, 1980), pp. 43-44.

17. U.S. Department of Agriculture, Forest Service, *An Analysis of the Timber Situation in the United States*, Appendix 3, pp. 93, 101.

18. U.S. Department of Agriculture, Forest Service, *U.S. Timber Production, Trade, Consumption, and Price Statistics: 1950-80*, Misc. Publication No. 1408 (Washington, D.C.: U.S. Department of Agriculture, 1981), p. 7.

19. Roland H. Ferguson and Neal P. Kingsley, *The Timber Resources of Maine*, U.S. Department of Agriculture, Forest Service, Resource Bulletin NE-26 (Washington, D.C.: U.S. Department of Agriculture, 1972), p. 20.

20. U.S. Department of Agriculture, Forest Service, *An Analysis of the Timber Situation in the United States*, p. 221.

21. *Ibid.*, p. 41.

22. U.S. Comptroller General, *To Protect Tomorrow's Food Supply, Soil Conservation Needs Priority Attention* (Washington, D.C.: General Accounting Office, 1977), p. 3; Tom Fulton and Peter Braestrup, "The New Issues: Land, Water, Energy," *The Wilson Quarterly* V(3):122 (1981).

23. U.S. Department of Agriculture, *Soil and Water Resources Conservation Act, 1980 Appraisal Part I, Soil, Water, and Related Resources in the United States: Status, Conditions and Trends* (Washington, D.C.: U.S. Department of Agriculture, 1981), pp. 157-158.

24. *Ibid.*, pp. 154-155.

25. U.S. Department of Agriculture, *Soil and Water Resources Conservation Act, 1980 Appraisal Part II, Soil, Water, and Related Resources in the United States: Analysis of Resource Trends* (Washington, D.C.: U.S. Department of Agriculture, 1981), p. 59.

26. U.S. Department of Agriculture, *Soil and Water Resources Conservation Act, 1980 Appraisal Part I, Soil, Water, and Related Resources in the United States*, p. 96.

27. U.S. Department of Agriculture, *1981 Program Report and Environmental Impact Statement, Soil and Water Resources Conservation Act* (Washington, D.C.: U.S. Department of Agriculture, 1981), p. 5.2.

28. *Ibid.*, p. 3.7.

29. U.S. Department of Agriculture, *Soil and Water Resources Conservation Act, 1980 Appraisal Part I, Soil, Water, and Related Resources in the United States*, p. 161.

30. David Pimentel, et al., "Land Degradation: Effects on Food and Energy Resources," *Science* 194(4261):150 (1976).

31. R. Neil Sampson, *Farmland or Wasteland, A Time To Choose: Overcoming the Threat to America's Farm and Food Future* (Emmaus, Pa.: Rodale Press, 1981), p. 127, Frederick N. Swader, "Soil Productivity and the Future of American Agriculture," in Sandra S. Batie and Robert G. Healy, eds., *The Future of American Agriculture as a Strategic Resource*, p. 91.

32. D.B. Ervin and C.T. Alexander, "Soil Erosion and Conservation in Monroe County, Missouri: Farmers Perception, Attitudes, and Performance," (unpublished) (Columbia, Mo.: University of Missouri, 1981); and Donald Baron, "Land Ownership Characteristics and Investment in Soil Conservation," Staff Report AGE 810911 (Washington, D.C.: U.S. Department of Agriculture, Economic Research Service, 1981), p. 29; *Soil Conservation Policies, Institutions and Incentives*, Harold G. Halcrow, Earl O. Heady, Melvin L. Cotner, eds. (Ankeny, Iowa: Soil Conservation Society of America, 1982), pp. 151-162, 163-183.

33. Don A. Dillman and John E. Carlson, "Influence of Absentee Landlords on Soil Erosion Control Practices," *Journal of Soil & Water Conservation* 37(1):37-41 (1982).

34. John F. Timmons, "Agriculture's Natural Resource Base: Demand and Supply Interactions, Problems and Remedies," in William C. Modlenhauer, pres., *Soil Conservation Policies: An Assessment* (Ankeny, Iowa: Soil Conservation Society of America, 1979), p. 55.

35. U.S. Department of Agriculture, *1979 Handbook of Agricultural Charts* (Washington, D.C.: U.S. Government Printing Office, 1979), p. 91.

36. U.S. Department of Commerce, Bureau of the Census, *1978 Census of Agriculture, Volume 1, Summary and State Data, Part 51, United States* (Washington, D.C.: U.S. Government Printing Office, July 1981), pp. 211, 214. Statistics compare total number of farms reporting cattle and calves (p. 214) with total number of farms reporting (p. 211).

37. *Ibid.*, pp. 331, 334.

38. R. Neil Sampson, *Farmland or Wasteland, A Time To Choose*, pp.380-385.

39. U.S. Department of Agriculture, Agricultural Stabilization and Conservation Service, *National Summary Evaluation of the Agricultural Conservation Program, Phase I* (Washington, D.C.: U.S. Department of Agriculture, 1978), p. 18 and calculated from information in Table 8, p. 26. (The estimate of 4.1 million tons of reduced erosion does not appear to be entirely consistent with the information presented in Table 8 of this report.)

40. U.S. Comptroller General, *To Protect Tommorrow's Food Supply*, pp. ii, 16-17.

41. U.S. Department of Agriculture, Economics, Statistics, and Cooperatives Service, *Natural Resource Capital in U.S. Agriculture: Irrigation, Drainage and Conservation Investments Since 1900* (Washington, D.C.: U.S. Department of Agriculture, March 1979), pp. 12-13; R. Neil Sampson, *Farmland or Wasteland, A Time To Choose*, pp. 58-59.

42. U.S. Department of Agriculture, Agricultural Stabilization and Conservation Service, *National Summary Evaluation of the Agricultural Conservation Program: Phase I*, p.18.

43. *Ibid.*, Executive summary, p. 2.

44. U.S. Department of Agriculture, Office of Governmental and Public Affairs, "USDA Announces Conservation Program Targeted to Problem Areas," press release, 276-82, March 10, 1982.

45. U.S. Comptroller General, *To Protect Tomorrow's Food Supply*.

46. R. Neil Sampson, *Farmland or Wasteland, A Time To Choose*, p.316.

47. U.S. Department of Agriculture, *Soil and Water Resources Conservation Act, 1980 Appraisal Part I, Soil, Water, and Related Resources in the United States* pp. 49-50.

48. Council on Environmental Quality, *National Agricultural Lands Study* (Washington, D.C.: U.S. Government Printing Office, 1981), p. 25.

49. Information provided by U.S. Department of Agriculture, Natural Resource Economic Division, Land Branch, March, 1982.

50. Council on Environmental Quality, *National Agricultural Lands Study*, pp. 8-9.

51. U.S., Congress, Senate Committee on Agriculture, Nutrition, and Forestry, *Ag-*

ricultural Land Availability: Papers on the Supply and Demand for Agricultural Lands in the United States, Committee Print, 97th Cong., 1st sess., p. 191.

52. Robert G. Healy and James L. Short, *The Market for Rural Land: Trends, Issues, Policies* (Washington, D.C.: The Conservation Foundation, 1981), p. 19.

53. *Ibid.*, pp. 28-29.

54. Council on Environmental Quality, *National Agricultural Lands Study*, p. 54.

55. *Ibid.*, pp. 9, 59.

56. U.S., Congress, Senate Committee on Agriculture, Nutrition and Forestry, *Agricultural Land Availability*, pp. 347-388.

57. *Ibid.*, p. 348.

58. *Ibid.*, pp. 135-139.

59. Council on Environmental Quality, *National Agricultural Lands Study*, p. 4.

60. *Ibid.*, p. 70.

61. *Ibid.*, pp. 70-71.

62. U.S. Department of Agriculture, Forest Service, *U.S. Timber Production, Trade Consumption, and Price Statistics*, Table 3, p. 7.

63. Erik Eckholm, *Planting for the Future: Forestry for Human Needs*, Worldwatch Paper 26 (Washington, D.C.: Worldwatch Institute, February 1979).

64. U.S. Department of Agriculture, Forest Service, *An Analysis of the Timber Situation in the United States,* pp. 287, 294.

65. *Ibid.*, pp. 279, 287, 294.

66. Sawtimber is being harvested at 2.5 to 3.0 times the rate it is growing on forest industry lands in the Pacific Coast region, a much higher percentage than on other ownerships; the forest industry is also harvesting over 6 percent of its sawtimber stock each year. (See U.S. Department of Agriculture, Forest Service, *An Analysis of the Timber Situation in the United States*, Appendix 3, Tables 11, 34, and 40).

67. U.S. Department of Labor, Bureau of Labor Statistics, *Producer Prices and Price Indexes: Data for August 1981* (Washington, D.C.: U.S. Department of Labor, September 1981), pp. 53-54, 79. The price index for all industrial commodities used here does not include the higher prices for energy and products made from fuels. The price index for lumber and wood products, excluding millwork, rose from 100 in 1967 to 315.5 in August 1980. Prices for softwood lumber and wood pulp rose the most, with their indices reaching levels of 347.7 and 396.6, respectively, in August 1981.

68. Forest Industries Council, *Forest Productivity Report*; U.S. Department of Agriculture, Forest Service, *An Analysis of the Timber Situation in the United States*, p. 9.

69. U.S. Department of Agriculture, Forest Service, *An Analysis of the Timber Situation in the United States*, p. 417. These projections of future demand are based on an assumed stable, relative price for forest products. Similarly, the supply projections are based on stable, relative prices for timber (that is, that investments in timber management will not increase in response to the higher prices.) In fact, free markets for timber will assure that supply and demand will be equal, but probably at prices significantly above those of today.

70. *Ibid.*, p. 290.

71. Forest Industries Council, *Forest Productivity Report*, p. 44.

72. G.K. Voigt, "Acid Precipitation Forest Ecosystems and Intensive Harvesting," *Proceedings, Impact of Intensive Harvesting on Forest Nutrient Cycling* (Syracuse, N.Y.: State University of New York, College of Environmental Science and Forestry, 1979), p. 33.

73. F.H. Bormann, "The Landscape: Air Pollution Stress and Energy Policy," in Carl Reidel, ed., *New England Prospects: Critical Choices in a Time of Change* (Hanover, N. H.: University Press of New England, 1982).

74. Henry A. Froehlich, "Soil Compaction from Logging Equipment: Effects on Growth of Young Ponderosa Pine," *Journal of Soil and Water Conservation* 34(6):276-78 (1979).

75. Forest Industries Council, *Forest Productivity Report*; U.S. Department of Agricul-

ture, Forest Service, *An Analysis of the Timber Situation in the United States.*

76. Forest Industries Council, *Forest Productivity Report*, p. 46.

77. U.S. Department of Agriculture, Forest Service, *An Analysis of the Timber Situation in the United States*, pp.496-499.

78. *Ibid.*, Table 6.14, p. 287; Forest Industries Council, *Forest Productivity Report*, p. 46.

79. U.S. Department of Agriculture, Forest Service, *An Analysis of the Timber Situtation in the United States*, Appendix 3, p. 103; Forest Industries Council, *Forest Productivity Report*, p. 46.

80. Forest Industries Council, *Forest Productivity Report*, p.47.

81. *Ibid.*, pp. 22, 27, 40, 46.

82. *Ibid.*, p. 45.

83. U.S. Department of Agriculture, Forest Service, *An Analysis of the Timber Situation in the United States*, Appendix 3, Table 4, p. 25.

84. *Ibid.*, p. 278.

85. *Ibid.*, Appendix 3, pp. 95, 103.

86. U.S. Department of Agriculture, Forest Service, *An Assessment of the Forest and Range Land Situation in the United States* (Washington, D.C.: U.S. Department of Agriculture, 1980), p. 556.

87. Phil Wheeler and Ed. Kerr, "The State of our Timber Resources, Part 3," *American Forests* 88(1):15 (1982).

88. Executive Office of the President, Office of Management and Budget, *Special Analyses, Budget of the United States Government*, p. 230; information provided by Congressional Research Service, Library of Congress, May 1982. The implications of the Economic Recovery Tax Act of 1981, which has been described as "the most far-reaching amendments to the Internal Revenue Code since the first tax act," on forest landowners is not included in these estimates. See William K. Condrell and George Neidich, "ERTA '81: Substantial Tax Relief for Timberland Owners," *American Forests* 88(2):12 (1982).

89. William E. Bruner and Perry R. Hagenstein, *Alternative Forest Policies for the Pacific Northwest*, Forest Policy Project, Washington State University (Springfield, Va.: National Technical Information Service, 1981), p. 6.54-6.73.

90. *Ibid.*, pp. 7.1-7.40.

91. A. Starker Leopold, "Wildlife and Forest Practice," in Howard P. Brokaw, ed., *Wildlife and America* (Washington, D.C.: U.S. Government Printing Office, 1978), p.108.

92. Paul Ehrlich and Ann Ehrlich, *Extinction: The Causes and Consequences of the Disappearance of Species* (New York, N.Y.: Random House, 1981), pp. 128-176.

93. U.S. Department of Agriculture, Forest Service, Pacific Northwest Region, *Draft Pacific Northwest Region Plan* (Portland, Oreg.: U.S. Department of Agriculture, 1981), p. 24.

94. A. Starker Leopold, "Wildlife and Forest Practice", pp. 109-111.

95. Jack Ward Thomas, ed., *Wildlife Habitats in Managed Forests: The Blue Mountains of Oregon and Washington*, Agricultural Handbook No. 553 (Washington, D.C.: U.S. Government Printing Office, 1979), pp. 282, 286.

96. David L. Mech, *The Wolf* (Garden City, N.Y.: Natural History Press, 1970).

97. U.S. Department of the Interior, Fish and Wildlife Service, "Kirtland's Warbler Recovery Plan" (Washington, D.C.: U.S. Fish and Wildlife Service, October 22, 1976).

98. Jack Ward Thomas, ed., *Wildlife Habitats in Managed Forests*, Appendix 6, pp. 200-245.

99. S. Dillon Ripley and Thomas E. Lovejoy, "Threatened and Endangered Species," in Howard P. Brokaw, ed., *Wildlife and America*, p. 372.

100. Paul Ehrlich and Ann Ehrlich, *Extinction*, p. 116; A. Starker Leopold, "Wildlife and Forest Practice", p. 113.

101. John C. Hendee, et al., *Wilderness Management*, U.S. Department of Agriculture,

Forest Service, Miscellaneous Publication No. 1365 (Washington, D.C.: U.S. Government Printing Office, October 1978), p. 222; Durward L. Allen, "The Enjoyment of Wildlife," in Howard P. Brokaw, ed., *Wildlife and America*, p. 28.

102. U.S. Department of the Interior, Fish and Wildlife Service, "Initial Findings from the 1980 National Survey of Fishing, Hunting, and Wildlife-Associated Recreation," paper presented at the 47th North American Wildlife and Natural Resources Conference, Portland, Oregon, March 28, 1982.

103. Michael J. Bean, "Federal Wildlife Law," in Howard P. Brokaw, ed., *Wildlife and America*, pp. 279-289.

104. Gustav A. Swanson, "Wildlife on Public Lands," in Howard P. Brokaw, ed., *Wildlife and America*, p. 429.

105. U.S. Comptroller General, *National Direction Required for Effective Management of America's Fish and Wildlife* (Washington, D.C.: General Accounting Office, 1981), p.9.

106. *Ibid.*

107. *Ibid.*, p. 43.

108. *Ibid.*

109. *Ibid.*, p. 42.

110. *Ibid.*, p. 47.

111. *Ibid.*, pp. 44-45.

112. U.S. Department of Agriculture, Forest Service, *Draft Pacific Northwest Regional Plan*, p. 29.

113. U.S. Department of Agriculture, Forest Service, Pacific Northwest Region, *Draft Environmental Impact Statement for Standards and Guidelines* (Portland, Oreg.: U.S. Department of Agriculture, 1981).

114. John S. Gottschalk, "The State-Federal Partnership in Wildlife Conservation," in Howard P. Brokaw, ed., *Wildlife and America*, pp. 290-301.

115. An assessment of wildlife habitat is included in U.S. Department of Agriculture, Forest Service, *An Assessment of the Forest and Range Land Situation in the United States*.

116. U.S. Department of the Interior, Fish and Wildlife Service, *1975 Survey of Hunting, Fishing and Wildlife-Associated Recreation* (Washington, D.C.: U.S. Department of the Interior, 1977), p. 63.

117. For one assessment of these laws see John C. Keene, et al., *Untaxing Open Space*, prepared for the Council on Environmental Quality (Washington, D.C.: U.S. Government Printing Office, April 1976).

118. For more information contact the Nature Conservancy, Suite 800, 1800 N. Kent Street, Arlington, Virginia 22209.

119. U.S. Department of Agriculture, Forest Service, *Draft Environmental Impact Statement*.

120. U.S. Comptroller General, "The Federal Drive to Acquire Private Lands Should be Reassessed" (Washington, D.C.: General Accounting Office, December 1979).

FIGURE REFERENCES

Figure 6.1

Livestock and crop production: (1967-1980)—U.S. Department of Agriculture, *1981 Handbook of Agricultural Charts*, Agricultural Handbook No. 592 (Washington, D.C.: U.S. Government Printing Office, 1982), p. 16. (1965-1979)—U.S. Department of Agriculture, *Agricultural Statistics, 1980*, (Washington, D.C.: U.S. Government Printing Office, 1981), p. 440. (1980-1981)—U.S. Department of Agriculture, Economic Reporting Service, *Agricultural Statistics, 1981* (Washington, D.C.: U.S. Department of Agriculture, 1982). Population: U.S. Department of Commerce, Bureau of the Census, *Statistical Abstract of the United States: 1980* (Washington, D.C.: U.S. Government Printing Office, 1981), p. 6.

Figure 6.2

(1967-1979)—U.S. Department of Agriculture, *Agricultural Statistics, 1980* (Washington: U.S. Government Printing Office, 1981), p. 417. (1980)—U.S. Department of Agriculture, *U.S. Foreign Agricultural Trade, Statistical Report, Calendar Year 1980* (Washington, D.C.: U.S. Department of Agriculture, 1981), p. 6. Index of agricultural exports is measured in terms of volume.

Figure 6.3

Cropland: U.S. Department of Agriculture, *Economic Indicators of the Farm Sector*, Statistical Bulletin 679 (Washington, D.C.: U.S. Government Printing Office, 1980), p. 20.; Fertilizers: *Ibid.*, p. 34.; Farm machinery: *Ibid.*, p. 51.; Farm labor: *Ibid.*, p 53.; Pesticides: (1964)—U.S. Department of Agriculture, *Quantities of Pesticides Used by Farmers in 1964*, Agricultural Economics Report 131 (Washington, D.C.: U.S. Government Printing Office, 1968), pp. 9, 13, 19, 26; (1966)—U.S. Department of Agriculture, *Farmers Use of Pesticides in 1971 - Quantities*, Agricultural Economics Report 252 (Washington, D.C.: U.S. Government Printing Office, 1974), pp. 8, 11, 15, 18; (1971 and 1976)—U.S. Department of Agriculture, *Farmers Use of Pesticides in 1976*, Agricultural Economics Report 418 (Washington, D.C.: U.S. Government Printing Office, 1978), pp. 6, 9, 15, 20; Irrigation: U.S. Geological Survey, *Estimated Use of Water in the United States in 1975*, Circular 765 (Washington, D.C.: U.S. Government Printing Office, 1977), p. 38 and previous quinquennial surveys; (1980)—Estimated at 83 billion gallons per day, a 3.7% increase between 1975 and 1980. See Second National Assessment.

Figure 6.4

(1969-1980)—U.S. Department of Agriculture, *1981 Program Report and Environmental Impact Statement, Soil and Water Resources Conservation Act, Revised Draft* (Washington, D.C.: U.S. Department of Agriculture, November, 1981), pp. 4-6.

Figure 6.5

U.S. Department of Agriculture, *Economic Indicators of the Farm Sector: Production and Efficiency Statistics*, Statistical Bulletin 657 (Washington, D.C.: U.S. Government Printing Office, 1980), p. 90; U.S. Department of Agriculture, *Agricultural Statistics 1980* (Washington, D.C.: U.S. Government Printing Office, 1981), p. 441; U.S. Department of Agriculture, *Agricultural Statistics, 1981* (in progress).

Figure 6.6

U.S. Department of Agriculture, Forest Service, *An Analysis of the Timber Situation in the United States, 1952-2030, Review Draft* (Washington, D.C.: U.S. Department of Agriculture, 1980), Appendix 3, pp. 93, 101.

Figure 6.7

(1950-1979)—U.S. Department of Agriculture, Forest Service, *U.S. Timber Production, Trade, Consumption, and Price Statistics, 1950-1980*, Miscellaneous Publication 1408 (Washington, D.C.: U.S. Department of Agriculture, August, 1981), p. 7; (1980)—U.S.

Department of Agriculture, Forest Service, *U.S. Timber Production, Trade, Consumption, and Price Statistics, 1950-1981* (in progress). Figure does not include data for exports and imports of logs, and exports of pulpwood chips.

Figure 6.8

U.S. Department of Agriculture, *1981 Program Report and Environmental Impact Statement, Review Draft* (Washington, D.C.: U.S. Department of Agriculture, November 1981), pp. 3-5; For sheet and rill erosion subtotals, see U.S. Department of Agriculture, *RCA Appraisal 1980: Review Draft, Part II* (Washington, D.C.: U.S. Department of Agriculture, 1980), pp. 59 (cropland), 64 (rangeland), 65 (pastureland), 66 (forestland).

Figure 6.9

U.S. Department of Agriculture, Soil Conservation Service, *1980 Appraisal Part I, Soil, Water, and Related Resources in the United States: Status, Conditions, and Trends* (Washington, D.C.: U.S. Department of Agriculture, March, 1981), Figure 24, p. 106, Figure 25, p. 108; For regional cropland use, see U.S. Department of Agriculture, Soil Conservation Service, *Natural Resource Inventory* (Washington, D.C.: U.S. Department of Agriculture, November 1979), Table 3a; For regional average annual sheet and rill erosion for 1977 cropland, see U.S. Department of Agriculture, Soil Conservation Service, *Natural Resource Inventory* (Washington, D.C.: U.S. Department of Agriculture, November, 1979), Table 16a.

Figure 6.10

U.S. Department of Agriculture, *1980 Appraisal Part I, Soil, Water and Related Resources in the United States: Status, Condition, and Trends* (Washington, D.C.: U.S. Department of Agriculture, March, 1981), pp. 112, 147.

Figure 6.11

U.S. Department of Agriculture, Forest Service, *An Analysis of the Timber Situation in the United States, 1952-2030*, Review Draft (Washington, D.C.: U.S. Department of Agriculture, 1980), Table 6.14, p.287, Table 6.16, p. 294.

Figure 6.12

U.S. Department of Agriculture, Forest Service, *An Analysis of the Timber Situation in the United States, 1952-2030*, Review Draft (Washington, D.C.: U.S. Department of Agriculture, 1980), Appendix C, pp. 20-25.

Figure 6.13

U.S. Department of Agriculture, Forest Service, *An Analysis of the Timber Situation in the United States, 1952-2030*, Review Draft (Washington, D.C.: U.S. Department of Agriculture, 1980), Table 6.15, p. 290.

WETLANDS

1. This is a 1971 figure from Council on Environmental Quality, *Environmental Trends* (Washington, D.C.: U.S. Government Printing Office, 1981), p. 18. Eighty-two million acres of continental U.S. wetlands were documented in 1954. See Council on Environmental Quality, *Our Nation's Wetlands, An Interagency Task Force Report* (Washington, D.C.: U.S. Government Printing Office, 1978), p. 49. Preliminary results from the National Wetland Inventory conducted by the Fish and Wildlife Service indicate, however, that 92 million acres of wetlands existed in the lower 48 states by the late 1970s. This inventory has relied on different definitions and more sophisticated techniques than past surveys. See U.S. Department of the Interior, Fish and Wildlife Service, National Wetland Inventory, "Statistical Analysis of Wetland Gains and Losses Between Mid-1950's and Late 1970's in the Conterminous United States" (Washington, D.C.: U.S. Department of the Interior, undated) and Bill O. Wilen and H. Ross Pywell, Fish and Wildlife Service, U.S. Department of the Interior, "The National Wetlands Inventory" (Washington, D.C.: Fish and Wildlife Service, 1981).

2. U.S. Department of Agriculture, Forest Service, *An Assessment of the Forest and Range Land Situation in the United States* (Washington, D.C.: U.S. Department of Agriculture, 1980), p. 218.

3. Council on Environmental Quality, *Our Nation's Wetlands, An Interagency Task Force Report*.

4. *Ibid.*, pp. 7-10.

5. Council on Environmental Quality, *Environmental Trends*.

6. U.S. Department of Agriculture, Forest Service, *An Assessment of the Forest and Range Land Situation in the United States*, p. 220.

7. U.S. Council on Environmental Quality, *Environmental Trends*, p. 18. Preliminary results from the National Wetland Inventory conducted by the U.S. Fish and Wildlife Service, which has re-evaluated wetland data from the 1950s, indicate that wetland losses may have actually averaged around 340,000 acres per year since that time.

8. Council on Environmental Quality, *Our Nation's Wetlands, An Interagency Task Force Report*, p. 50; and Council on Environmental Quality, *Environmental Trends*, p. 19.

9. R. Eugene Turner, et al., in "Bottomland Hardwood Forest Land Resources of the Southeastern United States," in *Wetlands of Bottomland Hardwood Forests*, J. R. Clark and J. Benforado, eds., (New York, N.Y.: Elsevier Scientific Publishing Co., 1981), p. 17.

10. U.S. Department of Agriculture, Forest Service, *An Assessment of the Forest and Range Land Situation in the United States*, p. 218.

11. *Ibid.*

12. Council on Environmental Quality, *Environmental Quality—1979* (Washington, D.C.: U.S. Government Printing Office, 1979), p. 501.

13. Jon A. Kusler, *Strengthening State Wetland Regulations*, performed for Fish and Wildlife Service, U.S. Department of the Interior (Washington, D.C.: U.S. Government Printing Office, 1978), pp. 7-8.

14. 33 U.S.C., sec. 1344 (1980). The Corps also has permitting authority under sec. 10 of the Rivers and Harbors Act of 1899, 33 U.S.C., sec. 403 (1980), over dredge and fill activities in traditional navigable waters, which includes some estuarine ecosystems.

15. Executive Order No. 11990, 3 C.F.R., sec. 121-123 (1978).

16. Fish and Wildlife Coordination Act, 16 U.S.C., sec. 661, *et. seq.* (1980). See also, Council on Environmental Quality, *Our Nation's Wetlands, An Interagency Task Force Report*, p. 62.

17. 16 U.S.C., sec. 1451, *et. seq.* (1980). See also, Council on Environmental Quality, *Environmental Quality—1979*, pp. 500-508.

Chapter 7

Land

The land of the United States, 2.3 billion acres in all,* is an incredibly rich resource, providing the space on which we live and on which we build our homes and communities, our roads and factories and offices. It supplies food, water, timber, grazing, minerals, recreation, wildlife habitat. It represents a significant portion of our national wealth.

Like other resources, land is subject to changing demands. Automobiles and interstate highways, for example, and preferences for spread-out patterns of settlement, have subjected ever larger areas to pressures for urban conversion. Rural population growth has intensified demands for homes in the countryside, even as expanding agricultural export markets impel farmers to seek additional areas for commodity production. Growing demands for outdoor recreation have intensified pressures on wilderness areas as well as on ski slopes and other places.

Even in times of slow national economic growth, the demands on land keep changing. Mineral development is booming in parts of the West, for example, bringing to that part of the country new employees and their families, who seek housing, shopping centers, and public services. Rural counties, some of them far from metropolitan areas, are coping with unfamiliar land-use problems.

NATIONAL PERSPECTIVES AND TRENDS

When U.S. land resources are viewed as a whole, trends may be clear from decade to decade; they are seldom so from year to year. Short-term trends are often difficult to identify or confirm. Even over the long term, changing definitions of the categories used for data collection often make comparisons among years difficult or

---

*This figure includes 108 million acres of streams, lakes, and other inland water bodies.[1]

inconclusive.*

National figures, moreover, cannot provide the detail needed to understand and address many land-use problems. Land capabilities, market demands, ownership, state and local public policies—all vary greatly from place to place. Because of this diversity, analysis and policymaking need to be based not only on national data but on information on regions, states, localities, even individual parcels.

Land Use

Demands on land are generally reflected in the way it is used. One perspective on American land use is provided by the "spatial continuum of development," from central cities at one extreme to wilderness at the other (figure 7.1). Urbanized areas within central cities and suburbs, where most of the population lives, occupy only 1.6 percent of our total land area, and only 10 percent of the 362 million acres included in metropolitan areas. Outside these metropolitan areas, urban forces are still strongly felt in an area almost two-thirds as large as metropolitan areas themselves.** The remaining land, the "countryside," occupies more than four times as much land as the metropolitan areas.

Another national perspective on land use is provided by major use categories. As of 1978, for every American, there were 10 acres of land: about 1.8 of cropland; 3.1 acres of forestland; 2.9 of grasslands, pasture, and range; 1.5 of marsh, desert, and tundra. The remaining 0.7 acre was devoted to "specialized uses," a broad category that includes urban areas as well as such diverse areas as parks and wildlife refuges, national defense sites, and flood control areas.†

Figure 7.2 shows changes in the distribution of land among major land-use categories from 1900 to 1978. From 1969 to 1978, grasslands declined (by 29 million acres, or 4.2 percent), as did forestland (by 20 million acres, or 2.8 percent). Cropland increased 11 million acres (2.9 percent) during this period, reversing the trend of the previous two decades, as a result of increased demand for agricultural

---

*The problem affects analyses of trends in this chapter: some data from different time periods are not completely comparable because of changed definitions and measurement techniques over the years.

**This "metropolitan impact" area consists of nonmetropolitan counties with 10 percent or more of their resident workers commuting to jobs in metropolitan areas.

†These figures changed in 1980 as a result of the Alaska National Interest Lands Conservation Act, which reallocated some 105 million acres.

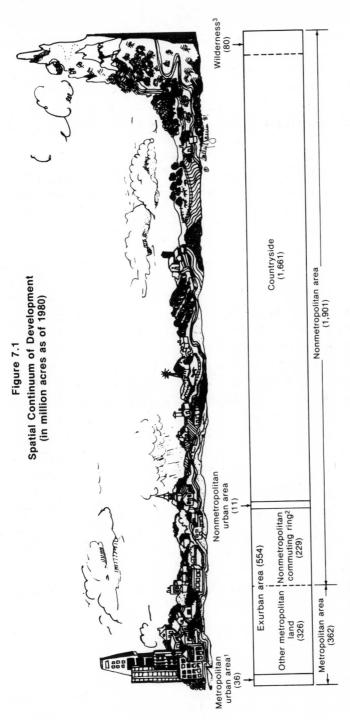

Figure 7.1
Spatial Continuum of Development
(in million acres as of 1980)

Metropolitan
urban area[1]
(36)

Nonmetropolitan
urban area
(11)

Wilderness[3]
(80)

Exurban area (554)

Other metropolitan
land
(326)

Nonmetropolitan
commuting ring[2]
(229)

Countryside
(1,661)

Metropolitan area
(362)

Nonmetropolitan area
(1,901)

Total U.S. land area is 2,264 million acres.

[1] Metropolitan urban area land includes: 12.1 million acres in central cities and 24.2 million acres in suburban areas.

[2] Nonmetropolitan counties with 10% or more of resident workers commuting to metropolitan areas.

[3] Wilderness includes land in the National Wilderness Preservation System only.

Source: U.S. Department of Commerce, Bureau of the Census, and The Conservation Foundation

Figure 7.2

Major Uses of Land in the United States, 1900-1978

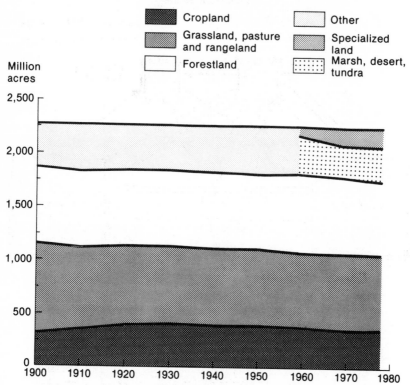

"Other" land (pre-1959) includes specialized land uses and marshes, deserts, tundra, and other lands of undetermined use.

"Specialized" land includes urban and built-up areas (cities and towns, rural highway and road rights-of-way, railroads, airports, and public institutions in rural areas) and nonurban special use areas (parks, recreational areas, federal and state wildlife refuges, national defense sites, flood-control areas, federal industrial areas, farmsteads, and farm roads).

Forestland excludes reserved forestland in parks, wildlife refuges, and other special-use areas.

Source: U.S. Department of Agriculture, Economic Research Service

production (see chapter 6).

These slowly changing totals mask considerable shifting back and forth among the different land-use categories. Figure 7.3 illustrates the dynamics of land-use conversions among nonfederal lands. Lands shift both to and from every category but "urban and built-up" land, which gains land from all the other categories.* For example, between 1967 and 1975, the total amount of land converted into

---

*The terms *urban* and *urban and built-up* are often used interchangeably, but they are not the same. The urban and built-up category used by the U.S. Department of Agriculture incorporates smaller settlements and more facilities than the urban category used by the

Figure 7.3
Land Use Conversions, 1967-1975
(in million acres)

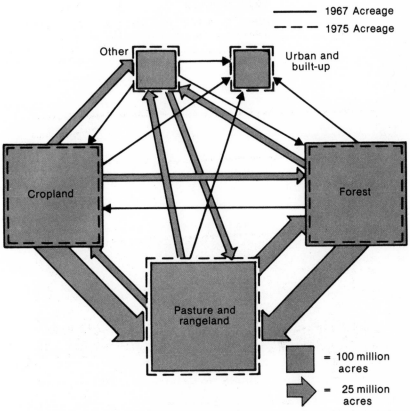

Boxes represent the total amount of nonfederal land in each category for a given year. Arrows represent amount of land converted from one use to another between 1967 and 1975.

Source: U.S. Department of Agriculture, Soil Conservation Service

or out of cropland equaled nearly 30 percent of the cropland base.[3]

The biggest percentage increase among major land-use categories from 1969 to 1978 (as illustrated by figure 7.2) was shown by the "specialized" uses, notably urban areas and parks and public recreation areas. Several factors account for this increase. One is the conversion of land to urban uses. About 3 million acres a year of forest, crop, pasture, or other types of land were transformed into urban uses between 1967 and 1977, as discussed in chapter 6.[4]

Bureau of the Census. According to the most recent available data, urban and built-up comprised 89 million acres (in 1977), while urban comprised only about 47 million acres (in 1980).[2]

Roads and highways have contributed to urban conversion by opening formerly inaccessible land to development. The interstate highway system helped industries to move to less expensive rural areas; urban freeways allowed firms to locate on the fringes of metropolitan areas. Starting in the mid-1950s, some 43,000 miles of interstate highways were built throughout the United States, directly consuming some 1.8 million acres of land.[5] Nevertheless, the total amount of land used by all nonfarm roadways has risen only slightly (to 21.5 million acres in 1978, up from 19.8 million in 1954).[6]

Reservoir and dam building, which began on a large scale in the 1930s, has also converted millions of acres—typically, of agricultural land—for energy, navigation, and flood control. Major areas of reservoir construction include the Tennessee Valley, Missouri River Basin, and Columbia River Basin.[7]

Another factor in the growth of specialized lands has been the increase in public areas set aside for recreation, wildlife, and wilderness (figure 7.4). State and national parks and wildlife refuges occupied about 186 million acres in 1980, about 0.8 acres for each person living in the United States.* The National Wilderness Preservation System, which includes some areas in national parks and wildlife refuges, grew from slightly more than 10 million acres in 1970 to nearly 80 million acres in 1980. While the acreage in these systems in the contiguous 48 states has grown, the dramatic national increases are largely attributable to the designation of national parks, wildlife refuges, and wilderness areas in Alaska. (The allocation of over 100 million acres of Alaskan land, in 1980, is discussed on pages 318, 319.)

Increased demands for specialized land uses over the last 50 years have caused profound changes. Care should be taken, however, in making extrapolations. Much of the expansion—reservoirs and roads, in particular—is no longer occurring at previous rates. The interstate highway system, for example, is virtually complete. Yet increasing demands for land uses such as public recreation areas, pipelines, and powerlines may result in some continuation of these trends.

Care must also be taken in making inferences from national data. Figure 7.5 shows how greatly land-use patterns in individual regions deviate from one another.

---

*This figure includes changes brought about by passage of the Alaska National Interest Conservation Lands Act. Excluding Alaska, the figure is about 89 million acres, or about 0.4 acres per person.

Figure 7.4
Parks, Wildlife Areas, and Wilderness, 1960-1980

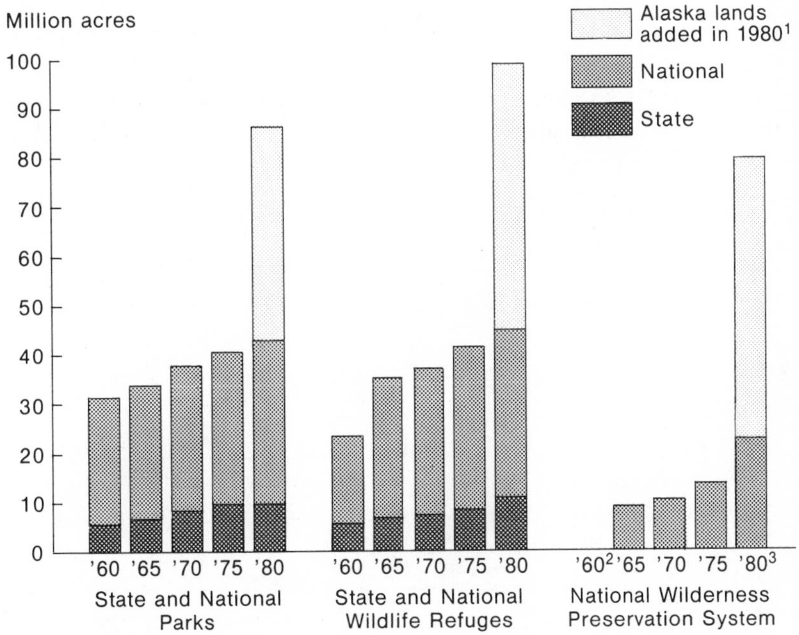

Million acres

[Legend: Alaska lands added in 1980[1]; National; State]

| | State and National Parks | State and National Wildlife Refuges | National Wilderness Preservation System |

[1] These lands were added under the Alaska National Interest Lands Conservation Act, enacted on December 2, 1980.

[2] The National Wilderness Preservation System was created in 1964.

[3] The National Wilderness Preservation System (NWPS) is composed of areas managed by four federal agencies. In 1980 the system included National Parks (35.3 million acres), National Wildlife Refuges (19.3 million acres), National Forests (25.1 million acres), and lands managed by the Bureau of Land Management (about 100,000 acres). Acreages shown above for the NWPS include some land also counted in parks and wildlife refuges.

Source: U.S. Department of the Interior, National Park Service, and U.S. Department of Agriculture, Soil Conservation Service

Land Capability

Just as demands on land vary regionally, locally, and even from one parcel to the next, so do the natural capabilities of land. Soils, climate, and topography make some places specially suitable for commercial production of pineapples or artichokes. Earthquake and flood hazards make other areas especially inappropriate for urban development.

Conflicts continually arise because some lands have a capability for more than one use. Productive farmlands, for example, may be suitable for industrial development as well. Productive grazing lands may have rich minerals underneath them. In many cases, moreover, users and regulating governments are uninformed about the full range of capabilities of particular parcels.

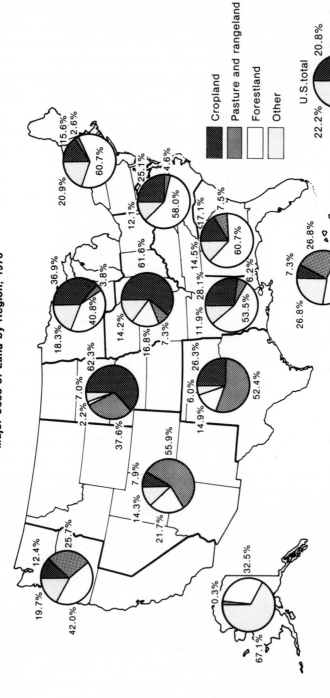

Figure 7.5

Major Uses of Land by Region, 1978

Cropland

Pasture and rangeland

Forestland

Other

U.S. total

Regions are U.S. Department of Agriculture farm production regions

"Other" land includes specialized and undetermined land uses (for definition see figure 7.2).

Source: U.S. Department of Agriculture, Economic Research Service

Land is often used in ways that do not respect its capabilities or even in ways that reduce or destroy unique capabilities: wetlands are drained for farming, for example, or factories are built on specialized cropland. Failure to respect land capability may also harm the user: building on floodplains can result in flood damages, and plowing steep slopes can cause severe erosion. In some cases, investments may extend capabilities, enabling land to satisfy more demands. Investments in irrigation allow some arid lands to become productive farms; reclaiming strip-mined lands can allow them to satisfy some useful purpose.

Special-capability lands are discussed in several parts of this book. Wetlands and floodplains, which are prominent among these lands, are examined in chapters 6 and 3, respectively. Prime farmlands are looked at in chapter 6. A fourth type of special-capability land—barrier islands—is discussed later in this chapter.

Landownership

The diversity of landowners also has an impact on the use of the country's land resources. The federal government owns 34 percent of the land, states and localities 6 percent, Indian tribes 2 percent.[8] The remaining 58 percent is held by some 34 million private landowners.* While nearly all cropland is privately owned, large acreages of grassland, forestland, and specialized land are owned by governments.[9]

Federal landholdings are distributed unevenly among numerous departments and agencies. As of 1979, principal holders included the Bureau of Land Management (17 percent of all land in the country), the U.S. Forest Service (8 percent), the National Park Service (3 percent), the Fish and Wildlife Service (2 percent), and the Department of Defense (1 percent).[10] As figure 7.6 illustrates, nearly half of all federal land is in 11 western states; 90 percent of the rest is in Alaska.[11] The proportion of land in federal ownership has not changed significantly during this century, except in Alaska, where substantial acreages have shifted to state and Indian tribe ownership.

Private land is owned predominantly by individuals (34 percent of all private land) and married couples (33 percent). Other family group ownerships, including family corporations, account for an-

---

*In the 48 contiguous states, the distribution is 22 percent federal, 6 percent state and local, 3 percent Indian tribes, and 69 percent private land.

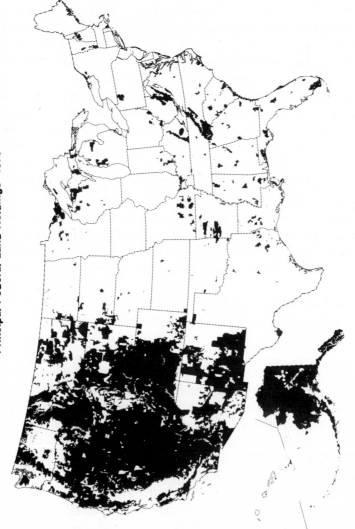

Figure 7.6

Principal Federal Land Holdings   1976

Source: U.S. Department of the Interior, Geological Survey

other 16 percent. Nonfamily corporations (11 percent), nonfamily partnerships (2 percent), and miscellaneous (4 percent) make up the remainder.[12] Private landownership is heavily concentrated; about 0.5 percent of the landowners have title to 40 percent of the private land, while 78 percent have title to only 3 percent of the private land.[13]

Tremendous regional variation exists in private landownership. For example, while individuals and married couples own 67 percent of private land in the nation as a whole, they own less than 50 percent of the private land in the Pacific region, but more than 80 percent in the Corn Belt and Lake States regions.[14]

One recent study of the rural land market found substantial increases over the past 20 years in the amount of rural land owned by absentees and former urban residents.[15] Although investments in land by foreign corporations and individuals have received media attention, current estimates place foreign ownership of farmland and forestlands at 7.8 million acres, just over 0.6 percent of U.S. agricultural land.[16]

There is also evidence of increasing "parcellation," or the division of rural land into small, noncommodity-producing parcels.[17] Land traditionally held in 80-acre to 640-acre plots is being converted into 5-acre to 40-acre tracts, sizes more suitable for second home sites and recreational use. More than one-fifth of private forestland is owned in units of less than 100 acres, and 6 percent (20 million acres) of all cropland is in units smaller than 50 acres.[18]

PROSPECTS AND ISSUES

The effect of some of the most significant potential influences on land—new energy and communications technologies, for example, and long-term demands for American agricultural products—cannot be confidently predicted. The continued unfolding of trends already observed, however, promises some far-reaching changes.

The American countryside is changing. As discussed in chapter 1, nonmetropolitan counties (those not near a major city) are growing faster than metropolitan areas for the first time in our history. Manufacturing has replaced agriculture as the largest employer in rural areas, where farmers are now a minority group.[19] Shops and services once labeled "urban" are springing up in rural places. In many parts of the nation, the appearance of the rural landscape is being transformed as population and employment grow. Impacts on resource productivity may also be substantial, as rural land is divided into smaller parcels for residential use, and as farming practices (manure spreading, for example, and use of pesticides and herbicides) are constrained by concerns of nonfarm residents.[20]

Some regions face the prospect of especially profound change. Employment between 1970 and 1978 in the West and South grew at almost three times the rate of that for the Northeast and North Central regions, gaining nearly 14 million new jobs.[21] (See chapter 1.) The rate of increase in manufacturing in the West and South, 2.4 percent annually during the 1970s, is expected to rise to 2.6 in the 1980s.[22] To cite another example, coal production in five western mountain states (Wyoming, Montana, Colorado, New Mexico, Utah) is expected to increase by 1985 to almost 15 times its 1967 level.[23]

Federal lands will continue to feel special pressures in the 1980s. These lands (including Outer Continental Shelf areas) contain about 85 percent of the nation's untapped oil, 35 percent of the coal, nearly half of the natural gas and geothermal resources, most of the tar sands and oil shale, significant quantities of many strategic minerals,[24] and a large proportion of the softwood timber. They also satisfy increasing demands for outdoor recreation. During the 1970s, the federal government established several land management processes to respond to pressures on federal lands.[25] Because of current budget limitations and proposals to reduce federal landholdings, it is uncertain whether these processes will be given an opportunity to work in the future.

Even though national land-use figures typically change slowly, the opposite can often be true at the metropolitan and local level: when a boomtown finds its school enrollment doubled in one year or the principal employer in town closes its doors, change may be rapid indeed. Chapter 8 considers some of the special prospects of central cities; these prospects, too, vary greatly from city to city.

Growth and change in the 1980s raise a host of concerns. Will familiar problems—sprawl, alteration of valuable resources, neglect of land capability—be repeated in areas of new growth? Will the lessons of the 1970s be applied to reconcile needs for environmental quality with pressures for new development?

The measures that will answer questions like these remain preeminently the responsibility of local governments and, to a lesser extent, of states. (See box on pages 304, 305.) In the past, the capability and willingness of these governments to address the consequences of growth and decline have varied greatly from place to place. Now, as voters opt for lower taxes and as federal financial and technical assistance are reduced, states and localities face additional challenges. Whether states and localities will fashion innovative, cost-effective ways to address the land-use issues of the 1980s, particularly in light of budgetary constraints and demands for less government intervention in private affairs, remains to be seen. (State and local institutional capabilities with respect to environmental programs are discussed in chapter 9.)

Some of the most effective means of addressing land-use problems—acquisition of parks and natural areas, for example, and providing seed money for private downtown development—cost money that states and localities may not have in the years just ahead. To address land-related problems, therefore, they may turn, even more than in the recent past, to regulations. The effectiveness and fairness of regulations accordingly promise to be significant issues. Rural localities will need to ask, for example, whether large-lot zoning is indeed protecting their agricultural areas or whether it is doing just the opposite—by forcing new rural residents to create larger lots than they really want. Localities will also need to seek more sophisticated ways of meeting public objectives without offending constitutional guarantees of fairness to landowners. What constitutes a regulatory "taking" of property, and what remedies are available when a "taking" occurs, will also be recurrent issues in the years ahead.

Even the most effective regulations, however, are likely to have only marginal influence on the use of the land. For land use is, as already suggested, the product of numerous forces: demands, natural capabilities, ownership patterns, and so on. And many of the decisions that most profoundly affect land use are made with little thought of the land. The company building a truck terminal to serve its market area, the local government building a treatment plant to end a pollution problem, the congressman writing a tax bill to stimulate business and investment—all may have profound influence on the use of land in a particular community, yet they may be unaware of that influence or unconcerned about it.[26] Too often, in fact, the web of decisions that affects land use is not well understood. Research during the 1980s may produce better understanding, creating opportunities to translate that understanding into more sophisticated, effective public policies for the land.

The diversity of land uses, capabilities, and ownership is reflected in numerous issues and policy choices. Growth and change in non-

Government Influences, the Courts, and Land Use

Government Influences,
the Courts, and Land Use

Government actions play a key role in determining how land is used. Some government actions, such as local zoning regulations, are intended to influence land use. Others, such as the building of regional wastewater treatment plants or the liberalization of depreciation rules for new commercial buildings, are principally intended to achieve other objectives but have land-use consequences as well.

Localities are the government units that most often intentionally influence land use—through permits, zoning, building codes, and the like. Of the approximately 3,000 county governments, 18,500 municipalities, and 17,000 townships in the United States, more than 14,000 engage in some type of land-use control.[1]* According to one study of government land-use programs:

> More than 10,000 have planning boards, and a slightly smaller number have a zoning ordinance or subdivision regulations. In addition to these general purpose governments, there are tens of

*See figure references at end of chapter.

thousands of special purpose agencies, including school districts, irrigation districts, pollution control agencies, and flood control districts, which influence land use by their siting and investment decisions and, occasionally, by direct controls.[2]

Land-use controls exercised by local governments in rural areas are increasing, but they remain small in number compared to similar initiatives in urban areas.[3]

During the 1970s, federal and state measures intended to influence land use also increased. Although some of the federal measures (such as section 404 of the federal Clean Water Act, under which the Corps of Engineers protects wetlands) operate directly, many others (such as the coastal zone management program and HUD's planning grants) seek to support state and local efforts. With the ending of some federal programs and deep cutbacks in others, states and localities will have even more land-use responsibilities in the 1980s.

Land-use planning in one form or another is authorized or required in half the states.[4] A majority of states

metropolitan areas throughout the country, for example, require reevaluating policies that affect those areas. So do increasing pressures for mineral development and recreation, which affect federal as well as private lands. Similarly, continuing development of sensitive lands, spurred on in part by public policies and funds, continues to alter the capabilitites of these lands. Among the many land issues, two have been singled out for discussion in this chapter—barrier island development and changing pressures on the National Park System.

Because of their fragile nature and scenic qualities, barrier islands and National Park System lands are confronted with some strong pressures—recreation, development, conservation of critical ecosystems or sites. Barrier islands, though unique, face problems

have environmental policy acts, modeled largely after the National Environmental Policy Act (NEPA), which require environmental impact statements for proposed projects that may significantly affect the environment.[5] Also, some states have established direct regulation of particular kinds of development (for example, energy facilities) or particular natural features (for example, coastal wetlands).[6] Many of the state programs, instead of authorizing direct controls on the land, establish requirements or support for local action.

State and local land-use regulations operate within constitutional bounds as interpreted by court decisions. Constitutional issues are often raised when regulations affect property, so courts play an important part in determining the impacts of state and local regulations. Substantial differences exist from state to state among court interpretations of land-use laws.

The issue of how far governments can regulate land use before running afoul of constitutionally protected property rights is not subject to any precise test. Instead, courts determine the constitutionality of regulations on a case-by-case basis.[7] Yet in the vast majority of reported decisions, courts have upheld land-use regulations against challenges that they "take," or unconstitutionally burden, private property. In fact, recent judicial trends have upheld a variety of controls, in-cluding open space[8] and landmark preservation,[9] and prime farmland[10] and wetland protection.[11]

When land-use regulations do unconstitutionally burden private property, what is the landowner's remedy? The traditional approach has been to try to invalidate the offending regulation or obtain authorization for the development to proceed.[12] Recent decisions suggest that an additional remedy may also be available: under certain circumstances, landowners may be entitled not only to invalidation of the regulations but also to money damages from the responsible government while the regulation is in effect.[13] The spectre of having to pay damages for land-use regulations could inhibit regulatory efforts by financially constrained local governments.[14]*

No matter what remedy is provided, of course, landowners are not entitled to any relief unless thay can prove a "taking." In any event, future court decisions on state and local land-use regulations will continue to have profound influences on the way land is used.

―――――
*The remedy issue has been made more pressing by recent developments under the Civil Rights Act of 1871, 42 U.S.C. Section 1983 (1980). Landowners have used this law to claim money damages when land-use regulations allegedly "take" their property.[15]

comparable to those confronting most sensitive lands. The National Park System, although facing stresses comparable to those affecting many recreation lands, has the distinction of being publicly owned and managed for specific purposes. Together, barrier islands and National Park System units constitute a small fraction of total land within the United States, but they illustrate the difficulty of designing policies for sensitive, diverse, highly valued, and heavily used lands.

Barrier Island Development

The nearly 300 barrier islands that fringe the Atlantic and Gulf Coasts are resilient and fragile.[27] They are resilient in their ability to alter their shapes and shift their positions in response to the rising sea level and to severe storms. They are fragile because almost any change in them alters a dynamic equilibrium of sediment supply, wave energy, surface shape, and water level.

In their natural state, barrier islands play a crucial role in helping to form the estuaries, bays, sounds, and lagoons that provide breeding grounds, habitats, and nutrients vital to wildlife and the fishing industry. Barrier islands also provide natural flood and storm protection to the coastline and estuarine systems, acting as efficient shock absorbers and dissipaters of storm energy.

These islands, with an area totaling some 2,600 square miles,[28] are also enormously attractive to developers. Data show that barrier islands were developed at a rate of some 6,000 acres per year between 1950 and 1973.[29]* Although urbanization of barrier islands is not new (witness Galveston, Atlantic City, Miami Beach), the urban area of barrier islands totaled only about 91,000 acres as recently as 1950.[31] By 1973, that figure had risen to 229,000 acres, equaling 14 percent of the total area of barrier islands, which is 1.6 million acres.[32] Between 1950 and 1973, barrier islands urbanized twice as fast as the nation as a whole.[33]

Although virtually every state with barrier islands has witnessed increased development of them, some states have been affected much more than others. Florida alone accounted for almost half of the total acres urbanized between 1950 and 1973. Other states showing major urbanization of these islands included North Carolina (16,000 acres), South Carolina (11,000), Texas (10,000), Louisiana (5,000), and New Jersey (5,000).[34]

A survey completed in the early 1970s showed that more than one-third of total barrier island acreage, or 625,000 acres, was protected against development as a result of ownership by federal, state, or local governments, or by land conservation organizations. Another 243,000 acres were already developed. The remaining 739,000 acres were unprotected.[35] The states with the largest amounts of undeveloped, unprotected land on barrier islands were Texas (240,000 acres), Florida (131,000), Georgia (86,000), and South Carolina (85,000).[36]

According to the survey, wetlands occupy just over 50 percent

---

*Barrier island data are generally based on estimates and vary from source to source. The most recent barrier island figures are U.S. Geological Survey data from 1972 to 1975. Recent estimates, however, suggest that the trends noted by the Geological Survey and presented here are continuing.[30]

of total barrier island acreage, about 840,000 acres.[37] Barren lands, typically beaches and dunes, make up another 230,000 acres (roughly 14 percent), and forestlands cover just over 150,000 acres (about 9 percent). Urban and developed areas occupy roughly 14 percent of total acreage, and the remaining 13 percent consists of agricultural lands, rangelands, and water bodies. All categories except urban or built-up areas have declined in recent years.

With more than one-third of the acreage of barrier islands protected, would it do any harm for development to spread to much of the rest? There are several reasons for concern.

Constantly changed by tidal and erosional forces, barrier islands provide a "first line of defense"—a barrier—against destructive ocean storms.[38] They protect, in addition to populated coastal mainlands, the lagoons, estuaries, and wetlands that nest and nourish millions of waterfowl, fish, and other wildlife.[39] Barrier islands and their associated estuaries serve as resting and feeding stops for migratory birds, including the endangered whooping crane and the peregrine falcon. Many other birds, including the bald eagle, nest on barrier islands, as do endangered sea turtles.[40] Although barrier islands are largely inhabited by small animals, they are also inhabited by large species like deer, alligators, and the famous wild ponies of Assateague Island.

The spawning and nursery areas, habitats, and food sources supplied by barrier island ecosystems are vital to America's offshore fishing industry. Development alters or destroys these resources. A recent Department of the Interior draft environmental impact statement on barrier island protection policies noted that:

> The condition of the estuaries is important to the commercial fishing industry because it is estimated that two thirds of the top-value Atlantic and Gulf Coast species of fish are directly dependent on conditions of the estuaries. Without the protection afforded the bay systems by the barrier islands, productivity would drop with obvious consequences to sport and commercial fishermen.[41]

Attempting to stabilize or build on barrier islands impedes their natural protective functions. Research, particularly on the Outer Banks of North Carolina, has shown that barrier islands naturally migrate due to dynamic ocean forces and that development can easily interfere with these forces, aggravating erosion and leading to alteration of the islands.[42] On many developed barrier islands, this has already happened, with costly results.

The forces that create and nourish the natural systems of barrier islands also present hazards for development. As a recent study put it:

> Development on barrier islands is a gamble between time and nature. The islands change position, often very rapidly, in response to storms, changes in water level, and changes in current patterns. The barriers are generally receding toward the mainland, responding to the progressive rise of sea level. Among the hazards are the migration of old inlets, formation of new inlets during storms, and storm overwash that can undermine the foundations by liquefying soil. The combination of rising water level, coastal storm surges, wave action, and high winds make development hazardous on many parts of the islands.[43]

Barrier islands often receive the most destructive impacts of the two types of harsh storms that hit the Atlantic and Gulf Coasts: the northeaster (or winter cyclone) and the hurricane (or summer cyclone). An average of two hurricanes a year strike these coasts, causing more combined damage than any other type of natural disaster.[44]

Development on barrier islands has not only altered natural systems and increased storm damage but has also added to costs incurred by the public. One source of expense is the continual task of resisting instability and natural movement. Roads, buildings, power lines—nearly all structures—are affected by barrier island movement. Continuing efforts to stabilize ground, prevent erosion, and strengthen structures are required. Shoring up buildings, repairing roads, reshaping dunes, are expensive and for many areas must be repeated frequently. In some instances, even huge expenditures prove futile: natural movement continues to reshape the island.

Miami Beach, one of the oldest developed barrier islands, lost all its beach right up to the supports of the luxury hotels. The first response, an expensive system of groins, ended up accelerating the erosion process. So the Army Corps of Engineers, beginning in 1977, recreated a beach 300 feet wide and 10 miles long, at a cost of $65 million; the federal government paid nearly half this cost. The annual federal cost of replacing the beach eroded away is estimated to be $1 million.[45]

Miami's problem is not unique. Beaches in North Carolina that have been replenished artificially generally disappear at a rate 10 times that of a natural beach. At Sea Bright, New Jersey, the beach now is gone, replaced by an intricately engineered granite and concrete seawall.[46]

These visible costs of maintaining and repairing public facilities are only a small element of total public expense. Other costs are potentially far larger, for the federal government as well as states and localities. Federal programs have borne much of the costs of bridges, roads, causeways, water supply, wastewater treatment, shore protection, disaster relief, and flood insurance on barrier islands. One recent Department of the Interior study found that nearly $500 million in federal funds were spent on these types of projects for barrier islands between 1976 and 1978 alone.[47]

Public expenditures to serve existing development of barrier islands appear likely to increase in the future, as property damaged or destroyed by storms is repeatedly repaired or replaced. Extension of barrier island development to additional areas would presumably increase those expenditures still further.

Yet another public cost of barrier island development results from alterations of natural systems that cause loss of fisheries; these costs can be reflected not only in higher prices for remaining fish and shellfish products, but also in the loss of related jobs. For example, a poorly designed causeway built in the 1960s to Sanibel Island, off the west coast of Florida, destroyed what was then a $1.5 million a year scallop industry; it has not returned.[48] St. George Island, a barrier off Florida's Panhandle in Appalachicola Bay, developed at a fast pace after causeway construction in the 1960s provided access to the mainland. But the inability of the island's soil to absorb sewage from new homes and businesses contributed to the bay's pollution, which caused the closing of the state's prime oyster beds for several months in 1980.[49]

Policies Promoting Development

Federal permits, licenses, and financial aid play a key part in barrier island development. Coast Guard permits, for example, are necessary for constructing any bridge or causeway to a barrier island.[50] And Corps of Engineers permits are necessary for filling barrier island wetlands.[51]

Federal financial aid has helped provide barrier island infrastructure. During a recent three-year period, the Economic Development Administration furnished more than $81 million in grants to roughly 150 barrier island projects such as roads, harbors, and sewage systems.[52] At the same time, the Farmers Home Administration awarded $26 million in grants and loans to barrier island communities, with 80 percent of the funds earmarked for water and wastewater treatment facilities.[53] Between 1975 and 1980, the Environmental Protection Agency funded over $450 million in wastewater construction projects that affected or had the potential to affect barrier island environments.[54] The federal government also bears much of the cost of bridges and causeways to barrier islands.[55]

Disaster relief is another public cost of barrier island development. Shortly after Hurricane Frederic destroyed the bridge to Dauphin Island, Alabama, the Federal Highway Administration authorized nearly $40 million to replace the bridge.[56] Altogether, disaster relief for barrier island communities—services, financial assistance, and infrastructure reconstruction—cost the federal government an annual average of more than $80 million from 1972 to 1979.[57]

The National Flood Insurance Program (NFIP) makes additional dollars available to barrier islands. Although the number of barrier island structures covered by National Flood Insurance is unknown, a recent study found NFIP coverage totaling almost $580 million in barrier island communities near four national seashores on the southeast Atlantic and Gulf of Mexico coasts. Just in these communities, $17.8 million in claims had been paid from 1978 to 1980.[58]

The same study documented the pattern of federal influence in accommodating and stimulating urbanization. A road, enlarged by a federal program, allows more housing; subsequently, federal funds improve water supply and wastewater treatment capacities, allowing still more development. According to the report, a cycle of development beyond infrastructure capacity, followed by continued rounds of expansion, upgrading, and reconstruction, is furthered by federal programs.[59] Using the most conservative estimates, the report found that:

> Documented federal expenditures in three of the study areas represent an average subsidy of $25,570 per developed acre in actual dollars expended or obligated, and a total expenditure of more than $96.7 million for 3,784 developed acres. When restated as 1980 replacement costs, federal subsidies in the three areas averaged $53,250 per developed acre.[60]

If current programs are continued, according to the same study, the federal cost of aiding development on undeveloped barrier islands could range from $5.56 billion to $10.77 billion over the next 20 years.[61]

Most of the federal programs that provide infrastructure assistance to barrier islands are "place neutral." That is, they are not focused on aiding barrier island development, but instead provide the same sorts of assistance provided to development elsewhere. In fact, however, federal programs may give relatively more aid to barrier islands than to other areas because of the expense of providing access and public facilities in these locations.

State and local actions also play a key role in furthering barrier island development. These governments frequently supply a portion of the public funds required for federally aided development, and their zoning and other regulatory controls often provide for expanded development. Within 10 months of Hurricane Frederic's destruction of Dauphin Island, building permits for nearly $20 million of construction on the island were issued by local governments.[62]

Policies Limiting Development

Governments at every level, as well as private conservation groups, have acted to protect barrier islands against spreading development. These protective actions take several forms, including acquisition, limitations on public assistance to barrier island development, and regulatory restrictions.

Acquisition. As already noted, some 625,000 acres of barrier islands—more than one-third the total acreage—are protected against development, as a result of ownership by federal, state, or local agencies or by conservation groups. States with large acreages of such protected land include Florida (234,000 acres), Texas (120,000), Georgia (71,000), and North Carolina (57,000).[63]

The federal government, largely through the National Park Service and the Fish and Wildlife Service, administers 439,000 acres of barrier islands.[64]* There are 12 barrier island units within the National Park System and 31 in Fish and Wildlife Service refuges. The 1970s saw substantial barrier island acreage added to the National Park System and large parts of 13 barrier islands, with nearly 50 miles of beach, acquired as wildlife refuges.[65] From 1965 to 1978, some $128 million was spent out of the Land and Water Conservation Fund to acquire barrier island areas for federal protection.[66]

State agencies administer over 177,000 barrier island acres, including many parks and wildlife refuges, and another 29,000 acres are administered by local governments.[67] Between 1965 and 1978, states and localities spent at least $100 million (including $51

*Some governmental holdings, such as those of the Department of Defense, are held for a variety of public purposes and are thus not considered "protected."

million from the Land and Water Conservation Fund) for acquisitions on 74 islands in 17 of the 18 barrier island states.[68] Private organizations owning property and having programs for acquisition of open space and coastal habitat protection include the Nature Conservancy, the National Audubon Society, the Maine Islands Trust, and both the Massachusetts and Long Island Heritage Trusts.[69]

Limitations on Public Assistance. Several measures in recent years have sought to limit or end various types of public assistance to barrier island development. Some of these measures have been directed specifically to barrier islands, while others are broader.

Of the measures focused specifically on barrier islands, the most significant is probably P.L. 97-35, which bars federal flood insurance, after October 1, 1983, for new construction or substantial modification of existing structures on undeveloped portions of barrier islands. Draft definitions and criteria for designating "undeveloped" islands were issued in January 1982 by the Department of the Interior.[70]

The Floodplains Management Executive Order and the Protection of Wetlands Executive Order, both issued by President Carter in 1977, may help to cut down the federal role in aiding barrier island development, although agency responses to the orders are still so recent that impacts are not yet clear. The Floodplains Executive Order is intended to prevent federal agencies from conducting, supporting, or allowing actions in or affecting floodplains unless no "practicable alternative" exists.[71] The Wetlands Executive Order is intended to avoid the alteration and destruction of wetlands by federal agency projects.[72] Since more than half the surface of barrier islands is occupied by wetlands, and since many of the islands are subject to serious flood hazards, the impact of these orders, combined with the Corps of Engineers wetland permitting authority under Section 404 of the Clean Water Act, may prove to be substantial.[73]

The Coastal Zone Management Act requires participating states to include barrier island and dune protection as a goal of their coastal plans and actions. All barrier island states except Georgia, Texas, and Virginia have federally approved coastal zone management programs or are expected to have them by the end of 1982.[74]

Regulatory Restrictions. Many states and localities have environmental, flood hazard mitigation, or wetland protection laws that limit—and, in some cases, prevent—urbanization of barrier islands.[75] Participation in the federally sponsored Coastal Zone Management Program has advanced many of these state and local measures.

As of 1979, eight Atlantic and Gulf Coast states had begun in various ways to restrict development and preserve remaining barrier islands.[76] Florida, for example, initiated an acquisition program along with regulatory measures.[77] Massachusetts, through executive order, prohibits state agencies from using any funds to "encourage growth in hazard prone barrier beach areas."[78]

Options for Conservation

A number of policy options exist to address barrier island development. These include eliminating financial aid for future development; strengthening regulations restricting development; and the "no action" or "place neutral" option, which continues current policy by making no distinction between barrier islands and other places. Some of these approaches have been reflected in legislative proposals.[79]

Elimination of Public Financial Support for Development. Financial support, particularly federal financial support, of future barrier island development could be eliminated, although permits and licenses would continue to be granted for facilities not requiring such support. Owners of private property on barrier islands would bear future costs of developing their property as well as future risks of damage and destruction. Also, if the federal government were to pursue this alternative, state and local governments would determine the extent to which they would bear the costs and risks of providing infrastructure.

Supporters of this option include proponents of economy in government as well as conservation groups. Indeed, the budget-cutting initiatives of the Reagan Administration are likely to reduce federal aid for development of barrier islands as well as for development elsewhere. Nevertheless, since some kinds of development aid will almost surely continue, pursuing this option would require some special treatment of barrier islands, as in P.L. 97-35 which, as already noted, amends the National Flood Insurance Program to deny federal flood insurance coverage for new development on undeveloped portions of barrier islands after October 1, 1983.[80]

To curtail federal aid more fully than P.L. 97-35 would presumably mean extending both the areas and the kinds of federal aid affected. That is, laws would need to deal with more than the "undeveloped" portions of barrier islands. Also, besides ending flood insurance, it would be necesary to end infrastructure aid and disaster assistance for repair or replacement of future development. Denial of disaster assistance is especially difficult politically, although present laws and regulations do provide for denial in some situations. For example, federal disaster assistance may be denied for repair of property that previously received it, but subsequently failed to secure or maintain adequate flood insurance coverage.[81]

Some of the policy arguments for discouraging development of barrier islands apply to other areas as well. For example, other islands respond to ocean forces and contain sensitive resources. Also, serious coastal flood hazards exist not only on barrier islands but on some mainland coasts. Some opponents of barrier island protection argue that it is unfair to single out barrier islands for restrictions that do not apply to comparable situations elsewhere. Proponents reply that broader restrictions (for example, barring federal aid for wastewater treatment plants that could encourage development of mainland coastal high hazard areas) would raise administrative and political difficulties that are not present when restrictions apply only to barrier islands.* Proponents of protection also argue that the conjunction of hazards and ecological sensitivity makes barrier islands uniquely worthy of protection.

Regulatory Restrictions. Going a step further, regulations could be strengthened to restrict development. In its most complete form, this would mean prohibiting permits or licenses for barrier island development. Proponents of this approach to inhibiting development draw attention to federal permits for bridges, roads, and other transportation facilities. Especially for the roughly 50 undeveloped islands that are still accessible principally by boat, prohibiting Coast Guard causeway and bridge permits might be sufficient by itself to prevent future development.[82] This option would call for denial not only of these permits but also other federal, state, and local development permits.

Proponents of this approach assert that withdrawal of financial support alone, although making future barrier island development more expensive, would not always make it impossible. Also, they suggest, cutting off disaster assistance is so difficult politically that regulatory measures are needed before development occurs.

A variant of this approach would provide federal incentives and

---

*It is noteworthy that P.L. 97-35 does apply to "coastal barriers," which includes a concept that is not necessarily limited to barrier islands. It includes, for example, spits or beaches that function as barriers.

support for state and local restrictions on barrier island development. The approach could be similar to that of the Coastal Zone Management program or could become part of that program. Or, individual state and local governments could strengthen barrier island restrictions without federal involvement.

"Place Neutral" Approach. A third option would make no distinction between barrier islands and other locations. Any assistance available for mainland development would also be available for barrier island development. Hazard areas and sensitive environmental areas might be restricted against development, but they would receive no additional protection because of their location on barrier islands.

Proponents of this approach essentially assert that barrier islands are too diverse to justify treating them all alike. They note economic and recreational benefits of development and claim that some islands, or at least parts of some islands, are neither so sensitive nor so hazardous as to be unsuitable for development. Opponents note that the measures used to date to protect sensitive areas and prevent development in hazard areas have proved insufficient to stop widespread development of barrier islands. They argue that this approach, in addition to environmental and safety impacts, will impose large future costs that could make this the most expensive of the three options.

Conclusion. As noted, state, local, and federal actions to protect barrier islands have increased in recent years. Development, however, has continued. In legislation pending before Congress, an alliance between budget cutters and environmentalists could prove a powerful force for providing additional protection. It remains to be seen whether additional protection will, in fact, result.

Changing Pressures on the National Parks

America's National Park System has long stood as a model for the world in preserving outstanding natural areas and cultural features and in providing for their enjoyment by the public. Both conservation and enjoyment are established by law as purposes of the parks.[83]

To achieve these goals in a changing society, the National Park System has continually evolved. Today, it encompasses far more than the "crown jewels"—parks like Yellowstone, Yosemite, the Grand Canyon—that "national park" first brings to mind. The system also includes national monuments of scientific or historic interest; lakeshores and seashores; recreation areas; parkways, rivers, and trails; and historic areas, battlefields, and buildings—more than 330 units in all.* (See figure 7.7.)

The 1970s were a decade of expansion for the National Park System. Seventy-five units were added through 1980.[84] In the contiguous 48 states, the acreage grew to 24.3 million in 1981, up from 21.8 million in 1970.[85] In Alaska, the addition of some 43.6 million acres more than doubled the size of the entire system. (See pages 318, 319.)

Many park system units, especially some of the newer ones, bear little resemblance to the massive rural domains of the traditional crown jewels. A number of the newer units, such as Gateway, in New York City, and Golden Gate, in San Francisco, are in or near metropolitan areas. Some of these units, moreover, have come into being not by the traditional method of designating as parks land already owned by the United States, but by purchasing land from private owners. In several of these units—Santa Monica Mountains, for example—publicly owned park lands are interspersed with extensive holdings that will remain private.[86]

Visitors are flocking to the parks in increasing numbers. Total visits to park system units exceeded 300 million in 1980, up from 172 million in 1970 and 79 million in 1960.[87] The addition of units to the system accounted for much of the recent increase in visitation: from 1976 to 1981, the bulk of the increases came at newly established units in or near metropolitan areas. Many of the "rural" units, however, also report continuing heavy use. Altogether, just over 50 of the more than 330 units each reported more than 1 million visits during 1980. Figure 7.8 shows the most visited units.

Pressures from heavy visitor use are producing strains on the national parks. Some of the most intensively used units—in rural as well as in metropolitan areas—experience problems usually associated with urban life: traffic jams, crime, deteriorating infrastructure. The General Accounting Office estimates needs of at least $1.6 billion to correct health and safety hazards by improving or replacing park system facilities such as water supplies, roads, and hotels.[88]

---

*The diversity of the system is reflected in a variety of titles assigned to its units. In addition to national parks, there are national monuments, national recreation areas, national seashores, national historical parks, and so on. For convenience, this discussion often refers to all as "units" or, simply, "parks."

Figure 7.7
National Park System

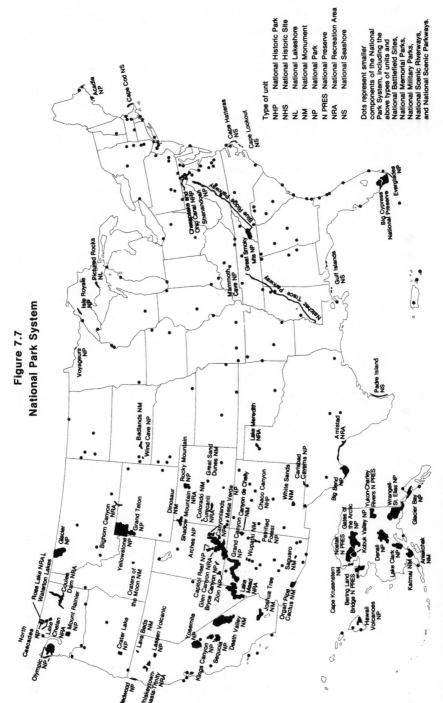

Type of unit
NHP   National Historic Park
NHS   National Historic Site
NL   National Lakeshore
NM   National Monument
NP   National Park
N PRES National Preserve
NRA   National Recreation Area
NS   National Seashore

Dots represent smaller
components of the National
Park System, including the
above types of units and
National Battlefield Sites,
National Military Parks,
National Memorial Parks,
National Scenic Riverways,
and National Scenic Parkways.

Source: U.S. Department of the Interior, National Park Service

Alaska Lands Allocation

The Alaska National Interest Lands Conservation Act (ANILCA),[1]* enacted in December 1980, protects 105 million acres of federally owned land—an area as large as California. The act has been termed the most important piece of land conservation legislation in decades.[2] Its significance has been equated with the enactment of the National Park Service Act in 1916 and the creation of the National Wilderness Preservation System in 1964.

Before Alaska became a state in 1958, less than one-half of 1 percent of its land was privately owned; virtually all the land was federal.[3] The Alaskan Statehood Act of 1958 gave Alaska 25 years to select about 104 million acres of federal land for transfer to the state. Disputes with Alaska's native population, however, stalled the land allocation process.

To resolve these disputes, the Alaska Native Claims Settlement Act in 1971 authorized conveyance of 44 million acres and nearly $1 billion to Eskimo, Aleut, and Indian organizations,

and federal withdrawal of up to 80 million acres of federally owned lands to study for possible preservation in the national interest.[4] Until such withdrawal by the federal government took place, the federal lands could not be conveyed to the state or native groups, or appropriated for mining and oil leasing. Because of no further action by Congress, this withdrawal authority threatened to expire in 1978. To protect the land from development until Congress could act, President Carter withdrew approximately 105 million acres under the authority of other laws.[5] These withdrawn lands spurred Congress to act and formed the basis of the conservation units established by ANILCA.

ANILCA was the product of intense congressional debate during 1978 and 1979 over the amount of acreage to be protected and the types of development to be allowed on protected land. In 1980, the House approved an environmentalist-supported bill that would have protected 127.5 million acres, largely as wilderness, parks, and wildlife refuges. Alaskan officials and development interests generally opposed these measures. The Senate

*See figure references at end of chapter.

Another set of problems, often unnoticed by the casual visitor, is of even greater long-run significance: degradation of the park resources themselves. At some parks, delicate artifacts are disintegrating, and some buildings and sites have fallen into disrepair. Although some of the damage results from natural causes such as harsh weather, much results from intense visitor use. Beaches are littered and springs polluted at Rio Grande Wild and Scenic River, while tons of fossil material are stolen each year from the Petrified Forest. The clearness of the water in Crater Lake has declined measurably in recent years.

There are also serious resource threats originating outside park boundaries. Even traditional national parks, once remote from population centers and often buffered by other public lands, are increasingly affected. There are smelters within close proximity of Glacier National Park, for example, and mineral and geothermal exploration is planned adjacent to Yellowstone. Smoke from distant

sought middle ground among the competing forces, and, in 1980, passed legislation to protect 104.2 million acres. The Senate bill called for less wilderness acreage than previous House bills and opened up the coastal plain of the Arctic Wildlife Range to oil and gas exploration; the House accepted the Senate legislation in the closing days of the 96th Congress.

ANILCA greatly enlarged the National Wildlife Refuge, Park, and Wilderness Preservation Systems.* The size of both the National Wildlife Refuge System, which gained 53.7 million acres—an area larger than Idaho—and the National Park System, which gained 43.6 million acres, more than doubled. Many new national parks, preserves, and monuments were established, and substantial additions were made to some existing park units. Unlike National Park System units elsewhere, the park lands incorporate, for the most part, entire ecosystems. Because of the fragile and pristine landscapes, visitor facilities will probably be less developed. Of the total ANILCA land area, 56.7 million

*In addition, 3 million acres, including two new national monuments, were added to national forests.[6]

acres (54 percent) received wilderness designation, including much of the new refuge and park land.[7]

The 1980 legislation[8] provides degrees of environmental protection to the new and expanded management units. Logging, mining, and motor vehicles will be prohibited in wilderness areas; more varied uses will be allowed on the remaining land. ANILCA also established specific management and use rules for each protection category. For example, management of refuges and forest wilderness areas in Alaska will be guided by legislative provisions that allow sport hunting to continue. Traditional subsistence hunting will be permitted in some national park areas. Also, cooperative agreements between federal agencies and the state, Alaskan native organizations, and private groups will be heavily relied on to manage land, fish, and wildlife resources.

With the bulk of Alaskan land allocation decisions made by enactment of ANILCA, proper management of these lands looms as the greatest challenge ahead. Current budgetary constraints on land managing agencies will tax the already limited abilities of these agencies to meet that challenge.

power plants creates a haze that obscures views of the Grand Canyon. Water is diverted away from the Everglades National Park. Underground rivers in Mammoth Caves carry sewage from nearby communities. Mineral extraction and processing pollutes air and water at Chaco Culture National Historical Park. Because of development in critical habitat around Yellowstone and Glacier National Parks, the grizzly bear is struggling to survive in its last strongholds in the continental United States.[89]

There are differences of opinion about the seriousness of the strains on park resources. Although some of the differences may stem from divergent interpretations of inconclusive data, disagreements run deeper. How much impairment of park resources is tolerable? And how much, even if undesirable, is simply unavoidable? There is no disagreement, however, that some strains on park resources do exist and that understanding and reducing the causes of these strains is essential to both enjoyment and conservation of park resources.

Figure 7.8
Most Visited Units of the National Park System, 1980

Unit	State	Million visits[1]
Golden Gate NRA	California	18.4
Blue Ridge Parkway	Virginia, North Carolina	13.4
Natchez Trace Parkway	Mississippi, Tennessee, Alabama	10.6
Gateway NRA	New York, New Jersey	9.1
Great Smoky Mountains NP	Tennessee, North Carolina	8.4
Colonial NHP	Virginia	6.3
George Washington Memorial Parkway	District of Columbia, Virginia, Maryland	6.3
Lake Mead NRA	Nevada	5.0
Cape Cod NS	Massachusetts	4.8
National Capital Parks[2]	District of Columbia	4.1
Valley Forge NHP	Pennsylvania	3.2
Chesapeake and Ohio Canal NHP	District of Columbia, West Virginia, Maryland	3.1
Acadia NP	Maine	2.8
Rocky Mountain NP	Colorado	2.6
Grand Teton NP	Wyoming	2.6
Gulf Islands NS	Mississippi, Florida	2.5
Yosemite NP	California	2.5
Delaware Water Gap NRA	Pennsylvania, New Jersey	2.5
Grand Canyon NP	Arizona	2.3
Yellowstone NP	Wyoming	2.0
Independence NHP	Pennsylvania	2.0

NRA = National Recreation Area NP = National Park
NHP = National Historical Park NS = National Seashore

[1] A visit is the entry of any person onto lands or waters administered by the National Park Service for recreation purposes. The number of visits is based mainly on vehicle counts and estimates of the average number of people per car, and does not reflect duration of the visits.

[2] The John F. Kennedy Center for the Performing Arts National Memorial (4.2 million visits in 1980) and the Lincoln Memorial (3.3 million visits) are administered separately by the Park Service and are not included in this total.

Source: U.S. Department of the Interior, National Park Service

Reactions to Pressure

In planning for the future of national parks, is it reasonable to expect continuing increases in visitor demands? Park Service forecasts anticipate that the number of park visits will continue to grow throughout the 1980s. After 1983, however, forecasts anticipate that the growth may increase more slowly than it did during the 1970s (assuming no major expansions of the system). In the 1990s and beyond, although no Park Service forecasts are available, it seems realistic to anticipate continued heavy park use: increasing overall demand for outdoor recreation has been projected well into the next century,[90] and there is no basis to believe that parks will not feel this demand.

Most observers expect visitor demand to change as well as grow. As the population ages, for example, there may be increasing demand for activities, such as interpretive walks, that retain high participation rates among the elderly.[91] The shift in population to the West, where there is more park system acreage than in the East and Middle West, is likely to result in heavier use of parks in this region. Even so, projections indicate that parks in and near metropolitan areas will continue to receive the most intense use.

Pressures from outside park boundaries also seem likely to increase as a result of projected economic growth and land development near many parks. Rural growth—the result of energy-related development in the West, industrial expansion in the South, and continued migration to nonmetropolitan areas across the country—could translate into greater inside-the-park pollution from outside sources and further disruption of critical wildlife habitats, among other problems.

In considering possible responses to strains on the parks in the future, it is useful to consider three dimensions of park policy during the 1970s: expansion of the park system, management of the system, and shifts of some costs to private groups and park users.

System Expansion. In recent years, National Park System expansion has increasingly been accomplished by acquiring private land. Congress typically authorizes such acquisition within specified unit boundaries; only later do funds become available. The acquisition of individual parcels may stretch out over a period of many years.

During the 1970s, Congress authorized numerous new units as well as expansion of several existing ones. (See figure 7.9.) Expenditures, for these acquisitions and others previously authorized, totaled $1.25 billion during the decade.[92] The expenditures averaged $155 million annually between 1976 and 1980, excluding the extraordinary expenditures in 1978 and 1979 for acquisition of the Redwoods National Park.[93]

Acquisition of land within established units is a continuing process. As of 1982, Congress had authorized the Park Service to acquire some $789 million worth of land (at 1982 prices), most of it within the boundaries of units where some acquisition has already taken place.[94] For practical reasons, some of these authorized acquisitions will undoubtedly occur. Owners of property inside authorized park boundaries, some of them promised years ago that the Park Service would buy them out, keep pressing for purchase. Park managers, too, press for purchase of some properties within park boundaries,

Figure 7.9
New Units Added to the National Park System, 1970-1980

Year authorized	Unit	State	Acreage[1]
1970	Apostle Islands NL	Wisconsin	42,009
1970	Andersonville NHS	Georgia	478
1970	Fort Point NHS	California	29
1970	Sleeping Bear Dunes NL	Michigan	71,105
1971	Gulf Island NS	Florida, Mississippi	139,975
1971	Voyageurs NP	Minnesota	219,128
1971	Lincoln Home NHS	Illinois	12
1972	Buffalo National River	Arkansas	94,146
1972	Puukohola Heiau NHS	Hawaii	77
1972	John D. Rockefeller, Jr., Memorial Parkway	Wyoming	23,777
1972	Grant-Kohrs Ranch NHS	Montana	1,528
1972	Longfellow NHS	Massachusetts	2
1972	Hohokam-Pima NM	Arizona	1,690
1972	Thaddeus Kosciuszko NM	Pennsylvania	<1
1972	Cumberland Islands NS	Georgia	36,545
1972	Fossil Butte NM	Wyoming	8,198
1972	Lower St. Croix NSR	Minnesota, Wisconsin	8,679
1972	Gateway NRA	New York, New Jersey	26,172
1972	Golden Gate NRA	California	38,677
1973	Lyndon Baines Johnson Memorial Grove on the Potomac	District of Columbia	17
1974	Big Cypress NPres	Florida	570,000
1974	Big Thicket NPres	Texas	84,550
1974	John Day Fossil Beds NM	Oregon	14,100
1974	Knife River Indian Village NHS	North Dakota	1,292
1974	Martin Van Buren NHS	New York	40
1974	Sewell-Belmont House NHS	District of Columbia	<1
1974	Springfield Armory NHS	Massachusetts	55
1974	Tuskegee Institute NHS	Alabama	74
1974	Clara Barton NHS	Maryland	9
1974	Cuyahoga Valley NRA	Ohio	32,460
1975	Canaveral NS	Florida	57,627
1976	Klondike Gold Rush NHP	Alaska, Washington	13,270
1976	Valley Forge NHP	Pennsylvania	2,466
1976	Ninety Six NHS	South Carolina	1,115
1976	Congaree Swamp NM	South Carolina	15,200
1977	Eleanor Roosevelt NHS	New York	180
1978	Lowell NHP	Massachusetts	134
1978	Chattahoochee River NRA	Georgia	8,515
1978	War in the Pacific NHP	Guam	1,923
1978	Santa Monica Mountains NRA	California	150,000
1978	Kaloko-Honokohau NHP	Hawaii	1,311
1978	Fort Scott NHS	Kansas	7
1978	Thomas Stone NHS	Maryland	322
1978	Upper Delaware Scenic & Recreational River	New York, Pennsylvania	75,000
1978	Edgar Allan Poe NHS	Pennsylvania	1
1978	*Palo Alto Battlefield NHS	Texas	50
1978	*Rio Grande Wild and Scenic River	Texas	9,600
1978	San Antonio Missions NHP	Texas	2,500

Year authorized	Unit	State	Acreage[1]
1978	Maggie L. Walker NHS	Virginia	1
1978	New River Gorge National River	West Virginia	62,024
1979	Frederick Law Olmstead NHS	Massachusetts	2
1980	Eugene O'Neill NHS	California	14
1980	Georgia O'Keeffe NHS	New Mexico	4
1980	Martin Luther King, Jr., NHS	Georgia	24
1980	Boston African American NHS	Massachusetts	0
1980	Aniakchak NPres	Alaska	376,000
1980	Aniakchak NM	Alaska	138,000
1980	Bering Land Bridge NPres	Alaska	2,457,000
1980	Cape Krusenstern NM	Alaska	560,000
1980	Denali NPres	Alaska	1,330,000
1980	Gates of the Arctic NPres	Alaska	900,000
1980	Glacier Bay NPres	Alaska	57,000
1980	Katmai NPres	Alaska	308,000
1980	Kenai Fjords NP	Alaska	567,000
1980	Kobuk Valley NP	Alaska	1,710,000
1980	Lake Clark NPres	Alaska	1,214,000
1980	Lake Clark NP	Alaska	2,439,000
1980	Noatak NPres	Alaska	6,460,000
1980	Wrangell-St. Elias NP	Alaska	8,147,000
1980	Wrangell-St. Elias NPres	Akaska	4,171,000
1980	Yukon-Charley Rivers NPres	Alaska	1,713,000
1980	*Salinas NM	New Mexico	1,113
1980	*Kalaupapa NHP	Hawaii	5,000
1980	*James A. Garfield NHS	Ohio	8
1980	*Women's Rights NHP	New York	2

NHP = National Historic Park   NPres = National Preserve
NHS = National Historic Site   NRA = National Recreation Area
NL = National Lakeshore   NSR = National Scenic River
NM = National Monument   N S = National Seashore
N P = National Park

*Authorized units for which acquisition funds have never been appropriated. Current acquisition costs for these units would total $9.5 million.

[1] Acreage figures are the areas within authorized unit boundaries, including areas not yet acquired and areas that will remain in nonfederal ownership.

Source: U.S. Department of the Interior, National Park Service

because the use or location of these properties creates administrative problems.* During fiscal year 1982, the Park Service plans to spend $93.2 million to acquire land within 24 units.[95]

The Park Service may use alternatives to full-fee acquisition. It may buy scenic easements, for example, or exchange lands, or secure cooperative agreements with private landowners. The Santa Monica Mountains and Jean Lafitte units, among others, rely on state and local planning and regulatory controls to supplement acquisition.[96] And at the Lowell National Historic Park, authorized in 1978,

---

*Some properties outside park boundaries create problems within the parks, too, but acquisition of these lands is generally not possible because there has been no congressional authorization. The Park Service can, however, accept donation of such lands.

federal incentives to state and local governments and private enterprise have been used instead of extensive acquisition.[97] Techniques such as these, although still experimental, can have significant advantages: reducing federal acquisition costs, accommodating property owners' desires, keeping property on local tax rolls and continuing its economic use. On the other hand, these techniques may result in higher administrative costs and problems of enforcement and resource protection.[98]

It is also noteworthy that, as national parks expanded during the 1970s, more people visited facilities run by states, private businesses, and other federal agencies than visited the National Park System. For example:

- State parks, although they have less than one-half as many acres as national parks (in the 48 contiguous states), have more than one and a half times as many visitors.[99] There were 3,851 state parks, totaling 9.4 million acres, in 1979; they had 596 million visits.[100] Between 1960 and 1979, state parks increased substantially both in number (up 44.6 percent) and in acreage (up 68.0 percent).[101] In addition to parks, states own and manage recreation areas, historic sites, forests, and fish and wildlife refuges. State lands are especially important in areas such as the Northeast and North Central region, where there are relatively few National Park System units.[102]
- Private facilities, such as theme parks and ski resorts, also serve millions of visitors each year. Disney World had 13.8 million visitors in 1979; Disneyland, 10.8 million; Georgia's Stone Mountain, 5 million.[103]
- Federal lands not part of the National Park System also provide important recreational opportunities. Six federal agencies besides the Park Service administer the majority of federal lands used for recreation: the Bureau of Land Management; the Bureau of Reclamation; the Corps of Engineers; the Fish and Wildlife Service; the Forest Service; and the Tennessee Valley Authority.[104] Recreational use of the national forests alone increased from 173 million in 1970 to 234 million in 1980.[105] The National Wilderness Preservation System, which is administered by four agencies, grew from 10.4 million acres in 1970 to nearly 80 million in 1980 (nearly 57 million in Alaska).[106] Over 750 federally owned reservoirs, containing 69,000 miles of shoreline, provide various types of water recreation.[107]

Park Management. Managing the parks presents the Park Service with surprisingly varied challenges. At some facilities, only traditional park services are offered: guides who interpret natural and historic sites and patrols to prevent vandalism and protect visitors. At major national parks, however, the Park Service also provides many of the facilities and services found in small cities. Buildings, roads, and water supply systems are constructed, maintained, and operated. Snow is removed. Yosemite and Grand Canyon have jails. In some parks, the Park Service oversees privately operated hotels and restaurants. At all units, the Park Service must comply with various federal and state requirements for air and water quality, health and safety, access for the handicapped, energy conservation, and so on.

Nontraditional units create additional demands. The 26,000-acre Gateway unit in New York City, for example, has half as many staff members (and four times as many visitors) as the 2.2-million-acre Yellowstone National Park.[108] Some of the nontraditional units also require nontraditional skills and management techniques. At Cape Cod and Indiana Dunes, for example, the Park Service works with surrounding communities on local land-use controls.

The Park Service staff grew during the 1970s, although it did not keep pace with the increase in the number of visitors to national parks. Staff size peaked in 1978 with almost 9,200 full-time staff, thereafter fluctuating near that level.[109]

Management expenditures nearly doubled (in constant dollars) during the 1970s, to a 1980 total of $399.3 million.[110] Toward the end of the decade, however, the real dollars available for operations and maintenance at some units actually declined. At 11 of the largest parks, for example, operation and maintenance funds declined 26 percent—from $56.3 million to $41.4 million (in constant 1978 dollars)—between 1978 and 1982.[111]

With fewer funds available, some parks have cut back visitor services, resources protection, and maintenance. Parks in the Rocky Mountain region, for example, were operating at reduced levels in the summer of 1981.[112] Visitor centers and campgrounds opened later in the summer and closed earlier in the fall. Some interpretive programs were curtailed. Resource protection projects were delayed, and garbage was collected less frequently. Some parks eliminated scheduled ranger patrols and responded only to emergency calls.

In allocating available management funds and in selecting management techniques, Congress and the Park Service have faced continuing choices as they try to provide facilities and services for today's park visitors, while conserving resources for future generations. Initiatives in both directions were evident in 1981. Responding, in part, to a Reagan Administration initiative, Congress approved $89 million for constructing and rehabilitating park facilities.[113] At the same time, the Park Service began to focus new attention on resource protection. It prepared a prevention/mitigation plan to address major resource problems. (Progress was slow; of four actions to be taken in 1981, only one—a resources management training program for superintendents—was implemented.)[114] The service also called for the preparation of revised plans for managing park resources.

Over the years, the Park Service has tried a number of innovative approaches to achieve its goals in the face of changing demands. It has closed part of Yosemite Valley to automobiles, for example, and instituted a free bus service. At a number of parks, it has established quotas for heavily used backcountry areas and restricted camping and waste disposal near rivers. It has built walkways over fragile sites to provide access as well as protection. It has adapted cultural resources and sites for uses, such as education centers and shops, in ways that will not damage an area's unique qualities.[115]

Some critics fault the Park Service, however, for failing to be sufficiently creative in response to changing needs. Innovative responses to heavy visitor use at Yellowstone's Old Faithful and in the Yosemite Valley, critics suggest, came only after the problems were extensively chronicled by interest groups and the media. The Park Service is slow, critics complain, to address problems that require nontraditional approaches—working with local governments, for example, to address problems created by activities outside park boundaries. As for recent Park Service attention to resource protection, critics see it as responding too much to congressional pressure, not enough as an initiative. Other observers, however, note the diversity of the service's responsibilities, the rapidity with which these responsibilities have grown and changed, and the extent to which political pressures force the service to respond to short-term needs—to repair a hotel roof or increase the frequency of snow removal—rather than to address less-visible problems such as threats to wildlife or water quality.

Shifting Costs. The 1970s brought more diversity in the services provided by concessioners, private companies, and other organizations that operate facilities within National Park Service units. Together, these groups grossed more than $260 million in 1980, up from $130 million in 1974, and they paid the Park Service nearly $5 million in franchise fees, as compared to about $2.3 million in 1974.[116] Park concessioners have recently taken more responsibility for a variety of services, such as conducting tours, providing inside-the-park transportation, and garbage recycling.

Nonprofit and volunteer organizations have also become heavily involved in a variety of activities, notably visitor education. At some historic and cultural sites, these organizations have undertaken resource protection and, in a few areas, acquisition. Other activities of extensive private sector involvement include trail construction and maintenance, skill training and safety, organized outings, and cleaning up park areas.

Visitor fees have risen only minimally in recent years. The Park Service charges entrance fees in 59 areas, user fees for certain facilities or services such as campgrounds, and various special permit fees.[117] It also receives revenues from such sources as fines and penalties, rents, royalties, concessions, and licenses. In fiscal year 1980, during which operation of the park system cost $390.9 million, park system revenues from all these sources totaled $22.2 million.[118]

Entrance fees, which generally range from $1 to $3, totaled $7.2 million.[119] These funds, along with sales of Golden Eagle Passports (a $10 card that waives all entrance fees for one year), user fees, and surplus property sales, go to the Land and Water Conservation Fund. The $16.1 million of revenues from these fees[120] are reduced, however, by the costs of collecting them; these costs, both direct and indirect, totaled $5.3 million in 1980.[121] Revenues raised by the Park Service from the other sources—which totaled $6.1 million in fiscal 1980—go to the U.S. Treasury.[122]

Policy Options

In examining options for future National Park System policy, it is convenient to use the 1970s as a backdrop. Of the four policy options discussed in the following pages, the first would essentially continue the emphases of the 1970s. The other three represent responses to federal budget stringency: reduced acquisition, reduced management expenditures, and cost shifting.

Expand the System. Accommodating visitor demands and continuing land acquisition are one option for national park policy during the 1980s. Although there does not appear to be strong current demand for the addition of many new units to the National Park System, this option would call for continued spending for land acquisition already authorized by Congress. If acquisitions continued at the rate typical in the late 1970s, the costs might approximate $155 million annually.

Management expenses under this option would need to respond to visitors' needs for facilities and services as well as to strains on park resources. New units added to the system would also add to management expenses. Management expenditures—estimated at $512.9 million in 1982[123]—would thus presumably continue to rise.

Proponents of this approach point to the magnificence of park resources and the importance of park experiences not only to Americans but to foreign visitors. Yet, they point out, public recreation needs are far from satisfied, and some important natural, historic, and cultural sites remain unprotected. The National Park Service, proponents argue, is an appropriate vehicle for making federal funds and management skills available to address these needs. Moreover, a static system cannot reflect, let alone satisfy, the demands of a changing society.

Stop Expansion. A second option for the 1980s would be to stop expanding the National Park System, perhaps even to cut it back. New units would not be added. Land acquisition to complete existing units would be minimized. Some existing units might be transferred to states or localities.*

One argument advanced for this option is that it would reduce federal expenditures; that spending cutbacks should be applied to park acquisition as fully as to other worthwhile programs. If acquisition of park land is to be resumed later, however, it is unclear that a moratorium on acquisition would be cost-effective. Land prices in the Santa Monica Mountains, for example, have been rising as rapidly as 40 percent a year.[125] If these increases should continue, postponing acquisition would increase the ultimate cost.

Some proponents of this approach also argue that many recreation and conservation demands are not the responsibility of the Park Service or, sometimes, of any federal agency. Rather, they argue,

---

*Memorandums drafted by officials of the Department of the Interior in 1981 raised the possibility that the department might recommend divestiture of a few units, although Secretary Watt subsequently denied that he had a "hit list" of parks to be severed from the system. There is some precedent for divesting Park Service areas—Shadow Mountain was exchanged with the National Forest Service for land incorporated into Rocky Mountain National Park. Any divestiture of units would, like acquisition, have to be approved by Congress.[124]

more of these demands should be addressed by states, localities, private companies, and conservation organizations.

Reduce Management Expenditures A third option is to reduce management expenditures. This would presumably bring more cutbacks of the kinds that some parks were already resorting to in 1981: opening facilities later in the season and closing them earlier, reducing interpretive services, and so on. Beyond these, difficult priority decisions would have to be made. At what point, for example, does resource impairment become so serious that resource protection must be given precedence over providing enjoyment for visitors? And how, for example, is the choice to be made between plowing snow in the spring, fixing the hotel roof, and providing ramps for access by the handicapped?

Rather than focusing cuts on particular park services, cutbacks could favor particular units or types of units over others. Full visitor services might be provided at fewer parks—perhaps the traditional "crown jewels"—while services at other units might be cut to minimal levels. Some units might be closed to the public altogether.

The principal argument for this approach is, again, budget stringency, the point that park management, like other programs, should bear its share of cuts. Another argument is that smaller budgets could, in some instances, disrupt established management practices and thus encourage needed innovation.

Shift More Costs. A fourth policy option for national parks in the 1980s would seek to avoid the impact of federal expenditure reductions by shifting responsibilities and costs to the private sector. The roles of concessioners and nonprofit organizations, already expanded during the 1970s, could be expanded further. Fees of all kinds—entrance, activity, special permit, franchise—could be increased. Even if resulting revenues did not go directly to the Park Service, they would, in effect, offset federal management costs.

The principal argument for this option is that it would help to provide for needed management services, yet still permit reduction of federal expenditures. Also, some proponents argue, it is appropriate that park users, rather than taxpayers, bear the cost of management.

Opponents suggest that some benefits of this cost shifting may prove illusory. They wonder how many services private organizations can, in fact, take over, and they point to costs and difficulties of collecting user fees. Also, some argue that parks should be accessible to everyone, regardless of ability to pay.

Conclusion

Whichever spending options are chosen, there are other, continuing issues that affect the National Park System today and will affect it in the future.

First, there is a continuing tension between two basic purposes of the National Park System: providing for visitor enjoyment and conserving resources for future generations. Even at generous spending levels, conservation of natural areas and historic buildings and artifacts is too easily overlooked, as spending and management attention are focused on accommodating intense visitor demands.

Second, there is a continuing tension between those who view the park experience simply as recreation, like any other vacation, and the view that it is—or should be—more educational, aesthetic, even spiritual. No amount of wise management will enable the 20,000 people who crowd into the Yosemite Valley on a busy summer day to repeat the wonder of 19th-century visitors who wandered in on horseback. There is a continuing question, however, which arises in contexts as diverse as the appropriateness of power boats in the Grand Canyon and cocktail lounges in Yellowstone, about what efforts the United States should make to retain traces of that experience.

Both of these tensions, as well as the four options identified above, need to be considered in searching for ways to address "strains on the parks." For these strains amount to the difficulties of adapting a magnificent resource to a changing environment in which neither public enjoyment nor resource conservation can be fully accomplished in traditional ways.

FURTHER READING

Land's diversity is reflected in the literature. While numerous references, books, reports, and periodicals exist, they typically are limited to certain kinds of land or particular land issues. Very few sources, if any, look at all aspects of land.

The Market for Rural Land, by Robert G. Healy and James L. Short, is a recent Conservation Foundation study that looks at the changing composition of rural lands, how the market for them works, who participates in it, what market trends imply for present and future use of this land, and what public policies are needed for the changes taking place.

Sensitive lands with unique capabilities— barrier islands, wetlands, floodplains—are the subject of numerous studies and books. *Alternative Policies for Protecting Barrier Islands Along the Atlantic and Gulf Coasts of the U.S. and Draft Environmental Statement*, prepared by five federal agencies for the Department of the Interior in 1979, and available at that department, is a thorough discussion of the ecological and socio-economic conditions of barrier islands as well as governmental policies that affect them. *Our Nation's Wetlands*, a 1978 federal government interagency task report coordinated by the Council on Environmental Quality, and available at the U.S. Government Printing Office, is a detailed, yet readable description of wetlands, the problems they face, and the federal policies designed to protect them. Jon A. Kusler, *Regulating Sensitive Lands* (Cambridge, Mass.: Ballinger, 1981), presents a number of principles for state and local governments to follow in managing a variety of lands, including parks, wetlands, floodplains, and erosion areas. Coastal lands and guidelines for their management are the topics of John Clark, *Coastal Ecosystem Management* (New York, N.Y.: John Wiley & Sons, 1977), and a Council on Environmental Quality report, *Coastal Environmental Management: Guidelines for Conservation of Resources and Protection against Storm Hazards* (Washington, D.C.: U.S. Government Printing Office, 1980).

Two recent, thought-provoking books on the National Park System are Alfred Runte, *National Parks: The American Experience* (Lincoln, Neb.: University of Nebraska Press, 1979), and Joseph Sax, *Mountains Without Handrails: Reflections on the National Parks* (Ann Arbor, Mich.: University of Michigan, 1980). Runte takes a historical look at the park system, why it was created and how it has evolved in the midst of vast changes and political pressures, while *Mountains Without Handrails* is a philosophical look at what types of recreation the parks should be providing. Two other sources, one governmental and one private, describe the resource problems parks and other publicly owned recreation lands face, largely as a result of developments on adjacent lands: National Park Service, *The State of the Parks - 1980* (Washington, D.C.: U.S. Department of the Interior, 1980), and William E. Shands, *Federal Resource Lands and Their Neighbors* (Washington, D.C.: The Conservation Foundation, 1979).

Because the federal role in land preservation and recreation is changing and may, in fact, be reduced over the next few years, innovative land acquisition techniques as well as past efforts and present capabilities of states and regions to provide recreation and preserve land need to be examined. Jon A. Kusler's report *Public/ Private Parks and Management of Private Lands for Park Protection* (Madison, Wis.: Institute for Environmental Studies, 1974) contains a design for creating "public/private parks," combining acquisition of lands needed for direct public use with state and local planning and land-use regulation for land that would remain in private ownership. The concept of multiple approaches to achieve resource protection objectives is further developed in a 1975 Congressional Research Service study, a Committee Print prepared for the Senate Committee on Interior and Insular Affairs, Subcommittee on Parks and Recreation, *Green-Line Parks: An Approach to Preserving Recreational Landscape in Urban Areas. Protecting Open Space: Land Use Control in the Adirondack Park* by Richard A. Liroff and G. Gordon Davis (Cambridge, Mass.: Ballinger, 1981) looks at land-use controls in the Adirondack Park and analyzes and evaluates New York's Adirondack Park Agency. Several of the lessons discussed are applicable to other state park lands.

In 1973, *The Use of Land, A Report of the Task Force on Land Use and Urban Growth* (New York, N.Y.: Thomas Crowell Co.), edited by William K. Reilly, identified a "new mood" toward land use and stimulated public interest in land-use issues. A range of recent publications examines government and judicial influences on land. *Land Use and the States*, by Robert G. Healy and John Rosenberg, 2d ed. (Washington, D.C.: The Johns Hopkins University Press, 1979) analyzes state involvement in land-use control, presents case studies of state activity, and recommends a series of alternative approaches for future state involvement. A recent revision of a landmark book, Samuel T. Dana and Sally K. Fairfax, *Forest and Range Policy: Its Development in the U.S.*, 2d ed. (New York, N.Y.: McGraw Hill, 1980) updates the analysis of federal policies affecting these types of land. Articles on current land-use planning and development regulation may be found in the *Journal of the American Planning Association*, the American Planning Association's *Planning* magazine, and *Urban Land* (Washington, D.C.: Urban Land Institute). *Land Use Planning Report* (Silver Spring, Md: Business Publishers, Inc.) is a weekly newsletter on land issues and government policies, and the *American Land Forum* (Bethesda, Md.: American Land Forum) is a quarterly containing thoughtful essays and commentary.

Legal land-use issues and the role of the courts are the subject of some noteworthy books, treatises, and periodicals. David Godschalk et.al., *Constitutional Issues of Growth Management*, 2d ed. (Chicago, Ill.: APA Planners Press, 1979) looks at local and regional efforts to guide land development and analyzes the important legal issues they face. Fred Bosselman, David Callies, and John Banta, *The Taking Issue* (Washington, D.C.: Government Printing Office, 1973), while nearly a decade old, remains an authoritative source on the limits of regulations as they affect property rights. The American Planning Association publishes monthly its *Land Use Law and Zoning Digest*, which covers the most recent cases and analyses on land-use law. For a more detailed look at land use and the courts, Robert C. Ellickson and A. Dan Tarlock's *Land-Use Controls* (Boston, Mass.: Little, Brown and Co., 1981), Donald G. Hagman's *Public Planning and Control of Urban and Land Development*, 2d ed. (St. Paul, Minn.: West Publishing Co., 1980), and Daniel R. Mandelker's *Land Use Law* (Charlottesville, Va.: Michie Co., forthcoming) contain valuable analyses and sources.

Aldo Leopold's *A Sand County Almanac* (New York, N.Y.: Oxford University Press, 1966) is a classic collection of essays on land conservation and what Leopold termed the "land ethic." On a more popular level, various writings of John McPhee and Edward Abbey, among others, have described the unique qualities of certain lands and the relationships people develop with them. Two notable titles include McPhee's *Coming into the Country* (New York, N.Y.: Farrar, Straus, and Giroux, 1978) on Alaska, and Abbey's *Desert Solitaire* (New York, N.Y.: Simon & Schuster, 1970) on the arid areas of the southwestern United States.

TEXT REFERENCES

1. U.S. Department of Agriculture, *Soil and Water Resources Conservation Act, 1980 Appraisal, Part I, Soil, Water, and Related Resources in the United States: Status, Condition, and Trends* (Washington, D.C.: U.S. Department of Agriculture, 1981), p. 72.

2. Information provided by Geography Division, U.S. Department of Commerce, Bureau of the Census, 1980 unpublished data; and U.S. Department of Agriculture, Soil Conservation Service, *Available Federal Data on Agricultural Land Use*, Technical Paper II, prepared by the Research Staff of the National Agricultural Lands Study (Washington, D.C.: U.S. Department of Agriculture, 1981), Table 1, p. 8.

3. U.S. Department of Agriculture, *Soil and Water Resources Conservation Act, 1980 Appraisal, Part I, Soil, Water, and Related Resources in the United States: Status, Condition, and Trends*, p. 50.

4. *Ibid.*, p. 49.

5. Philip M. Raup, "Competition for Land and the Future of American Agriculture," in *The Future of American Agriculture as a Strategic Resource*, Sandra S. Batie and Robert G. Healy, eds., (Washington, D.C.: The Conservation Foundation, 1980), p. 49.

6. Council on Environmental Quality, *Environmental Statistics 1978* (Springfield, Va.: National Technical Information Service, 1979), p. 33.

7. Philip M. Raup, "Competition for Land and the Future of American Agriculture," pp. 52-53.

8. James A. Lewis, "Landownership in the United States, 1978," U.S. Department of Agriculture, Economics, Statistics, and Cooperatives Service, Agriculture Information Bulletin, No. 435 (Washington, D.C.: U.S. Department of Agriculture, 1980), p. 3.

9. Thomas H. Frey, "Major Uses of Land in The United States: 1978" (Washington, D.C.: U.S. Department of Agriculture, Economic Research Service, 1981), pp. 32-33.

10. U.S. Department of Interior, Bureau of Land Management, *Public Land Statistics: 1980* (Washington, D.C.: U.S. Government Printing Office, 1980), Table 9, pp. 13-31.

11. *Ibid.*, p. 9.

12. James A. Lewis, "Landownership in the United States, 1978," p. 4.

13. *Ibid.*, p. 5.

14. U.S. Department of Agriculture, *Soil and Water Resources Conservation Act, 1980 Appraisal Part I, Soil, Water, and Related Resources in the United States: Status, Condition, and Trends*, p. 21.

15. Robert G. Healy and James L. Short, *The Market for Rural Land: Trends, Issues, Policies* (Washington, D.C.: The Conservation Foundation, 1981), p. 15.

16. *Ibid.*, p. 61.

17. *Ibid.*, p. 19.

18. *Ibid.*, pp. 17-21.

19. Charles E. Little and W. Wendell Fletcher, "Buckshot Urbanization: The Land Impacts of Rural Population Growth," *American Land Forum* 2(4):11 (1981); Robert G. Healy and James L. Short, *The Market for Rural Land*, p. 4.

20. Philip M. Raup, "Competition for Land and the Future of American Agriculture," p.55.

21. U.S. Department of Commerce, Bureau of the Census, *Statistical Abstract of the United States: 1980*, 101st ed., (Washington, D.C.: U.S. Government Printing Office, 1980), p. 412.

22. "America's Restructured Economy", *Business Week*, June 1, 1981, p. 64.

23. "Rocky Mountain High," *Time*, December 15, 1980, p. 32.

24. U.S. Department of Energy, *Securing America's Energy Future, The National Energy Policy Plan: A Report to the Congress Required by Title VIII of the Department of Energy Organization Act* (Washington, D.C.: U.S. Department of Energy, 1981), p.1.

25. For example, the Forest and Rangeland Renewable Resources Planning Act, 16 U.S.C. sec. 1601-13 (1975), the National Forest Management Act of 1976, codified in 16 U.S.C., and the Federal Land Policy and Management Act of 1976, codified in various sections of Titles 7, 16, 30, 40, and 43 U.S.C. set in place management laws, goals, and processes for vast amounts of federal acreage.

26. For example, changes made in the federal tax code by the Economic Tax Recovery Act of 1981, were made to create a more profitable business climate and stimulate business and industrial investments. The act provides direct tax cuts to businesses that should equal about $164 billion between 1982 and 1986. See Robert G. Healy, *America's Industrial Future: An Environmental Perspective* (Washington, D.C.: The Conservation Foundation, forthcoming, 1982). Larger and more accelerated depreciation allowances on commercial buildings may encourage new facility construction, expansion of existing facilities, and investment in capital-intensive equipment. By speeding up the rate of change, the act, for example, encourages those industries contemplating moves, say, to rural areas or sunbelt locations, to go ahead and do so quickly. One recent analysis of the Internal Revenue Code added up all the federal "tax expenditures" (revenues foregone) that directly or indirectly affected land use and concluded that the annual total was somewhere near $50 billion. See "Land Use and the Tax Code," *American Land Forum* 2(3):18 (1981).

27. Council on Environmental Quality, *Environmental Quality—1980* (Washington, D.C.: U.S. Government Printing Office, 1980), p. 345. See also, U.S. Department of the Interior, Heritage Conservation and Recreation Service, *Alternative Policies for Protecting Barrier Islands Along the Atlantic and Gulf Coasts of the United States, Draft Enivronmental Statement* (Washington, D.C.: U.S. Department of the Interior, 1979), pp. 57-60. Barrier islands also occur near the Pacific Coast and parts of the Great Lakes, but attention has focused on the Atlantic and Gulf Coast islands, largely because of their abundance and use.

28. Harry F. Lins, Jr., *Patterns and Trends of Land Use and Land Cover on Atlantic and Gulf Coast Barrier Islands*, U.S. Geological Survey Professional Paper 1156 (Washington, D.C.: U.S. Government Printing Office, 1980), p. 11.

29. Council on Environmental Quality, *Environmental Quality - 1980*, p. 345.

30. Council on Environmental Quality, "Barrier Island Development Near Four National Seashores," prepared by Sheaffer & Roland, Inc. (Washington, D.C.: Council on Environmental Quality, 1981), p. 1. See also, H. Crane Miller, "The Barrier Islands: A Gamble with Time and Nature," *Environment* 23(9):7 (1981).

31. U.S. Department of the Interior, Heritage Conservation and Recreation Service, *Alternative Policies for Protecting Barrier Islands Along the Atlantic and Gulf Coasts of the United States*, p. 117.

32. *Ibid.*

33. *Ibid.*, p. 118.

34. *Ibid.*, p. 117. See also, Harry F. Lins, Jr., *Patterns and Trends of Land Use and Land Cover on Atlantic and Gulf Coast Barrier Islands*, Table 4, p. 5.

35. U.S. Department of the Interior, Heritage Conservation and Recreation Service, *Alternative Policies for Protecting Barrier Islands Along the Atlantic and Gulf Coasts of the United States*, pp. ii, 64.

36. *Ibid.*, Table 2, p. 64.

37. *Ibid.*, Table 15, p. 117. See also Lins, *Patterns and Trends of Land Use and Land Cover on Atlantic and Gulf Coast Barrier Islands*, Table 3, p.4.

38. Council on Environmental Quality, "Barrier Island Development Near Four National Seashores," p. 1.

39. U.S. Department of the Interior, Heritage Conservation And Recreation Service, *Alternative Policies for Protecting Barrier Islands Along the Atlantic and Gulf Coasts of the United States*, p. ii.

40. *Ibid.*, Table 6, pp. 80-81.

41. *Ibid.*, p. 123. See also William J. Siffin, "Bureaucracy, Entrepreneurship, and Natural Resources: Witless Policy and the Barrier Islands," *Cato Journal* 1(1):294 (1981)

42. U.S., Congress, House, Committee on Interior and Insular Affairs, Subcommittee on Public Lands and National Parks, *Hearings to Establish a Barrier Islands Protection System*, H.R. 5981, 96th Cong., 2d sess., March 1980, pp. 107-110. See also William H. MacLeish, "Our Barrier Islands Are the Key Issue in 1980, the 'Year of the Coast,'" *Smithsonian Magazine*, September 1980, p. 56.

43. Council on Environmental Quality, *Barrier Island Development Near Four National Seashores*, p.1.

44. U.S. Department of the Interior, Heritage Conservation and Recreation Service, *Alternative Policies for Protecting Barrier Islands Along the Atlantic and Gulf Coasts of the United States*, p. 92.

45. Jennie C. Myers, *America's Coasts in the 80s: Policies & Issues* (Washington, D.C.: Coast Alliance, 1981), p. 129; William H. MacLeish, "Our Barrier Islands are the Key Issue in 1980, the 'Year of the Coast,'" p. 55.

46. U.S., Congress, House, Committee on Interior and Insular Affairs, Subcommittee on Public Lands and National Parks, *Hearings to Establish a Barrier Islands Protection System*, p. 107.

47. U.S. Department of the Interior, Heritage Conservation and Recreation Service, *Alternative Policies for Protecting Barrier Islands Along the Atlantic and Gulf Coasts of the United States, Draft Environmental Statement*, p. xv.

48. U.S., Congress, House, Subcommittee on Public Lands and National Parks, *Hearings to Establish a Barrier Islands Protection System*, p. 478-482.

49. *Ibid.*, pp. 113-114.

50. U.S. Department of the Interior, Heritage Conservation and Recreation Service, *Alternative Policies for Protecting Barrier Islands Along the Atlantic and Gulf Coasts of the United States, Draft Environmental Statement*, p. A-55.

51. Rivers and Harbors Appropriation Act of 1899, as amended 33 U.S.C., sec. 404 (1980), Clean Water Act of 1977, 33 U.S.C., sec. 1344 (1980); see also, U.S. Department of the Interior, Heritage Conservation and Recreation Service, *Alternative Policies for Protecting Barrier Islands Along the Atlantic and Gulf Coasts of the United States, Draft Environmental Statement*, p. A-36.

52. William J. Siffin, "Bureaucracy, Entrepreneurship, and Natural Resources: Witless Policy and the Barrier Islands", p. 299.

53. U.S. Department of the Interior, Heritage Conservation and Recreation Service, *Alternative Policies for Protecting Barrier Islands Along the Atlantic and Gulf Coasts of the United States, Draft Environmental Statement*, pp. A-63,64.

54. William J. Siffin, "Bureaucracy, Entrepreneurship, and Natural Resources: Witless Policy and the Barrier Islands", p. 299.

55. U.S. Department of the Interior, Heritage Conservation and Recreation Service, *Alternative Policies for Protecting Barrier Islands Along the Atlantic and Gulf Coasts of the United States, Draft Environmental Statement*, pp. A-57,58; see also H. Crane Miller, "The Barrier Islands: A Gamble with Time and Nature", p. 9.

56. Robert R. Kuehn, "The Shifting Sands of Federal Barrier Islands Policy," 5 *Harv. Env't. L. Rev.* 232 (1981). See also H. Crane Miller, "The Barrier Islands: A Gamble with Time and Nature", p. 9.

57. Robert R. Kuehn, "The Shifting Sands of Federal Barrier Islands Policy," p. 239.

58. Council on Environmental Quality, "Barrier Island Development Near Four National Seashores," p. 6.

59. *Ibid.*, p. 59.

60. *Ibid.*, p. 6.

61. H. Crane Miller, "The Barrier Islands: A Gamble with Time and Nature," p. 41.

62. William H. MacLeish, "Our Barrier Islands Are the Key Issue in 1980, the 'Year of the Coast'," p. 53.

63. U.S. Department of the Interior, Heritage Conservation and Recreation Service, *Alternative Policies for Protecting Barrier Islands Along the Atlantic and Gulf Coasts of the United States, Draft Environmental Statement*, Table 2, p. 64.

64. *Ibid.*, p. 105.

65. *Ibid.*, pp. vii, 107-109.

66. *Ibid.*, p. 4.

67. *Ibid.*, p. 105.

68. *Ibid.*, p. vii, 5.

69. Jennie C. Myers, *America's Coasts in the 80s: Policies & Issues*, p. 39.

70. Department of the Interior, Coastal Barrier Task Force, Draft, *Undeveloped Coastal Barriers: Definitions and Delineation Criteria* (Washington, D.C.: U.S. Department of the Interior, 1982).

71. Executive Order No. 11988, 3 C.F.R., sec. 117-120 (1978).

72. Executive Order No. 11990, 3 C.F.R., sec. 121-123 (1978).

73. By June 1980 only one-half of the 32 federal agencies affected by the Executive Orders had established final procedures to implement them. See Robert R. Kuehn, "The Shifting Sands of Federal Barrier Islands Policy," p. 223, footnote 44.

74. Office of Coastal Zone Management, "CZM Information Exchange" (Washington, D.C.: Office of Coastal Zone Management, December 1981), p. 11.

75. Council on Environmental Quality, *Environmental Quality - 1979* (Washington, D.C.: U.S. Government Printing Office, 1979), pp. 501-503.

76. *Ibid.*, p. 503.

77. Outdoor Recreation and Conservation Act, *Fla. Stats. Ann.*, sec. 375.031 (1980); Beach and Shore Preservation Act, *Fla. Stats. Ann.*, sec. 161.011 *et. seq.* (1981).

78. Commonwealth of Massachusetts, Executive Order No. 181, (August 13, 1980).

79. Four bills to lessen development of barrier islands are pending before the 97th Congress. S. 1018 (introduced by Senator John Chafee, R-R.I.) and H.R. 3252 (Rep. Thomas Evans, R-Del.) would create a Coastal Barrier Resources System, consisting of undeveloped barriers, and prohibit new federal expenditures and financial assistance, with some specificied exceptions, to areas within the system. S.96 (Senator Dale Bumpers, D-Ark.) would restrict federal agencies from issuing licenses or permits to most construction projects on designated Barrier Islands as well as prohibit federal expenditures or financial assistance. Finally, H.R. 857 (Rep. Phillip Burton, D-Cal.) goes one step beyond denying federal funds or licenses; it authorizes the creation of barrier islands national parks through land donations, purchases, or exchanges by the Department of the Interior. For a complete description of these bills, see Robert R. Kuehn, "The Shifting Sands of Federal Barrier Islands Policy," pp. 242 -256.

80. Title 111, Part 4 of the Omnibus Budget Reconciliation Act of 1981, Public Law 97-35, sec. 1321, (Aug. 13, 1981), 95 Stat. 419, amending 42 U.S.C., sec. 4028, 4081 and 26 U.S.C., sec. 170.

81. National Flood Insurance Act, 42 U.S.C., sec. 5154 (1980).

82. H. Crane Miller, "The Barrier Islands: A Gamble with Time and Nature", pp. 37-38.

83. National Park Service Act of 1916, 16 U.S.C., sec. 1 (1980).

84. U.S. Department of the Interior, National Park Service, *Index, National Park System and Related Areas, 1979* (Washington, D.C.: Government Printing Ofice, 1979); and U.S. Department of the Interior, National Park Service, "Areas Added to the National Park System Since Publication of 'Index of the National Park System' on June 30, 1979." Other areas have been added to Park Service management responsibilities since 1970, but are not considered part of the National Park System. These include wild and scenic rivers such as the Flathead and New Rivers, national trails like the Continental Divide National Scenic Trail, and various "affiliated areas" such as the Pinelands National Reserve and the Jamestown National Historic Site, which are neither federally owned nor directly administered by the Park Service but which receive Park Service assistance.

85. Information provided by Land Resources Division, National Park Service, May 12, 1982.

86. National Parks and Recreation Act of 1978, Public Law 95-625, sec. 507 (1978), 16 U.S.C., sec. 460kk, *et seq.* (1980).

87. U.S. Department of the Interior, National Park Service, *Public Use of the National Parks: A Statistical Report, 1960-1970*, p. 5; U.S. Department of the Interior, National Park Service, *National Park Statistical Abstract, 1980* (Washington, D.C.: U.S. Department of the Interior, 1980), p. 13.

88. U.S. Comptroller General, *Facilities in Many National Parks and Forests Do Not Meet Health and Safety Standards* (Washington, D.C.: General Accounting Office, 1980), pp. 6, 102-103.

89. See U.S. Department of the Interior, National Park Service, *State of the Parks: 1980, A Report to the Congress* (Washington, D.C.: U.S. Department of the Interior, 1980).

90. For more information on outdoor recreation demands, see U.S. Department of Agriculture, Forest Service, *An Assessment of the Forest and Range Land Situation in the United States* (Washington, D.C.: U.S. Department of Agriculture, January 1980), pp. 97-105.

91. U.S. Department of the Interior, Heritage Conservation and Recreation Service, *The Third Nationwide Outdoor Recreation Plan, The Assessment* (Washington, D.C.: U.S. Government Printing Office, 1979), pp. 31-31.

92. Information provided by Land Resources Division, National Park Service, May 12, 1982.

93. *Ibid.*

94. *Ibid.*

95. *Ibid.*

96. National Parks and Recreation Act of 1978, 16 U.S.C., sec. 460 kk (1980), and 16 U.S.C., sec. 230 (1980).

97. 16 U.S.C. Sections 410cc *et. seq.* (1981). See also, U.S. Department of the Interior, National Park Service, *Index, National Park System and Related Areas 1979*, p. 36.

98. U.S., Senate, Committee on Energy and Natural Resources, *Workshop on Public Land Acquisition and Alternatives*, 97th Cong., 1st sess., October 1981.

99. U.S. Department of Commerce, Bureau of the Census, *Statistical Abstract of the United States, 1980*, p. 244.

100. *Ibid.*

101. *Ibid.*

102. U.S. Department of Agriculture, Forest Service, *An Assessment of the Forest and Range Land Situation in the United States*, p. 114.

103. U.S. Travel Data Center, *National Travel Barometer* (Washington, D.C.: U.S. Travel Data Center, 1980), p. 26. Increasing amounts of private lands are being used to satisfy intense demands for recreation. Yet because of the diversity of areas and lack of standardized data, it is more difficult to quantify acreage and usage of private recreation land than of publicly owned land. A report by the Heritage Conservation and Recreation Service of the Department of the Interior, *The Third Nationwide Outdoor Recreation Plan* (Washington, D.C.: Government Printing Office, 1979), p. 77, concluded that "a majority of the lands available for recreation, recreation development, and special services for recreation are in the hands of the private sector." These lands include second home developments, theme parks, ski areas, and so on. The report also found that: "Approximately 32 percent of the noncorporate land acreage in the United States (about 217 million acres) and 59 percent of noncorporate forest and range acreage (about 40 million acres) are now designated by the owners as open to the public for recreation. An additional 31 percent of noncorporate and 13 percent of corporate land are currently available to employees or special groups for recreation purposes. . . . The location of usable private lands, as opposed to public lands, spreads recreational opportunity more evenly throughout the United States."

104. U.S. Department of Agriculture, Forest Service, *An Assessment of the Forest and Range Land Situation in the United States*, p. 110.

105. U.S. Department of Agriculture, Forest Service, Recreation Information Management System, unpublished data.

106. *Ibid.*; see also, Randel F. Washburne and David N. Cole, "Problems and Practices in Wilderness Management: Results of a Survey of Managers" (Missoula, Mt.: U.S. Forest Service, Intermountain Forestry and Range Experiment Station, unpublished manuscript, 1981).

107. U.S. Department of Agriculture, Forest Service, *An Assessment of the Forest and Range Land Situation in the United States*, p. 112.

108. Information provided by National Park Service staffs at both units, February 1982. Yellowstone National Park has a total of 599 full, part-time, and seasonal staff, while Gateway National Recreation Area has 311.

109. Daniel B. Tunstall and William E. Shands, "National Park Trends, 1960-1980" (prepared for a meeting of The Conservation Foundation Board of Trustees, November 13, 1981).

110. Information provided by Budget Office, National Park Service, May 1982.

111. U.S., Congress, House, Committee on Appropriations, Subcommittee on the Department of the Interior and Related Agencies, *Department of the Interior and Related Agencies Appropriations for 1982*, Hearings, Part 12, 97th Cong., 1st sess., 1981, p. 784.

112. *Ibid.*, p. 775.

113. P.L. 97-100, 95 Stat. 1396 (1981).

114. U.S. Department of the Interior, National Park Service, *State of the Parks: A Report to the Congress on a Servicewide Strategy for Prevention and Mitigation of Natural and Cultural Resources Management Problems* (Washington, D.C.: U.S. Department of the Interior, 1980); testimony of William E. Shands, The Conservation Foundation, before the U.S. Congress, House Committee on Interior and Insular Affairs, Subcommittee on Public Lands and National Parks, *Threats to the Natural and Cultural Resources of the National Park System*, Hearings, 97th Cong. 2d sess., February 4, 1982.

115. 1980 amendments to the National Historic Preservation Act, codified at 16 U.S.C., sec. 470H-3 (1981), authorize the Park Service to lease historical properties and keep the revenues generated for administration.

116. 1980 figures are based on information provided by Concessions branch, National Park Service, February 1982. 1974 figures are from U.S., Congress, House, H.R. Rep. No. 869, 94th Cong., 2d sess. 1976, pp. 4, 85.

117. U.S. Department of the Interior, Heritage Conservation and Recreation Service, *Federal Recreation Fee Report 1980, Including Federal, State and Private Sector Recreation Visitation and Fee Data* (Washington, D.C.: U.S. Department of the Interior, 1980), pp. 15, 17.

118. U.S., Congress, House, Committee on Appropriations, Subcommittee on the Department of the Interior and Related Agencies, *Department of the Interior and Related Agencies Appropriations for 1982, Part 1*, Hearings, 97th Cong., 1st sess., 1982, pp. 1169-1173.

119. U.S. Department of the Interior, Heritage Conservation and Recreation Service, *Federal Recreation Fee Report 1980, Including Federal, State and Private Sector Recreation Visitation and Fee Data*, p. 18. Entrance fees currently being raised.

120. U.S., Congress, House, Committee on Appropriations, Subcommittee on Department of the Interior and Related Agencies, *Department of the Interior and Related Agencies Appropriations for 1982, Part 1*, p. 1169.

121. U.S. Department of the Interior, Heritage Conservation and Recreation Service, *Federal Recreation Fee Report 1980, Including Federal, State and Private Sector Recreation Visitation and Fee Data*, p.19.

122. U.S., Congress, House, Committee on Appropriations, Hearings before Subcommittee on the Department of the Interior and Related Agencies, *Department of the Interior and Related Agencies Appropriations for 1982, Part 1*, p. 1169.

123. Executive Office of the President, Office of Management and Budget, *Budget of the United States Government, Fiscal Year 1983* (Washington, D.C.: U.S. Government Printing Office, 1982).

124. Information provided by Office of Park Planning, National Park Service, February 1982.

125. Information provided by Santa Monica Mountains National Recreation Area, September 1981.

FIGURE REFERENCES

Figure 7.1

"Metropolitan and nonmetropolitan areas": U.S. Department of Commerce, *Statistical Abstract of the United States: 1981*, 102d ed. (Washington, D.C.: U.S. Government Printing Office, 1982), Appendix II, Table C, p. 919.

"Metropolitan urban area": includes "urbanized area" as determined by the U.S. Department of Commerce, Bureau of the Census, Geography Division, unpublished data; and "other urban land" in metropolitan areas estimated by The Conservation Foundation.

Exurban: "Other metropolitan land": Computed by the Conservation Foundation.

Exurban: "Nonmetropolitan commuting ring": Estimate based on more than 10 percent of employees commuting to SMSAs. Robert G. Healy, *The Market for Rural Land: Trends, Issues, Policies* (Washington, D.C.: The Conservation Foundation, 1981), Figure 8, p. 23, adjusted to include all 50 states.

"Nonmetropolitan urban area": U.S. Department of Commerce, Bureau of the Census, Geography Division, unpublished data, and the Conservation Foundation estimate of amount of "other urban land" in and out of SMSAs.

"Countryside": Estimated by The Conservation Foundation

"Wilderness": Council on Environmental Quality, *Environmental Statistics* (Springfield, Va.: National Technical Information Service, 1979), Table 2-7, p. 44; and Paul J. Culhane, *Public Land Politics* (Baltimore, Md.: Johns Hopkins University Press, 1981), p. 109.

Figure 7.2

(1900-1974) — Council on Environmental Quality, *Environmental Statistics* (Springfield, Va.: National Technical Information Service, 1979), Table 1-12, p. 29.; (1978) — Thomas H. Frey, "Major Uses of Land in the United States: 1978" (Washington, D.C.: U.S. Department of Agriculture, Economic Research Service, 1981), Table 2, p. 3. "Specialized uses" includes urban land for all years.

Figure 7.3

U.S. Department of Agriculture, *1980 Appraisal, Part 1, Soil, Water and Related Resources in the United States: Status, Condition, and Trends* (Washington, D.C.: U.S. Department of Agriculture, 1981), p. 50. For revised data on "pasture," "range," and "forest," see U.S. Department of Agriculture, *National Agricultural Lands Study*, "Available Federal Data on Agricultural Land Use", Technical Paper II (Washington, D.C.: U.S. Department of Agriculture), p. 8.

Figure 7.4.

State and National Parks: U.S. Department of the Interior National Park Service, *Index of the National Park System and Affiliated Areas as of January 1, 1975* (Washington, D.C.: U.S. Department of the Interior, 1975); "Updated Addenda of October 22, 1976" for the *Index, 1975*, National Recreation and Park Association; *State Park Statistics, 1970* (Washington, D.C.: National Recreation and Park Association, 1971), p. 9; U.S. Department of Commerce, Bureau of the Census, *Statistical Abstract of the United States: 1976* (Washington, D.C.: U.S. Government Printing Office, 1977), p. 216; National Recreation and Park Association, *State Park Statistics, 1975* (Washington, D.C.: National Recreation and Park Association, 1976), p. 28; Paul J. Culhane, *Public Land Politics* (Baltimore, Md.: Johns Hopkins University Press, 1981), p. 109.

State and National Wildlife Refuge System: U.S. Department of the Interior, Division of Realty, *Annual Report of Lands Under Control of the U.S. Fish and Wildlife Service as of Sept. 30, 1980 and Addendum—Dec. 2, 1980* (Washington, D.C.: U.S. Department of the Interior, 1981) pp. 3, 4, 17 and previous annual issues; Thomas H. Frey, "Major Uses of Land in the United States: 1978" (Washington, D.C.: U.S. Department of Agriculture, Economic Research Service, 1982), Table II, p. 30; Council on Environmental Quality, *Environmental Statistics* (Springfield, Va.: National Technical Information Service, 1979), Table 2-12, p. 50; Paul J. Culhane, *Public Land Politics* (Baltimore, Md.: Johns Hopkins University Press, 1981), p. 109.

National Wilderness Preservation System: (1964-1976) — Council on Environmental Quality, *Environmental Statistics* (Springfield, Va.: National Technical Information Service, 1979); Table 2-7, p. 44; (1977-1980) — U.S. Department of Agriculture, Forest Service, Recreation Management Staff, "Wilderness Fact Sheet," February 15, 1979 and December 31, 1980; Unpublished data from Forest Service, National Park Service, U.S. Fish and Wildlife Service, and Bureau of Land Management. See also, Paul J. Culhane, *Public Land Politics* (Baltimore, Md.: Johns Hopkins University Press, 1981) p. 109.

Figure 7.5

Thomas H. Frey, "Major Uses of Land in the United States: 1978" (Washington, D.C.: U.S. Department of Agriculture, Economic Research Service, 1982), Table 3, p. 9.

Figure 7.6

U.S. Department of the Interior, Geological Survey Special Maps Division (Washington, D.C.: U.S. Geological Survey, 1977). Shaded areas may include small amounts of land in private ownership.

Figure 7.7

Council on Environmental Quality, *Environmental Trends* (Washington, D.C.: U.S. Government Printing Office, 1981), p. 29 Designation of areas since 1979 from the National Park Service.

Figure 7.8

U.S. Department of the Interior, National Park Service, *National Park Statistical Abstract: 1980* (Washington, D.C.: U.S. Department of the Interior, 1980), Table 4.

Figure 7.9

U.S. Department of the Interior, National Park Service, *Index, National Park System and Related Areas, 1979* (Washington, D.C.: U.S. Government Printing Office, 1979), and U.S. Department of the Interior, National Park Service, "Areas Added to the National Park System Since Publication of 'Index of the National Park System' on June 30, 1979." Other National Park System units, such as the Jean Lafitte National Historical Park and Preserve in Louisiana, were redesignated and substantially enlarged during this period.

GOVERNMENT INFLUENCES, THE COURTS, AND LAND USE

1. Robert G. Healy and John S. Rosenberg, *Land Use and the States*, 2d ed. (Baltimore, Md: The Johns Hopkins University Press, 1979), p. 7.
2. *Ibid.*
3. Robert G. Healy and James L. Short, *The Market for Rural Land: Trends, Issues, Policies* (Washington, D.C.: The Conservation Foundation, 1981), pp. 82-83.
4. Daniel R. Mandelker and Edith Netter, "A New Role for the Comprehensive Plan," *Land Use Law & Zoning Digest*, 33(9):6-8, (September 1981), pp. 6-8.
5. Council on Environmental Quality, *Environmental Quality—1979* (Washington, D.C.: U.S. Government Printing Office, 1979), Table 10-3, pp. 595-602.
6. *Ibid.*, pp. 485-508.

7. *Penn Central Transportation Co. v. New York City*, 438 U.S. 104, 123-124 (1978).

8. *Agins v. City of Tiburon*, 100 S. Ct. 2138 (1980).

9. *Penn Central Transportation Co. v. New York City*, 438 U.S. 104, *op. cit.*

10. *Hodel v. Indiana*, 101 S. Ct. 2376 (1981); see also *Hodel v. Virginia Surface Mining and Reclamation Association, Inc.*, 101 S. Ct. 2352 (1981).

11. *Graham v. Estuary Properties, Inc.*, 399 So. 2d 1374 (Fla. 1981); *Deltona Corp. v. U.S.*, 657 F. 2d 1184 (Ct. Cl., 1981).

12. See, *Pamel Corp. v. Puerto Rico Highway Authority*, 621 F. 2d 33 (1st Cir. 1980); *Fred F. French Investing Co. v. City of New York*, 350 N.E. 2d 381, *appeal dismissed* 429 U.S. 990 (1976); *Gary D. Reihart, Inc. v. Township of Carroll*, 409 A. 2d 1167 (Pa. 1979); *Holaway v. City of Pipestone*, 269 N.W. 2d 28 (Minn. 1978); *Davis v. Pima County*, 590 P. 2d 459 (Ariz. App. 1978), *cert. denied*, 442 U.S. 942 (1979); *Agins v. City of Tiburon*, 598 P. 2d 25 (Cal. 1980), *aff'd* 100 S. Ct. 2138, *op. cit.*

13. *San Diego Gas & Electric Co. v. City of San Diego*, 101 S. Ct. 1287 (1981); *Burrows v. City of Keene*, 432 A. 2d 15 (N.H. 1981); *Hernandez v. City of Lafayette*, 643 F. 2d. 1188 (5th Cir. 1981), *rehearing denied*, 649 F. 2d 336 (5th Cir. 1981).

14. See, Christopher J. Duerksen and Michael Mantell, "Interim Damages: A Remedy in Land Use Cases?," *Land Use Law and Zoning Digest*, 33(4):6-12 (April 1981), pp. 6-12.

15. *Hernandez v. City of Lafayette, op. cit.*; *Pamel Corp. v. Puerto Rico Highway Authority, op. cit.*; *Lake Country Estates, Inc. v. Tahoe Regional Planning Agency*, 440 U.S. 391 (1979).

ALASKA LANDS ALLOCATION

1. P.L. 96-487, 16 U.S.C., sec. 3101-3233 (1981).

2. Paul J. Culhane, *Public Lands Politics: Interest Group Influence on the Forest Service and the Bureau of Land Management* (Baltimore, Md.: published for Resources for the Future by The Johns Hopkins University Press, 1981), p. 97.

3. John McPhee, *Coming Into the Country* (New York, N.Y.: Farrar, Straus, Giroux, 1977), p. 17.

4. "Congressional Stall Prompts Administrative Actions to Protect the Alaska National Interest Lands," 8 ELR 10245 (1978); see also Paul J. Culhane, *Public Lands Politics: Interest Group Influence on the Forest Service and the Bureau of Land Management*, pp. 96-97; and Regina Marie Hopkins, "The Alaskan National Monuments of 1978: Another Chapter in the Great Alaskan Land War," 8 *B.C. Envtl. Aff. L. Rev.* 59, 66-70 (1979).

5. The other laws President Carter used were the Antiquities Act of 1906, 16 U.S.C., sec. 431 (1980) and the Federal Land Policy and Management Act, 43 U.S.C. sec. 1702 (1980). See, Presidential Proclamation Nos. 4611-4627 (1980), 43 Fed. Reg. 57009-57132 (1978). See also Paul J. Culhane, *Public Lands Politics: Interest Group Influence on the Forest Service and the Bureau of Land Management*, p. 97.

6. Paul J. Culhane, *Public Lands Politics: Interest Group Influence on the Forest Service and the Bureau of Land Management*, p. 109, *supra*. note 56.

7. *Ibid.*, pp. 97,109.

8. P.L. 96-487, *op. cit.*

Chapter 8

The Urban Environment

Achieving a viable urban environment deserves a high place among environmental goals. The lands on which our towns, villages, cities, and suburbs have been built are irrevocably committed to urban use. Urban areas represent major investments in homes, public buildings, commerce and industry, utilities, streets, and parks. Distinctive urban structures and places have historic, cultural, and architectural importance for urban residents and for the nation's common heritage.

At no time since World War II has there been more uncertainty about prospects for our urban areas. The past decade has brought a great deal of visible renovation of older homes and enlivening of moribund commercial areas. Physical resources in cities and older suburbs have been adapted to changing living arrangements, tastes, and local economies. These events point to the continued attractiveness and usefulness of existing structures and communities.

But other kinds of changes have also occurred: housing starts and resales are at an all-time low, and subsidies are being withdrawn; new tax incentives and a recession are influencing investor and business decisions; local budgets for community and economic development are strained by inflation and taxpayer revolts; federal support is declining. The search for jobs is intensifying, especially among young people deciding where to establish their homes. All of these events, and others, will profoundly affect our urban areas— but we don't yet know how. Uncertainty is accentuated by the debate over what government can and ought to do in the face of the changes urban areas are experiencing.

Nevertheless, the decade of the 1970s encompassed a subtle shift in urban prospects. Whereas in 1970 it was difficult to point to a single encouraging trend in the social and economic circumstances particularly of America's older central cities, by 1982 nearly every city could point to one or more older areas undergoing improvement.

343

Although statistics do not yet establish the extent of these areas, the taste for city living evident among a segment of middle-class Americans is significantly influencing older cities.

URBAN TRENDS

Despite an immense land base and agricultural economy, the United States is one of the most urbanized countries in the world. Approximately three-fourths of the population, or almost 169 million people, live in Standard Metropolitan Statistical Areas (SMSAs).* The number of people living in SMSAs increased 10.2 percent in the 1970s, slightly less than the national population growth rate of 11.4 percent.[1] (See figure 8.1 and chapter 1.)

Metropolitan Areas

Overall, metropolitan areas continue to increase in number, in inhabitants, and in land area. In 1950, there were 169 SMSAs.

Figure 8.1

Population in Metropolitan and Nonmetropolitan Areas, 1950-1980

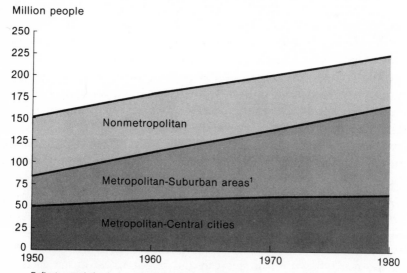

Reflects population in areas as defined at each census.

[1] The suburban area population includes people living in suburbs, small cities and towns and all other residents within the SMSA boundaries except those in central cities.

Source: U.S. Department of Commerce, Bureau of the Census

---

* Standard Metropolitan Statistical Areas (SMSAs) almost always include a central city or urbanized area of 50,000 or more, the county containing the urban center, and neighboring counties closely associated with the central area by daily commuting ties.

These occupied 6 percent of the land and contained 56.1 percent of the nation's population, or 85 million people. By 1970, the number of SMSAs had increased to 243. These occupied 11 percent of the land and had 139.5 million inhabitants, 68.6 percent of the population. By 1980, there were 318 SMSAs, occupying more than 16 percent of the land, with 74.8 percent of the population, that is, 169.4 million inhabitants, 29.9 million more than in 1970.[2]

The region in which an SMSA is located is a major influence on its population trends. Most of the SMSAs designated since 1970 are in the South and West, and previously designated SMSAs in these regions are growing. In the Northeast and North Central regions, by contrast, many metropolitan areas between 1970 and 1980 grew at rates far below the national average, and some experienced actual decline. Total metropolitan populations in both these regions declined during the decade. (See figures 8.2 and 1.4.)

Population trends in SMSAs also vary considerably by size of SMSA:

Large SMSAs. A total of 38 SMSAs had more than a million residents in 1980. In all, almost 92.9 million people, or 41.0 percent of the nation's population, lived in these SMSAs, an increase of 6.3 million (7.3 percent) since 1970. (See figure 8.3.)

Middle-sized SMSAs. A total of 112 SMSAs had between 250,000 and a million residents in 1980. These middle-sized SMSAs contained 52.6 million persons—23.2 percent of the nation's population. The rate of increase since 1970 was 13.6 percent, somewhat above the U.S. average, representing an additional 6.3 million persons.

Small SMSAs. The remaining 168 SMSAs had fewer than 250,000 inhabitants each. In 1980, 23.7 million people, or 10.5 percent of the population, lived in these SMSAs. This represented a rate of increase of 15.6 percent since 1970, an additional 3.2 million inhabitants. Although this growth rate is high, small SMSAs do not account for a major share of the nation's population increase.

Between 1970 and 1980, the U.S. population increased by 23.2 million persons (see chapter 1). Approximately 15.8 million of this increase is accounted for by growth in metropolitan areas and 7.4 million in nonmetropolitan areas. (Trends in nonmetropolitan area population are shown in figure 1.5.) Most of the population growth during the decade, however, took place in the suburban areas of SMSAs. Those areas in 1980 had 101.3 million residents; in 1950, they contained about 35 million.[3]

Figure 8.2
Metropolitan and Nonmetropolitan Population by Region, 1970 and 1980

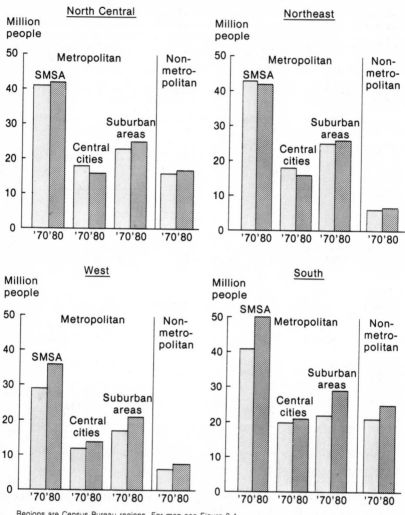

Regions are Census Bureau regions. For map see Figure 8.4.

Source: U.S Department of Commerce, Bureau of the Census

Central Cities

Overall, the population of central cities remained virtually unchanged during the 1970s. This aggregate statistic, however, hides great differences among individual cities.

Population is contracting in some cities, growing in others. Some cities, established in colonial days, prospered early, benefiting from

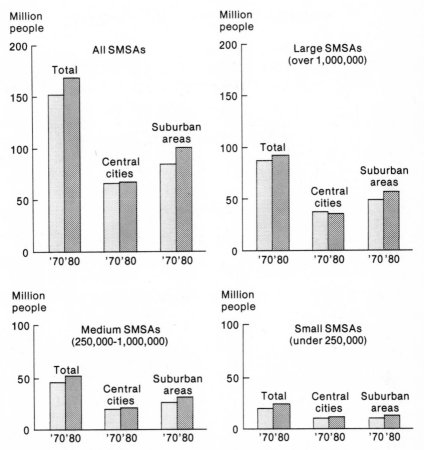

Figure 8.3
Metropolitan Population by Size of SMSA, 1970 and 1980

In 1980 there were 318 SMSAs, of which 38 were large, 112 were medium-sized, and 168 were small.

Source: U.S. Department of Commerce, Bureau of the Census

the right combination of water, labor, and transportation access for the Industrial Revolution. Many of these now have obsolescent economies. Economies in some other cities, however, are performing well relative to national averages.

*Large Central Cities.** Especially in the Northeast and North Central regions, large central cities with aging industrial economies are

---

*The term large central city as used in this section refers to central cities in SMSAs of more than a million residents. These central cities range in size from 7,071,030 (New York) to 270,444 (Ft. Lauderdale-Hollywood, Florida). Twenty-five have populations of more than 500,000.

becoming less dense, and less "central" to the metropolitan areas they helped spawn and once dominated. Overall, central cities in the 38 largest SMSAs lost 1.7 million people during the 1970s, a 4.6 percent decline. Twenty-three of the 38 largest SMSAs had central cities that lost population; 17 lost more than 10 percent of their population, and 6 lost more than 15 percent. (Cleveland lost 23.6 percent; St. Louis, 27.2 percent; Pittsburgh, 18.5 percent; Buffalo, 22.7 percent; Washington, D.C., 15.7 percent; and Detroit, 20.5 percent.) Seventeen of the 38 also lost population in the 1960s, but, in every case, losses increased in the 1970s.[4]

As figure 8.4 shows, most large central cities with contracting population are located in the Northeast and North Central regions. Some large central cities in the South and West, however, also lost population: Seattle, Portland, Atlanta, Denver, New Orleans, Oakland, Baltimore, Washington, D.C., and San Francisco.

Fourteen large central cities gained population. All of them, except Columbus, Ohio, are located in the West or South. In four of the cities—Houston, San Diego, Phoenix, and San Antonio—population grew at a rate greater than the national average. The growth of these cities reflects both a vibrant economy and a propensity to annex. Houston and San Antonio grew by adding population to existing territory and by annexing adjacent communities. San Diego had annexed large areas in the 1950s and 1960s. Columbus, the only large central city in the North Central region that registered a population increase, also has annexed territory in recent years.

Medium- and Small-sized Central Cities. In contrast to central cities in large SMSAs, those in medium and small SMSAs showed population gains of 5.0 percent and 9.8 percent, respectively, between 1970 and 1980. Some—for example, Shreveport, Austin, Nashville, and others located in the South and West—have grown considerably faster than the national average. Cities such as Johnstown, Pennsylvania, and Akron, Ohio, on the other hand, located in the Northeast and North Central regions, have contracting populations and are experiencing the same type of demographic and economic changes as the large central cities.

Suburban Areas

In all regions, the suburban areas—that is, areas within SMSAs but outside central cities—have been growing. (See figure 8.4.) Overall, the growth rate of suburban portions of SMSAs in the 1970s was

Figure 8.4
Population Growth and Decline in Large Metropolitan Areas, 1970-1980

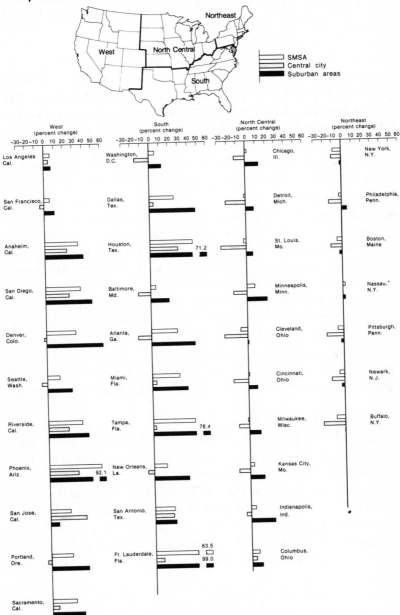

Large metropolitan areas are SMSAs with a population greater than 1 million in 1980.

Regions are Census Bureau regions.

* The SMSA of Nassau does not have a designated central city.

Source: U.S. Department of Commerce, Bureau of the Census

18.3 percent, or 15.7 million persons.[5]

In large SMSAs, the growth rate was 16.5 percent, or 8.1 million persons. Between 1970 and 1980, the proportion of residents in large SMSAs who lived in suburbs increased from 56.9 percent to 61.7 percent of the SMSA total.[6]

Although suburbs in general are growing in the Northeast, in a number of large SMSAs in this region—around Boston, New York City, Pittsburgh, Newark, and Buffalo—the suburban population was virtually unchanged or declined. In some of the other older SMSAs where overall suburban population increased, some close-in older suburbs lost population.[7]

Household Formation and Density

As noted in chapter 1, the rate of household formation in the 1970s was far greater than the rate of increase in the nation's total population. The size of households has declined, reflecting a significant drop in the birthrate as well as an increase in the number of persons living alone. Within SMSAs, household size in central cities is smaller than in the suburbs (a median of 2.58 persons per occupied unit in central cities compared to 2.85 persons per occupied unit outside central cities).[8] Compared with the suburbs, in 1980 a higher proportion of households in central cities consisted of unmarried couples, single persons, and households without children—all household types that increased significantly during the 1970s.

As a result of these changes in household formation and composition, many cities that lost population showed a smaller decline, or even an increase, in the number of households. In Boston, for example, the number of households registered a small increase, despite a 12.2 percent population loss.[9]

One outcome of the significant demographic changes discussed here is a decline in density in SMSAs. Within SMSAs, density in areas outside the central city has increased, while density inside central cities has fallen off sharply. (See figure 8.5.)

Jobs

Population growth and decline have been accompanied by changes in the number and location of jobs. Regionally, jobs have moved from the Northeast and North Central regions to the growing South and West. Within metropolitan areas, jobs and industry—like population—have moved steadily outward to the fringes. Studies show that during the 1970s, new businesses were established and old ones

Figure 8.5
Population Density, 1940-1978

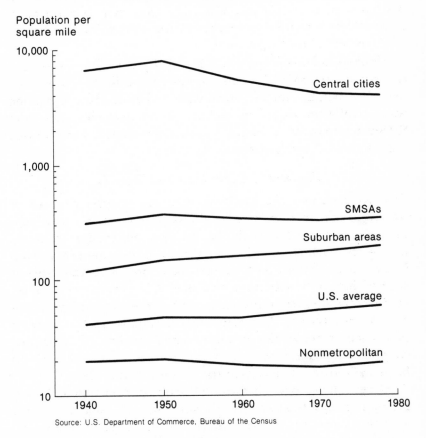

Population per
square mile

Central cities

SMSAs

Suburban areas

U.S. average

Nonmetropolitan

Source: U.S. Department of Commerce, Bureau of the Census

expanded in greater numbers in the suburbs than in central cities. Regionally, many more of these new suburban businesses were begun in the South and West than in the Northeast and North Central regions.

Employment in the suburbs of the largest metropolitan areas expanded considerably during the 1970s in all employment categories. (See figure 8.6.) Retail trade and professional and related services provided the largest number of new jobs. Although experiencing a relatively low rate of growth (6 percent between 1970 and 1977), manufacturing remains the largest single employer in the suburbs. (Nationwide, approximately two out of every three metropolitan manufacturing jobs are now located in the suburbs.) Other industries exhibiting large growth in the suburbs during the

Figure 8.6
Growth and Decline in Employment by Industry, 1970-1977

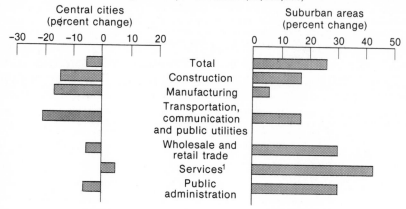

Large metropolitan areas (≥1,000,000)

Central cities
(percent change)

Suburban areas
(percent change)

Total
Construction
Manufacturing
Transportation,
communication
and public utilities
Wholesale and
retail trade
Services[1]
Public
administration

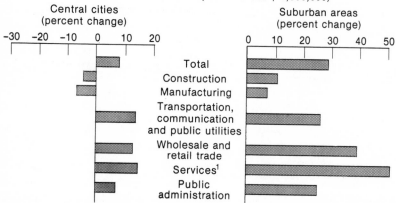

Medium and small metropolitan areas (<1,000,000)

Central cities
(percent change)

Suburban areas
(percent change)

Total
Construction
Manufacturing
Transportation,
communication
and public utilities
Wholesale and
retail trade
Services[1]
Public
administration

Data exclude workers in agricultural and mining industries.
[1] Services include the following industries: finance, insurance and real estate; business and repair services; entertainment and recreation; and professional and related services.
Source: U.S. Department of Commerce, Bureau of the Census

1970s include transportation, construction, business services, personal services, and retail trade.

In contrast, the number of people employed in large central cities (that is, central cities of metropolitan areas with more than a million inhabitants) declined by approximately 900,000, or 6 percent, between 1970 and 1977, the latest year for which comparable data are available.* Central city job losses were sharpest (15 percent or

*Not yet available from the 1980 Census are the data for industrial employment by central city and suburban areas, or the socioeconomic data with which to compare central

more) in transportation, manufacturing, and construction. Wholesale and retail trade and public administration also registered substantial declines.

Although these traditional sources of employment in large cities declined, opportunities in other industries were growing. Jobs in service industries of all kinds increased by over 250,000, or 5 percent, making this the major source of employment in large central cities. Within this category, business and repair services increased by 14 percent, and entertainment and recreation services by 21 percent.

Unlike employment trends in large central cities, employment in smaller central cities increased by more than 800,000 jobs, or 8 percent, between 1970 and 1977. These cities registered employment gains in every category except construction and manufacturing, with sizable gains in professional and related services, wholesale and retail trade, finance and insurance, and entertainment. Employment in manufacturing declined by 7 percent (substantially less than the decline in the large central cities) during this period.

With each successive downturn in the national economy, employment in large central cities has declined more than in the nation as a whole and much more than in adjacent suburbs. Following each recession, employment in these cities did not return to its prerecession levels.

This trend is strongest in the Northeast and North Central regions, where employment growth in many of the large cities stopped during the 1971 recession, and subsequent recessions led to further declines in cities such as St. Louis, Boston, and Philadelphia. A few large cities such as Washington, D.C., and San Francisco, however, managed to maintain their employment levels during and after national economic recessions.[11] Still others, including Houston, San Antonio, and San Diego, registered substantial increases in employment even during periods of national economic slowdown.[12]

Regional differences in central city employment are highlighted in a study of 20 selected cities with populations between 220,000 and 1 million, conducted by the Center for Urban Policy Research at Rutgers University. The 10 cities of this size most dependent

city and suburban areas for large SMSAs. However, a few summary socioeconomic characteristics of large SMSAs were released in April 1982 by the Census Bureau in a preliminary report, "Provisional Estimates of Social, Economic, and Housing Characteristics, Supplementary Report from the 1980 Census of Population and Housing," PHC 80-51-1 (Washington, D.C.: U.S. Department of Commerce, Bureau of the Census).

on federal or state aid experienced a 16.6 percent decline in numbers of jobs between 1970 and 1977, compared to an 15.1 percent growth in employment in the nation as a whole. All of these cities are located in the Northeast and North Central regions. The 10 cities of this size least dependent on federal and state aid experienced a 56.7 percent growth in jobs. Of these cities, all except one (Columbus, Ohio) are located in the Sunbelt.[13]

Overall, unemployment rates in the large central cities reached 9.8 percent for males in 1977, compared to 4.9 percent in 1970; the rates in adjacent suburbs were 6.4 percent in 1977 and 3.3 percent in 1970.[14] Unemployment rates in large central cities were consistently 1 or 2 points higher than in the central cities of SMSAs with under 1 million inhabitants.

The decline in overall employment opportunities in large central cities has resulted in a mismatch between the workforce and available jobs, which is especially evident in unemployment among minorities. Too often, jobs created in these cities require educational levels and skills that many of the poorer residents do not possess. Unemployment rates for black males increased from 7.1 percent in 1970 to 17.3 percent in 1977; for black females, from 6.8 percent in 1970 to 13.3 percent in 1977. Unemployment rates for workers of Spanish origin increased from 5.8 percent to 10.7 percent for males and from 8.0 percent to 10.4 percent for females over the same years.[15]

Income

Levels and changes of income are good indicators of the economic well-being of a community. Increases in income translate into greater demand for goods and services and, over time, into more investment, production, and jobs. A community with declining levels of income will have difficulty maintaining its standard of living.

The median income of families living in the largest central cities (central cities in SMSAs of more than a million inhabitants) declined by 8 percent between 1969 and 1976. (See figure 8.7.) In constant 1976 dollars, annual income declined from $14,912 in 1969 to $13,700 in 1976. Incomes of families living in adjacent suburban areas experienced a small decline during the same period. As a result of these changes, the ratio of central city to suburban family income declined from 0.81 to 0.75. In metropolitan areas with less than a million population, family incomes in both central cities and the suburbs remained virtually the same (in constant dollars) between

Figure 8.7

**Median Family Income by Size of Metropolitan Area, 1969 and 1976
(in constant 1976 dollars)**

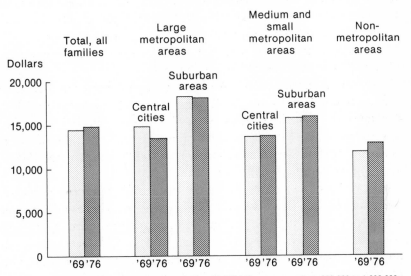

Large metropolitan areas have a population of 1,000,000 or more; medium, 250,000 to 1,000,000; and small, less than 250,000.

Source: U.S. Department of Commerce, Bureau of the Census

1969 and 1976.

In the South and West, central city incomes are higher than in the Northeast and North Central regions, and income differences between the central city and suburban areas are considerably smaller.

Central city families have become increasingly dependent on sources of income other than earnings, principally social security, public assistance, and other income. Some cities, such as San Antonio, Phoenix, and San Diego, have relatively high levels of transfer income because they have higher proportions of retired civilian and military workers. The high percentage in 1975 of transfer income in cities like Boston (32 percent), Philadelphia (27 percent), and St. Louis (28 percent) reflects significant federal spending for social programs aimed at distressed persons.[16]

The number and percentage of poor people living in central cities in large SMSAs increased during the 1970s, especially in the largest ones. In 1969, there were approximately 5 million people, or 14.8 percent of the population of these cities, living in poverty. (See figure 8.8.) By 1976, this number had increased to more than 5.4 million, and the percentage in poverty had increased to 17.1 percent.

Figure 8.8

Persons Below the Poverty Level by Size of Metropolitan Area, 1969 and 1976

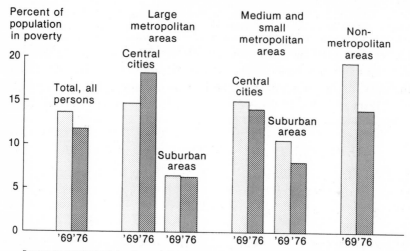

Persons are classified as being above or below the poverty level using the index adopted by a federal interagency committee on poverty in 1969. The poverty level varies by farm and nonfarm status, and by family size and composition.

Large metropolitan areas have a population of 1,000,000 or more; medium, 250,000 to 1,000,000; and small, less than 250,000.

Source: U.S. Department of Commerce, Bureau of the Census

During the same period, the number and percentage of people living in poverty in suburban and in nonmetropolitan areas declined. About 60 percent of the increase in the poverty population in large central cities is accounted for by individuals living in female-headed families.

At the other end of the scale, the number and percentage of higher income families living in large central cities declined between 1970 and 1977. Families with incomes above $25,000 per year declined from 18 percent to 16 percent of the population. The percentage of families in adjacent suburbs with incomes above $25,000 increased from 26 percent to 28 percent. [17]

Because family characteristics have been changing markedly in the United States, useful comparisons call for attention to per capita as well as family or household income. The income needs and income-generating capacity of families vary by the number of family members, sex, age, health status, and other characteristics. In the study of 20 cities referred to earlier, per capita income in the 10 cities most dependent on state or federal aid increased 15.5 percent between 1970 and 1977; per capita income in the 10 cities least dependent on outside aid increased 22.8 percent during the same period.[18] (Trends in real per capita income are measured in constant 1977 dollars.)

Among the cities in the study, Newark has the lowest rate of income growth; Cleveland and Rochester also registered relatively low rates of growth. Nashville-Davidson more than doubled its real per capita income over the past two decades. Overall, per capita incomes in the cities most dependent on outside aid lagged behind per capita incomes in cities least dependent on outside aid by 18.5 percent between 1960 and 1977.

REVITALIZATION AND FISCAL SURVIVAL

Suffering from economic obsolescence and the trend toward decentralization, central cities must adapt to changing circumstances if their resources are to be conserved. Despite contracting economies and population losses, a number of our older cities have an urban style, distinctiveness of place, and sense of community that many Americans have in recent years increasingly valued. Dynamism vies with continuing decline, while fiscal constraints and shifts in federal policy present new stumbling blocks.

The Revitalization of Older Cities

Sometime in the 1970s, observers began to detect the phenomenon we now know as "revitalization." Private market interest in older urban neighborhoods rekindled as young people with choice and money bought homes in run-down areas and started to renovate. "Gentrification" brought middle-class residents to neighborhoods where they would not have ventured a decade before.* A 1981 survey of housing directors in the nation's 25 largest cities found neighborhood revitalization occurring in every one of the cities.**[19]

---

* The term *gentrification*, imported from England, has class connotations with which many Americans feel uncomfortable. The term *back-to-the-city* has been used to refer to the same phenomenon, although with less precision. Both terms have an additional inadequacy because they leave out stable city populations whose renewed confidence in their neighborhoods is perceived by many experts as a benefit of middle-class resettlement, essential to significant neighborhood revitalization.

** The indicators of neighborhood revitalization used in the survey, and the percentage of officials responding positively are: young professionals renovating older, single-family homes (96 percent); condominium conversion (80 percent); rent and housing prices rising faster than inflation (72 percent); the revival of neighborhood stores (68 percent); and complementary public investment (92 percent). The survey was undertaken as part of a collaborative project on Revitalization and the Elderly conducted by The Conservation Foundation and the Urban Institute from 1979 to 1981.

More recently, private investment has enlivened moribund downtowns. Some development is of boom proportions. Investors speak of the economic successes of "urban marketplaces," restaurants, condominiums, in-town hotels, and new office buildings. People are returning to the streets, parks, squares, and waterfronts of the old centers of town.

It is against the backdrop of urban decline that this revitalization phenomenon has particular importance. New industrial technology, improved communications, and the automobile have deprived older central cities of advantages that once made them grow and thrive. For decades, these cities have lost population, as people who could exercise the choice have moved away, leaving a growing proportion of residents in need of public support. As the industrial economies of many central cities have shrunk, physical neglect of buildings and public facilities has increased.

For decades, governments have tried to respond to the needs of declining industrial cities. A succession of expensive programs has sought to reverse the losses of jobs and residents, or at least to address their economic and social consequences. Today, there is consensus that some of the programs—such as massive razing of blighted areas—destroyed more than was rebuilt. Typically, government programs have focused on problems, on what is wrong with cities. They have paid far less attention to cities as places where people choose to live, work, have fun, or invest.

How should governments, particularly the federal government, respond to the phenomenon of revitalization? Should they seek to aid it, in hopes of creating more viable urban economies and improved urban environments? Should they try to extend it so that its effects will be transferred to places where, unaided, private investment would not go? Or should they ignore it (or seek only to limit harmful side effects), concentrating available public resources on direct aid to poor and disadvantaged people?

Particularly in a time of budgetary stringency, these questions pose a dilemma. Government assistance to revitalization could promote the growth of a smaller "city of the elite" engulfed by the "city of the poor," in the words of urban expert George Sternlieb. It could also displace the poor and replace them with middle-class "gentry."

Yet, if governments ignore the signals in market forces, they could miss an opportunity, lacking in so many earlier strategies, to strengthen and expand these forces rather than fighting them or trying to replace them. If older cities are to live up to their potential as resources, they need the private energies and investment that revitalization brings. They need public energies and investment as well, however, and the revitalization phenomenon could represent an unprecedented opportunity to make public investment effective.

Revitalization Trends

For all the talk about revitalization, how significant a trend is it, really? In trying to answer this question, it is useful to distinguish neighborhood revitalization from commercial reinvestment.

Neighborhood Revitalization. Despite considerable evidence that residential revitalization is occurring in a number of older cities, much about the phenomenon is not well understood, and data about its extent remain inconclusive. Information from the 1980 Census is still being analyzed.

The "new demographics" are clearly important. In city after city, reported housing demand has a familiar pattern: home buyers are predominantly from the "baby boom" generation—young professionals who, compared with their parents, are setting up independent households earlier, marrying later or not at all, having fewer children, or postponing them, and earning more money.[20] They are making housing choices in response to preferences about interesting architecture and neighborhoods, accessibility to work, and urban amenities rather than concerns about the best environment in which to raise a family.

Increased interest in homeownership and renovation has worked in favor of older cities. Dizzying appreciation in real estate prices and generous tax incentives have impelled households—even single-person households—to buy homes rather than rent. Prices of single-family homes, particularly those in need of renovation, are often lower in revitalizing neighborhoods than in the suburbs. Growing interest in historic preservation and, more broadly, rehabilitation, has aided neighborhood revitalization by conferring value on the old buildings that abound in cities.

Until more complete data become available from the 1980 Census, researchers must rely on two kinds of studies to try to understand neighborhood revitalization. Neither provides definitive evidence of the extent of the phenomenon. Studies of the first type, close-up examinations of particular neighborhoods, are subject to challenge as not being "representative." In the second, multicity studies, market patterns accompanying revitalization tend to wash out in a sea of diversity.[21]

Data from the 1980 Census that are expected to provide reliable information about economic and social change since 1970 in city residential neighborhoods will not be available until late 1982. The citywide data that are already available show that many central cities have continued to lose population. Other recent information indicates that the proportion of people in poverty has continued to increase. The income gap between residents of cities and suburbs continues.[22]

The percentage of owner-occupied housing in all central cities did increase slightly between 1970 and 1980—by 1.4 percent, as compared with a .7 percent increase during the previous decade. More significantly, owner occupancy increased by 2.8 percent in Northeast central cities between 1970 and 1980. Nonetheless, the growth of owner-occupied housing in the United States as a whole, 2.7 percent between 1970 and 1980, continues to outpace the growth of such housing in central cities.[23]

These data have led some experts to conclude that revitalization is either a mirage or of limited significance. While the data are sobering, however, such conclusions are premature. The extent and significance of residential revitalization remain to be documented by more detailed information from the Census.

Commercial Reinvestment. Evidence of reinvestment in the commercial areas of older cities parallels that of residential revitalization: many impressions, but few confirming statistics. Reports from business groups and investors have been highly encouraging. In 1981, for example, mortgage bankers noted significantly increased investment activity in Chicago, Boston, and Philadelphia, and predicted that Minneapolis, Pittsburgh, and Columbus were emerging growth centers.[24] A 1981 survey of 17 cities reported that 10 had less than 3 percent of their downtown office space available for rent. Office rentals had experienced a "dramatic rise in rental rates," 21 percent in a year compared to 12 percent in suburban locations.[25]

The "urban marketplace" model, pioneered in the Ghirardelli Square renovation in San Francisco, has sparked creative reuse of old buildings in many cities. Designs for rebuilding old commercial areas, emphasizing harmonious blending of old and new development, a variety of uses, and "people activities," have had striking successes. Even more than neighborhood renovation, the revival of profitable downtown enterprise has generated considerable optimism about the future of older cities.

The statistics now available are insufficient to support (or, for that matter, to undermine) this optimism. The federal census of business is less reliable than the census of population, and the economic conditions it reports are more volatile. Data are still being analyzed from the 1977 business census, and new data (from the 1982 business census) will not be available until 1984 or 1985. County business data, reported annually, provide more current information, but only for the few cities where county and city boundaries coincide. Local indicators—changes in assessed property values, construction and renovation permits, and so on—are difficult to compile because of differing local practices in gathering information.

Government Assistance for Revitalization

Federal actions aiding revitalization have involved a combination of new responses and adaptation of existing programs. Most, although not all, have focused on cities as "distressed places." Legislation has been enacted to ensure an equitable flow of credit by lending institutions to older cities. The Urban Development Action Grants (UDAG) program was established to stimulate public-private partnerships in economic development projects in distressed urban areas.[26] Grants to neighborhood groups have encouraged community-based housing and commercial development. The broad terms of established programs, like the Community Development Block Grants program, have enabled cities to use funds flexibly for revitalization projects—to make revitalization happen faster, or to stimulate revitalization in places where it could benefit low- and moderate-income people.

City governments, too, have aided revitalization by such means as providing low-interest loans for new homeowners in targeted urban neighborhoods, reforming building codes that hinder rehabilitation, encouraging protection of historic buildings and districts, fostering neighborhood planning and resident participation, and providing tax abatements and other incentives to encourage downtown and neighborhood development.

Baltimore, for example, has ably used its distinctive ethnic neighborhoods, row housing and old lofts, open waterfront, old squares, and other resources as assets. It has made pioneering efforts in home-repair programs for elderly homeowners, provided financial assistance to enable moderate-income renters to become homeowners, and supported conversion of apartment buildings to low-yield cooperatives for low-income renters. Its unusually successful program combines aggressive city leadership and complementary public spending to encourage private investment in the downtown.

State targeting of activities to distressed urban areas, although growing, is still limited. States have provided funds for urban parks and waterfront development, and they have assisted economic development ventures. Massachusetts, for example, has authorized $35 million in capital spending to establish eight Heritage Parks in old mill towns.[27] Ohio granted $673,830 to Cleveland to help purchase a key waterfront park site.[28] New York State has provided technical assistance to distressed urban areas. Some states have funded infrastructure improvements to attract developers to cities.

In addition to providing funds, states have aided revitalization in other ways. Examples include enactment of enabling legislation for historic preservation; reforms in building codes to encourage rehabilitation; regulation to ensure that lenders do not discriminate against city borrowers; and authorization for cities to float tax-exempt revenue bonds to fund housing purchase and rehabilitation and economic development.

It would be useful to have good information about the effectiveness of the various government actions encouraging revitalization. For most programs, however, especially those that are highly decentralized, good information about effectiveness is lacking. Two evaluations of federal programs that encourage private investment in rehabilitation—one of UDAG and another of tax incentives for historic preservation—have influenced the continuance of these programs.[29] Such useful analyses are few, however, and cutbacks in federal funds for research and program assessment are likely to reduce their number still further.

Displaced People and Threatened Landmarks

Revitalization, while bringing needed investment, can have injurious side effects. Displacement of people is one risk, as "gentrification" results in condominium conversions and rents too high for the poor residents of neighborhoods. Historic buildings are also sometimes threatened, particularly where downtown reinvestment entails market interest in massive new construction.

Displaced People. How extensive is displacement? Like the revitalization that causes it, the existence of displacement is clear but its extent is not well documented. Moreover, while we have some information about the immediate impact on individuals, we know less about lasting effects. Displacement studies are plagued by difficulties of definition and data collection; finding people who have moved is expensive and time consuming. Studies have generally concluded that displaced people pay more for their next housing, but often stay in the same neighborhood.

In October 1981, the Department of Housing and Urban Development (HUD) estimated that, nationwide, between .8 and 1.1 percent of U.S. households (1.7 to 2.4 million people) were displaced by private activity in 1979.* In specific cities, local estimates range from 1 to 7 percent. HUD has concluded that displacement is a problem of local rather than national concern, except for displacement that results directly from federally funded activities.[30]

To reduce displacement resulting from federally aided projects, HUD's policies provide "regulatory and administrative protections," encouraging local review of projects to determine alternatives to displacement.[31] The National Housing Law Project charges, however, that HUD has been "sluggish in requiring cities to counter displacement."[32]

Some states and localities have responded to concern about displacement. Some cities have adopted condominium conversion regulations, for example, that require converters to permit elderly residents to remain as tenants for a certain period if they cannot afford to buy their apartments, or that require developers to pay relocation payments to low-income tenants. A San Francisco ordinance requires developers to replace razed or rehabilitated skid row hotel units (or pay into a city fund established for this purpose).[33] Proponents of such compensation typically stress the hardship of relocation and the scarcity of affordable rental housing, while opponents argue that the costs imposed on developers will likely slow revitalization.

Threatened Landmarks. Revitalization can also threaten buildings of significant historic, cultural, and architectural merit. It is true that recent revitalization has drawn inspiration from historic preservation. Yet, as older areas increase in value, developers often advance plans for larger-scale redevelopment. Clashes between preservationists and developers have occurred in the UDAG program, for example, in federally aided projects in Charleston (South Carolina), New Brunswick (New Jersey), Pittsfield (Massachusetts),

---

* This estimate, based on responses to a new question in the Annual Housing Survey, does not sharply distinguish between displacement that may result from revitalization and displacement that may result from other causes.

New York City, and New Orleans. The clashes have involved proj-
ect-related demolition of landmark-quality buildings and the design
of new development in historic districts.[34]

When federally aided projects threaten landmark-quality buildings, federal law has provided some protection. The law calls for
federal and state review of impacts on historic landmarks and areas
that are listed in the National Register of Historic Places or are
eligible for listing.[35] In addition, the National Environmental Policy
Act (NEPA) requires consideration of a broad range of effects that
a federally aided project may have on the urban environment.[36]

Efforts to streamline federal and state review processes—to reach
decisions more rapidly and concentrate more authority in local governments—increased in the late 1970s. In 1981, the federal Advisory
Council on Historic Preservation adopted regulations that limit the
time allowed for federal and state comments on the effects on historic
buildings of proposed UDAG projects.[37] Under review are regulations that would streamline federal review of non-UDAG projects.

In a number of communities, state and local historic preservation
programs also defend threatened buildings. New York City and
Washington, D.C., for example, have protected a number of buildings and districts, and local legislation provides for administrative
reviews of developers' plans to demolish landmark buildings.[38] These
reviews, triggered by a request for a demolition permit, set the
stage for negotiations over any economic hardship that retention of
the landmark would cause. Unless a project is federally funded,
state and local measures like these provide the primary legal defense
against destruction of landmark-quality buildings.

Policy Options

Governments' responses to the revitalization phenomenon are part
of their overall responses to the needs of central cities. The future
form of these overall responses is less clear today than it has been
for many years. Even the broadest questions are unsettled: how
much money should be spent to aid poor people and distressed
places, what forms should the spending take, what measures besides
spending should be used, and which governments should do what.
Substantial government involvement will unquestionably continue.
The key question is how governments should factor the revitalization
phenomenon into their urban strategies.

Subsidies for Revitalization. One option is for government to provide
financial aid for revitalization. Attracting middle-class residents and

commercial development remain objectives of many central cities, and this option would pursue them with dollar support.

With respect to neighborhood revitalization, the maneuvering room for governments is currently constrained by high interest rates. The large spread between what buyers can afford and the market costs of credit make it difficult to design attractive financing packages with subsidies from such sources as block grants or state tax exempt bonds. A federal initiative to stimulate the housing market generally could benefit older cities, even if it were not targeted to them, since trends favoring purchase of homes in older urban areas continue.

To aid economic development, governments could focus subsidies on attracting private investment to urban marketplaces, cultural and tourism activities, adaptive reuse of distinctive underused commercial structures, and waterfronts, parks, and well-designed public spaces. At the federal level, emphasizing such commercial revitalization could include continuation or expansion of programs such as the Urban Development Action Grants (UDAG). Block grants and other public funds might emphasize, more than in the past, capital improvements for downtown and neighborhood economic development, including small business activities, which have been shown to be very important in the urban economy.

Some states and localities have provided limited amounts of their own dollars, particularly in recent years, to assist economic development. Apart from funds made available from the federal government, most state aid to development has not been targeted to cities, however.

Proponents of providing subsidies for revitalization argue that subsidies are needed to make development in cities competitive with development in the suburbs or Sunbelt. Also, they argue, past assistance has been effective. The World Trade Center in Baltimore, constructed by the state of Maryland, and the Town Square development in St. Paul, Minnesota, aided by UDAG and other public funds, are examples of projects that seem to have successfully stimulated other profitable privately funded downtown development. A Department of Housing and Urban Development study has concluded that most UDAG projects would not have occurred without federal assistance.[39]

Others are less confident that direct subsidy programs have been effective or efficient. They are not convinced that the successful projects needed government funds. Moreover, the fragile economic position of some urban projects (such as Renaissance Center in Detroit, which was aided substantially by the city) testifies to the difficulty of projecting market forces when public aid is involved. Questions have also been raised about whether aided projects create new economic activity or simply move it around.

Both proponents and opponents of subsidies call attention to regulations accompanying aid from the federal (and to a lesser extent, state) government. Regulations accompanying federal aid have had important effects on such matters as landmark review, public participation, and spending directed to particular groups. The Reagan Administration has indicated its intent to reduce such regulation (as well as federal aid).

Financial Aid to Extend Revitalization to Needy People. Government spending for revitalization might alternatively be focused on needy people and places that the market would not otherwise help. UDAG and other subsidized economic development programs have been criticized as stimulating too many office buildings, hotels, and convention centers. And "gentrification" has been criticized for displacing low-income residents. Focusing aid on the needy would respond to these criticisms by trying to spread the benefits of revitalization more widely.

Like other revitalization strategies, this option would call for building on the physical and social strengths that all neighborhoods, even poor ones, have. In practice, it would seek to encourage conservation of the housing stock for existing residents. There is precedent for this approach. In a number of cities, for example, funds have been made available to help low-income and moderate-income people renovate their homes, and housing subsidies have been provided to enable low-income people to stay in "gentrifying" neighborhoods. Funding has also been provided to community groups with a track record of accomplishment in rehabilitation, community and economic development, and other self-help efforts.

Support for such efforts is found among those who believe it is government's function to act on behalf of the people the market does not help, as well as among those who argue that conserving old cities cannot be accomplished politically unless aid is extended to current residents. Opponents of these efforts argue that such subsidies perpetuate dependency by keeping people in places where they can no longer earn a living.

Increased private support for needy people and places is possible. The Local Initiatives Support Corporation and the Inner City Ventures Fund of the National Trust for Historic Preservation, both funded entirely by the private sector, provide grants to community initiatives emphasizing physical and economic rebuilding of low- and moderate-income neighborhoods. Philanthropy, while always important, has not totaled anywhere near the amount of money provided by government, however. The President's Task Force on Private Sector Initiatives has been formed to stimulate additional corporate support for community self-help activities.

Another source of private aid for needy people involves subsidies from development profits. Two examples are the Enterprise Foundation, which will funnel funds from development ventures to community-based housing projects, and local laws that require developers, as a condition of obtaining a permit, to contribute to a fund for low- or moderate-income housing.

No Subsidies for Revitalization. Another option is to end dollar subsidies for revitalization. This approach would let revitalization happen, or not happen, as market forces dictate.

Quite disparate arguments have been advanced for this option. Market proponents argue that urban investments should be made in response to market forces—or not at all. Subsidy programs are costly and have brought governmental standards, especially federal standards, into the revitalization process: environmental reviews, protection for historic buildings and districts, relocation expenses, and so on. Subsidy opponents emphasize the delay and expense caused by these reviews, and question their effectiveness.

A very different sort of argument for this option is made by people who see revitalization as a threat to the poor. Private reinvestment in neighborhoods, convention centers, urban marketplaces, and downtowns may enliven cities, they assert, but there is no proof that it helps the "city of the poor." Moreover, if governments focus on revitalization, their attention and resources may be distracted from continuing problems of urban poverty. To address those problems, according to this view, governments should focus not on revitalization, but on programs that provide funds for needy people and that create jobs suitable for unemployed city dwellers.

Nonsubsidy Incentives. Governments might provide nonsubsidy aid to revitalization in a variety of ways—through regulation, for example, or tax incentives. Relevant federal regulatory strategies that have been tried include requirements that credit be extended without discrimination to urban areas, that agencies examine the effects of proposed actions on urban areas (urban impact statements), and that city mayors be notified of pending federal aid to outlying new shopping centers and permitted to request analysis of the effects of that development on cities' existing retail centers.

Proponents of this approach argue that such regulations encourage private investments in the existing city and that federal aid to distressed cities should not be undermined by other federal actions that diminish the impact of the aid. Opponents assert that such regulations not only create unnecessary paper work and impede the marketplace, but also are inappropriate at the federal level because of America's diversity.

At the state and local level, regulatory strategies to aid revitalization include facilitating condominium conversion, changing single-family zoning to permit several households to share large old houses, encouraging infill of bypassed urban lots before new development is permitted, and zoning to require design amenities and mixed use in commercial projects.

Governments at every level—federal, state, and local—provide various kinds of tax incentives that have aided some revitalization projects. Federal tax credits for rehabilitation and preservation, first passed in 1976, work in favor of older cities and the type of rehabilitation and preservation development increasingly popular in revitalization strategies.[40] The Economic Recovery Tax Act, enacted in 1981, extended these incentives substantially for both rehabilitation of older buildings and preservation of historic structures.[41] Examples of state incentives include enabling legislation for cities to provide tax abatements for development and tax-exempt financing for both residential and commercial development. Some states provide distressed areas with technical assistance for economic development.

A widely discussed new proposal involving incentives to attract investment to distressed older cities is the urban enterprise zone. In addition to tax incentives, this concept is identified with reduced regulation and other state and local inducements intended to free the market to make better use of available human and economic resources.

In general, proponents of tax incentives argue they are cheaper and more effective than direct subsidies. Further, these incentives, once put in place, usually require less governmental intervention than direct subsidies, and thus less delay and expense to developers and entrepreneurs. Opponents of such incentives contend that because tax incentives reduce government income, they can cost as much as, or even more than, subsidies. Further, they regard as an advantage the opportunity subsidies provide for governments to scrutinize and shape projects.

The Fiscal Condition of Cities

For many cities, the immediate issue is fiscal survival. To create and maintain environments in which people want to live, every city must spend money on services and amenities. Yet cities face a numbing combination of increased demands, rising costs, reduced resources, electorates unwilling to pay more taxes, and reductions in the federal aid on which cities and their citizens have increasingly depended in recent years.

This set of fiscal circumstances is particularly serious in cities in the Northeast and Midwest, and is worse for cities in these areas with populations over a million. In 1980, even before the budget cuts initiated by the Reagan Administration, the Joint Economic Committee found that nearly 80 percent of 300 cities it surveyed expected operating deficits in 1981, a substantial increase over 1979 and 1980. Of the 29 survey cities that had over 250,000 population, all but four expected to be in the red.[42]

Overall, Sunbelt cities are less threatened. Their spending per capita is lower. Their residents are less heavily taxed. Their tax bases mostly are increasing, especially in the many cities that annex growing fringe areas. There are fiscal problems, of course, even in Sunbelt cities. Some, growing rapidly, are postponing needed spending on infrastructure and public amenities. Not all Sunbelt cities are located in wealthy, expanding metropolitan areas, and not all can or do annex to follow taxpayers to new fringe developments. On the whole, however, the fiscal problems of Sunbelt cities are less critical than those of older cities in the Northeast and Midwest.

Federal budget cuts promise to intensify the cities' fiscal problems. Since the 1960s, and especially since the late 1970s, cities have come to depend on federal and state funds to cope with the problems created as money and jobs have moved out, leaving diminished resources and an increasingly dependent, unemployed, and under-educated population. Some of this aid has gone to city governments (for example, CETA funds); some of it (food stamps, for example) has gone directly to poor people, many of whom would otherwise have looked to the cities for support. Budget cuts during 1981 reduced the federal contribution, and the Reagan Administration is proposing deeper cuts for the future.

Figure 8.9
Municipal Financial Performance by Stage of Industrialization, 1975

Stage of industrialization (number of cities)	Local taxes as percent of personal income	Local taxes per capita	Current operating expenses per capita	Intergovernmental revenue as percent of total local revenue	City government employment as percent of total local employment
Old industrialized cities (9)	9.5%	$407	$604	38.0%	8.0%
Maturing industrial cities (13)	5.5%	$254	$518	40.7%	4.3%
Young industrial cities (44)	4.9%	$239	$451	32.1%	3.1%
Average, all cities studied (66)	5.7%	$265	$485	34.6%	4.0%

Cities were grouped according to two key factors of industrial aging — population decline and manufacturing employment decline.

Source: James M. Howell and Charles F. Stamm, *Urban Fiscal Stress*

As funds grow scarce, the services essential to a quality living environment decline. Schools close, libraries reduce their hours, buses run less often, snow stays on the streets. Municipal employees strike, and the arguments among politicians and their constituents become increasingly acrimonious.

Fiscal health will have much to do with the ability of cities to attract people who have a choice among urban, suburban, and rural life-styles. Dissatisfaction with the urban environment—crime, congestion, noise, service levels—ranks high among the reasons people give for moving out of cities. Each wave of public consciousness aroused by strikes of sanitation workers or teachers, cutbacks in public transit, homeless "street people," and closings of libraries and cultural facilities takes its toll. Public loss of confidence becomes part of a cycle of defeat in which it is hard to persuade investors or residents to cast their lot with cities. Instead of "cultural magnets," cities become "distressed places," to be shunned in favor of the suburbs or the countryside beyond.

Financial Demands on Cities

One side of cities' fiscal balance consists of costly demands. Cities spend most of their money providing public services—including education, health care, welfare, and parks and recreation—and facilities such as sewers and streets and highways.

The amounts cities spend on services and infrastructure have, in general, been rising faster than the cost of living.[43] Some of the higher costs are associated with efforts to improve the quality of service—better training and up-to-date equipment for police, better art and music education. Some cities have also been doing new things—promoting business investment, sponsoring fairs and other city "events."

Municipal expenditures tend to be higher in central cities that are large, or have declining populations or obsolescent industry (frequently, a city has two or three of these characteristics). In one study, for example, the operating costs of a group of cities with aging industrial economies were much higher than those in a group of newly industrializing cities: $604 per capita compared to $451 (figure 8.9). And in another study, the costs of police and fire protection were higher in cities that were losing population than in cities with growing populations (figure 8.10).

For all cities, wages of municipal employees increased 225 percent between 1955 and 1976, about one-fourth faster than private-sector wages.[44] The number of city employees increased 200 percent during the same period. In a study of old cities, municipal employees represent a far higher percentage of total local employment than in

Figure 8.10
Municipal Government Outlays for Selected Common Services, 1977

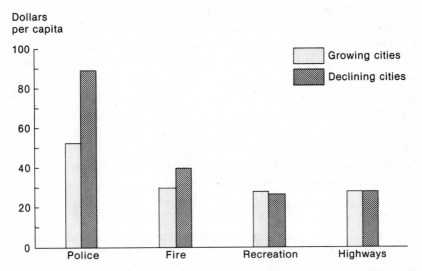

Growing cities include: Dallas, San Antonio, Houston, San Diego, Phoenix, San Jose, Jacksonville, and Oklahoma City. Declining cities include: New York, Buffalo, Detroit, Cleveland, Philadelphia, Pittsburgh, St. Louis, and Chicago. These were the fastest growing and declining cities of those with populations of at least 500,000 in 1970.

Source: U.S. Department of Commerce, Bureau of the Census

newer ones. Employee pensions are among the most rapidly growing fixed costs in municipal budgets. Detroit, with an unfunded pension liability of $818 million, spent 18 percent of its general fund expenditures on pension contributions in 1978.[45]

High public spending does not necessarily produce quality services. In a group of cities with population losses, for example, outlays for education increased 96.6 percent per pupil between 1972 and 1977, as school population fell 12.6 percent (the cost of living increased 44 percent during the same years).[46] Yet public schools in these cities are typically held in low esteem, and the proportion of students attending private schools in many cities is the highest ever.

Two components of increased demand merit special attention: capital spending for infrastructure and welfare spending for dependent populations.

Capital spending has typically been the first item cut as cities struggling with budgets try to make cuts that "don't show." Such deferred spending is evident both in expanding cities, which need to build new facilities to serve growing populations, and in old cities, which need to maintain or replace worn-out physical plants.

A study of selected public works in nine cities found the streets and mass transit systems of eight to be in poor condition. Bridges in six cities were deteriorating badly or in need of major repair. In New York City alone, according to another report, investment of over $40 billion is needed within nine years to "repair, service, and rebuild . . . 1,000 bridges, two aqueducts, one large water tunnel, several reservoirs, 6,200 miles of paved streets, 6,000 miles of sewers, 6,000 miles of water lines, 6,700 subway cars."[47]

Public awareness of cutbacks in capital spending rises as poor maintenance becomes more visible, and as poor facilities impede efforts to attract new economic development.

The costs of dependency—persons who cannot afford the basic costs of food, shelter, clothing, and health, or who need special services they cannot pay for—are another significant source of demands on central cities. The numbers of elderly persons, new immigrants to the United States, and households headed by women are increasing in central cities.

Shrinking Resources

Local taxation provides much of the revenue used by cities to meet costly demands for municipal services and facilities. The single largest source of local tax revenue is the property tax. In addition, local income and sales taxes, and a variety of other taxes, provide increasing proportions of local tax revenues. Miscellaneous local fees and charges provide significant nontax revenue.[48]

Declining cities typically impose a heavier local tax burden than do growing ones. In 1975, local taxes per capita in a group of old, industrialized cities were $407, for example, but only $239 in a group of newly industrializing cities. (See figure 8.9.)

For the past two decades, receipts from local taxes have increased steadily, although they leveled off in 1979 in response to taxpayer resistance. Taxpayer revolts affect cities in all parts of the country. They have an especially serious impact in states—such as Massachusetts—where cities have depended heavily on the property tax, have few alternative resources to tax, and are prevented by state law from turning to new sources of revenues. Overall, as a result of increased state and federal aid as well as more recent taxpayer resistance, the importance of the property tax in municipal revenue has fallen dramatically, from 44.2 percent in 1962 to 24.7 percent in 1978.[49]

In some cities, opportunities for property taxation are further reduced by declines in the value of taxable property. In one study, of six cities that were losing population, five experienced a decrease in the real market value of all property between 1971 and 1976.[50] Large declines in the real value of nonresidential property occurred in Detroit and Milwaukee; in New York, Philadelphia, and Pittsburgh, these values declined slightly or remained stable. Values for single-family homes fared somewhat better, except in Detroit.

Two cities that show a different pattern are Washington, D.C., and Baltimore. Despite population losses, the value of single-family homes in the nation's capital, where "gentrification" has been strong, rose even more than in San Diego. Baltimore, which has become known nationally for strong city leadership in efforts to renew its neighborhoods and downtown, experienced modest increases in market values of both residential and nonresidential properties.

Many Sunbelt cities have been able, through annexation, to maintain their property tax bases as taxpayers move to the fringes. Older cities in the Northeast, by contrast, typically lack annexation opportunities. Hemmed in by other jurisdictions and state restrictions, these cities have watched helplessly as their taxpayers fled to the suburbs.

To cover gaps between revenue and expenditures, cities typically rely on borrowing. Although Sunbelt cities continue to borrow, reflecting their financial health and good credit ratings, cities with declining populations have been borrowing less. This does not reflect a stronger fiscal condition, but rather the difficulty they face in borrowing: low credit ratings and consequent increased interest rates and the competition of other tax-exempt investments.

State and Federal Reaction

As already noted, many cities have become increasingly dependent on aid from higher levels of governments, especially the federal government. The "most important development in the finances of the largest 45 cities in the past decade," says one expert, "has not been the rate of growth in expenditures, but rather the revolution in the way cities have been financing them."[51] Direct and indirect infusions of federal aid to municipalities increased steadily during the 1960s and most of the 1970s. In 1962, municipalities received 5 cents of federal aid for each dollar of locally raised revenue; by 1978, the figure had risen to 26 cents, although it dropped to 23 cents in 1980.[52]

Reliance on federal aid varies greatly among cities. One study found an average of $14 in federal aid per resident in cities under 50,000 population, compared to an average of $74 per resident in cities with over 250,000 people.[53]

In 1981, an estimated $39.5 billion in federal grants provided cash and in-kind benefits to individuals based on need.[54] Because cities have high concentrations of needy people, city residents received a high proportion of this aid. For example, the 30 percent of American households who live in central cities account for 54.7 percent of housing subsidy recipients, and 41.2 percent of those receiving Medicaid.[55]

In addition, federal grants fund a range of local government activities. Although much of this money flows first to states, an increasing proportion flows directly from the federal government to cities. These direct federal grants, which increased from $2.6 billion in 1970 to $21.1 billion in 1980, include revenue sharing and grants for activities in education, energy, transportation, and justice, as well as programs targeted to distressed places—CETA, Community Development Block Grants, Urban Development Action Grants, and antirecessionary public works grants.[56] The targeted programs have been especially important components in a number of central city budgets.

Unlike federal aid, state dollar aid to distressed cities has not significantly increased during the past decade. States have, however, helped cities by assuming large portions of education costs and, to a lesser extent, welfare costs. States have provided assistance to distressed cities in other forms: tax incentives, loan guarantees, and technical assistance for economic development and housing. The Advisory Commission on Intergovernmental Relations argues that the states' most important role is not as "banker" but in these other activities. Yet it comments that "only a small number of the 50 have made extensive use of the full range of powers and tools at their disposal [to help distressed communities]."[57]

Policy Options

Cities have faced fiscal problems for a long time. Today, with fiscal pressures on them intensifying, what are their choices?

Cut Expenditures. One option is to cut expenditures. This can be done by deferring capital spending, reducing employment or other costs of providing services, or reducing services.

With respect to capital spending, there may be limited opportunities for deferral, since cities have been exercising this option for years. Indeed, as neglect in repairing facilities results in costly or dangerous situations, expenditures may well have to be increased. The current budgets of some cities (and states) do reflect increases, not decreases, in this area.

Another direction is to reduce the number of municipal employees and reduce employee salaries. Opportunities for these kinds of cost reductions are suggested by high levels of municipal employment and per capita municipal spending in a number of distressed cities. Municipal employment in these cities has already begun to decline in recent years, according to some analyses. Contracting out services to private companies has reduced employment in some cities. Such "privatization" of services is increasing, and results are reportedly promising.

Yet there are serious impediments to cutting employment. Not the least of these is the political power of municipal employees and their unions, which are strong in some of the most distressed cities. Also, labor-saving equipment imposes capital costs that cities sometimes find hard to meet. Cutting employment also runs afoul of the view that governments should serve as the "employer of last resort."

Another way to cut costs is to cut services, but this, too, can prove exceedingly difficult. Service levels may be mandated by the federal government, states, or courts. In addition, proposals to cut services are likely to cause local protests and to require politically difficult choices—for example, between parks and cultural facilities, which improve the quality of life and can help to stimulate economic development, and special services such as compensatory education that can help integrate poor people into the mainstream of society. Debate over such issues promises to become acute if cutbacks in federal funds force cities to allocate increasing proportions of their budgets to alleviate the immediate distress of their residents.

Still other ways of cutting municipal costs are to charge residents for services or to turn over more governmental responsibilities to volunteer and neighborhood groups. User fees have been a growing source of nontax revenue for local governments. The many innovative examples of local volunteer action in recent years—from cleaning up local parks to preserving historic buildings to rehabilitating multifamily housing—are evidence that such efforts have value as well as appeal across the political spectrum.

Reliance on user fees or local self-help raises important questions, however. Will volunteer efforts be more effective in affluent neighborhoods than in poorer ones? Which self-help efforts are likely to remain effective after their novelty wears off? Should user fees be structured so that poorer residents can obtain services even if they are unable to pay the full cost of the service? In view of issues like these, both user fees and self-help efforts seem more likely to supplement than to replace publicly funded activities.

Raise revenues. Cities—at least some cities—may have ways to increase their revenues, despite eroded tax bases and overtaxed residents. One way is to try to increase the tax base. Another, of course, is to raise taxes.

Although cities' destinies are determined, to a remarkable extent, by factors beyond their control—what region they are located in, for example—many have been trying to improve the asset side of their ledgers by attracting luxury hotels, intown retail centers, and high-income housing, including condominiums. To do this, some cities have adopted tax abatement policies to attract private investment or have issued tax-exempt bonds to attract middle-class buyers to renovating neighborhoods. One problem is that these efforts cost money now, while many of the benefits are long-term, if indeed the payoff comes.

Another way to raise revenues is to raise taxes. The conventional wisdom is that this is politically impossible, because cities in need are often heavily taxed already; or suicidal, because it will cause more people and businesses to leave; or legally impossible, because of state-imposed limitations on cities' taxing powers. Citizen tax revolts have cast an additional pall on raising taxes, either at the city or state level.

Yet 15 out of 24 cities in one study raised local tax rates at least once between 1977 and 1980, and two more imposed new taxes.[58] Some cities are also imposing a range of user and miscellaneous charges. The Advisory Commission on Intergovernmental Relations foresees "real growth" in revenue from income and sales taxes in the 1980s, although it believes property taxes will continue to decline.[59]

Shift Expenditures to Other Governments. Another option is to shift expenditures from city governments to the states and to the federal government. As we have seen, this option has been vigorously pursued in recent years, but the movement today is to turn back more funding responsibility to cities themselves.

One broad argument for shifting expenditures to higher levels of government is that some expenses are not place-specific: they are necessary to help particular people wherever they are. The Advisory Commission on Intergovernmental Relations has long argued that the federal government should take over the costs of welfare, for example.

Another broad argument for shifting expenditures is that demands for public spending—particularly on behalf of dependent people—are sometimes concentrated in places with unhealthy tax bases. In some cases this argues for shifts to the state level. In others, it argues for federal responsibility, since some of the cities most in need are located in states that are themselves hard pressed financially (for example, Michigan).

A principal argument on the other side is that state and federal taxpayers feel unfairly burdened by the costs of increasing grants-in-aid to cities and city residents. Moreover, they argue, the difficult measures needed to reduce inefficiency in city government will be avoided so long as outside funds are available to pay for services.

Effective responses to the fiscal problems cities face will, of course, require a combination of actions. This is illustrated by the experience of New York City and Cleveland, both of which came close to bankruptcy during the 1970s. Both cities were able to orchestrate comprehensive solutions using an array of public and private measures affecting many interests. Services were cut back, workers were laid off, private businesses guaranteed loans or offered below-market terms, and so on. In Cleveland, corporations loaned personnel to government agencies to help improve snarled management procedures, and voters approved a tax increase by referendum. In both cities, the mayors were reelected overwhelmingly after the budgets were balanced, and—despite cuts in municipal services—private sector investment and city rebuilding have increased since the stringent measures were implemented.

Mayors of both cities have said, however, that their success stories could not be repeated if the cities faced an array of federal budget cuts, recession, high interest rates, and cutbacks of CETA workers. They have also indicated that their newly balanced budgets are teetering, and they have proposed new taxes and user fees.

CONCLUSION

The problems of contracting central cities have been for decades the nub of concerns about urban areas. Today, government responses being advanced—decentralization, defederalization, public-private partnerships, voluntarism, and self-help—sound quite different from the ones we have been accustomed to hearing. These ideas will have an important influence on the viability of the urban environment.

But government responses alone will not be decisive. Change is inevitable in the urban environment as it is in the natural environment. Demography changes, the economy changes, tastes change. Areas decline and prosper. Buildings need to be kept in repair, altered for new uses, marketed, or demolished and rebuilt.

While the future of aging urban areas must today be acknowledged as uncertain, the 1970s have provided unmistakable evidence of market revival in some parts of older central cities. The magnitude of this change, and its impact on city economies, may well hold the key to the continued adaptation of these cities.

FURTHER READING

The literature on decline in older cities is extensive. Two comprehensive studies based on data from Census statistical series are U.S. Department of Housing and Urban Development, *The 1980 President's Urban Policy Report* (Washington, D.C.: U.S. Government Printing Office, 1980), and Anthony Downs, Kenneth A. Small, and Katharine L. Bradbury, *Urban Decline and the Future of American Cities* (Washington, D.C.: The Brookings Institution, forthcoming).

A collection of articles on the research evidence and theoretical and policy issues posed by revitalization appears in Shirley Bradway Laska and Daphne Spain, *Back to the City: Issues in Neighborhood Renovation* (New York, N.Y.: Pergamon Press, 1980). Two recent studies focusing primarily on displacement are Richard Legates and Chester Hartman, "Displacement," *Clearinghouse Review*, 15(3):207-249 (1981), and George and Eunice S. Grier, "Displacement: Where Things Stand, A Report to the Ford Foundation" (Bethesda, Md.: Grier Partnership, 1981). Both include comprehensive bibliographies of the revitalization literature and attempt, from somewhat different perspectives, to define the nature of displacement, sort out conflicting evidence about its extent, and discuss the policy implications. In fulfillment of a congressional mandate to report on the extent of privately and publicly caused displacement, the Department of Housing and Urban Development, Office of Policy Development and Research, has prepared two documents: *Displacement Report* (Springfield, Va.: National Technical Information Service, February 1979), and *Residential Displacement: An Update* (Springfield, Va.: National Technical Information Service, October 1981). While the HUD reports review all the displacement research, they focus particularly on national evidence reported in the Annual Housing Survey and the implications for federal policy.

A Conservation Foundation publication addressing the question of the impact of revitalization on urban elderly residents is Phyllis Myers, *Aging in Place: A Sourcebook of Ideas to Help the Elderly Stay in Revitalizing Neighborhoods* (Washington, D.C.: The Conservation Foundation, forthcoming).

The issues posed in reconciling historic preservation and environmental impact reviews with economic development goals in federally aided projects is discussed in greater depth in Phyllis Myers, "UDAG and the Urban Environment," *Journal of the American Planning Association*, 48(1):99-109 (1982).

Case studies of models of private and public cooperation and a discussion of policy issues especially focused on increased responsibilities of state and local governments and the private (for-profit and nonprofit) sector in the face of a declining federal role appear in Committee for Economic Development, *Public-Private Partnerships: An Opportunity for Urban Communities* (Washington, D.C.: Committee for Economic Development, 1981).

Dr. Stuart M. Butler has written a seminal publication advocating the enterprise zone approach to job creation in declining urban areas: *Enterprise Zones: Pioneering in the Inner City* (Washington, D.C.: The Heritage Foundation, 1980).

Comprehensive analyses of the range of fiscal issues facing central cities, particularly the old industrial ones, appear in Robert W. Burchell and David Listokin, eds., *Cities Under Stress: The Fiscal Crises of Urban America* (New Brunswick, N.J.: Rutgers University, Center for Urban Policy Research, Rutgers University, 1981). A more detailed study of the most recent economic, social, and demographic data available on what the authors call the "intergovernmental city" (characterized by a high dependence on federal and state aid) appears in a report by Robert W. Burchell, James Carr, and Richard L. Florida, *Restructuring the Intergovernmental City* (New Brunswick, N.J.: Rutgers University, Center for Urban Policy Research, Rutgers University, forthcoming).

Congressional studies of the fiscal problems of central cities, emphasizing the impacts of Reagan Administration cutbacks, appear in U.S., Congress, Joint Economic Committee, *The Regional and Urban Impacts of the Administration's Budget and Tax Proposals*, Joint Committee Print, 97th Cong., 1st Sess., 1981; and *Emergency Interim Survey: Fiscal Conditions of 48 Large Cities*, Joint Committee Print, 97th Cong., 1st Sess., 1982.

In 1980 and 1981, the Advisory Commission on Intergovernmental Relations surveyed trends in state aid to distressed cities. For the most recent survey, see Advisory Commission on Intergovernmental Relations, *The States and Distressed Communities: A 1981 Report* (Washington, D.C.: U.S. Government Printing Office, 1982).

The October 1981 *Conservation Foundation Letter*, "Can We Afford to Maintain Our Physical Plant?" presents a concise overview of the growing concern about the condition of the urban infrastructure and prospects for addressing the needs.

These needs are discussed in greater depth in Pat Choate and Susan Walter, *America in Ruins: Beyond the Public Works Pork Barrel* (Washington, D.C.: The Council on State Planning Agencies, 1981), while a range of institutional and financing mechanisms to address the needs are analyzed in George E. Peterson and Mary J. Miller, "Financing Options for Urban Infrastructure" (Washington, D.C.: Urban Institute, August 1981).

TEXT REFERENCES

1. Philip M. Hauser, "The Census of 1980," *Scientific American* 245(5):53-57.

2. U.S. Department of Commerce, Bureau of Census, *Statistical Abstract of the United States: 1981* (Washington, D.C.: U.S. Government Printing Office, 1982), pp. 917-919.

3. U.S. Department of Commerce, Bureau of Census, *Census of Population: 1980*, Supplementary Reports PC80-S1-5 (Washington, D.C.: U.S. Government Printing Office, 1981), pp. 1-46.

4. U.S. Department of Commerce, Bureau of the Census, Press Release CB81-61 (Washington, D.C.: U.S. Department of Commerce, Bureau of the Census, 1981), p. 1.

5. Calculated from U.S. Department of Commerce, *Census of Population: 1980*, pp. 1-46.

6. *Ibid.*, pp. 1-46.

7. *Ibid.*, pp. 1-46.

8. *Ibid.*, p. 3.

9. Bryant Robey, ed., "1980 Guide to Metropolitan Areas," *American Demographics* 3(11):26; and U.S. Department of Commerce, Bureau of Census, *County and City Data Book: 1977* (Washington, D.C.: U.S. Government Printing Office, 1978), p. 675.

10. David L. Birch, "Who Creates Jobs?" *The Public Interest*, no. 65 (Fall 1981), pp. 6-7.

11. Franklin J. James, "Economic Distress in Central Cities," in Robert W. Burchell and David Listokin, eds., *Cities Under Stress: The Fiscal Crises of Urban America* (New Brunswick, N.J.: Rutgers University, The Center for Urban Policy Research, 1981), p. 30.

12. U.S. Department of Labor, Bureau of Labor Statistics, *Supplement to Employment and Earnings, States and Areas, Data from 1977-80*, Bulletin 1370-15 (Washington, D.C.: U.S. Government Printing Office, 1981), pp. 25, 236, 238.

13. Robert W. Burchell, et al., *Restructuring the Intergovernmental City*, draft, (New Brunswick, N.J.: Rutgers University, The Center for Urban Policy Research, forthcoming) Chapter III, Exhibit 2.

14. U.S. Department of Commerce, *Social and Economic Characteristics of the Metropolitan and Nonmetropolitan Population: 1977 and 1970*, pp. 64-65.

15. *Ibid.*, pp. 68-71.

16. U.S. Department of Housing and Urban Development, "The Urban Fiscal Crisis: Fact or Fantasy? (A Reply)," in Robert W. Burchell and David Listokin, *Cities Under Stress: The Fiscal Crises of Urban America* (New Brunswick, N.J.: Rutgers University, The Center for Urban Policy Research, 1981), pp. 154-155.

17. U.S. Department of Commerce, *Social and Economic Characteristics of the Metropolitan and Nonmetropolitan Population: 1977 and 1970*, pp. 104-105.

18. Robert W. Burchell, et al., *Restructuring the Intergovernmental City*, Chapter IV, Exhibit 2.

19. Phyllis Myers, *Aging in Place: A Sourcebook of Ideas to Help the Elderly Stay in Revitalizing Neighborhoods* (Washington, D.C.: The Conservation Foundation, forthcoming 1982).

20. Shirley Bradway Laska and Daphne Spain, ed., *Back to the City: Issues in Neighborhood Renovation* (New York: Pergamon Press, 1980), pp. 10-11.

21. For example, a multi-city study initiated by HUD, undertaken with carefully designed methodology, did not find similar patterns of speculation, owner investment, renovation, and price changes in revitalizing neighborhoods. See, Frank F. deGiovanni, *Private Market Revitalization: Its Characteristics and Consequences*, draft report (Research Triangle Park, N.C.: Research Triangle Institute, 1981).

22. U.S Department of Commerce, Bureau of Census, *City to Suburb Income Gap: Is It Being Narrowed by a Back-to-the-City Movement?* (Washington, D.C.: Bureau of Census,

March 1980), p. 5.

23. U.S. Department of Census, Bureau of Census, *1960 Census of Housing*, HC(1)-1 (Washington, D.C.: U.S. Government Printing Office, 1960), p. I-40; and U.S. Department of Commerce, Bureau of Census, *Annual Housing Survey, Part A, General Housing Characteristics*, H-150-80 (Washington, D.C.: U.S. Government Printing Office, 1980), p. 1.

24. "Slants and Trends," *U.S. Census Report*, January 13, 1981, p. 1.

25. "Immediately Available Office Space is Tight in Most Major Cities," *Land Use Digest*, May 15, 1981, p. 2.

26. 42 U.S.C., sec. 5318 (1981).

27. Letter from Christopher Green, Heritage State Parks Planning Coordinator, Massachusetts Department of Environmental Management, to Phyllis Myers, March 5, 1982.

28. *Cleveland Press*, November 19, 1981.

29. U.S. Department of Housing and Urban Development, Office of Policy Development and Research, *An Impact Evaluation of the UDAG Program* (Germantown, Md.: HUD User, Feb., 1982); and U.S. Department of the Interior, Heritage Conservation and Recreation Service, *Federal Tax Provisions to Encourage Rehabilitation of Historic Buildings: An Assessment of their Effect* (Washington, D.C.: U.S. Government Printing Office, 1979).

30. U.S. Department of Housing and Urban Development, Office of Policy Development and Research, *Residential Displacement: An Update* (Springfield, Va: National Technical Information Service, 1981), p. iii.

31. *Ibid.*, p. 66.

32. Richard T. Legates and Chester Hartman, "Displacement," *Clearinghouse Review* 15(3):210 (1981).

33. "Residential Hotel Conversion and Demolition Ordinance," Ordinance 330-81, City of San Francisco, approved June 26, 1981.

34. Phyllis Myers, ed., *Urban Conservation and Federally Funded Economic Development in Cities: Putting it Together*, Proceedings of a Symposium Cosponsored by The Conservation Foundation and the National Trust for Historic Preservation (Washington, D.C.: The Conservation Foundation, 1980), pp. II-1-34.

35. National Historic Preservation Act of 1966, 16 U.S.C., sec. 470 *et. seq.* (1980).

36. National Environmental Policy Act of 1978, 42 U.S.C., sec. 4321 *et. seq.* (1980).

37. 46 Fed. Reg. 42426 (1981).

38. Historic Landmark and Historic Preservation Act of 1978, D.C. Code 5-1001 *et. seq.* (1981); and Landmarks Preservation Law of 1965, N.Y.C. Administrative Code, Ch. 8-A, 205-1.0 *et. seq.* (1976).

39. U.S. Department of Housing and Urban Development, *An Impact Evaluation of the UDAG Program*.

40. U.S. Department of the Interior, *Federal Tax Provisions to Encourage Rehabilitation of Historic Buildings: An Assessment of their Effect*, pp. 45-57.

41. Economic Recovery Tax Act of 1981, P.L. 97-34, Title II, Subtitle B, sec. 212.

42. U.S., Congress, Joint Economic Committee, *The Regional and Urban Impacts of the Administration's Budget and Tax Proposals*, Committee Print, 97th Cong., 1st Sess., 1981, p. 20.

43. Thomas Muller, "Changing Expenditures and Service Demand Patterns of Stressed Cities," in Robert W. Burchell and David Listokin, eds., *Cities Under Stress: The Fiscal Crises of Urban America*, p. 292.

44. George E. Peterson, "Transmitting the Municipal Fiscal Squeeze to a New Generation of Taxpayers: Pension Obligations and Capital Investment Needs," in Burchell and Listokin, *Cities Under Stress: The Fiscal Crises of Urban America*, p. 251.

45. Harold Wolman and Barbara Davis, *Local Government Strategies to Cope with Fiscal Pressure* (Washington, D.C.: Urban Institute, 1980), p. 19.

46. Thomas Muller, "Changing Expenditures and Service Demand Patterns of Stressed

Cities," in Robert W. Burchell and David Listokin, *Cities Under Stress*, pp. 288-89.

47. Pat Choate and Susan Walter, *America in Ruins: Beyond the Public Works Pork Barrel* (Washington, D.C.: The Council of State Planning Agencies, 1981), p. 2.

48. Advisory Commission on Intergovernmental Relations, *Significant Features of Fiscal Federalism: 1979-80* (Washington, D.C.: U.S. Government Printing Office, 1980), p. 82.

49. Advisory Commission on Intergovernmental Relations, *Significant Features of Fiscal Federalism: 1979-80* (Washington, D.C.: U.S. Government Printing Office, 1980), p. 83.

50. Dick Netzer, "The Property Tax in the New Environment," Burchell and Listokin, eds., in *Cities Under Stress: The Fiscal Crises of Urban America*, p. 466-469.

51. John E. Petersen, in "Transmitting the Municipal Fiscal Squeeze to a New Generation of Taxpayers: Pension Obligations and Capital Investment Needs," pp. 234-5.

52. Advisory Commission on Intergovernmental Relations, *Significant Features of Fiscal Federalism: 1980-81* (Washington, D.C.: U.S. Government Printing Office, 1981), p. 62.

53. U.S., Congress, Joint Economic Committee, *The Regional and Urban Impacts of the Administration's Budget and Tax Proposals*, p. 8.

54. Information provided by Dr. John Palmer, Senior Fellow of the Urban Institute, May, 1982.

55. U.S. Congress, *The Regional and Urban Impacts of the Adminsitration's Budget and Tax Proposals*, p. 7.

56. Advisory Commission on Intergovernmental Relations, *Significant Features of Fiscal Federalism: 1980-81*, p. 59.

57. Advisory Commission on Intergovernmental Relations, *The States and Distressed Communities: 1981 Report* (Washington, D.C.: Advisory Commission on Intergovernmental Relations, 1982), p. 113.

58. Harold Wolman and George E. Peterson, "State and Local Strategies for Responding to Fiscal Presssure, *55 Tulane Law Review* 813 (1981).

59. Advisory Commission on Intergovernmental Relations, *Significant Features of Fiscal Federalism; 1979-80*, p. 83.

FIGURE REFERENCES

Figure 8.1

U.S. Department of Commerce, Bureau of the Census, *1980 Census of Population, Supplementary Reports*, PC 80-51-5 (Washington, D.C.: Bureau of the Census, October 1981), p. 1.

Figure 8.2

U.S. Department of Commerce, Bureau of the Census, *1980 Census of Population, Supplementary Reports,* PC 80-51-5 (Washington, D.C.: Bureau of the Census, October 1981), p. 55, 56.

Figure 8.3

U.S. Department of Commerce, Bureau of the Census, *1980 Census of Population, Supplementary Reports,* PC 80-51-5 (Washington, D.C.: Bureau of the Census, October 1981), p. 1.

Figure 8.4

"The 1980 Guide to Metropolitan Areas," *American Demographics*, 3(11):25-30 (1981).

Figure 8.5

Council on Environmental Quality, *Environmental Trends* (Washington, D.C.: U.S. Government Printing Office, 1981), p. 48.

Figure 8.6

U.S. Department of Commerce, Bureau of the Census, *CPR, P-23*, No. 75 (Washington, D.C.: Bureau of the Census, November 1978), pp. 88, 89.

Figure 8.7

U.S. Department of Commerce, Bureau of the Census, *CPR, P-23*, No. 75 (Washington, D.C.: Bureau of the Census, November 1978), p. 104, 105.

Figure 8.8

U.S. Department of Commerce, Bureau of the Census, *CPR, P-23*, No. 75 (Washington, D.C.: Bureau of the Census, November 1978), Table 20, pp. 116, 117.

Figure 8.9

James M. Howell and Charles F. Stamm, *Urban Fiscal Stress: A Comparative Analysis of 66 U.S. Cities* (Lexington, Mass.: Lexington Books, 1979), Table 1.4, p. 11.

Figure 8.10

Thomas Muller, "Changing Expenditures and Service Demand Patterns of Stressed Cities," in *Cities Under Stress, the Fiscal Crisis of Urban America*, Robert W. Burchell and David Listoken, eds. (New Brunswick, N.J.: Rutgers University, Center for Urban Policy Research, 1981), p. 291.

Chapter 9

The Reagan Administration and Institutional Change

During the 1970s, considerable responsibility for protecting environmental quality gravitated to the federal government. Strong public demand, limited state regulatory capability, the national scope of many environmental problems, industry's desire for national uniformity in environmental regulation, and other factors prompted a substantial enlargement of the federal purview. Congress enacted numerous environmental, health, and safety laws; new executive agencies were created to implement the laws; and the agencies elaborated detailed regulations, specifying how states, local governments, and the private sector should comply.

Many of the new laws were enacted amidst uncertainty surrounding scientific information on pollutants and their effects. In the face of incomplete information, the statutes encouraged regulatory action rather than delay. Moreover, in the setting of standards, greater weight was assigned to protecting health than to protecting the economic well-being of industries that dispersed pollutants threatening public health. The new laws and regulations also provided for extensive public participation in developing and implementing programs and regulations, to prevent administrative foot dragging and to preclude dominance of regulatory agencies by the regulated. The statutes authorized and funded considerable research designed to enhance understanding of ecological systems, pollution, and techniques for pollution control. Because much of the responsibility for implementing federal environmental laws would be borne by the states, substantial grant programs were developed to support state environmental agencies.

Since the federal government itself had often caused environmental problems, the National Environmental Policy Act of 1969 (NEPA) was enacted to increase agencies' attention to the environmental consequences of their actions. NEPA took effect January 1, 1970. It encouraged impact assessment, interagency review, and public

385

scrutiny, all designed to identify, anticipate, and minimize environmental problems.

Among the new institutions created to formulate and implement environmental policy, NEPA established the Council on Environmental Quality in the Executive Office of the President. Pollution control programs, which had been scattered among several different departments, were brought together under the Environmental Protection Agency. The Consumer Product Safety Commission and the National Institute of Occupational Safety and Health were formed to strengthen protection of consumers and workers. The Heritage Conservation and Recreation Service was created (building upon the former Bureau of Outdoor Recreation) to implement a national heritage program designed to identify and protect significant cultural and natural resources. All major federal agencies created offices to examine the environmental impacts of agency actions.

New statutes were also enacted to improve planning for protection and use of federally owned lands. The Forest and Rangeland Renewable Resources Planning Act of 1974, the National Forest Management Act of 1976, and the Federal Land Policy and Management Act of 1976, all promoted more systematic and comprehensive planning by the Forest Service and the Bureau of Land Management.

Following the oil embargo in 1973, increased attention began to be paid to the economic and energy impacts of environmental programs. More and more concern was also shown for the proliferation of federal regulations, the lack of coordination among programs, and growing paper-work burdens. The changing priorities prompted a number of reorganizations and policy initiatives in the Nixon and Ford Administrations — for example, creation of the Federal Energy Administration and review of inflation impact statements by the President's Council on Wage and Price Stability. The Carter Administration's concern about these problems was reflected in creation of the Department of Energy, to overcome fragmented responsibility for energy policy; creation of the Regulatory Analysis Review Group, to examine the economic impact of proposed regulations; creation of the U.S. Regulatory Council, to improve coordination of federal regulatory activities; a proposal for an Energy Mobilization Board, to reduce delays in the permitting of proposed energy projects; and promulgation of new rules for implementing NEPA, to reduce delay, duplication, and paper work.

Ronald Reagan campaigned for the presidency on a platform that stressed reduction of the federal government's involvement in American life. Candidate Reagan supported less federal regulation; reduced federal spending and taxation; a return of responsibility to state and local government; greater reliance on the marketplace to solve social problems; greater attentiveness to the costs of environmental, health, and safety regulation; and accelerated resource development on federal lands.

This chapter assesses some of the Reagan Administration's attempts to implement these principles, beginning with a review of budget decisions involving energy, public lands, regulatory agencies, research, and related matters. The Administration's "regulatory relief" efforts are also examined, as are its efforts to reorganize the federal government and to enhance the Office of Management and Budget's (OMB's) authority to constrict the flow of new regulations. Since the federal system is one of checks and balances, congressional and judicial reactions are briefly noted.

The chapter also explores the capabilities of state and local governments to adopt the responsibilities being relinquished by the federal government. The concluding section discusses public opinion on the balance that ought to be struck among environmental, economic, and energy concerns.

THE FEDERAL BUDGET

For much of 1981, the Reagan Administration focused its attention almost exclusively on national economic problems, especially on reducing federal nondefense spending and federal taxes. The economic criteria used by the Administration in cutting the federal budget included: applying rigorous standards to economic subsidy programs that have "made our economic problems worse by interfering with the workings of the marketplace"; stretching out public sector capital investment programs; and recovering allocable costs by means of user fees.[1]

The budget-cutting process for fiscal year 1982 proceeded through several complex stages.* The President and Congress haggled over proposed cuts; the federal government shut down partially when the President vetoed a congressional spending bill that he regarded as too extravagant; and the Office of Management and Budget used its administrative authority to implement reductions sought by the President but not yet enacted by Congress. Many individual ap-

---

*The federal fiscal year begins on October 1 and ends on September 30 of the following year. Fiscal year 1982 began on October 1, 1981.

propriations bills had not been passed by Congress as the year ended, and presidential vetoes of some pending bills were threatened. In February 1982, the President presented Congress with his proposed budget for fiscal year 1983, a proposal that continued the domestic budget-cutting priorities of fiscal year 1982.

Figure 9.1
Federal Agency Employment, 1981 and 1983
(number of positions)

Agency	FY1981 actual	FY1983 estimated	Percent change 1981-1983
Office of Surface Mining, DOI	1,036	638	−38.4%
Consumer Product Safety Commission	789	556	−29.5
EPA (excluding Superfund)	10,498	8,129	−22.6
Federal Trade Commission	1,587	1,235	−22.2
Occupational Safety and Health Administration, DOL	3,009	2,354	−21.8
Mine Safety and Health Administration, DOL	3,808	2,996	−21.3
National Highway Traffic Safety Administration, DOT	755	645	−14.6
Bureau of Indian Affairs, DOI	13,152	11,410	−13.2
National Oceanic and Atmospheric Administration, DOC	13,563	11,794	−13.0
Federal Highway Administration, DOT	4,020	3,500	−12.9
Urban Mass Transportation Administration, DOT	575	509	−11.5
Corps of Engineers — Civil Works, DOD	27,445	24,689	−10.0
Coast Guard, DOT	6,321	5,773	−8.7
National Park Service, DOI	9,945	9,291	−6.6
Fish and Wildlife Service, DOI	4,914	4,600	−6.4
Bureau of Mines, DOI	2,699	2,559	−5.2
Geological Survey, DOI	9,517	9,070	−4.7
Bureau of Reclamation, DOI	7,351	7,371	+0.3
Forest Service, USDA	29,818	29,975	+0.5
Nuclear Regulatory Commission	3,277	3,303	+0.8
Bureau of Land Management, DOI	6,041	6,096	+0.9
EPA — Superfund	270	516	+91.1

Employment figures include permanent positions only.
Source: Executive Office of the President, Office of Management and Budget

Concern about the size of the federal nondefense budget was a motivating factor behind many of the Administration's proposed cuts, but President Reagan noted that he was not cutting the budget simply for the sake of sounder financial management: "Those of us who call ourselves conservative have pointed out what's wrong with government policy for more than a quarter of a century. Now we have an opportunity . . . to change our national directions."[2] Secretary of the Interior James Watt, echoing the President, stated, "We will use the budget system to be the excuse to make major policy decisions."[3]

One of those decisions has been to propose substantial personnel cuts throughout the government in agencies responsible for implementing environmental, natural resource, consumer protection, and worker health and safety programs (figure 9.1).

Environmental Protection Agency

The Environmental Protection Agency's (EPA's) budget for fiscal year 1982 initially was cut 12 percent from its 1981 level, and another 12 percent cut was proposed in late 1981.[4] Even deeper cuts discussed for fiscal year 1983 raised widespread concern whether EPA will be able to fulfill its statutory obligations, particularly with respect to recently created programs for control of hazardous wastes and toxic substances.[5]

EPA Administrator Anne Gorsuch defended the proposed cuts, arguing that the agency can do its job much more efficiently than it has in the past. However, the magnitude of the fiscal year 1982 cuts, and those proposed for fiscal year 1983, indicates either that there was an inordinate amount of inefficiency at EPA in the past or that the agency will have great difficulty carrying out its statutory mandates in the future.

The fiscal year 1983 Administration proposals to Congress are based largely on EPA's suggestions, EPA having successfully resisted even deeper cuts proposed by OMB.[6] The 1983 proposals, and EPA's actual budget for fiscal year 1981, are shown in figure 9.2. The reductions in proposed spending for nearly all programs are quite dramatic.[7]

Air programs would be cut by nearly 20 percent. This cut is spread relatively evenly across major program components. "Abatement, control and compliance," which is the component responsible for developing regulations and overseeing the general implementation of the statute, would be reduced 20 percent. Enforcement

Figure 9.2
EPA Expenditures by Program, 1981 and 1983
(million dollars)

Program	FY1981 actual	FY1983 request	Percent change 1981-1983
Air	$ 235.4	$ 188.6	−19.9%
Water quality	318.2	192.3	−39.6
Drinking water	79.3	71.8	−9.4
Hazardous waste	141.4	106.4	−24.8
Pesticides	64.8	52.3	−19.4
Radiation	14.2	10.6	−25.4
Noise	12.2	0.0[1]	−99.7
Interdisciplinary	13.9	20.9	+50.4
Toxic substances	94.1	73.2	−22.2
Energy	84.6	42.5	−49.8
Other[2]	233.2	260.3	+11.6
Total expenditures	$1,291.3	$1,018.8	−21.1%
Budget authority[3]	1,347.0	958.4	−28.8

[1]FY1983 Noise budget: $40,000.
[2]"Other" includes management and support and reimbursable obligations.
[3]"Budget authority" differs from "Total" because of unobligated balances and transfers.
Source: Executive Office of the President, Office of Management and Budget

would be reduced 30 percent and research and development 15 percent. Some of these reductions reflect a proposed shifting of responsibilities to state authorities, although financial assistance to states is also being cut. The enforcement reduction also reflects a shift of some enforcement responsibilities to other parts of EPA. Development of national emission standards for hazardous pollutants under the Clean Air Act would be slowed; and inspections of stationary sources of air pollution would drop dramatically.[8]

The resources devoted to water quality protection would be cut almost 40 percent. The biggest cut in both absolute and percentage terms is in "abatement, control, and compliance," where proposed 1983 expenditures are only 57 percent of actual 1981 expenditures. Much of this cut would be in grants made to the states to help them implement water quality improvement efforts. Other reductions reflect a lower rate of funding for municipal sewage treatment plants (which are not included in figure 9.2) and the Administration's proposal to transfer substantial management responsibility to the states (in spite of reducing the funds available for carrying out these responsibilities). The proposed budget reductions may also reflect a reduced emphasis on implementing the provisions of the Clean Water Act dealing with control of toxic substances (see chapter 3).

Water quality research would be reduced substantially, because the Administration believes that most of the necessary research in this area will have been completed by fiscal year 1983. Water quality enforcement would be reduced 22 percent. It is not clear whether this reduction will allow the timely reissuance of permits required under the Clean Water Act, particularly if these are to include limitations on toxic discharges.

The reduction in the hazardous waste program, though less than in some other programs, is noteworthy because this program is still in the process of being formulated (see chapter 4). Given the substantial public concern with the problem of hazardous waste, and the complicated requirements of the Resource Conservation and Recovery Act (RCRA), this program might have been expected to grow significantly rather than shrink. In a comparison of 1981 and 1983, most of the reduction occurs in "abatement, control, and compliance," although the proposed 1983 level for these activities is only slightly less than the 1982 budget level. Again, financial assistance to states is an area in which substantial cuts have been proposed, even though the Administration expects the states to take over primary responsibility for implementing RCRA. Enforcement efforts would receive the largest percentage cut—83 percent. This reflects an assumption that the states will have primary enforcement authority and that some enforcement responsibilities will be transferred to other parts of EPA.

Among other agency programs, the most notable changes are the elimination of the noise control program, a substantial decrease in the radiation program (in spite of the renewed Administration emphasis on nuclear energy and the general growing concern about the government's inability to find an acceptable disposal method for nuclear wastes), and a general reduction in programs devoted to controlling toxic substances. The proposed reduction in the pesticides program would reduce the rate at which EPA reviews the hazards associated with pesticides that are currently in use. The reduction in the toxic substances program would similarly reduce the amount of activity devoted to reviewing and controlling existing chemicals that may be hazardous.

The sole increases between 1981 and 1983, in the "inter-disciplinary" and "other" categories, reflect reorganizations that concentrate enforcement in the new EPA Office of Legal and Enforcement Counsel. EPA's defense of its reduced spending contains numerous references to streamlining and efficiency, increased voluntary compliance, increased responsibility for state and local governments, improved priority-setting by states, elimination of low-priority efforts, slowing of synthetic fuels development, and completion of long-term projects. It remains to be seen whether the EPA budget represents cost-effective use of federal resources or an abdication of responsibility that will adversely affect human health and welfare.[9]

Energy

The Administration's budget recommendations, and the extent to which it fought to have them adopted by Congress, reflected a mix of economic principles, energy development desires, and political motivations. For example, even though major cutbacks were made in most energy programs, the Administration recommended funding for the Clinch River breeder reactor. The Carter Administration had tried several times to terminate this project, but Congress had insisted on funding it. The Reagan Administration's support for the breeder was a product both of its preference for nuclear power in domestic energy supplies and of the support for the project shown by Republican Senate Majority Leader Howard Baker. The Clinch River breeder reactor represents 25 percent of the nondefense budget for nuclear fission programs in 1983. (Figure 9.3 shows the distribution of funds within the various nuclear fission programs.) Conventional reactors, in contrast, represent only 3 percent of the fission budget, a decrease of 10 percent from 1981; the absolute decrease in spending for conventional reactors is $71 million. Yet the independent Energy Research Advisory Board recommended to the secretary of energy that funding for the Clinch River breeder reactor be delayed or terminated and that research funds for con-

Figure 9.3
Nuclear Fission Budgets, 1981 and 1983
(million dollars)

Program	FY1981 actual	FY1983 request	Percent change 1981-1983
Clinch River breeder reactor	$172	$ 253	+47.1%
Other breeder reactors	464	324	−30.2
Conventional reactors	103	32	−68.9
Other programs	247	407	+64.8
Total nuclear fission	$986	$1016	+ 3.0%

The data for this budget table are from the House Appropriations Committee, and differ slightly from those in OMB's budget appendix for 1983.

Source: U.S. Congress Environmental and Energy Study Conference

ventional reactors be increased.[10] The *Wall Street Journal*, in an editorial criticizing the breeder, quoted OMB Director David Stockman's 1977 comment that federal support for the breeder "is totally incompatible with our free market approach to energy policy."[11]

On the other hand, consistent with his free market philosophy, President Reagan was less supportive than was President Carter of the federal government's synthetic fuels program. This dismayed congressional supporters of the program, such as Democratic House Majority Leader Jim Wright. However, over the objections of OMB Director David Stockman, President Reagan agreed with the recommendation of Secretary of Energy James Edwards, Senate Budget Committee Chairman Pete Domenici, Senate Majority Leader Baker, and Senate Minority Leader Robert Byrd and approved federal price supports and loan guarantees for three major synthetic fuels projects.[12] Over $2 billion in loan guarantees was provided to the Great Plains coal gasification project in North Dakota; over $1.1 billion in loan guarantees was provided to a Tosco oil shale project in Colorado; and a commitment was made to purchase jet fuel at a fixed price from a Union Oil Company oil shale project. The oil shale contract could cost the federal government millions of dollars more than purchases of jet fuel in the free market.

The restructuring of the federal budget clearly indicated the Administration's energy priorities. Figure 9.4 illustrates the shifts, both in actual dollars and in percentages of the Department of Energy (DOE) budget, between actual 1981 expenditures and the 1983 budget request.* The strong shift toward defense activities and away from energy efficiency and renewable energy is evident. More specifically:

- Demonstration programs were curtailed or eliminated, with the exception of the Clinch River breeder reactor.
- Information programs were curtailed or eliminated.
- Research, development, and demonstration programs for energy conservation and for fossil fuel research both took large budget cuts.
- Programs in support of nuclear energy were the only nondefense sector of the Department of Energy's budget that increased rather than decreased.

---

*The Administration's fiscal year 1983 budget request, anticipating dissolution of the Department of Energy, programmed most funds for energy into the Department of Commerce. The discussion here assumes this reorganization will not occur.

Figure 9.4

Department of Energy: Selected Program Budgets, 1981 and 1983
(million dollars)

Program	FY1981		FY1983		
	Actual	Percent of total energy budget	Request	Percent of total energy budget	Percent change 1981-1983
Atomic energy defense activities	$ 3,668	29%	$ 5,506	47%	+50.1%
Solar and conservation	1,212	10	94	1	−92.2
(solar)	(500)	(4)	(72)	(<1)	(−85.6)
(conservation)	(712)	(6)	(22)	(<1)	(−96.9)
Nuclear	1,362	11	1,460	13	+7.2
(fusion)	(376)	(3)	(444)	(4)	(+18.1)
(fission)	(986)	(8)	(1,016)	(9)	(+3.0)
Strategic Petroleum Reserve	2,791	22	2,316	20	−17.0
All other programs	3,655	29	2,456	21	−32.8
Total	$12,688	100%[1]	$11,832	100%[1]	−6.7%

The data for this budget table are from the House Appropriations Committee, and differ slightly from those in OMB's budget appendix for 1983.

[1] Figures do not add to total because of rounding.

Source: U.S. Congress Environmental and Energy Study Conference

- Solar energy research and development programs were cut or eliminated; support for the Solar Energy Research Institute, the national laboratory dedicated to solar research, was curtailed.
- Support for state and local programs dealing with supply and efficiency improvements was severely curtailed.
- Energy activities related to defense are up sharply, representing 47 percent of DOE's 1983 budget. (See "atomic energy defense activities" in figure 9.4.) Only 1 percent of the money is proposed to be used for safeguards and security of nuclear materials and an additional 1 percent for developing verification technologies. On the other hand, 58 percent is for developing, producing, and maintaining nuclear weapons, 18 percent for producing weapons-grade nuclear materials, 7 percent for developing naval nuclear propulsion, and 7 percent for storage and disposal of military nuclear waste materials.[13]*

---

*Because of undelivered orders, these percentages only add up to 92 percent.

Strong philosophical disagreements exist between the Administration and Congress. Congress systematically increased the amounts appropriated in 1982 above the 1982 request; the 1983 budget requests virtually kill the conservation and solar programs (figure 9.5), but whether Congress will follow this set of priorities is highly uncertain.

The Administration's approach to energy is also reflected in its budget for activities not under the control of the Department of Energy. Two of the more important areas are energy leasing (discussed in the following section under "Energy and Minerals De-

Figure 9.5
Energy Conservation and Solar Energy Program Budgets
of the Department of Energy, 1981 and 1983
(million dollars)

Program	FY1981 actual	FY1983 request	Percent change 1981-1983
Energy Conservation			
Buildings and community systems	$ 64	$ 0	−100.0%
Industrial programs	43	0	−100.0
Transportation	93	0	−100.0
State and local programs	405	4	−99.0
Low income weatherization	175	0	−100.0
Schools and hospitals	150	0	−100.0
Energy Extension Service	20	0	−100.0
State energy conservation programs	48	4	−91.7
Emergency conservation	2	0	−100.0
Multi-sector programs	27	18	−33.3
Deferred to FY1982	67	na	na
Total, energy conservation	$712	$22	−96.9%
Solar Energy			
Active solar	$ 41	$ 0	−100.0%
Passive solar	32	0	−100.0
Photovoltaics	139	27	−80.6
Wind energy	60	5	−91.7
Ocean energy	35	0	−100.0
Industrial solar	169	25	−85.2
Other solar	24	12	−50.0
Total, solar energy	$500	$72	−85.6%

na = not applicable
Source: U.S. Congress Environmental and Energy Study Conference

velopment") and strip-mining control (discussed in the "Other Programs" section).

Natural Resources

President Reagan's fiscal year 1983 budget proposals reflect the Administration's emphasis on development of natural resources and deemphasis of resource planning and environmental protection. For example, funds for the expansion of timber production and the acceleration of energy leasing have received top priority and are slated for major increases above fiscal year 1981 levels. These proposed increases have been accompanied by planned sharp reductions in water and soil conservation, wildlife and coastal zone protection, and land acquisition for parks.

Water Resources. Heated battles have been fought in recent years over federal spending on water resources development projects. President Carter jousted with Congress over a lengthy "hit list" of projects that he and his advisers regarded as economically and environmentally unsound. He also sought to impose fees on users of navigable waterways and tried to increase the states' share of water project costs. His efforts were politically damaging and only marginally successful.

The Reagan Administration has also sought to raise fees for users of navigation projects, to increase the states' share of water project costs, and to raise prices for water purchased from federal projects.[14] The Administration has, in addition, slashed the budget of the Soil Conservation Service's small watershed program (see "watershed and flood prevention operations" in figure 9.6), which environmentalists complain "has dammed and channelized hundreds of small streams, with little effect on floods and less regard for soil erosion and other environmental damage."[15]

On the other hand, reflecting its professed support for water projects, the Administration hopes to begin construction on new projects that satisfy its criteria for nonfederal financing and cost-sharing. Moreover, it has increased the Bureau of Reclamation's construction funding by 15.7 percent, and the bureau's operation and maintenance budget by 32.5 percent.[16] The Administration cut the Corps of Engineers' budget a substantial 24.1 percent between 1981 and 1983, but much of this reduction was from delaying construction of recreational facilities and other less important features of Corps projects, and from the normal winding down of several large projects.[17]

Figure 9.6
Water Resources: Selected Program Budgets, 1981 and 1983
(million dollars)

Program	FY1981 actual	FY1983 request	Percent change 1981-1983
Watershed and flood prevention operations, USDA	$ 192.5	$ 117.7	−38.9%
Construction, Bureau of Reclamation, DOI	576.1	666.6	+ 15.7
Operation and maintenance, Bureau of Reclamation, DOI	106.3	140.8	+ 32.5
General construction, Army Corps of Engineers, DOD	1,593.9	1,209.3	−24.1
General operation and maintenance, Army Corps of Engineers, DOD	967.9	1,011.0	+ 4.5
Water Resources Council	19.8	0.0	−100.0

Source: Executive Office of the President, Office of Management and Budget

There is some irony in the gentle budgetary treatment of water projects, because these projects have the longest history of being subject to cost-benefit analysis, and have long been criticized as poor investments by the General Accounting Office (GAO).[18]* Congress has often chosen to ignore critical GAO appraisals of the Corps of Engineers' and Bureau of Reclamation's calculations. This symbiotic relationship between Congress and the water project agencies has produced politically valuable water projects that in some cases are environmentally destructive and have little economic justification.

One of the most heavily criticized projects has been the Tennessee-Tombigbee Waterway, supported by many southern politicians, including Senate Majority Leader Baker.[19] The Administration did not recommend termination of this project, although fiscal year 1982 funding of $189 million was only narrowly approved by the House of Representatives. The *Wall Street Journal*, at the same time it criticized the breeder reactor, noted that the plan for the Tennessee-Tombigbee Waterway is "economic nonsense"; the *Journal*

*The GAO has issued numerous reports on the mathematical errors, erroneous assumptions, inconsistent methods, and other miscalculations made by the Corps and by the Bureau of Reclamation. Critics have argued that the Corps has inflated benefits, understated costs, undervalued environmental amenities, and otherwise manipulated quantitative analytical techniques.

observed that the Corps "will move more dirt than was required to construct the Panama Canal in order to provide a parallel waterway to the wider Mississippi River."[20]

The Administration has proposed elimination of the Water Resources Council, which formulated environmentally sensitive principles and standards for water resource development projects during the Carter Administration.[21] These principles contained strong language intended to assure that the environmental consequences of water projects were examined. In addition, the Administration is curtailing the Fish and Wildlife Service's involvement in reviews of other agencies' water development projects.[22]

In sum, despite some commendable reform efforts, the Administration appears to have foregone significant money-saving opportunities.

Forestry. The 1983 proposed budget for the Forest Service reflects the Administration's budgetary preference for resource development. Commercial resource extraction has become the dominant use of the National Forest System. According to Administration budget documents, "priority was placed on programs which could help improve the Nation's economic condition while maintaining a minimum level of protection for the Nation's natural resource base."[23]

In the proposed 1983 budget, minerals area management, which evaluates energy leasing and minerals development proposals in the national forests, increases 64.5 percent over 1981 levels (figure 9.7). Because timber sales are a major source of revenue from national forests, the 1983 Reagan budget calls for a 21.1 percent increase in the timber sales administration and management program. To

Figure 9.7
Forest Service: Selected Program Budgets, 1981 and 1983
(million dollars)

Program	FY1981 actual	FY1983 request	Percent change 1981-1983
Minerals area management	$ 15.2	$ 25.0	+64.5%
Timber sales administration and management	155.5	188.3	+21.1
Construction (Roads)	247.7 (224.8)	297.5 (271.6)	+20.1 (+20.8)
Soil and water management	30.6	23.9	−21.9
Forest research	127.8	98.0	−23.3

Source: U.S. Department of Agriculture, Forest Service

facilitate timber harvesting, the budget allocation for road construction increases by over 20 percent. Administration budget documents acknowledge that timber "is the driving force behind the major portion of the roads program."[24]

The Reagan Administration's proposed timber sales policy has been sharply attacked because an enormous backlog of sold but unharvested timber already exists. In addition, the Forest Service has noted that road construction in more difficult terrain will be necessary to meet timber harvesting goals.[25] Road construction is a major cause of soil erosion, and the risks of erosion undoubtedly increase in rough terrain.

Management activities for hunting, fishing, and recreation are to be reduced.[26] The Forest Service's soil and water management program is to be curtailed by 21.9 percent in fiscal year 1983. Moreover, the budget allocation for forest research is due to decline by nearly 25 percent. Within the research category, resource development programs have top funding priority: timber management and genetics, and forest products and engineering, will be cut slightly or not at all. However, resource protection research programs, including those dealing with habitat requirements for threatened and endangered species, consequences of forest and rangeland management practices on water quality and yield, and surface environment and mining will all be cut back significantly.[27]

Fish and Wildlife. The 1983 Reagan budget for the Fish and Wildlife Service (FWS) further reflects the Administration's lack of interest in resource protection. FWS's role in energy development decisions is being severely downgraded. The service's involvement in the oil shale, geothermal, and tar sands leasing programs has been scratched from the proposed 1983 budget.[28] Previously, the Fish and Wildlife Service had analyzed the environmental effects of energy development with the purpose of minimizing loss of habitat and wildlife and the degradation of soil and water quality. The environmental contaminant evaluation program, which examines both agricultural and industrial chemicals, is also due to be cut, and resource impact assessments of contaminants from mining and smelting will be discontinued.[29]

Instead of expanding the National Wildlife Refuge System, the Administration has decided to focus its efforts on the operation and maintenance of existing refuges and on visitor-related services. The only major Fish and Wildlife Service program expected to receive a funding increase in fiscal year 1983, above 1981 budget levels, is wildlife resources (9.3 percent), which manages existing wildlife refuges[30] (figure 9.8). At the same time, however, research programs on wildlife resources would be curtailed. For example, research on refuges and on the impact of disease on wildlife resources would be decreased, and support to states for research on migratory and upland game birds would be discontinued.

Although the proposed 1983 budget for the Fish and Wildlife Service ($416.1 million) declines only 3 percent below 1981 levels ($427.6 million), a significant reallocation of funds would occur. Reductions in conservation programs are most evident. Funds would be slashed for habitat preservation (29.0 percent), endangered species (26.0 percent), and fishery resources (8.9 percent).

The Administration proposes to eliminate the $4.4 million co-operative research program at state universities.[31] In addition, monitoring activities would be sharply reduced and categorical grants for state programs to conserve endangered species habitat would be terminated. Fisheries management might suffer: anadromous fish matching grants to states, which are used for restoration of the Atlantic salmon, would receive no funds in 1983; 31 federal hatcheries would either be turned over to states or be closed.[32]

Parks. President Reagan's 1983 budget proposals for the National Park Service reflect the Administration's interest in the rehabilitation and maintenance of facilities in existing parks, rather than the acquisition of new parkland. To improve visitor-related services, the Administration requests a 13.6 percent increase for the operation of the National Park System, including a 16.9 percent increase for the park management program. In addition, the construction budget skyrockets 185.0 percent over 1981 levels[33] (figure 9.9). It is widely acknowledged that park facilities are in need of improvement, and the Administration has been praised for this particular effort.

Figure 9.8

Fish and Wildlife Service: Selected Program Budgets, 1981 and 1983 (million dollars)

Program	FY1981 actual	FY1983 request	Percent change 1981-1983
Wildlife resources	$98.5	$108.6	+9.3%
Habitat preservation	43.8	31.1	−29.0
Endangered species	22.3	16.5	−26.0
Fishery resources	36.1	32.9	−8.9

Source: Executive Office of the President, Office of Management and Budget

Figure 9.9

**National Park Service: Selected Program Budgets, 1981 and 1983
(million dollars)**

Program	FY1981 actual	FY1983 request	Percent change 1981-1983
Operation of the National Park System (Park management)	$ 475.0 (412.7)	$ 539.7 (482.5)	+13.6% (+16.9)
Construction	43.4	123.7	+185.0
Land and Water Conservation Fund (State grants) (Federal acquisition)	288.6 (173.7) (114.9)[1]	69.4 (0.0) (69.4)	−76.0 (−100.0) (−39.6)
National recreation and preservation	16.4	7.0	−57.3
Historic Preservation Fund	26.0	0.0	−100.0

[1] Includes $7.6 million appropriation for administrative expenses.

Source: Executive Office of the President, Office of Management and Budget, and U.S. Department of the Interior, National Park Service

Land acquisition, however, has dropped dramatically. Federal purchases of parkland, using money from the Land and Water Conservation Fund, are to be severely reduced in 1983 (39.6 percent). Federal grants to states have been eliminated, and the proposed federal funding for fiscal year 1983 will be used almost exclusively to pay court awards on lands already taken or condemned. These Administration actions have aroused concern that, in the face of rising demand for outdoor recreation, opportunities to acquire additional parcels of land will be lost.

Protection and preservation of important natural and cultural resources by the National Park Service would be curtailed because of a proposed cutback of more than 50 percent for the national recreation and preservation program. This cutback encompasses the elimination of funds for future studies of potential wild and scenic rivers, and scenic and historic trail routes.[34] Two related cultural programs in the National Park System are also to be abolished: the Urban Park and Recreation Fund and the Historic Preservation Fund. Both provide grant money to state and local governments.

Energy and Minerals. A Department of the Interior budget document declares that "one of the Department's highest priorities is to accelerate and streamline its energy leasing activities and encourage the development of the Nation's energy resources in order to strengthen the economy, increase Federal revenue and reduce our dependence on foreign sources of energy."[35] The 1983 budget proposals for the Bureau of Land Management (BLM) reflect this trend.

Although BLM's energy and minerals management program is actually projected to decrease 14 percent below 1981 levels (figure 9.10), it would increase by more than 10 percent over 1982 budget estimates.[36]

BLM funding for environmental planning and protection has been slashed. BLM's renewable resource management program, which is responsible for grazing management, wild horse and burro management, soil, water, and air management, and wildlife habitat management, would fall 21.3 percent below 1981 levels. This reduction is expected to be met primarily by cutting back on environmental analyses and other studies. BLM will also be cutting its planning and data management program by 35.9 percent. Land development decisions may now be made without carefully examining their effects on environmental quality.

The Administration's emphasis on resource development and deemphasis of environmental protection is also evident in the budget figures of other Department of the Interior agencies. For example, in fiscal year 1983 the Bureau of Mines' mineral resources technology program jumps 36.1 percent above 1981 levels.[37] This program concentrates on the recovery and conservation of critical and strategic

Figure 9.10

**Energy and Minerals: Selected Program Budgets
of the Department of the Interior, 1981 and 1983
(million dollars)**

Program	FY1981 actual	FY1983 request	Percent change 1981-1983
Energy and minerals management, Bureau of Land Management	$115.0	$ 98.9	−14.0%
Renewable resource management, Bureau of Land Management	130.0	102.3	−21.3
Planning and data management, Bureau of Land Management	31.2	20.0	−35.9
Mineral resources technology, Bureau of Mines	24.9	33.9	+ 36.1
Minerals information, Bureau of Mines	17.2	25.8	+ 50.0
Minerals health and safety technology, Bureau of Mines	57.7	37.8	−34.5
Minerals environmental technology, Bureau of Mines	25.3	6.2	−75.5

Source: Executive Office of the President, Office of Management and Budget

materials. The minerals information program climbs 50.0 percent. At the same time, however, the bureau's minerals health and safety technology program will be cut 34.5 percent and the minerals environmental technology program, which studies mine waste materials and mined land reclamation, is expected to decrease by more than 75 percent.

Perhaps the Department of the Interior's most important and highly controversial energy development proposal is the Outer Continental Shelf (OCS) oil and gas leasing program, which is managed by BLM. BLM is one of the largest collectors of nontax revenue for the U.S. Treasury. It estimates that it will collect $18.0 billion from offshore oil and gas leasing in fiscal year 1983.[38]

OCS energy programs comprise nearly half of BLM's energy and minerals management program budget. The expansion and acceleration of offshore oil and gas leasing activities is a potential threat to coastal environments. But funding for Coastal Zone Management (CZM) programs, within the National Oceanic and Atmospheric Administration (NOAA), declines precipitiously in President Reagan's 1983 budget request.[39]

Other Programs

The Consumer Product Safety Commission was another agency hit hard in the budget process. The Reagan Administration initially sought to abolish the commission, or have it absorbed by the Department of Commerce, but settled for a substantial reduction in its budget.[40] The commission's budget was cut back 20 percent between fiscal year 1981 and fiscal year 1983.[41]

The Occupational Safety and Health Administration (OSHA), one of the most controversial federal agencies, has reduced its staff considerably.[42] The work force dropped by over 15 percent, and the inspection staff by more than 25 percent. These reductions were consistent with the Administration's effort to reduce safety inspections by OSHA and to emphasize enforcement by the states. The National Institute of Occupational Safety and Health (NIOSH), which develops the information on which OSHA's occupational health standards are based, was also cut back substantially.[43]

The federal Office of Surface Mining has been reorganized; the number of federal mining inspectors is being reduced; and federal funding for state programs is increasing—all part of the effort to promote state primacy in regulation of strip mining. As of early 1982, 17 of 27 coal-producing states had attained primacy; that is, they were delegated responsibility for administering the federal surface mining law, having demonstrated to the federal government their ability to enforce the law's standards. The Department of the Interior anticipates that 7 others will attain primacy by mid-1982, and 2 additional ones in fiscal year 1983.[44] The department also expects that the number of full-time federal inspectors will drop from 115 to 69 by the end of fiscal year 1983.[45] In past years, litigation has delayed states' assumption of responsibility for regulating strip mines.[46] In the future, if states are unable to assume primacy as rapidly as projected by the federal government, because of additional litigation or for other reasons, the federal inspection program may be understaffed.

Research and Public Information. Federal nondefense research and development funding in 1981 was $17.2 billion, having risen steadily from a 1969 level of $7.2 billion. It is expected to drop, however, to an estimated $16.8 billion in fiscal years 1982 and 1983.[47] The President of the National Academy of Sciences and leaders of the nation's scientific community have expressed grave concern about the substantial reductions in federal funding for research.[48] As noted, EPA's research budget has been reduced considerably. Estimated 1983 funding of $216 million represents a 40 percent reduction from 1981 spending of $358 million.[49] Research on the Great Lakes will suffer from cuts in several agencies' budgets. The National Oceanic and Atmospheric Administration's Great Lakes Environmental Research Laboratory is slated for abolition in fiscal year 1983; EPA's Large Lakes Research Laboratory in Grosse Ile, Michigan, has had its budget reduced; and the Great Lakes Basin Commission has been dismantled.[50]

Gathering of data on environmental trends was also reduced, as was production of key reports. These curtailments can substantially diminish our ability to monitor and understand environmental conditions. For example, compilation and validation of nationwide rankings on the Pollution Standards Index for air pollution is being discontinued because funds supporting this work have been cut from the Council on Environmental Quality's budget.[51] The staff of the EPA office that assembles and analyzes ambient air quality trends was reduced by 40 percent, and data processing funds for the National Emissions Data System, which is used to develop national emission estimates, were cut 90 percent in the proposed 1983 budget. The proposed forecasting budget of EPA's Office of Research and Development was cut in half, and there are no concrete plans to prepare EPA's *Environmental Outlook* report in 1983. This report, last published in 1980, provided detailed projections of air and water pollution emissions up to 1985 and the year 2000, and was a key input in identifying EPA's research needs.

In late 1981, CEQ released *Environmental Trends*, a compendium of charts, maps, and prose, recording key changes in the environment and related social conditions over the past few decades. There are no plans within CEQ or the cosponsoring agencies to maintain and update the trends data base of over 400 key series or to update the publication.

Finally, the federal government has done little to follow up on the landmark *Global 2000* report published in 1980. In December 1981, CEQ chairman A. Alan Hill announced the Administration's plans to establish an Interagency Working Group on Global Issues and a complementary Global Forecasting Team. The latter would be technical staff assigned to improve data sets and models. But as of mid-April 1982, the working group had met only once, and the global forecasting team had not met.

The budget reductions at many federal agencies also included substantial cuts in programs that fund groups or individuals to conduct public participation workshops, to publish materials facilitating participation, or to participate in agency rule making. Congress had begun cutting back consumer and environmental representation programs in 1980, by disapproving public participation appropriations for several federal agencies.[52]

The budget cuts for public participation and information were part of a broader effort to reduce the flow of environmental and consumer information and to reduce the adversary character of relations between government and business. For example, in March 1981, the new Director of the Occupational Safety and Health Administration banned circulation of 50,000 government booklets on brown lung disease. The action was taken because the booklet pictured on its cover a victim of the disease, and the text reported that the victim had died.[53] Similarly, and perhaps in reaction to the "chemical of the month" syndrome of the 1970s, EPA reduced the flow of information and toned down its rhetoric about hazardous chemicals in the environment. For example, the EPA public affairs office decided not to publicize new agency findings that certain wood preservatives might cause cancer. The office also was reportedly trying to avoid using words, such as "cancer-causing," that might alarm the public.[54]

The Reagan Administration places great faith in the marketplace, but apparently believes the government role in providing information to the consumer should be limited. The government's most popular consumer publication, *The Car Book*, will not be reprinted when existing supplies are exhausted.[55] The Administration also substantially reduced funding for public information programs on energy conservation and solar energy, contending that "with rising energy prices, consumers are demanding and manufacturers are producing more energy-efficient products and buildings."[56]

OTHER ADMINISTRATION ACTIONS

The Administration's efforts to bring about significant changes in environmental, natural resource, consumer protection, and other health and safety regulatory programs have not been limited to budget cuts. Some major administrative changes are also being undertaken. Two of the most significant involve regulatory relief and reorganization.

Regulatory Relief

On January 22, 1981, President Reagan announced creation of a Presidential Task Force on Regulatory Relief, chaired by Vice President George Bush.[57] The task force is supposed to review major regulatory proposals by executive branch agencies, assess regulations already in effect, and make proposals to the President on regulatory reform. Much of the task force's work is conducted by the Office of Management and Budget in response to a presidential executive order, described further below, requiring cost-benefit analysis for existing and proposed regulations.

A week after creating the task force, the President asked agency heads to postpone the effective dates of regulations that otherwise would become effective in the following 60 days, and to refrain from issuing any new final regulations during the same period. The purpose of this request was to allow the Administration time to review numerous regulations that had been issued during the last month of the Carter Administration. Of the more than 150 final regulations issued during that last month, over 100 were scheduled to become effective before March 29. In the Reagan Administration's view, these regulations would impose substantial new burdens on the economy.

The review process was carried out by OMB, the task force, and federal agencies. The review effort was concentrated in OMB. The new OMB director, David Stockman, had written in a November 1980 "Economic Dunkirk" memo that "unless swift, comprehensive, and far-reaching regulatory policy corrections are undertaken immediately, an unprecedented, quantum scale-up of the much discussed 'regulatory burden' will occur during the next 18-40 months."[58]

On March 25, the task force reported progress on regulatory relief, noting that 30 of the 172 postponed final regulations would be further postponed and reconsidered, while the balance had been issued or would be released by March 30.[59] The task force also targeted for review a number of existing regulations, including EPA's hazardous waste disposal rules; EPA's regulations for pretreatment by industry of wastewater discharges to publicly owned sewage treatment plants; and the Department of the Interior's surface mining regulations.

The Vice President's task force invited comments from state and local governments, trade associations, and others about existing rules perceived as most burdensome. In mid-August, a "hit list" was published of additional existing regulations scheduled for review.[60] It included EPA's regulations for lowering the amount of lead that can be added to gasoline; premanufacture notification requirements under the Toxic Substances Control Act; regulations applying NEPA and the National Historic Preservation Act to Community Development Block Grant programs; and regulations under the Fish and Wildlife Coordination Act requiring consideration of wildlife resources in government funding of projects affecting wetlands. Of the 30 regulations targeted, 18 were the focus of complaints by state and local governments.

The impact of the new Administration's attack on regulation has been quite evident at EPA. In November 1981, most of the 183 regulations listed in EPA's regulatory agenda of January 14, 1981, were, according to the Congressional Research Service, in "various states of delay, reconsideration, or inaction."[61]

The Reagan Administration has been particularly concerned about providing regulatory relief for the automobile industry. The Bush task force listed 18 relief steps that might be taken by EPA and 18 by the National Highway Traffic Safety Administration. Suggested changes in EPA regulations included relaxed emission standards and eased vehicle testing requirements.[62]

As part of its regulatory relief efforts, the Reagan Administration also has sought to settle industry lawsuits against regulations. Environmentalists and others have been concerned that EPA has been somewhat too anxious to settle with industry out of court, rather than defend itself. In at least one case, ethical questions were raised about a meeting between two senior EPA officials and industry attorneys to discuss a settlement, without an invitation being extended to the EPA and Justice Department attorneys of record in the litigation.[63]

The Administration also took the unusual step of seeking to have returned to OSHA a regulation that had been upheld by the D.C. Circuit Court of Appeals and that was scheduled for argument before the U.S. Supreme Court.[64] The appeals court had held that cost-benefit analysis could not be used as a basis for setting an occupational health standard for cotton dust, and this issue was to be debated before the Supreme Court. OSHA wanted its standard returned for administrative review prior to the argument before the Supreme Court so that it could be revised on the basis of a cost-benefit test that the agency believed it should apply. This effort to regain jurisdiction over the regulation failed, and the Supreme Court subsequently ruled that Congress did not intend for cost-benefit analysis to be used by OSHA as the basis for setting occupational health standards.

Discussions with industry prior to making decisions to issue regulations have also been part of the regulatory relief program. Like the settlement negotiations, some of the discussions between EPA officials and industry representatives have raised issues of procedural fairness. For example, EPA Deputy Administrator John Hernandez held a series of meetings with industry representatives regarding formaldehyde and di-2-ethylhexyl phthalate (DEHP).[65] EPA was considering whether both chemicals should be regulated. No consumer or environmental group representatives were invited and, although the meetings supposedly were designed to examine scientific matters, industry attorneys were present. Perhaps in another Administration more sympathetic to environmental regulation, such meetings would not attract much attention. But in an Administration avowedly wary of environmental regulation, such meetings are indicative of the changes that have been made. The regulated industries, rather than the environmental groups, have become the primary constituency of EPA and the other resource and environmental agencies.

Existing regulations have been cancelled in anticipation of the end of selected federal programs. For example, in August 1981,

EPA suspended enforcement of reporting and record-keeping requirements that were part of its program for controlling noise from compressors, trucks, motorcycles, and garbage trucks. The Reagan Administration proposed virtually no funding for the noise program in fiscal year 1983, even though the noise standards themselves would remain in effect. An EPA spokesman conceded that, in the absence of record-keeping and enforcement activities, EPA would not know if a new product complied with the standards.[66]

EPA's efforts to suspend various regulatory activities have prompted litigation by environmentalists. For example, EPA's lack of action on standards for permits issued to existing disposal sites under the Resources Conservation and Recovery Act and the agency's suspension of some Clean Air Act requirements for new sources of air pollution were challenged, respectively, by the Environmental Defense Fund and the Natural Resources Defense Council.[67]

A final component of the regulatory relief effort has been EPA's reduced enforcement of environmental laws. EPA plans to increase its efforts to bring criminal enforcement actions against illegal handlers of hazardous waste and filers of false environmental monitoring reports, but it also asked the Justice Department to drop 49 pending actions against polluters. EPA maintained the 49 cases did not merit prosecution because enforcement action was being taken by states; the cases were "insignificant" or "stale"; the polluting facilities had come into compliance or were closed; or the regulations on which cases were based were being litigated.[68]

Reorganization

As part of its effort to redirect government efforts toward desired policy goals, the Reagan Administration reorganized parts of the federal government, abolishing some agencies and shifting responsibilities among others. For example, it abolished the Heritage Conservation and Recreation Service (HCRS), incorporating some of HCRS's responsibilities into the National Park Service. It also sought to abolish the Water Resources Council, seeking to replace it with a smaller water policy office in the Office of the Secretary of the Interior. It considered abolishing both the Council on Environmental Quality and the Consumer Product Safety Commission, but settled instead for reduced budgets and personnel.

In late 1981, the President began to honor a campaign promise to eliminate the U.S. Department of Energy, by proposing a reorganization that would shift most of the department's duties and budget to the Department of Commerce.[69] Under the proposal, the Commerce Department would collect statistical data on energy, develop contingency plans for supply disruptions, and set policy for the Strategic Petroleum Reserve (SPR). A new agency, tentatively named the Energy Research and Technology Administration, would operate the nuclear weapons program and oversee other research programs, and would report to the President through the secretary of commerce. The Federal Energy Regulatory Commission would become an independent commission, as had been its predecessor, the Federal Power Commission, and the Department of the Interior would manage the SPR. The proposed plan encountered significant congressional opposition.

Reorganizations within agencies also were proposed. For example, Interior Secretary Watt announced his intention to reorganize the Office of Surface Mining, reducing its field offices from 37 to 20 and replacing 5 regional offices with 2 technical service centers. The reduction would reflect a change in orientation for the strip-mining office, from a substantial federal regulatory role to one emphasizing cooperation with and assistance to state strip-mine control efforts. The proposed reorganization encountered initial resistance in Congress, but most of it was approved when Congress passed the Interior Department appropriations bill.[70]

The Department of the Interior also sought to shift primary responsibility for oil and gas studies in the Arctic National Wildlife Refuge from the U.S. Fish and Wildlife Service to the United States Geological Survey. However, in response to an environmentalist complaint, a federal district court ruled that the transfer violated federal law.[71]

A hallmark of the Reagan reorganization has been assignment to OMB of considerable authority to review proposed federal regulations.[72] On February 17, 1981, President Reagan issued Executive Order 12291 which (1) emphasized the importance of measuring the costs and benefits of federal regulations, (2) stressed the significance to be given the resulting analyses, and (3) strengthened OMB's oversight to ensure compliance by federal agencies. Pursuant to the executive order, OMB absorbed the roles played in the Carter Administration by the Council on Wage and Price Stability and the Regulatory Analysis Review Group, gaining a much stronger voice in regulatory matters than its predecessor review agencies had.

Reagan's executive order establishes criteria for making and analyzing regulatory decisions, and for clearing regulations and analyses through OMB and through the Presidential Task Force on Regulatory Relief. The Reagan program applies to major rules, defined as: (1) rules having an annual effect on the economy of $100 million or more; (2) rules imposing a major increase in costs or prices on particular industries, agencies, consumers, or geographic regions; (3) rules producing significant adverse effects on competition, investment, innovation, productivity, or employment; and (4) regulations designated as major by the OMB director. The OMB director may also designate existing rules for review.

The executive order states that, to the extent permitted by law, all agencies must adhere to the order's substantive criteria in their regulations. These include: (1) refraining from regulatory action unless potential benefits outweigh potential costs to society; (2) choosing regulatory objectives that maximize net benefits to society; (3) selecting the alternatives that will impose the least net cost to society while achieving regulatory objectives; and (4) setting regulatory priorities to maximize aggregate net benefits to society, taking into account factors such as the condition of the national economy and of particular industries.

The OMB director can review agencies' regulatory documents—proposed and final rules, and preliminary and final impact analyses—prior to their publication in the *Federal Register*. He must provide reviews within fixed periods specified in the executive order, although he can also simply inform the agency within the specified periods that he intends to submit views in the future on proposed rules and preliminary impact analyses, thus postponing action on the regulation. The agency, unless otherwise required by statute or court order to publish a proposed rule, must then refrain from publishing until the review is concluded. The agency also must refrain from publishing its final rule and analysis until it has responded to the director's views and has incorporated those views and its own response in the rule-making record.

The Congressional Research Service (CRS) has noted that the order appears to establish "a formal, comprehensive, centralized, and substantively oriented system of control of informal rule making that is without precedent."[73] Other concerns expressed by CRS are that: (1) "in the context of the unfettered authority that may be wielded," OMB could displace the discretionary rule-making authority placed by statutes in agency officials; (2) by removing from the hands of agencies the prerogative of whether or not to make a rule, the order may conflict with the Administrative Procedure Act;

and (3) the order creates a new entry point for those interested in influencing the outcome of a particular rule making, but it provides "no explicit safeguards to protect the integrity of the process or the interests of the public against secret, undisclosed, and unreviewable contacts."

The CRS study concluded that, because the order arguably conflicts with the Adminstrative Procedure Act, there is a substantial risk that a court challenge to rules promulgated pursuant to it may succeed on the ground that the President exceeded his authority in issuing it. Furthermore, a court might rule that, because the order fails to protect the integrity of the policymaking process from influence by secret, undisclosed, and unreviewable contacts by governmental and nongovernmental interests, it may on its face deprive interested persons of their due process rights to meaningful participation in the decision-making process, to a reasoned agency decision based on some kind of record, and to the possibility of effective judicial review.

OMB issued guidelines governing informal contacts with private parties in the review process, relying on advice from the Department of Justice.[74] A report prepared for a consortium of public interest groups has criticized this "policy of minimal disclosure."[75]

Some of the executive order's provisions are incorporated in omnibus regulatory reform bills that are under consideration in the House and Senate. Concern about potential abuse of the authority given OMB is reflected in the provisions of S.1080, the regulatory reform bill passed by the Senate in March 1982. The bill excludes certain agencies from regulatory analysis requirements, places time limits on OMB's review, and requires agencies to disclose changes made in rules in response to OMB comments.[76]

In December 1980, just before the Reagan Administration took office, Congress handed OMB a potent weapon for control of agency actions when it enacted the Paperwork Reduction Act of 1980.[77] The act created in OMB an Office of Information and Regulatory Affairs and gave OMB the power to approve or disapprove forms agencies use to gather information. The General Accounting Office has complained that the new office has given priority to implementing Executive Order 12291 at the expense of the Paperwork Reduction Act.[78] Nevertheless, the authority to review information requests may assume greater importance in the future, perhaps rivaling OMB's authority to review agency budgets.

Through December 28, 1981, the Office of Information and

Regulatory Affairs had reviewed 2,781 submissions.[79] Of these, 2,412 were consistent with the executive order, without change; 134 were found consistent with minor changes; and 91 were returned to agencies or withdrawn. The remainder were exempt from the order. About 25 percent of those returned or withdrawn were from EPA, and included some of the regulations caught in the regulatory freeze discussed earlier.[80] In mid-1981, OMB was reluctant to disclose to Congress why it had begun to reject proposed regulations, and not until a congressional subpoena was issued in September 1981 did OMB start supplying to Congress explanations for its actions.[81]

In addition to reorganizing, the Reagan Administration moved carefully in its appointments to ensure that those serving in policymaking positions share the President's wariness of federal regulation and his desire to open up federal lands for development. Many of the President's appointees, and subordinates hired by these appointees, have come from industries that are regulated by the federal government or that are the beneficiaries of federal resource policies. These appointments are in marked contrast to those of the Carter Administration, in which many environmental and consumer activists served. For example, the new assistant EPA administrator for air quality programs, a former lobbyist for the timber and paper industries, replaced an attorney who had worked for the Natural Resources Defense Council.

Coinciding with new appointments were firings of existing staff. The Reagan Administration fired the entire staff of the Council on Environmental Quality. The Administration also dismissed about half of the negotiating team involved with the Law of the Sea Treaty, having rejected the treaty's provisions.

In March 1981, the Department of the Interior announced the firing of 28 lawyers from its solicitor's office. The office produces legal opinions for the department and works with the Justice Department in filing and defending lawsuits. The department contended that the office had exceeded its hiring ceiling and that the personnel had been hired illegally by the Carter Administration, but the moves were widely regarded as being designed to remove lawyers sympathetic to environmental concerns.[82]

There have been mutual recriminations between some of the new appointees and career civil servants. Newspaper and magazine reports of ill will between EPA Administrator Gorsuch and career EPA staff have been widespread. Indeed, one of the causes of the rapid departure from EPA of Administrator Gorsuch's newly appointed associate administrator for policy and resource management (the third highest post in the agency) reportedly was his defense of the career personnel beneath him.[83]

CONGRESS AND THE COURTS

Relationships among the three branches of government can work smoothly when there is a consensus on what the nation's policies should be. The Reagan Administration has to deal with a House of Representatives controlled by the opposing party and with courts that have been widely used to force government to act quickly and aggressively to protect the environment.

Congressional Oversight

When Ronald Reagan was elected president and the Republican Party gained control of the U.S. Senate in 1980, the Democratic Party retained control of the U.S. House of Representatives. Following the election, President Reagan's appointees acted quickly to dismantle many programs that, with strong Democratic backing, had started or had grown significantly during the 1970s. Among these were many designed to protect environmental quality and to promote conservation of natural resources. The stage was set for a confrontation between Administration officials and House oversight committees chaired by Democrats.

For example, the House Interior Committee used Section 204(e) of the Federal Land Planning and Management Act to declare an "emergency" that would prevent Secretary of the Interior James Watt from issuing leases for mineral exploration in the Bob Marshall Wilderness Area. Under the Wilderness Act of 1964, the secretary of the interior has authority to issue leases until December 31, 1983, but none of Secretary Watt's predecessors had ever done so. Secretary Watt disputed the constitutionality of Section 204(e), and his former employer, the Mountain States Legal Foundation, sued to have the congressional action overturned on constitutional grounds. The federal judge hearing the case ruled that the committee can withdraw lands on an emergency basis, but the secretary of the interior has authority to set the duration of such a ban.[84] Prior to the court's decision, only an agreement by Secretary Watt to give Congress advance notice of proposed lease approvals in wilderness areas, or to lease only following formal environmental review, forestalled consideration by the committee of an "emergency" resolution that would have banned leasing in all wilderness areas.[85]

Administration efforts to weaken environmental laws have also been the focus of Senate hearings chaired by moderate Republicans concerned about environmental quality. The Senate Environment and Public Works Committee, concerned about EPA's loosening of Clean Air Act requirements, has proposed a revision of the Clean Air Act that would narrow EPA's regulatory discretion. Specifically, the committee decided to prevent the relaxation of emission standards for heavy duty trucks, a policy change that had been contemplated by EPA.[86]

Congressional committees involved with revision and oversight of environmental laws have become an important target for the activities of political action committees (PACs). For example, Common Cause, in a report entitled "Dirty Money . . . Dirty Air?" estimated that $1.14 million in industry PAC contributions were made to members of House and Senate committees involved in rewriting the Clean Air Act.[87] Environmentalists have begun to increase their attention to congressional elections, having formed their own political action committees and having targeted particular campaigns for door-to-door organizing.

Judicial Review

Beginning in the late 1960s and continuing into the early 1970s, federal courts were used by environmentalists to promote environmental values. For example, the Refuse Act of 1899 was resurrected as a device for regulating discharges of pollution into navigable waters, prior to creation of the National Pollutant Discharge Elimination System (NPDES) permitting program by amendments enacted in 1972 to the Federal Water Pollution Control Act. In 1970, the National Environmental Policy Act (NEPA) was signed into law, and litigants used the act's spare language to ensure that federal officials took seriously its message that their agencies were obliged to protect environmental quality. Legislative proponents of the Clean Air Act and Federal Water Pollution Control Act regarded citizen group litigation as so important that liberal "citizen suit" provisions were included in these and nearly every other significant statute designed to protect the environment. These provisions, designed in part to overcome legal objections to the standing of such groups to seek judicial redress, were used by environmental groups to promote administrative adherence to the deadlines and criteria established by Congress for regulatory action.

Regulated industries filed large numbers of lawsuits during the 1970s, challenging actions by EPA and other agencies. In the late 1970s, these industry efforts were supplemented by those of new types of "public interest groups" that emerged to litigate in support of "free enterprise and limited government." These groups, reported the *Wall Street Journal*, were "out to tame environmental extremists and rabid regulators." Industry also began to turn NEPA to its advantage by using the act to delay regulations or other actions to which it objected. By 1979, NEPA litigation initiated by industry was about equal to that initiated by environmental groups.[88]

Environmental groups were aided during the 1970s not only by explicit citizen suit provisions, but by expansive judicial holdings that made it easy to gain standing to sue. By the late 1970s, the division of the U.S. Justice Department defending the federal government against environmental lawsuits had dropped its practice of routinely challenging the standing of public interest groups to sue. However, in 1981, the Reagan Administration announced that this policy would be revised and that, henceforth, standing would be challenged.[89] This policy would affect all types of public interest groups, but it increased the possibility that the basis for gaining standing would be narrowed, because standing would once again become an issue in a number of cases.

The U.S. Supreme Court, under the leadership of Chief Justice Warren Burger, has complained about the overloading of court agendas and has tried to discourage judicial activism. In recent years, the Court has rebuked lower courts that were too aggressive in second-guessing administrative decisions.[90] During 1981, the Court ruled against the bringing of lawsuits over water pollution on the basis of federal common law, thereby calling into question the development of federal common law against other kinds of pollution.[91]

Despite some congressmen's complaints about judicial activism and efforts by the Supreme Court to rein in federal judges, other congressmen have attempted to broaden judicial review of regulatory agency actions. The so-called Bumpers amendment states that, for purposes of judicial review, there should be no presumption that any rule or regulation of any agency is valid. This amendment to the Administrative Procedure Act, and variations on it, would eliminate the existing basis for judicial deference to administrative judgments. Related amendments included in proposed regulatory reform bills would give judges greater authority to review and weigh independently factual matters contained in administrative records.

The Judicial Conference of the United States expressed its wariness of congressional tinkering with the basis for review of administrative actions.[92]* The conference declared that proposed language changes might require duplication of agency decisions by reviewing courts, and that it appeared inappropriate for judicial review to "become equated with complete oversight and redetermination of administrative agency decisions including factual decisions." The conference contended the broad scope of review would increase the incentive to litigate agency decisions.

A decision in 1981 by the D.C. Circuit Court of Appeals suggests both the breadth of judicial review currently possible under existing administrative law and the demands placed on judges as a result.[94] In a decision over 200 pages long, the court upheld new source performance standards for coal-fired power plants, promulgated by EPA pursuant to the Clean Air Act. Judge Patricia Wald noted in her conclusions:

> We reach our decision after interminable record searching (and considerable soul searching). We have read the record with as hard a look as mortal judges can probably give its thousands of pages. We have adopted a simple and straightforward standard of review, probed the agency's rationale, studied its references (and those of appellants), endeavored to understand them where they were intelligible (parts were simply impenetrable), and on close questions given the agency the benefit of the doubt out of deference for the terrible complexity of its job. We are not engineers, computer modelers, economists or statisticians, although many of the documents in this record require such expertise—and more.
>
> Cases like this highlight the enormous responsibilities Congress has entrusted to the courts in proceedings of such length, complexity and disorder. Conflicting interests play fiercely for enormous stakes, advocates are prolific and agile, obfuscation runs high, common sense correspondingly low, the public intent is often obscured.
>
> We cannot redo the agency's job. . . . So in the end we can only make our best effort to understand, to see if the result makes sense, and to assure that nothing unlawful or irrational has taken place. In this case, we have taken a long while to come to a short conclusion: the rule is reasonable.[95]

---

*The Administrative Conference of the United States has also recommended against enactment of the Bumpers amendment and other legislation that reverses the presumption of validity presently attached to agency judgments. The conference has suggested that the existing presumption of validity does not shield a regulation from close judicial scrutiny.[93]

The future role of judicial review during the Reagan Administration is unclear. Informal relations between the environmental community and many senior officials of federal agencies are strained or nonexistent, but relations between the Administration and those being regulated have improved immensely. The lack of access by environmentalists to the Administration, and the Administration's attempts to dismantle environmental programs, may prompt environmental groups to seek relief in the federal courts.

If officials are careless in observing procedural requirements, or take steps to dismantle environmental safeguards on the basis of insufficient research, their efforts to alter environmental programs may bog down in litigation. Changes in regulation may be subject to especially searching judicial review if judges are given greater leeway by Congress to substitute their views for those of administrative agencies. Many federal judges, particularly those appointed by President Carter when the federal judiciary expanded during the late 1970s, may be especially unsympathetic to the proposed administrative actions. President Reagan has begun to nominate conservative judges to the federal courts, but it may take some time for their influence to be felt.

STATE AND LOCAL GOVERNMENT

During the 1970s, responsibility for maintaining and enhancing environmental quality was increasingly vested in the federal government. State and local agencies directed their efforts toward implementing federal laws, and became heavily dependent on federal monies for substantial portions of their planning and operating budgets. The Reagan Administration now expects to increase state and local responsibility for programs, and to reduce federal aid, but it is not clear whether states and localities are either willing or able to shoulder the burdens that will be passed to them.

State and local governments have played and will continue to play an active role in environmental quality management. As implementers of federal laws and by their own initiatives, many states have developed well-established programs and institutional structures. For example:

- 49 states, plus the District of Columbia and several territories, have air quality programs. These programs employ 9,000 people, approximately seven times the number working in air programs at EPA.
- 42 states currently have been delegated authority to administer

at least some portion of the program for construction of sewage treatment plants; 46 states and territories are expected to have such authority by the end of fiscal year 1982.

- 33 states have programs for issuing permits to dischargers of water pollutants. These programs employ 1,200 people.
- All but 6 states and the District of Columbia control the quality of public drinking water, under the Safe Drinking Water Act.
- 54 states and territories have pesticide enforcement programs.[96]

Figures such as these are used by the Administration to support its view that reductions in federal programs and personnel will be adequately compensated at the state and local levels. Representatives of state environmental programs contend, however, that federal efforts to increase state responsibilities even further have not been accompanied by provision of necessary funds.

The effectiveness of many state air quality programs already has been limited by inadequate levels of funding and trained personnel.[97] Salaries for state and local employees have tended to be too low to employ and retain people with sufficient skills; at the end of 1979, 8.5 percent of state and 10 percent of local agency positions were vacant.[98] These vacancies occurred even though EPA was providing considerable support for state programs. (Figures for 1980 indicate that EPA grants totaled over $89 million, and constituted from 20 to 60 percent of the budgets of many state and local air pollution control agencies.[99]) With federal aid now declining, some states may simply decide that, since the federal government establishes so many regulatory requirements, the burden should fall on the federal government, rather than states, to implement the requirements. This will increase the permitting and enforcement burden on already reduced EPA regional office staffs.

Reductions in EPA grants and personnel appear comparably threatening to state water quality programs. State programs for implementation of the Clean Water Act and Safe Drinking Water Act had position vacancy rates in 1979 of 10.7 percent and 14.7 percent, respectively.[100]

The capability of state and local governments to provide funds for existing environmental programs is, of course, closely linked to their general financial health. Most of the states are not in good financial condition. The total of all federal grants-in-aid to the states is projected to fall from $88 billion in 1980 to $78.6 billion in 1983.[101] The significance of this cut becomes clearer when inflation is taken into account. An annual inflation rate as low as 5 percent would mean that the grant reductions represent a decrease of 23 percent in actual spending power. Because categorical grants were being combined into block grants, the Administration stated that it expected its cuts in federal assistance to the states to be compensated by savings resulting from fewer paper-work requirements with which states would have to comply. But when the Reagan programs passed through Congress, only 57 categorical programs, rather than the 90 proposed by the Administration, were consolidated into block grants.[102] Consequently, states will get reduced funding without the appreciable increase in discretionary spending power for which they had hoped.

The energy-rich states of the Rocky Mountains and Southwest, benefiting from booms in severance tax revenues, will be able to cope better with reductions in federal aid than will states lacking such revenues. In 1981, for example, seven states received more than 20 percent of their revenues from severance taxes levied on the production of oil, gas, coal, and other minerals.[103]

Some states may be hurt financially not only by cuts in direct federal assistance, but also by changes in the federal tax code. Some 30 states tie their tax systems to federal taxes. Unless they decouple their systems from the federal system, their tax rates will drop along with reductions in federal tax rates. The state of Kentucky, for instance, expects to lose $30 million in revenue this year because of changes in federal depreciation rules.

State and local efforts to borrow money have also become more difficult. Tax-free state and local bonds have been made less attractive as tax shelters for investors because of Reagan Administration measures such as lower taxes on upper income brackets, tax-exempt All Savers' certificates, and widened eligibility for Individual Retirement Accounts. To stay competitive, state and local governments may have to pay increased interest on their bonds, a step that would further deplete their coffers.[104] Because of recent record-high interest rates, some local governments with shaky finances have been closed out of credit markets or have reached the limit of their borrowing authority.

To compensate for losses of federal revenues and address general financial problems, states may decouple their tax system from the federal one, or increase tax rates. A Tax Foundation study reported that, through September 1981, 30 state legislatures had already moved to raise taxes a total of $2.5 billion, the highest annual increase since 1971. Most of these tax increases were initiated before the Reagan Administration's cutbacks in funding for state and local governments, and reflected state needs to cope with inflation and high interest rates.[105]* It should also be noted that voter initiatives such as Proposition 13 in California and Proposition 2½ in Massachusetts may limit states or local governments in their ability to raise certain taxes.

Federal budget cuts are having a significant effect on city budgets. (See chapter 8.) A survey of 100 cities by the U.S. Conference of Mayors in November 1981 reported massive layoffs of workers, service reductions, tax increases, and postponements of needed capital investments. Of 96 cities responding, 41 percent had raised or intended to raise taxes. Many cities' taxing abilities, however, are restricted: 40 states do not allow local governments to levy income taxes; local sales taxes are not allowed in 24 states.[106] And, in states such as Massachusetts, measures like Proposition 2½ limit the levying of property taxes by cities. Many states may simply pass on to localities those programs and responsibilities newly relegated to them by the federal government, although local governmental units generally have the smallest tax capacity and tax base. [107]

Tax increases by state and local governments do not necessarily ensure the continuation of environmentally related programs. Recreation and park programs, for instance, are likely to be a low priority for cities worried about maintaining basic services such as police and fire protection and sanitation. The federal government has never played a large role in the financing of urban parks and recreation systems; however, reduced federal assistance in other areas forces cities to divert funds from them. According to the survey by the U.S. Conference of Mayors, "parks and recreation" was the service area most commonly cut; 20 percent of the 93 cities responding had made such a reduction. Toledo, for example, in addition to cutting the frequency of garbage collection in half, has virtually eliminated park and recreation activities.[108]

State construction programs for sewage treatment plants have financial problems as well. The National Governors' Association has warned that Clean Water Act deadlines will not be met without federal funds. In 1981, the Reagan Administration provided no fiscal year 1982 funds for the sewage treatment grant funding pro-

*About a third of the tax increase was in the form of general sales tax and another third was in the form of higher tax rates on motor fuel. Twelve states established new severance taxes on minerals and fossil fuels or raised existing ones.

gram, which had provided 75 percent of the costs of construction for conventional state and local sewage treatment plants, until Congress agreed to make changes in the design of the program. The temporary halt in funding had a significant impact on states and cities, stopping the construction of major sewage treatment plants, including eight major projects in Texas and several in California.[109] In late 1981, Congress enacted reform legislation, and the Administration requested a supplemental 1982 appropriation of $2.4 billion for the program. The reforms include reducing the components and types of projects eligible for federal funding, particularly those designed to accommodate future population growth. The federal share for future projects will also drop, to 55 percent.[110]

Raising taxes and eliminating programs are but two of the responses to financial problems available to state and local governments. One trend likely to continue is an increased reliance on the private sector for funding and maintenance of environmental programs. For some municipalities under the financial constraints of inflation, decreasing revenues, and legally imposed bonding limits, leasing has been a successful alternative to bond-financed purchases of wastewater treatment projects. Philadelphia, Oakland, and Neola (Iowa) are examples of cities that found lease-purchase agreements to be a more practical and economical method of financing the purchase of water treatment facilities and equipment. The advantages of leasing include avoidance of the costs and delays of bond referenda and its suitability for projects too small to be considered for a bond issue, yet too large to be funded by current revenues.[111] Some cities are turning their sewers, water supplies, and other facilities over to independent operating authorities who (through pricing and bonding power) have their own revenue sources. Although this approach usually results in healthier financing and better maintenance, it limits the flexibility of governments to shift funds among municipal services to meet the most pressing priorities as they arise.

As funds for recreation have dwindled, there has been a steady increase across the United States in the contracting of recreation services to private firms. The city of Detroit's park department acquired a golf course by leasing idle land to a private firm which designed, built, developed, and maintains the course. Fair Oaks, California, coped with Proposition 13 by contracting with a private firm to manage the city's Recreation and Park District; private management reduced expenditures by more than half, yet increased recreation services to the community.[112]

Declining state and local budgets may also alter the role of nonprofit private groups that have worked cooperatively with public agencies in conservation programs. For example, the Nature Conservancy traditionally has transferred most of its purchased land to state and local governments for maintenance and stewardship. As states and localities have become less willing to assume that responsibility, the conservancy has compensated by increasing its budget and fund-raising efforts for stewardship.*

There has also been greater reliance on user fees. In 1981, Oregon established an admission price at nine major state parks and greatly increased overnight camping fees to pay for park maintenance and operation.[114] Several cities have added charges for the use of swimming pools and tennis courts. Increases in license fees are being sought by 21 of the nation's fish and wildlife agencies, which find themselves without the funds to keep their conservation programs running effectively. Their budget problems have stemmed from a reluctance of state legislatures to raise the fees and, for the 19 agencies with incomes that include an average of 22 percent from state general funds, from an indirect pinch attributable to the reduction of federal aid to the states.[115]

It is not yet clear to what extent American cities will rely on user fees to fund other municipal services threatened by federal budget cuts and measures such as Propositions 13 and 2½. In Canada, where user charges made up 4 to 5 percent of municipal revenues between 1974 and 1978, cities substantially recovered the costs of certain services such as public transportation, sewage, and the provision of water.[116] Sixty percent of the U.S. cities surveyed by the U.S. Conference of Mayors reported that fare increases for public transportation had occurred in the last six months, and 53 percent expected another fare increase in less than a year.[117] Problems with reliance on user fees for revenue include additional costs for the administration and collection of charges and questions of equitability. It can be argued that charging for certain basic services (and thereby limiting the user population to those who can afford them) is unfair to the poor, whose only recourse is the government.

---

*For example, in Ohio, the budget of the state's division of Natural Areas and Preserves was cut drastically. The division has responsibility for managing natural areas, including much property acquired by the Ohio Nature Conservancy. The conservancy responded to the budget cut by increasing its stewardship budget fourfold.[113]

In sum, state and local governments will have difficulty accepting the burdens being passed to them by the federal government. Many states have appropriate environmental agencies and statutory authority, but they lack the financial resources with which to develop state plans, retain skilled personnel, and carry out adequate oversight and enforcement functions.

PUBLIC OPINION

Debate over major changes in national environmental policies will be influenced by perceptions of the public's opinion on environmental matters. An extensive survey of American public opinion in 1980, sponsored by CEQ, indicated that citizens' concern for environmental quality, first evidenced on a massive scale in the early 1970s, was enduring.[118] Numerous surveys made in 1981 by major polling organizations, news magazines, and newspapers reinforce the conclusion that support for pollution control remains strong.[119] Referring to his poll results, Louis Harris testified before Congress that "when you obtain such lopsided majorities on any issue, it is evident that there is a broad and deep consensus across the land." He added, "This message on the deep desire...of the American people to battle pollution is one of the most overwhelming and clearest we have ever recorded in our 25 years of surveying public opinion."[120]

Figure 9.11 demonstrates the public's enduring commitment to strong environmental laws. When asked in October 1973, "Do you think environmental protection laws and regulations have gone too far, or not far enough, or have struck about the right balance," 66 percent of those responding replied that the laws either struck the right balance or did not go far enough.[121] In September 1981, such sentiments were expressed by 69 percent of those responding. In the intervening years, the percentage of those expressing such sentiments has never fallen below 65 percent, and the percentage of those stating that the environmental laws do not go far enough has never fallen below 25 percent.

In recent years, some commentators have advanced the notion, based on case studies and surveys of environmental groups, that the environmental movement is an elitist force seeking to protect the privileged position of its members. These commentators often place the upper socioeconomic classes at loggerheads with those disadvantaged individuals who might benefit from the economic growth that environmentalists allegedly impede. This view has been pop-

Figure 9.11

Public Perception of Environmental Laws and Regulations, 1973-1981

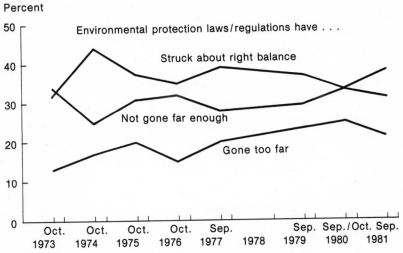

The question asked was: There are . . . differing opinions about how far we've gone with environmental protection laws and regulations. At the present time, do you think environmental protection laws and regulations have gone too far, or not far enough, or have struck about the right balance?

"Don't know/no answer" responses (not plotted) ranged between 10 and 21 percent.

Source: Roper Organization Polls, 1973-1981

ularized by William Tucker, who, citing union and black criticism of the environmental movement, writes:

> This neopopulist revolt against environmentalism has been literally a quarrel between the "haves" and the "have-nots," between the urban and suburban liberal establishment intent on protecting its positions of privilege and the broad reaches of lower-middle-class and poor people, who feel that they do not yet have enough.[122]

Writing less polemically several years ago, researcher Everett Carll Ladd suggested in *Public Opinion* magazine that there are significant differences in environmental preferences among classes.[123] But Ladd has since reconsidered and, writing in *Public Opinion* in March 1982, admits, "We were wrong."[124] He adds that the few environmental questions that reflect class alignments are the exception rather than the rule. He observes that Americans have come to regard a clean environment as a basic material value. "This accounts," he writes, "for both the persisting high support for environmental protection and the absence of significant group differences."

Poll results must be interpreted with care. Questions about environmental attitudes can be asked in many different ways. They can be directed at those who have considerable knowledge, and at

Figure 9.12

Public Opinion on the Environment — Selected Polls, 1981

A. Economic Growth and Environmental Quality

	Agree	Disagree	Other
Government regulations and requirements to protect the environment are worth the extra costs added to the products and services the average person buys. (1)	58%	36%	6%
It is possible to maintain strong economic growth in the United States and still maintain high environmental standards. (1)	75	17	8
We need to relax our environmental laws in order to achieve economic growth. (2)	21	67	12
In order to help solve our energy problems, we should slow down the rate at which we are working to improve the environment. (1)	36	55	9
Protecting the environment is so important that requirements and standards cannot be too high, and continuing environmental improvements must be made regardless of cost. (2)	45	42	13

B. Clean Air and Energy

	Stricter	Same	Less strict	Other
Congress will soon reconsider the Clean Air Act . . . Given the costs involved in cleaning up the environment, do you think Congress should make the Clean Air Act stricter than it is now, keep it about the same, or make it less strict? (5)	29%	51%	17%	2%

	Favor	Oppose	Other
Do you strongly favor, mildly favor, mildly oppose, or strongly oppose "temporarily relax[ing] some pollution controls so that greater use can be made of coal and high-sulphur oil"? (3)	59%	36%	5%
Do you favor or oppose . . . relaxing clean-air requirements to permit industry to burn more coal rather than imported oil? (1)	55	36	9
Do you favor or oppose . . . reducing auto-exhaust regulations that add to the price of new cars? (1)	42	53	5

C. Energy, Minerals, Public Lands, and Wilderness

	Favor	Oppose	Other
Do you favor or oppose . . . easing restrictions on strip mining to provide more coal? (1)	48%	39%	13%
Do you strongly favor, mildly favor, mildly oppose, or strongly oppose "speed[ing] up the development of our coal reserves"? (3)	86	10	4
Do you favor or oppose . . . increasing oil exploration and other commercial uses of Federal lands (not including national parks)? (1)	76	19	5
Would you favor or oppose allowing drilling for oil and natural gas in federal wilderness areas — those areas which were originally set aside by the government to remain natural and undeveloped? (2)	45	45	10

C. Energy, Minerals, Public Lands, and
Wilderness (continued)

	Favor	Oppose	Other
How do you feel about changing the use of wilderness areas so that roads could be built and the natural resources, such as timber, gas, oil and other minerals could be developed as long as developers covered up all signs of use afterward? Would you favor or oppose such use if developers restored the environment, as nearly as possible, to its original state? (4)	57%	39%	4%

	Favor	Risks too great	Other
Would you favor increasing drilling for oil and natural gas off the California and Atlantic Coasts, or do you think the risks of oil spills are too great? (2)	61%	26%	13%

	Favor	Oppose	Other
Do you strongly favor, mildly favor, mildly oppose, or strongly oppose "more drilling for oil and natural gas offshore in U.S. waters"? (3)	82%	16%	2%

"Other" includes the responses "don't know" and "no answer."
Numbers in parentheses refer to source of questions.

Source: Newsweek/Gallup Poll, June 1981 (1)
New York Times/CBS News Poll, September 1981 (2)
Opinion Research Corporation Poll, March 1981 (3)
Opinion Research Corporation Poll, March 12-15, 1981 (4)
Harris Poll, September 1981 (5)

those who have little knowledge. They can inquire about national policies without giving consideration to economic effects, or they can ask those questioned to take national, local, or personal economic effects into account. Queries may or may not balance environmental protection and energy development concerns. The questions reproduced in figure 9.12 are drawn from polls conducted by the *New York Times* and *CBS News*, by *Newsweek* and the Gallup Organization, by the Opinion Research Corporation (ORC), and by Louis Harris.

The results in Section A of figure 9.12 indicate strongly that Americans are willing to bear the general costs of pollution control, that they do not believe that economic growth and environmental quality are incompatible, and that they are not willing to sacrifice environmental quality generally for economic growth. However, the last question in Section A suggests that, while many Americans are willing to disregard costs in protecting the environment, an almost equal percentage believes that we should not be totally oblivious of costs.

Because the Clean Air Act will be amended by Congress, several polls have included questions about public attitudes toward this statute. Section B of figure 9.12 reproduces four of the many questions that have been asked. The first indicates that, even taking costs into account, the public is willing to keep the Clean Air Act strict, or make it even stricter.* Pollster Louis Harris commented, on the basis of this and similar responses, "Clean Air happens to be one of the real sacred cows among the American public."[126]** The second and third questions in Section B suggest public willingness to see Clean Air Act requirements eased to permit coal burning. However, in a March 1982 speech, Harris reported that, by 66 to 29 percent, the public opposed relaxing pollution standards to allow burning of higher sulfur coal and oil.[127] The fourth question in Section B reinforces the responses reported in Section A, indicating that the public is willing to absorb the cost of cleaning automotive fumes.

Polls of environmental attitudes in 1981 also focused on energy development on public lands, including the outer continental shelf and existing and proposed wilderness areas. There appears to be considerable public support for energy exploration on the outer continental shelf, as indicated in the last two questions in Section C of figure 9.12. The variation in the percentages of support reported suggests how important the language of questions can be in eliciting positive or negative responses.

The balance of the questions in Section C emphasize on-shore exploration. The first two focus on mining: the differences between the enthusiastic endorsement of mining in the second question and the less enthusiastic endorsement in the first may be attributable to differences in their language. The third question, which does not specifically mention wilderness areas, suggests considerable public support for exploration on federal lands. But the fourth, which does mention existing wilderness areas, shows that the public is quite split on exploration of such lands. The fifth question implies greater public support for exploration in wilderness areas, if damage to them can be repaired.

The general public support for environmental concerns evidenced in recent polls has been reflected in increasing support for environ-

---

*ORC's poll for the U.S. Chamber of Commerce notes, however, that the public is willing to accept changes in the Clean Air Act that ease procedural requirements, provided that air quality is not adversely affected. It also indicates a low level of knowledge by the public of specifics of the Clean Air Act.[125]
**Harris' comments were generally supported by two other pollsters willing to comment on his remarks.

mental groups. For example, the Sierra Club's membership increased by over 100,000 in 1981, to approximately 300,000.[128] This growth is a response to the widespread perception that the Reagan Administration will undercut the nation's environmental safeguards.

CONCLUSIONS

The view of the President and his appointees is that environmental policies and regulations have imposed unnecessary costs on the private sector and that many conservation and environmental programs and agencies should be severely altered, reduced in size, or eliminated. These views coincide with a more general goal of curtailing or abolishing many federal domestic programs.

The effect of the Administration's policies on environmental institutions has already been dramatic and promises to become even more evident during the coming year. New regulatory initiatives of EPA, OSHA, the Office of Surface Mining, and similar agencies have almost ceased, except for some proposals to ease the burden on regulated industries. Research on environmental problems has been sharply reduced. Efforts to encourage public participation and to disseminate information have been abandoned. The Office of Management and Budget, with its almost exclusive focus on reducing spending and paper work, has been given a central role in approving agency regulations and information collection activities.

The Administration has taken major steps to pass to the states, or to leave to the private sector, responsibilities that the federal government had assumed during the 1970s. It is far from certain that these responsibilities can and will be dealt with any better by the private sector and by the states. Many Americans resent federal paternalism, but they also recognize that substantial environmental improvements have flowed from the strong federal efforts of the 1970s, which backstopped and sometimes forced state government actions. The public greatly fears hazardous and toxic pollutants in air and water, and strongly desires firm government responses. Much can be done by state and local governments and the private sector to address environmental problems, but the federal government risks a great deal of its legitimacy as a protector of public health and safety if it refuses to assume those responsibilities for which it is best suited. Many environmental problems are inherently regional or national in scope, and can only be addressed through federal legislation. Industry can be hurt by conflicting state and local regulations. And hazards to public health will not be reduced simply because the federal government learns less about them.

Public opinion, to some extent the Congress, and perhaps the courts are forces that are working against full implementation of the Administration's environmental policies. The tension between these forces and the initiatives of the executive branch creates a high degree of uncertainty over what the government's policies are or will be. How far the pendulum will swing in the direction of reduced environmental requirements and increased resource exploitation is hard to predict, but it is clear that it has already swung a significant distance during the past year.

FURTHER READING

For general background on the development of pollution control programs in the late 1960s and early 1970s, see J. Clarence Davies III and Barbara S. Davies, *The Politics of Pollution*, 2d. ed. (Indianapolis, Ind.: Pegasus Books, 1975). A more recent overview of pollution control and natural resources policies during the 1970s is found in Helen M. Ingram and Dean E. Mann, "Environmental Policy: From Innovation to Implementation," and Paul J. Culhane, "Natural Resources Policy: Procedural Change and Substantive Environmentalism," in Theodore J. Lowi and Alan Stone, eds., *Nationalizing Government: Public Policies in America* (Beverly Hills, Calif.: Sage Publications, Inc., 1978). For a broad, topical review of environmental issues during the 1970s, see Rice Odell, *Environmental Awakening* (Cambridge, Mass.: Ballinger Publishing Company, 1980). *Environmental Awakening* is based on the *Conservation Foundation Letter*, which Odell has edited for the past 15 years.

Regulatory relief is the Reagan Administration's program for regulatory reform. Regulatory reform, in a broader sense, refers to such alternative approaches as effluent charges, marketable pollution privileges, labeling and other forms of disclosure, and insurance and other forms of risk-sharing. A good summary of these other kinds of regulatory reform is found in *Framework for Regulation*, Vol. VI, one in a series issued by the Senate Governmental Affairs Committee entitled *Study on Federal Regulation*, 95th Cong. 2d. Sess., December 1978. The Project on Alternative Regulatory Approaches of the now-defunct U.S. Regulatory Council published numerous reports on regulatory reform. See, for example, *Alternative Regulatory Approaches: An Overview* (1981). U.S. Regulatory Council publications are available from the Adminstrative Conference of the United States, 2120 L Street, N.W., Washington, D.C. 20037.

The costs and benefits of wider use of cost-benefit analysis in environmental programs are explored in Daniel Swartzman, Richard A. Liroff, and Kevin G. Croke, eds., *Cost-Benefit Analysis and Environmental Regulations: Politics, Ethics, and Methods* (Washington, D.C.: The Conservation Foundation, 1982). For discussion of the benefits of environmental programs, see Roger C. Dower and Daniel C. Maldonado, *An Overview: Assessing the Benefits of Environmental, Health and Safety Regulations* (Washington, D.C.: U.S. Regulatory Council, 1981), and Allen R. Ferguson and E. Phillip LeVeen, *The Benefits of Health and Safety Regulation* (Cambridge, Mass.: Ballinger Publishing Company, 1981).

Information on state and local government capabilities and problems is available from many organizations that are researching federalism or representing state and local governments. These include the Advisory Committee on Intergovernmental Regulations, Suite 2000, 1111 20th Street, N.W., Washington, D.C. 20575; the U.S. Conference of Mayors, 1620 Eye Street, N.W., Washington, D.C. 20006; the National Governors' Association, 444 North Capitol Street, N.W., Washington, D.C. 20001; and the Council of State Governments, Iron Works Pike, Lexington, Kentucky 40511.

For information on the budget process, the congressional *Environmental and Energy Study Conference Weekly Bulletin* (available from U.S. Congress, 515 House Annex 2, Washington, D.C. 20515) tracks the President's budget requests and committee authorization hearings. This year, a special "Fact Sheet" from the conference (March 8, 1982) analyzed environmental, energy, and natural resource budgets. And every spring, the *Conservation Foundation Letter* devotes an issue to environmental budget analysis.

Many environmentalists have sharply criticized the Reagan Administration's policies. Summaries of their principal concerns can be found in two 1982 publications: *Shredding the Environmental Safety Net: The Full Story Behind the EPA Budget Cuts* (available from the National Wildlife Federation, 1412 16th Street, N.W., Washington, D.C. 20036), and *Indictment: The Case Against the Reagan Environmental Record* (available from Information Services, Sierra Club, 530 Bush Street, San Francisco, California 94108).

TEXT REFERENCES

1. The Administration's criteria are recorded in Executive Office of the President, Office of Management and Budget, *Fiscal Year 1982 Budget Revisions* (Washington, D.C.: U.S. Government Printing Office, 1981), p. 9.

2. "Reagan's First 100 Days," *New York Times Magazine*, April 26, 1981.

3. "Administration Seeks Greater Role for Entrepreneurs at Federal Parks," *New York Times*, March 29, 1981.

4. The two 12 percent cuts are not necessarily cumulative. See Lawrence Mosher, "Move Over, Jim Watt, Anne Gorsuch Is the Latest Target of Environmentalists," *National Journal* 13(43):1899-1902 (1981).

5. The costs proposed by EPA in its budget request for fiscal year 1983 are documented in detail in "EPA Takes Major Hit in FY-83, Purchasing Power Halved, 2,000 in Staff Cuts," *Inside E.P.A. Weekly Report*, October 2, 1981, pp. 1, 5-10.

6. The OMB proposals are described in detail in "OMB Chops Gorsuch's FY-83 Budget by Another 20%, Down 34% From FY-82," *Inside E.P.A. Weekly Report*, November 20, 1981, p. 1. The text of Gorsuch's protest to OMB is reprinted in *Inside E.P.A. Weekly Report*, November 27, 1981, special report. Industry is also concerned about the deep cuts in the EPA budget. See "An Unlikely Alliance Against New EPA Cuts," *Business Week*, December 7, 1981, p. 40.

7. The following discussion of the components of the Environmental Protection Agency's budget is based primarily on a staff working paper by the Congressional Budget Office, Natural Resources and Commerce Division, "The Environmental Protection Agency: Preliminary Analysis of the Proposed 1983 Budget" (Washington, D.C.: Congressional Budget Office, March 1982).

8. *Environment Reporter—Current Developments*, November 27, 1981, pp. 941-44.

9. For a critical view of the budget reductions, see National Wildlife Federation, "Shredding the Environmental Safety Net: The Full Story Behind the EPA Budget Cuts" (Washington, D.C.: National Wildlife Federation, 1982).

10. U.S. Department of Energy, Energy Research Advisory Board, Research & Development Panel, *Federal Energy Research & Development Priorities* (Washington, D.C.: U.S. Department of Energy, 1981), p. 20.

11. "Flowing Rivers," *Wall Street Journal*, July 29, 1981.

12. The synfuel subsidies are noted in Eliot Marshall, "Reagan's Cabinet Split on Synfuels Funding," *Science* 213(4509):742 (1981); Eliot Marshall, "Reagan Endorses Two More Synfuel Loans," *Science* 213(4510):848 (1981). See also, "Reagan Hears Strong Support for Interim Program, But Defers Decision," *Synfuels Newsletter*, July 24, 1981, p. 1.

13. Executive Office of the President, Office of Management and Budget, *Budget of the United States Government, Fiscal Year 1983, Appendix* (Washington, D.C.: U.S. Government Printing Office, 1982).

14. "An Age of Economies and Stilled Water Projects," *New York Times*, August 9, 1981.

15. Friends of the Earth, et al., *Indictment: The Case Against the Reagan Environmental Record* (San Francisco, Calif.: Sierra Club, March 1982), p.24.

16. Executive Office of the President, Office of Management and Budget, *Budget of the United States Government, Fiscal Year 1983, Appendix*.

17. "Water Projects Sail On, Despite Budget Cuts," *Washington Post*, February 24, 1982.

18. The discussion in this paragraph is drawn from Richard A. Liroff, "Cost-Benefit Analysis in Federal Environmental Programs," in Swartzman, Liroff and Croke, eds., *Cost-Benefit Analysis and Environmental Regulations: Politics, Ethics, and Methods* (Washington, D.C.: The Conservation Foundation, 1982), and the sources cited therein.

19. R. Jeffrey Smith, "The Waterway that Cannot be Stopped," *Science* 213(4509):741-742 (1981).

20. "Flowing Rivers," *Wall Street Journal*.

21. Laurence Mosher, "Water, Water Everywhere," *National Journal* 14(5):207 (1982).

22. U.S. Department of the Interior, *Budget Justifications, F.Y. 1983, Fish and Wildlife Service* (Washington, D.C.: U.S. Department of the Interior, 1982).

23. U.S. Department of Agriculture, *1983 Budget Explanatory Notes For Committee on Appropriations, Forest Service* (Washington, D.C.: U.S. Department of Agriculture, 1982), p. 8, and sources therein.

24. *Ibid.*, p. 212.

25. *Ibid.*

26. *Ibid.*, p. 8.

27. *Ibid.*, pp. 7, 16-17.

28. U.S. Department of the Interior, *The Interior Budget, Highlights, Fiscal Year 1983* (Washington, D.C.: U.S. Department of the Interior, February 1982), p. 4.

29. *Ibid.*, p. 50.

30. U.S. Department of the Interior, *Budget Justifications, F.Y. 1983, Fish and Wildlife Service.*

31. *Ibid.*

32. U.S. Department of the Interior, *The Interior Budget, Highlights, Fiscal Year 1983*, pp. 50-51.

33. U.S. Department of the Interior, *Budget Justifications, F.Y. 1983, National Park Service* (Washington, D.C.: U.S. Department of the Interior, 1982).

34. *Ibid.*

35. U.S. Department of the Interior, *The Interior Budget, Highlights, Fiscal Year 1983*, p. 3.

36. U.S. Department of the Interior, *Budget Justifications, F.Y. 1983, Bureau of Land Management* (Washington, D.C.: U.S. Department of the Interior, 1982).

37. Executive Office of the President, Office of Management and Budget, *Budget of the United States Government, Fiscal Year 1983, Appendix.*

38. Department of the Interior, News Release on Departmental FY 1983 Budget, February 8, 1982, p. 8.

39. Executive Office of the President, Office of Management and Budget, *Budget of the United States Government, Fiscal Year 1983, Appendix*; see also, U.S. Congress, Environmental and Energy Study Conference, "Fact Sheet—President Reagan's FY 1983 Budget Request for the Environment, Energy and Natural Resources" (Washington, D.C.: Environmental and Energy Study Conference, February 1982), p. 13.

40. Wendy Swallow, "Consumer Product Agency is Battling for its Independence and Its Life," *National Journal* 13(26):1163-65 (1981); and "U.S. Dismantling Consumer Programs," *Washington Post*, November 1, 1981.

41. Executive Office of the President, Office of Management and Budget, *Budget of the United States Government, Fiscal Year 1983, Appendix.*

42. Michael Wines, "They're Still Telling OSHA Horror Stories, But the 'Victims' are New," *National Journal* 13(45):1985-89 (1981).

43. See Marjorie Sun, "Reagan Reforms Create Upheaval at NIOSH," *Science* 214(4517):166-68 (1981).

44. Department of the Interior news release on Departmental FY 1983 budget, p. 25.

45. U.S. Environmental and Energy Study Conference, "Fact Sheet—President Reagan's FY 1983 Budget Request for the Environment, Energy and Natural Resources," p. 11.

46. See OSM's discussion of litigation delays at 46 Fed. Reg. 54495 (1981).

47. Executive Office of the President, Office of Management and Budget, "The Budget of the United States Government, 1983, Special Analysis K, Research and Development" (Washington, D.C.: U.S. Government Printing Office, 1982), p. 29.

48. Barbara J. Culliton, "Frank Press Calls Budget Summit," *Science* 214(4521):634-35 (1981).

49. Information provided by Kay Pettit, Environmental Protection Agency, Budget Office, February 22, 1982.

50. *Ann Arbor News*, February 8, 1982.

51. The three paragraphs in the text on environmental data are based on testimony by Conservation Foundation Senior Associate Daniel Tunstall, before the U.S., Congress, House Committee on Post Office and Civil Service, Subcommittee on Census and Population, Hearings, 97th Cong., 2nd sess., March 16, 1982. Tunstall directed the research and development of the *Environmental Trends* report discussed in the text.

52. For details, see "Budget Cuts Raise Ominous Questions," *Conservation Foundation Letter* (May 1981); see also, "Agencies Curtail Access to Data and Decisions," *Conservation Foundation Letter* (November 1981).

53. The booklet-banning episode is recounted in a copyrighted story by the *St. Louis Post-Dispatch*, cited in "OSHA Official Has Cotton Dust Booklets Destroyed," in the *Washington Post*, March 27, 1981.

54. Frank Greve, "Trying Not To Say What They Mean," *Boston Globe*, August 31, 1981.

55. There had been controversy over the accuracy and usefulness of some data in the book, and the federal government will provide a toll-free safety hotline in its stead. An updated version has been published commercially by a former staff member of the National Highway Traffic Safety Administration.

56. Executive Office of the President, Office of Management and Budget, *Fiscal Year 1982 Budget Revisions—Additional Details on Budget Savings* (Washington, D.C.: U.S. Government Printing Office, 1981), p. 114.

57. The discussion in the first two paragraphs of this section of the text draws from a February 18, 1981 Fact Sheet, "President Reagan's Initiatives to Reduce Regulatory Burdens," issued by the Office of the Press Secretary, The White House. This and many of the other presidential, vice-presidential, and OMB documents cited in this section are reprinted in U.S., Congress, House Committee on Energy and Commerce, Subcommittee on Oversight and Investigations, *Role of OMB in Regulation*, 97th Cong., 1st sess., 1981, Serial No. 97-70.

58. Stockman is quoted in Lawrence Mosher, "Reaganites, With OMB's List in Hand, Take Dead Aim at EPA's Regulations," *National Journal* 13(7):256-59 (1981). See also, Timothy B. Clark, "OMB to Keep its Regulatory Powers in Reserve in Case Agencies Lag," *National Journal* 13(11):424-29 (1981).

59. The discussion in this paragraph draws from material accompanying a statement by Vice President George Bush, issued by the Office of the Press Secretary, the Vice President, March 25, 1981.

60. "30 More Regulations Targeted for Review," *Washington Post*, August 13, 1981. See also, "White House Targets 30 More Regulations," *National Journal* 13(33):1479 (1981).

61. The Congressional Research Service analysis is cited in *Environment Reporter—Current Developments*, November 13, 1981, p. 870.

62. The status of the regulatory relief effort for the auto industry is described in "Auto Reg. Relief Update: EPA Rules Need More Work, Most NHTSA Work Done," *Inside O.M.B.*, November 9, 1981, p. 5. See also EPA's notice regarding auto industry regulations under review, 46 Fed. Reg. 21628 (1981).

63. This incident is discussed in *Environment Reporter—Current Developments*, September 4, 1981, p. 556, and September 25, 1981, p. 647.

64. See "OSHA's Latest Recall of Carter Era Rules," *Business Week*, April 27, 1981, p. 48; "A High Court Win for OSHA," *Newsweek*, June 29, 1981, p. 59; and "Supreme

Court Upholds OSHA's Cotton Dust Standard, Deals Setback to Cost-Benefit Analysis," 11 ELR 10163 (1981).

65. For discussion of the meetings, see Marjorie Sun, "EPA May be Redefining Toxic Substances," *Science* 214(4520):525-26 (1981); and Marjorie Sun, "Gorsuch Defends EPA Meetings with Industry," *Science* 214(4521):636-37 (1981).

66. See "U.S. to Ignore Some Noise Rules," *Washington Post* August 15, 1981. The EPA notice is published in the Federal Register, 46 Fed. Reg. 41057-41059 (1981).

67. *Environment Reporter—Current Developments*, September 18, 1981, p. 604, and October 23, 1981, p. 791.

68. "Sullivan: Civil Cases, Penalties Cut; State, Criminal Actions Stressed," *Inside E.P.A. Weekly Report*, November 13, 1981, pp. 13-14; *Environment Reporter—Current Developments*, November 27, 1981, p. 937.

69. This description of the energy reorganization is based on a report in *Energy Users Report*, December 24, 1981, pp. 1821-22.

70. See "Conferees Agree to 3.7 Billion for Interior; OSM Tech Center Move Barred," *Federal Lands Newsletter*, November 9, 1981, p. 3.

71. Trustees for *Alaska v. Watt*, 16 ERC 1679 (D. Alaska, 1981).

72. The discussion of E.O. 12291 in the text, in this and the succeeding two paragraphs, is based on Liroff, "Cost-Benefit Analysis in Federal Environmental Programs," and the sources cited therein.

73. See U.S., Congress, House, Committee on Energy and Commerce, *Presidential Control of Agency Rulemaking*, Committee Print, 97th Cong., 1st sess., 1981, pp. 70-73.

74. Memorandum (No. M-81-9) from David A. Stockman for Heads of Executive Departments and Agencies, "Certain Communications Pursuant to Executive Order 12291, 'Federal Regulation,'" June 11, 1981.

75. Charles E. Ludlam, *Undermining Public Protections: The Reagan Administration Regulatory Program* (Washington, D.C.: The Alliance for Justice, 1981), p. 45.

76. See revised sections 553(F) and 553(G), and new sections 621(3), 621(4), and 624(b), of Title 5 of the U.S. Code, in U.S., Congress, Senate, *Congressional Record*, 97th Cong., 2d sess., 1982, pp. S2714-S2715.

77. Pub. Law 96-511, 44 U.S.C., sec. 3502 *et seq.* and various sections of Title 5, 20, 40, and 42.

78. See testimony of U.S. Comptroller General Charles A. Bowsher before the U.S., Congress, House, Committee on Government Operations, Subcommittee on Legislation and National Security, *Implementation of the Paperwork Reduction Act*, Hearings, 97th Cong., 2nd sess., October 21, 1981.

79. The statistics on OMB's activity are found in a fact sheet, "Year-End Summary of the Administration's Regulatory Relief Program," issued by the Vice-President's Press Secretary, December 30, 1981.

80. "OMB Analysis Shows EPA With Major Portion of Returned or Withdrawn Rules," *Inside O.M.B.*, November 19, 1981, p. 7.

81. Charles E. Ludlam, *Undermining Public Protections*, pp. 25-26.

82. For a summary of the factual details that cast suspicion on the department's explanation, see "How Interior is Changing, From the Inside," *Washington Post*, January 8, 1982.

83. "Political Realities Slow Up EPA's Chief, But She Still Manages to Jolt the Agency," *Wall Street Journal*, October 20, 1981.

84. *Pacific Legal Foundation v. Watt*, 16 ERC 1825 (D. Montana, 1981).

85. "Watt and Wilderness Leasing: He'll Back Off—But Won't Stop Trying," *Federal Lands Newsletter*, November 30, 1981, pp. 1-3.

86. *Environment Reporter—Current Developments*, November 27, 1981, p. 924.

87. "Sens. Abdnor and Symms Each Got $180,000+ From CAA-Minded Industry Groups," *Inside E.P.A. Weekly Report*, May 29, 1981, pp. 8-9.

88. Richard A. Liroff, "NEPA Litigation in the 1970s: A Deluge or a Dribble?" 21 *Natural Resources Journal* 315 (1981); see also, "Alternative Public-Interest Law Firms Spring Up With Nader et al. As Target," *Wall Street Journal*, August 21, 1979.

89. "Justice Agency Plans Greater Opposition to Environment Suits," *Wall Street Journal*, May 13, 1981.

90. The most noteworthy rebuke in an environmental case is found in *NRDC v. NRC*, 435 U.S. 519, 8 ELR 20288 (1978), also known as the *Vermont Yankee* decision.

91. Some lower court decisions in the 1970s had raised hopes that such a common law could be developed. See "Requiem for the Federal Common Law of Nuisance," 11 ELR 10191 (1981).

92. Letter to Representative George Danielson, Chairman Subcommittee on Administrative Law and Governmental Relations, from William E. Foley, Director, Administrative Office of the U.S. Courts, cited in "Judiciary Wary of Reg Reform Bills, Sees Problems With Increase in Cases," *Air/Water Pollution Report*, July 27, 1981, p. 295.

93. See its recommendation published in 46 Fed. Reg. 62805 (1981).

94. *Sierra Club v. Costle*, 15 ERC 2137 (D.C. Cir., 1981).

95. *Sierra Club v. Costle*, 15 ERC 2137, 2225 (D.C. Cir., 1981). For further discussion of judicial deference and technical capability, see "D.C. Circuit Upholds NAAQS for Lead and Ozone, Defers to EPA's Rulemaking Discretion Under Air Act," 11 ELR 10197 (1981); and Sheila Jasanoff and Dorothy Nelkin, "Science, Technology, and the Limits of Judicial Competence," *Science* 214(4526):1211-15 (1981).

96. Many of these figures were cited in EPA Administrator Ann Gorsuch's testimony before the Oversight and Investigations Subcommittee of the U.S. House Energy and Commerce Committee. See "Mrs. Gorsuch Defends Budget Cuts, Says Agency Can Still Function Effectively," *Environmental Health Letter*, Dec. 1, 1981, pp. 4-5; see also, U.S. Comptroller General, *States Compliance Lacking in Meeting Safe Drinking Water Regulations* (Washington, D.C.: General Accounting Office, 1982); and U.S. Environmental Protection Agency, Office of the Comptroller, "Summary of 1983 Budget" (Washington, D.C.: U.S. Environmental Protection Agency, 1982).

97. Final Report of the National Commission on Air Quality, *To Breathe Clean Air* (Washington, D.C.: U.S. Government Printing Office, 1981) pp. 89-90.

98. *Ibid.*, p. 93.

99. *Ibid.*, p. 90.

100. U.S. Comptroller General, *Federal-State Environmental Programs—The State Perspective* (Washington, D.C.: General Accounting Office, 1980), p. 60.

101. "Special Report: State and Local Government in Trouble," *Business Week*, October 26, 1981, pp. 135-181.

102. See "'New Federalism', Old Rap," *Newsweek*, August 24, 1981, p. 20; *Business Week*, October 26, 1981.

103. *Ibid.*

104. *Ibid.*

105. Tax Foundation, "State Tax Action in 1981," *Tax Review* 42(8):31-34 (1981).

106. United States Conference of Mayors, *The FY82 Budget and the Cities: a Hundred City Survey* (Washington, D.C.: U.S. Conference of Mayors, Nov. 20, 1981).

107. This possibility is considered highly likely by members of the National Association of State Budget Officers, according to member John T. Herndon, Florida's budget and planning director. See *National Journal* 13(50):2183 (1981).

108. U.S. Conference of Mayors, *A Hundred City Survey*, pp. 8, 10.

109. "Governors, Stockman Meet in Effort to Gain FY-82 Construction Grants Funds," *Inside E.P.A. Weekly Report*, October 2, 1981, pp. 1, 9-10.

110. See *Environment Reporter—Current Developments*, December 11, 1981, p. 971; January 1, 1982, p. 1051.

111. *Environmental Finance* 1(2):3-4 (1981).

112. National Recreation and Parks Association, "Private Contractors Spell Relief for Many," *Dateline NRPA* 4(3) (1981).

113. Information provided by the Ohio Nature Conservancy.

114. "Experimental Park Fee Called a Success," *The Oregonian*, July 9, 1981.

115. National Wildlife Federation *News Release*, "Survey of State Fish and Wildlife Agencies Reveals 21 Have Serious Financial Problems," October 2, 1981.

116. Bruce Kiernan, "Thinking About User Fees," *Impact: 2½*, No. 7, August 1, 1981, p. 2.

117. U.S. Conference of Mayors, *A Hundred City Survey*, p. 38.

118. See Council on Environmental Quality, *Environmental Quality—1980* (Washington, D.C.: U.S. Government Printing Office, 1980), pp. 401-25.

119. Among the polls are the following: Harris Survey telephone poll of 1,250 adults, May 6-10, 1981, summarized in "Substantial Majorities Indicate Support for Clean Air and Clean Water Acts," released June 11, 1981 by the Chicago Tribune-New York News Syndicate, Inc.; Newsweek Poll conducted by the Gallup Organization, a phone survey of 745 adults on June 17-18, 1981, reported in "Public Opinion About Environmental Protection and Defense Spending," June 1981, and published in part in *Newsweek*, June 29, 1981, p. 29; Opinion Research Corporation phone survey of 1,008 adults, March 12-15, 1981, reported in part in *LTV Looking Ahead—Part I*, "More Access to Federal Lands—for Oil, Gas, Minerals, Timber, and Water," and poll of 1,008 adults, March 1981, reported in *LTV Looking Ahead—Part V*, "Can the U.S. Become Energy Self-sufficient?" (advertising materials sponsored by the LTV Corporation); Harris Survey telephone poll of 1,249 adults, September 19-24, 1981, the results of which were discussed at a hearing, U.S., House Committee on Energy and Commerce, Subcommittee on Health and Environment, October 15, 1981, and reported in "Pollster Lou Harris to Politicians: 'Hands Off' Environmental 'Sacred Cow,'" *Inside E.P.A. Weekly Report* October 23, 1981, pp. 1, 7-8; New York Times/CBS News telephone survey of 1,479 adults, September 22-27, 1981, summarized in "Poll Finds Strong Support for Environmental Code," *New York Times*, October 4, 1981; NBC News telephone survey of 1,598 persons, October 25-26, 1981, noted briefly in *Air/Water Pollution Report*, November 23, 1981, p. 451; Opinion Research Corporation poll of 1,400 adults, November 20-22, 1981, commissioned by the U.S. Chamber of Commerce and summarized in *Environment Reporter—Current Developments*, December 11, 1981, p. 973; Roper Survey of 2,000 adults, September 19-26, 1981, cited in "Opinion Roundup—Environmental Update," *Public Opinion*, 5(1):32 (1982).

120. Harris is quoted in "Pollster Lou Harris to Politicians: 'Hands Off' Environmental 'Sacred Cow,'" *Inside E.P.A. Weekly Report*, pp. 1, 7-8.

121. Survey by the Roper Organization, September 19-26, 1981, cited in "Opinion Roundup—Environmental Update," *Public Opinion* 5(1):32 (1982).

122. William Tucker, "The Environmental Era," *Public Opinion* 5(1):46 (1982).

123. Everett Carll Ladd, "The New Lines are Drawn: Class and Ideology in America," *Public Opinion* 1(3):48-53 (1978).

124. Everett Carll Ladd, "Clearing the Air: Public Opinion and Public Policy on the Environment," *Public Opinion* 5(1):18 (1982).

125. *Environment Reporter—Current Developments*, December 11, 1981, p. 973.

126. See "Pollster Lou Harris to Politicians: 'Hands Off' Environmental 'Sacred Cow,'" *Inside E.P.A. Weekly Report*; "Two Pollsters Generally Support Harris View of Environment as Sacred Cow," *Inside E.P.A. Weekly Report* December 4, 1981, pp. 10-11.

127. Address by Louis Harris before the Environmental Industry Council, Washington, D.C., March 12, 1982. Printed text, p. 7.

128. Frances Gendlin, "A Talk With Mike McCloskey," *Sierra* 67(2):36 (1982).

FIGURE REFERENCES

Figure 9.1

Executive Office of the President, Office of Management and Budget, *Budget of the United States Government, Fiscal Year 1983, Appendix* (Washington, D.C.: U.S. Government Printing Office, 1982).

Figure 9.2

Ibid.

Figure 9.3

U.S., Congress, Environmental and Energy Study Conference," Fact Sheet—President Reagan's FY 1983 Budget Request for the Environment, "Energy and Natural Resources" (Washington, D.C.: Environmental and Energy Study Conference, February, 1982).

Figure 9.4

Ibid.

Figure 9.5

Ibid. Data received from U.S., Congress, Environment Energy Study Conference for FY 1981 expenditures for specific state and local conservation programs did not add to total.

Figure 9.6

Executive Office of the President, Office of Management and Budget, *Budget of the United States Government, Fiscal Year 1983, Appendix.*

Figure 9.7

U.S. Department of Agriculture, *1983 Budget Explanation Notes for Committee on Appropriations, Forest Service* (Washington, D.C.: U.S. Department of Agriculture, 1982)

Figure 9.8

Executive Office of the President, Office of Management and Budget, *Budget of the United States Government, Fiscal Year 1983, Appendix.*

Figure 9.9

Ibid. For 1981 budget totals for the Land and Water Conservation Fund and for the National Recreation and Preservation Program, see U.S. Department of the Interior, *Budget Justifications, F.Y. 1983, National Park Service* (Washington, D.C.: U.S. Department of the Interior, 1982). 1983 budget figures for the Land and Water Conservation Fund are based on information provided by the National Parks and Conservation Association, Washington, D.C.

Figure 9.10

Executive Office of the President, Office of Management and Budget, *Budget of the United States Government, Fiscal Year 1983, Appendix.*

Figure 9.11

Roper Opinion Poll Surveys, most recent was one of 2,000 adults (September 19-26, 1981). This survey is only the latest in a series that began in October, 1973. See "Opinion Roundup—Environmental Update," *Public Opinion* 5(1):32 (1982).

Figure 9.12

Newsweek poll conducted by the Gallup Organization, a phone survey of 745 adults on June 17-18, 1981, see "Public Opinion about Environmental Protection and Defense Spending", June 1981 and published in part, in *Newsweek*, June 19, 1981, p. 29. *New York Times*/CBS News telephone surveys of 1,479 adults, September 22-27, 1981, see "Poll finds Strong Support for Environmental Code," *New York Times*, Oct. 4, 1981. Opinion Research Corporation phone survey of 1,008 Adults, March 12-15, 1981, see *LTV Looking Ahead—Part I*, "More Access to Federal Lands—for Oil, Gas, Minerals, Timber, and Water" and Poll of 1,008 adults, March 1981, see *LTV Looking Ahead— Part V*, "Can the U.S Become Energy self-sufficient", advertising materials sponsored by the LTV Corporation. Harris Survey Telephone poll of 1,249 adults, September 19-24, 1981. Results of this survey were discussed at a hearing of the House Committee on Energy and Commerce, Subcommittee on Health and the Environment, October 15, 1981, and reported in *Inside EPA Weekly Report*, October 23, 1981, pp. 1, 7-8.